-7

The Inspectors' Calling:
HMI and The Shaping of Educational Policy 1945–1992

Stuart Maclure

Hodder & Stoughton

A MEMBER OF THE HODDER HEADLINE GROUP

For the reproduction of copyright material, the publishers would like to thank the following:

Faber and Faber for the extract from *Turbulent Years: My Life in Politics* by Kenneth Baker; Article by Sheila Browne which appeared in *Accountability in Education* published by Ward Lock Educational; Article on 'The Yellow Book' (15 October 1976), article by John Hudson (3 October 1986) and letters written by Kenneth Clarke and Eric Bolton (18 October 1999) are reproduced with permission by The Times Educational Supplement. Her Majesty's Stationery Office for permission to reproduce the following: *Yellow Book or School Education in England: Problems and Initiatives* (DES, 1976); DES Reports of Education No.49 Colleges of Education Graph; *Statistics of Education*: Teachers 1962 (DES) Table 40; *HMI Inspectors' Handbook* (1954); White Paper on Educational Reconstruction Cmnd 6458 (1943); The Ruskin Speech, delivered by the Prime Minister at Ruskin College, Oxford Monday 18th October; Martin Roseveare, SCI cited in *Challenge and Response: An Account of the Emergency Scheme for the Training Of Teachers* (Pamphlet 17 1950); The Rayner Report in *Study of HM Inspectorate in England and Wales* (1982); *Reading Ability: Some suggestions for Helping the Backward* (Pamphlet 18 1950); Primary Education in Wales (1968). Crown copyright is reproduced with the permission of the Controller of Her Majesty's Stationery Office.

Every effort has been made to trace the copyright holders of material reproduced in this book. Any rights omitted from the acknowledgements here or in the text will be added for subsequent printings following notice to the publisher.

The author and publisher would also like to thank the following for the use of photographs:

Mrs Jean Ross (Sir Martin Roseveare); Mrs Dorothy Wilson (Percy Wilson); Mrs Karin Elliott (Bill Elliott); Harry French (photo of himself and Sir Edward Boyle). All other photographs occur courtesey of Times Newspapers, Insight, Associated Press, and Oxford and County Newspapers.

Front cover appears courtesy of News Team International.

Orders: please contact Bookpoint Ltd, 78 Milton Park, Abingdon,Oxon OX14 4TD. Telephone (44) 01235 827720, Fax: (44) 01235 400454. Lines are open from 9.00–6.00, Monday to Saturday, with a 24 hour message answering service. E-mail address: orders@bookpoint.co.uk

British Library cataloguing in Publication Data
A catalogue record for this title is available from The British Library

ISBN 0 340 753919

Typeset by Fakenham Photosetting Ltd
Printed in Great Britain for Hodder & Stoughton Educational, a division of Hodder Headline Plc, 338 Euston Road, London NW1 3BH by Redwood Books Ltd.

Table of Contents

Part 1: Reconstruction and Reorganisation – 1945–70

Part 2: Reaction – 1970–76

Part 3: Reform – 1977–86

Part 4: Revolution – 1986–92

Preface

I have received help from many people in writing this book and wish to express my thanks to all who have agreed to share their knowledge of the events covered here, or have otherwise helped to make it possible. In particular I must thank the Trustees of the Nuffield Foundation and Dr Helen Quigley for the generous support which has enabled the project to go forward. Lois Reynolds and Brian Arthur (a former HMI of distinction) have acted as research assistants. It would have been impossible to cope with the volume of material to hand without their skilled and unstinting help. Professor Geoff Whitty of the University of London Institute of Education kindly took the project under his wing and I am grateful for his interest and support.

A special word of thanks goes to the Institute of Education Library, the HMI (Jack Kitching) Archive and Jenny Haynes, and to Arabella Wood at the Library of the Department for Education and Employment, for the help they have extended to Lois Reynolds and Brian Arthur.

Simply to list the people who have helped with information and guidance seems an inadequate way of thanking those who gave interviews, wrote to me, spoke on the telephone or otherwise offered their help, but it is all I can do here to acknowledge their generous assistance. They include Rosemary Ballard, Arthur Balls, John Banks, Lord Baker of Dorking, Mrs N. M. Brown, Richard Bird, Eric Bolton, Clive Booth, Sheila Browne, Geoffrey Caston, Jeff Crozier, Geoffrey Cockerill, Pat Collings, Anne Corbett, Charles Creall, Jack Curtis, Michael Duffy, John Dunford, Dr D. Ernaelsteen, Alec Evans, Bill Finch, Sir David Hancock, John Hedger, John Hudson, Richard Jameson, Harry Judge, June Keyte, Maurice Kogan, Petra Laidlaw, David Leadbetter, George Lowe, John Mann, David and Mary Medd, Terry Melia, Dave Metzger, John Mills, Don Neave, Sir Peter Newsam, Christopher Price, Brian Smith, Caroline St. John Brooks, Geoffrey Stone, Nick Stuart, Norman Thomas, John Thompson, Peter Thorpe, John Tomlinson, Roy Wake, D. A. Watkins, Sir Toby Weaver, David G. Williams, Lady Williams of Crosby, Jack Wright and Joe Young. If I have omitted anyone inadvertently, please forgive me.

I am indebted to a number of people who have read and commented on the manuscript or parts of it. The marginalia which resulted would have made another, no doubt, more interesting book. My thanks to Eric Bolton, Sheila Browne, Howard Monks, Norman Thomas, Terry Melia, Don

Porter, Nick Stuart, Roy Wake, John Slater, Peter Wynn and Tom Wylie. Collectively their commentary was illuminating as well as humbling, offering wise suggestions and saving me from foolish errors. This said, there is no one to blame for the final outcome but me.

I am deeply indebted to the group of former HMI who decided to collect from their colleagues personal accounts of the life and work of the Inspectorate during the period covered by this book. The product of their initiative runs to well over a million words and has provided part of the background – and much of the foreground – of this book. The exercise owes a great deal to Brian Arthur who organised the material and put it in order. My thanks to all who contributed; their names are recorded at the back of this book.

I would be at fault if I did not refer to John Dunford's excellent *Her Majesty's Inspectors of Schools since 1944,* The Woburn Press, London, 1998. This appeared shortly after I began work on this book. If I have unconsciously borrowed from this work without acknowledgement I apologise.

Finally my thanks to Mary Maclure for her patience and long-suffering, particularly during the period towards the end of the writing of this book, as of any book when the author begins to wish he had never agreed to do it and takes it out on his nearest and dearest.

Stuart Maclure
31 May 2000.

The author and publisher would also like to thank the following for the use of photographs:

Mrs Jean Ross (Sir Martin Roseveare); Mrs Dorothy Wilson (Percy Wilson); Mrs Karin Elliot (Bill Elliot); Harry French (photo of himself and Sir Edward Boyle).

About this Book

This book is about aspects of the evolution of the education system in England and Wales in the second half of the twentieth century. It focuses on the making of education policy and the way policy unfolded, beginning with the Education Act of 1944 – R. A. Butler's Act which incorporated wartime hopes for a better world – and ending with the world turned upside down by Kenneth Baker's Education Reform Act of 1988, and the clatter of bills which followed, like aftershocks in the wake of the seismic event. It concludes in 1992 with the setting up of the Office for Standards in Education.

The last fifty years of the century was a period of rapid and vigorous growth in the education system. It saw the transformation of what at the beginning had been a highly decentralised system, run by strong local authorities and a weak Ministry of Education, to one in which an all-powerful Department for Education and Employment is in total command and the local authorities have been reduced to little more than ciphers.

This book does not attempt to cover the waterfront. It is mainly about schools and further education; universities only come into the story when they are involved with teacher education and training. The angle of vision is narrow: that of the policy makers, looking outward from the centre. And moving from the background to the foreground are Her Majesty's Inspectors of Schools.

How their role changed at different stages within the period is one of the principal themes of the book. This study has been able to draw on personal accounts provided by some 200 members of the Inspectorate who were active in the period under consideration – notes varying in length and substance from a few pages of typescript to longer essays in autobiography. These have provided invaluable background information and insight into the work they did individually and collectively, the way they interacted with teachers and with the Office – that is, with ministers and their senior officials. It is hoped that extensive quotation from these sources will convey something of the diversity of the work of HMI. There can be no claim that the sample chosen here is in any strict sense representative – how could it be? – these were HMI who responded to a general invitation. But given the fallibility of memory and the passage of time, these edited personal views provide authentic snapshots, sufficiently numerous and diverse to add depth to the narrative.

The contribution of HMI to the making of policy became increasingly important as the role of the Department of Education and Science evolved in the 1970s and 1980s. 'The Inspectorate is without doubt the most forceful single agency to influence what goes on in schools, both in kind and in standards.' This was the Department's own verdict in 1976. It was echoed six years later in the Rayner Report on the Inspectorate, which testified to HMI's 'crucial contribution to the development of policies for the education service by central government'.

The story comes in four parts:

Reconstruction and Reorganisation

This is the post-war period when policy is determined by what has to be done to bring the Act (or most of it) into operation. The Ministry of Education's main concerns are building schools and the recruitment and training of teachers. Money is tight, but there is some expansion for the further education colleges and the further education avenue to higher education is being strengthened. Hopes are high for adult education. The big disappointment is the failure to do anything about county colleges. The completion of the Hadow reorganisation remains a preoccupation into the 1960s before 'reorganisation' got another meaning and Anthony Crosland issued Circular 10/65. The decision of the Labour government to 'nationalise' the organisation of secondary education as an educational issue, marks the first serious challenge to the post-war division of power between central and local government.

HMI play a part in every phase of post-war reconstruction – teacher training, school building, further education, the creation of post-war primary education and the developments at the secondary level including the work on ways of going comprehensive. The major inquiries mounted by the Central Advisory Councils lean heavily on HMI. After the wartime interruption there is a huge backlog of inspection to be completed by the end of the 1950s. This is the heyday of the general and district HMIs going about their routine business. But by the end of the 1960s HMI is in need of a new sense of direction.

Reaction

This extends far beyond education. It marks the end of the 'post-war' period when optimism and liberal hopes for a better world covered a multitude of sins. The schools come in for severe criticism – primary schools for failing to teach the basic subjects, secondary schools for failing to prepare young people for a hostile world where unemployment is rising. Teachers come under fire as surrogates for a liberal orthodoxy. One of the side effects of the reaction of the early 1970s is to prompt questions about the function of the Department of Education and its ability to respond to public concerns about the schools. In 1976, James Callaghan decides to make a major speech on education at Ruskin College, Oxford, which reclaims the school curriculum as a matter of legitimate public concern and, more generally, signals a determination to get to grips with education at the national level.

For rather different reasons, during the years leading up to Ruskin, the Inspectorate is under pressure. It has to find ways of adapting to changes within the system which are stretching the demands made on HMI. The outcome is more control over the Inspectorate's programme of work by the Senior Chief Inspector and the Chief Inspectors who form the senior management team.

Reform

The next 10 years mark the step-by-step attempts of the Department to develop its authority over the curriculum, the examination system and the training of teachers. The Secretary of State has to push his way into the Secret Garden by initiating public debate on curricular matters, forcing the debate into the open with a series of circulars, White Papers and discussion documents, and by talking with the local authorities and the teachers' unions. There is a continuity of policy which stretches from the time of Shirley Williams to that of Keith Joseph. It is he who works out a method of enabling the partners in the education system to come to a collective mind on the curriculum without resorting to legislation.

The 'Reform' period sees HMI move much closer to the policy makers. They are the Department's main source of information on the curriculum and the facts which lie behind the arguments about primary and secondary education: they set up the necessary inquiries to be able to provide evidence-based answers to the questions which ministers and officials put to them about patterns of teaching in primary and secondary schools. They do this without losing the detachment and impartiality which give them credibility. The closer the Inspectorate gets to the Office, the more important it becomes to defend HMI's professional autonomy.

Revolution

The arrival of Kenneth Baker at the Department of Education and Science in 1986 marks the end of Keith Joseph's attempts at consensual reform. A long-drawn-out dispute over teachers' salaries and conditions of service had done nothing to help Joseph achieve his aims. His approach needed time – time which had run out. Major legislation follows to create a new structure for the education system, with a much stronger role for the Department of Education. The Education Reform Act chops away at the powers of the local authorities. Where Joseph had tried to achieve a national curriculum by consensus and persuasion, Baker relies on Statute and Parliamentary Order. The Education Reform Act which replaces large sections of the 1944 Education Act, is followed by a succession of lesser bills which deal with higher and further education, teacher training and the

Inspectorate. As in the 'Reform' period, the Department relies heavily on HMI for help in pushing the National Curriculum through at high speed.

A massive reorganisation of the Inspectorate is inevitable if the National Curriculum is to be policed by universal, formal, external, inspection. The critical decision is to take OFSTED (and therefore HMI) right outside the Department for Education and Employment when quite by chance questions of inspection become entangled with the Citizen's Charter.

England and Wales

England and Wales share an education system and a common body of legislation. For the first half of the period covered by this book, Welsh education was dealt with by officials of the Ministry, and latterly the Department of Education and Science, in London in much the same way as an English region. In HMI terms Wales was, in effect a division, like the 10 other divisions in England, receiving only a brief mention in the *Inspectors' Handbook* (see Chapter 5). There had usually been dutiful nods towards the particular needs of the Principality in circulars and White Papers – there was a separate Central Advisory Council for Education in Wales – but it was not till 1970 that the Welsh Office took over administrative responsibility for Welsh schools, and in 1978, for further education in Wales. Most education White Papers since then have been jointly issued by the two Secretaries of State.

The distinguishing mark of Welsh education over the past half century has been the development of robust policies on the Welsh language and the adaptation of the education system to the needs of a bilingual community. HMI have played a leading part in the promotion of these policies which are only incidentally touched on in these pages. From the perspective of this book the English and Welsh education systems go together because the main lines of educational policy are common to the two countries and have evolved together – always acknowledging, as for instance in the National Curriculum, the significance of the Welsh language in all aspects of the life of Wales and in the life of every Welsh educational institution.

A Note about Chronology and Nomenclature

While, in the main, the scheme of the book follows this chronology, some of the topics, themes and individuals stubbornly refuse to be confined neatly to these periods and some degree of overlap is unavoidable. And nothing is more tedious than having constantly to interrupt the flow to explain that Joe Bloggs has by now become Sir Joseph Bloggs and later turns up again as Lord Bloggs of Wherever. This narrative will not therefore be scarred by 'Joe Bloggs (as he then was)' or similar formulations. Such biographical details as are necessary will be conveyed in the text or the notes.

Prologue – Brave New World

Bankrupt but Hopeful. A New Education Act. HMI – The Roseveare Reorganisation.

Bankrupt but Hopeful

On August 10 1945, Terence Rattigan paid a visit to Sir Henry Channon MP at his home in Belgrave Square. Channon (Chips to his friends) was an indefatigable diarist and kept a note of the occasion:[1]

> *Terry came to lunch about 12.55pm. He said (he is a wireless addict) – 'turn on the news'; and we did as we sipped our pre-prandial cocktails. The wireless announced that Japan had asked for peace, but insists on the rights of the Emperor ... At long last the war is over or ending. The streets were crowded with celebrating people singing, and littered with torn paper.*

VJ day was four days later when the nation celebrated officially. No one who thronged Trafalgar Square and the Mall or the centre of any other town or city across the realm, could forget the occasion – the singing and cheering, the joy and delight in long-awaited victory, the release of tension and the excuse for a party.

A new era was dawning. The post-war period had begun. The war in Europe had ended three months earlier. The nation had voted in a general election – exit Winston Churchill; enter as prime minister, Clement Attlee, to lead the first Labour government with a working majority in the House of Commons. The Labour and Conservative Parties had vied for the electoral mandate to preside over the reconstruction of Britain: each offered a prospectus for national revival, and the electors had chosen Labour's vision. The size of the majority in the House of Commons was a quirk of the 'first-past-the-post' voting system, but nobody doubted that Labour had indeed won, nor yet that the public mood demanded the building of a new Jerusalem in England's green and pleasant land.

Hugh Dalton, the new Chancellor of the Exchequer, had already opened up the books and begun to come to terms with the enormity of the economic problems which faced the new Government. His diary (August 17) records some mild annoyance at the distractions of public rejoicing: 'Work in these last few days has been much interrupted by Victory celebrations. I have been receiving good advice, in addition to pep pills, from [Lord] Horder [the King's Physician]. I have sometimes felt pretty tired, but seem as well to have a good deal of resilience.'[2] A good deal of resilience (and plenty of pep pills) were, no doubt, what the situation demanded. There was a great deal to do to put Britain back on its peacetime feet, and the resources with which to do it were scarce.

There were two sets of interlocking problems: one set was economic and industrial; the other was social and psychological.

The economic difficulties were massive. The war was over and the immediate military hazards were at an end but other dangers were looming. Peter Hennessy, in *Never Again* provides a brilliant account of Britain in the first six years after the war had ended, which shows in graphic detail the magnitude of the challenge which faced the country and its new Government.[3] Britain finished the war with five million men and women in uniform in Europe, the Middle East, North Africa, India and South-East Asia. Royal Air Force squadrons were deployed in all the theatres of war in numbers never seen before or since. The Royal Navy had more than 1,000 warships and submarines, and 6,500 assorted patrol boats, landing craft and auxiliaries at varying states of readiness, spread out across the seven seas.

The resettlement of demobilised servicemen and their integration into productive employment meant juggling priorities and release dates for different groups of personnel. (Captain Anthony Crosland, an intelligence officer with General Alexander's army in northern Italy, was one who exchanged the prospect of an immediate posting to the Far East for the first steps on his return to Oxford.[4]) The call-up continued for 18-year-olds while the release of those who had served their time went forward.

Well before the end of the war, a Government department – the Ministry of Reconstruction, headed by Lord Woolton – had begun overseeing plans for the transition. The Ministry of Labour's plans for demobilisation included the package of further education and training grants to help former servicemen and women pick up the threads of civil life. In July 1944, Martin Roseveare, the newly appointed senior chief inspector of schools, was already making a case[5] for the immediate recruitment of 25 HMIs for:

> 1. *preparing schemes of training for Service folk between armistice and demob for War Office,* 2. *same for Min of Lab.*

The later years of the war and the outbreak of peace had seen a rapid increase in the workload of the Army Education Corps and educational activities in the other services.

Full employment was a cardinal policy for the new Government. But employment depended on recreating strong export industries and bringing about a speedy return to former patterns of production, consumption and trade. Investment in the war years had been wholly subordinated to the war effort. There was an urgent need to re-equip industry and modernise – a need which had to be balanced against the consumer demands of a nation hoping to emerge from the austerities of wartime.

Correlli Barnett's influential study of Britain's wartime industrial performance, published in 1986 under the title of *The Audit of War*, brought home to a later generation the extent of the deficiencies of the British engineering and armaments industries exposed by the demands of the war. There was a wide gap in productivity between the British and German factories; the British came badly out of most of the comparisons. There was the familiar story of ingenious inventions poorly exploited. The British were less good at combining high-quality design with efficient production engineering to make possible economical and speedy manufacture. It took fewer man-hours to build a Messerschmitt than a Spitfire because the designers of the German plane had a better understanding of the production engineering requirements. (The German management and unions were also more flexible in their working arrangements.)

No less daunting was the financial situation – the state of the currency, the balance of payments and the Government's credit. Britain's war effort had been sustained by American credits. The Lease-Lend arrangements through which this had been done, came to an abrupt end with the outbreak of peace. A large American loan had to be negotiated – and as John Maynard Keynes, Britain's chief negotiator, well knew – as a virtual bankrupt, there was no way Britain could afford a loan on ordinary commercial terms. After lengthy negotiations a deal was agreed for a $3.75 billion loan at 2 per cent interest. The terms provided for no interest to be paid for five years, after which repayment would begin and be spread over 50 years. The most significant clause in the agreement, however, was a condition of the loan that Britain should agree to make sterling convertible. The dangers of such a move were obvious – the sterling area was hedged around with controls which prevented the outflow of funds. Lift these controls and there was a very strong probability that holders of sterling would promptly exchange their pounds into dollars. On 15 July 1947, sterling began to melt away and the following month controls were reimposed.

The day was saved by the Marshall Plan and renewed American aid, but not before the usual group of top civil servant insiders had spelled out to the Cabinet what the devastating consequences would have been in terms of even tighter rationing and a much stricter siege economy if the Americans had not relented. The financial troubles continued with the devaluation of the pound in 1949 and the economic consequences of the Korean War (and British rearmament) in 1950–1.

The truth is that the politics and the social development of Britain in these years were overshadowed by these recurring economic misfortunes. The financial cards were heavily stacked against the Labour government from the start. No doubt the Americans also suspected their socialist rhetoric and their collectivist instincts – perhaps the insistence on sterling convertibility might have been less implacable if it had been a Churchillian government which sent Keynes cap in hand for a loan.

Arthur Marwick sums up the early post-war years with images of a dark and stormy scene enlightened by glimpses of something better. 'Many of the conditions of war were ... to continue until early 1950 with rationing and controls enduring still longer ... Between 1945 and 1950 the country lay in a crepuscular zone with the shadows of night as firm upon the landscape as the heartening hints of the rising sun.'[6]

Looking back with the benefit of hindsight, what stands out is the long-drawn-out nature of Britain's industrial and financial troubles – the relative decline of the British economy which had started long before the Second World War and went on for most of the twentieth century. The immediate post-war period was particularly bad; recovery was slow and patchy; crises recurred again and again. Special budget cuts or economy measures were introduced in 1951, 1956, 1961, 1965, 1968 and 1973 – the last date heralding the Middle East oil crisis and the sustained economic pressures which eventually forced Britain to call in the International Monetary Fund and submit to a programme of financial measures as a condition of IMF support.

The sequence of crises provides a counterpoint to the history of education for most of the four decades which followed the Second World War. Financial stringency was the order of the day, most of the time. When new restrictions were introduced or new cuts imposed, people would cheerfully look back to some imagined time when the education system was flush with money, but taken as a whole these were years of modest growth and indifferent economic performance in Britain. For a quarter of a century the worst evidence of structural weakness in industry was concealed by the sustained growth of the world economy. During the 1970s and 1980s, the full extent of the weakness of the low-wage, low-skill economy began to become apparent with the rise in unemployment (including youth unemployment) and the collapse of the heavy industries which had long recruited large numbers of 14- and 15-year-old school-leavers.

Inevitably the question arises: to what extent was the story of relative economic decline written in the stars – the consequence of external events which presented Britain with insuperable difficulties in the post-war world? Or (as seems much more likely) was the failure man-made – a failure of economic management, an unwillingness to tackle the underlying weaknesses in the economy, and a failure of politics which offered voters easy but ineffectual options?

Barnett combines his analysis of Britain's industrial shortcomings with his own explanation of what went wrong. He blames the post-war Labour government (and its Conservative successors) for not making industrial and technological modernisation their first priority. He saw the creation of the welfare state – the building of the new Jerusalem – as an economic and political distraction from the main task which was to make Britain into a first-class industrial power, able to earn a good living in a fiercely competitive world economy. According to his hypothesis, technical education and industrial training ought to have taken precedence over all other educational aims in the post-war period.

His was a formidable attack on the failure of British Governments to tackle the shortage of skilled manpower and the shortcomings of the education system. But it is far from clear that any British Government, dependent on winning a parliamentary majority in a general election, could have successfully imposed the kind of measures needed for the single-minded subordination of civil society in general, and the education system in particular, to the needs of economic recovery. There will be occasion, later, to note the half-hearted way in which post-war Governments approached the matter of technical schools and the provision of technical education as a component in secondary schooling, and to comment on the low priority which British companies gave to industrial training. But Barnett's recipe would have demanded a far more draconian approach than simply an emphasis on technical education. Given the politics of post-war Britain it is difficult to imagine any post-war Parliament accepting the kind of authoritarian measures which would have been needed.

Part of Barnett's case attributed the blame for the failure of political direction to the mindset of a complacent and technologically illiterate ruling class, reared on the educational ideals established by Dr Arnold in the middle of the nineteenth century and adopted (and adapted) by generations of English public and grammar schools in the years that followed. In his hypothesis, this watered-down Christian classical heritage – pacifist and tender-minded – was an added disabling factor.

Barnett's book made a considerable impact when it appeared. Among those who admitted to being impressed by it was Nigel Lawson, when he was Chancellor and chipping into the education debate in the 1980s.[7] Unfortunately the intemperate enthusiasm of Barnett's writing – which greatly contributes to its readability – frequently betrays him. His main thesis does not stand up if the evidence from the rest of Western Europe is taken into account. Barnett implies that Britain's commitment to the welfare state was specially damaging, mopping up public spending and crowding out investment in industrial reconstruction. But what was happening elsewhere in Europe lends no support to this argument. By the end of the 1940s, West Germany, Austria and Belgium were all spending a larger proportion of gross domestic product on the welfare state than Britain; by the mid 1950s, they had been joined by France, Denmark, Italy and Sweden.

Pointing this out,[8] Dr Jose Harris, the biographer of Beveridge, also looked at Barnett's canard about a Christian conspiracy and found no evidence to back it up among those most closely involved in setting out these policies. As it happened, however, in 1942 a group of Christians with Conservative affiliations led by Geoffrey Faber, the publisher, did try to persuade R. A. Butler and the Conservative Party's Central Council, to adopt a truly radical package of plans for educational reconstruction. These included taking over the public schools, introducing compulsory technical and vocational training, conscripting young people into youth movements, replacing the classics in the curriculum with science and technology and inculcating an ideology of public spirit based on state-prescribed Christian doctrine. As Harris observed, 'with the exception of the emphasis on Christian doctrine, this programme was an almost exact replica of the kind of policies that Corelli Barnett appears to think *should* have been adopted by Britain's wartime planners.'

The proposals were rejected out of hand by the Conservatives as 'stark totalitarianism'. As it happened, about the same time Ernest Bevin[9] was also toying with radical notions for educational reform which also envisaged universal technical and vocational training and putting 16–18-year-olds in boarding schools to learn a mixture of academic and practical skills, using the industrial hostels and military camps which would become available when the war was over. This, too, had no takers and he did not follow it up.

To turn from the economic to the psychological and social considerations is to introduce less clear-cut and measurable factors into the discussion. By 1945 there was a widespread war-weariness, a sense that 'make-do and mend' had become part of the British way of life for too long. The end of hostilities brought patriotic rejoicing and a determination to make sure better things were on the way. What people felt about the post-war world had brought Labour to power with a mandate for a radical transformation of British society. People did not want simply a restoration of the *status quo ante*. They wanted a bigger share of the good things of life.

Britain remained a highly disciplined country – where else did rationing continue into the 1950s? – and demobilisation was carried through fairly and in an orderly fashion. But the war aims of ordinary people had been articulated by the wartime coalition Government: the Beveridge Report had caught the imagination of a nation which believed in a fairer, more decent Britain. The welfare state was an abstraction, but jobs, homes, schools, pensions and hospitals were not – after six years of war, people could be forgiven for believing it was time to redeem the pledges given to sustain the war effort.

Post-war Britain had a lively recollection of the 1930s – the Depression and heavy unemployment particularly in the Midlands and the north of England. Labour advertising played on this, urging new voters to 'ask your dad' if they were in any doubt about what the post-war priorities should be. Only the realisation of the wartime ideals and aspirations would justify the wartime austerities which had been cheerfully – and collectively – shared. The patriotic unity of the war years had indeed been remarkable but was not to be presumed upon: it had certainly not obscured the demand for better ways of conducting affairs than those which prevailed pre-war. Moreover these hopes and expectations were by no means confined to the self-conscious working class – they had become national aims. It was more than 30 years before the welfare state came under serious attack.

There were also the psychological consequences of having 'won' the war to contend with. National pride had been a major contributing factor to the war effort and people delighted in patting themselves on the back because 'in the darkest days of the war they had stood alone against the might of Hitler's Germany.' The words come out almost automatically in inverted commas because they became a sort of a national mantra – a ritual incantation with which to bolster the national ego.

It was only natural to look across the Channel to continental Europe, devastated by war and starting to build up again from scratch, and to feel a certain smugness. But smugness was mixed with envy when people discovered that the French ate much better than the rationed British and that shops in many continental countries were better stocked than those at home. Starved of civilian travel for the war years, the British became avid travellers and purchasers of cheap package holidays. Armed with their passports, endorsed for £50 worth of francs or pesetas, they set off to discover 'abroad'. What they found was evidence of rapid renewal and rebuilding, much of it financed by the Marshall Plan and the recovery of international trade. On a cynical view losing the war and rebuilding from scratch seemed a better bet than being on the winning side.

When the war ended it was still politically correct to talk of the British Empire. There was all that red on the map and London was an imperial capital. Britain had a seat at the top table which she considered hers by right. The Attlee government began the process of changing Empire into Commonwealth and took rapid steps to end British rule in the Indian subcontinent. As the colonial era came to an end in the coming decades, this would be celebrated with one ceremonial lowering of the Union flag after another. But lowering the flag in front of Government House has been much easier than lowering it in the popular mind or the tabloid imagination. Delusions of grandeur have taken a long time to fade. British politics have been distorted by the continuing desire to play a leading international role – 'to punch beyond our weight' as a distinguished modern foreign secretary liked to put it – without the military, and industrial strength to back it up. Britain's relations with Europe were dogged by these geopolitical illusions which General de Gaulle rightly said Britain would have to eschew if she were ever to become a good European. Events have shown how right he was and what a long way the British had to travel to shrug off the historic past.

A New Education Act

Peter Gosden in his *Education in the Second World War* [10] has given a blow-by-blow account of how the wartime coalition Government came to draft and enact the 1944 Education Act. R. A. Butler, the Conservative architect of the Act, has told the story more briefly and with his own wry humour, in *The Art of the Possible*.[11] At the end of 1940, four and a half years before the war ended, the first moves were taken inside the Board of Education to plan the post-war reform of the education system. A group was set up to prepare an outline of what needed to be done which produced a draft that was widely circulated but not formally published.

By the time Butler succeeded Herwald Ramsbotham as President of the Board (with Chuter Ede as his Labour deputy) it was already fairly clear what, in general terms, would be in a new education Act. It was clear, also, what the most obvious stumbling block might be – the 'dual system', which allowed the Churches to participate in the provision of public education alongside the local authorities. Churchill had formally warned Butler off the idea of preparing an education bill because the fierce controversies about the dual system which plagued the Liberal government of 1904, were still fresh in his mind 30 years later. For Churchill, an education Act meant revisiting the contentious issues of church schools and how to pay for them, which had caused Welsh ratepayers to withhold their taxes and rail against 'Rome on the Rates'. Butler and Ede were not deterred. There was a lot of spadework to do before a bill could be brought forward – work they could put in hand without committing the Government to legislation.

Butler's patient and skilful negotiation of the church school issue was his great contribution to what became known as the Butler Act. The question of the voluntary schools – meaning, in most cases, the Church schools – was the critical issue which had to be settled first. The 'religious question' could scupper everything else in the bill including all the things people were agreed about, if it got to the floor of the House of Commons without some sort of agreed or at least tolerable compromise having been worked out.

In 1938, there were 10,553 church schools, 85 per cent of them Anglican, attended by about a third of all pupils in the system. Many of these schools dated back to the previous century and would have to be rebuilt or replaced. Other schools would be needed to cope with expansion and the raising of the school leaving age. It was common ground on all sides that there was no way in which the Churches themselves could pay for all that needed to be done to their existing schools, unless they received generous assistance from public funds. What had to be worked out was a deal with the Churches under which they traded some of their independent control over their schools in return for capital grants.

There was a fine line to be trod: politically there was a limit to what Butler could do to help the Churches; the Nonconformists (who were not large-scale school providers) were strongly opposed to financing Church school building and wanted to take the opportunity to do away with the 'dual system' . Many Labour MPs shared this view.[12] The Roman Catholics, on the other hand, were equally determined to keep control and favoured the Scottish system which would have transferred all the capital cost to the State. The Anglicans, under the leadership of Dr William Temple, the Archbishop of Canterbury, had most to lose if they could not find a compromise because they would have to pay out most to maintain their historic role in public education.

The compromise which emerged from Butler's long and patient negotiations provided for two categories of voluntary schools: aided and controlled. Aided status would give governors more denominational control, but in return they would have to bear 50 per cent of any capital expenditure. Controlled schools governors, on the other hand, were offered less denominational control but all their capital costs would be met from public funds. Current costs in both kinds of school were to be met by the local education authority (LEA). No fees were to be charged in either type of school.

When it came to the crunch, Temple backed Butler's proposals and secured the support of his colleagues, but not before Butler forced the Church of England to face up to the true state of their schools and what was required to put them in order. (More than half the names on the Board's 'blacklist' were those of Anglican schools.) Temple's expectation was that 90–95 per cent of Church of England schools would become controlled; in the event, a third chose the more expensive aided status.

The Roman Catholics remained unappeased, never accepting what people called the 1944 Act religious 'settlement'. With one solitary exception, their schools became aided and they accepted the financial burden which this implied, the number of Roman Catholic aided schools increasing from 1,266 in 1938 to 2,049 by the end of the century, by which time the Church of England had 1,985 aided and 2,808 controlled schools. After 1998, both aided and controlled schools came within the foundation category.

Over the years, amending legislation brought the share of capital expenditure which voluntary bodies have to raise, down to 15 per cent. The Free Churches opposed the settlement but without making much impact in or outside Parliament and raised no serious opposition when denominational liabilities were cut. Falling church attendances have since encouraged more ecumenical attitudes and the 'religious question' which used to be argued most hotly *between* the Churches has come to unite them against the indifferent majority.

Sections 25–28 of the 1944 Act enshrined the religious compromise in law. Religious instruction was made the one compulsory subject, and there was provision for a daily act of worship. These contentious matters disposed of (at least temporarily), Butler and Ede could address the rest of the educational reform agenda. A White Paper on *Educational Reconstruction* (1943) had articulated the conventional wisdom about educational reform. Under legislation passed in 1936, the school leaving age had been due to go up to 15 in 1939 but this had been aborted at the outbreak of war. The 1944 Act reaffirmed the raising of the school leaving age to 15 within 2 years, and to 16, 'as soon as [the Minister] is satisfied it has become practicable'.

What was new was the generous spirit in which reconstruction of the education system was conceived and the conscious sense of legislating for the long term. It was a big bill in terms of the number of sections, clauses and schedules, and a big bill, too, in the flexible provision it made for future development by the blend of powers and duties it gave the LEAs. This added up to the expectation that, without too much fuss – and certainly without violence – there was going to be a social revolution based on fairness and a redistribution of wealth and privilege. The Act carried powerful messages about equality of opportunity – a noble, but insidious phrase which crumbles under analysis yet remains potent as a reforming principle. Butler gave his own assessment of its potentially revolutionary social objectives in a stilted filmed interview for an American audience: leaning negligently against an elegant mantelpiece, and speaking like a parody of an upper-class English gent, he said:

> *The effect as I see it will be as much social as educational. I think it will have the effect of welding us into one nation when it's got thoroughly worked out instead of the two nations Disraeli talked about.*[13]

The first section of the Act provided for the appointment of a Minister 'whose duty shall be to promote the education of the people of England and Wales and the progressive development of institutions devoted to that purpose, and to secure the effective execution by local authorities, under his control and direction, of the national policy for providing a varied and comprehensive educational service in every area'. It was the responsibility of the LEAs to secure 'adequate provision of primary and secondary education' including nursery and special schools. They would employ the teachers and provide the schools. They were given responsibility for the curriculum in county schools. In the case of voluntary schools the curriculum was to be a matter for the governors of each school.

The weakness of the Minister's position on curricular matters reflected the assumptions of the time. The same assumptions made LEAs reluctant to use their powers to intervene in the curriculum. Butler saw value in having the Central Advisory Councils (CACs), linked to the 'central authority' (ie the Ministry), which would 'pay some attention to what is taught in schools and to all the most modern and up-to-date methods, and by reviewing the position continually, consider the whole question of what may be taught to the children'.[14]

The main weakness of the education system as it appeared to wartime reformers was that there was too little of it and too small a proportion of the population benefited from it. Only 14.34 per cent of children in England and Wales aged 11 in 1938 had gone on to secondary education – more in Wales, less in England.

The content of education was not seen as the problem; what was needed was more of it, better provided, and with wider access to it. Governments and LEAs had to make this possible. As Butler had reminded Churchill, when urged to make sure that all children learned about Wolfe storming the Heights of Abraham,[15] it was not thought to be the business of Parliament and ministers to decide what children should be taught. Such matters were best left to the teachers and professionals who ran the system.

It was, nevertheless, clearly the intention when the bill was drafted that the Minister should have greater powers than those of the President of the Board under previous legislation. Unfortunately, one of the mechanisms which might have provided strength to the Minister's elbow – the development plan which every LEA was to draw up – proved ineffective as an instrument of control. There were specific sections of the Act which empowered the Minister to call LEAs to order. But in a sense they were too powerful, 'blunderbuss-type' clauses which were hardly ever invoked. What the Minister could do by the exercise of executive authority was very little. The Act put a premium on indirect influence and persuasion – on the working of what was called a partnership. All went reasonably well till the politics of education changed and ministers wanted to enforce their will. Then, when they reached for the levers of power they found them ineffective. This is a recurring theme which leads to the eventual decision in the 1980s to change the power structure of the education system and replace the 1944 Act with the Education Reform Act of 1988.

The central provision of the Act required LEAs to provide primary, secondary and further education in 'three progressive stages'. For children up to the age of 11 there were to be primary schools; for those above the age of 11, secondary schools. Transfer from the primary to the secondary stage was to be determined by age alone. Before 1944, the only schools known as secondary were grammar schools. The Act made secondary education a universal entitlement without specifying what sort of curriculum was to be offered. The White Paper had assumed a differentiated system of grammar, modern and technical schools along the lines put forward in the Norwood Report, but this was not in the Act which was content to define the LEA's responsibility as follows:

> *The schools available in an area shall not be deemed to be sufficient unless they are sufficient in number, character and equipment to afford for all pupils opportunities for education offering such variety of instruction and training as may be desirable in view of their different ages, abilities and aptitudes, and of the different periods for which they may be expected to remain at school, including practical instruction and training appropriate to their respective needs.*

The ending of elementary education also meant an end to the elementary school teacher. In future qualified teachers would be qualified to teach in any primary or secondary school. The Act reorganised the Burnham Committees (where teachers' salaries were negotiated) to take account of this.

LEAs were required to start work immediately on development plans for approval by the Minister, showing how they proposed to provide primary and secondary education under the Act. These were meant to be the key strategy documents, the means by which ministers concentrated the minds of the LEAs on what needed to be done.

Separate plans were required for FE which had its own lengthy coverage in the Act. It was expected that there would have to be a big expansion of technical education and courses designed to meet the demands of industry. Plans for day continuation schools which had figured in the 1918 Act – and had never been put into force because of financial cuts –

reappeared in the 1944 Act in a new form. County colleges were to provide part-time day-release courses for all young school-leavers. In the years which followed the Act there was much interest in the possibilities which such colleges would open up. It could not be foreseen that these provisions, like their predecessors, would remain a dead letter for lack of money, to be repealed almost as an afterthought in the Education Reform Act of 1988.

The Act placed a duty on the Minister to 'cause inspections to be made of every educational establishment at such intervals as seem to him to be appropriate' and to arrange for special inspections where desirable. This was the rubric under which Her Majesty's Inspectorate operated. LEAs were empowered to appoint their own local inspectors.

Part 3 of the Act dealt with independent schools which HMI also inspected as a matter of routine. The Minister was to appoint a registrar of independent schools to set up and maintain a register of such schools 'open for public inspection at all reasonable times'. It would fall to HMI to inspect schools seeking registration. The Minister was given the power to deny registration to any school which was found to be unsatisfactory, subject to appeal to the Independent Schools Tribunal.

The 1944 Act, then, was the framework within which a reconstructed education system could be built. It was a programme for a generation, to be worked through a bit at a time with progress dependent on the supply of funds. It was backed by a general consensus between the main political parties and (no less important) between the politicians and the professionals.

There were no short cuts. Priority was given to schools and schooling. County colleges and the introduction of compulsory part-time education for school-leavers went on the back-burner, not for a lack of supporters ready to argue the importance of FE, but because the statutory requirements for 11 years of compulsory schooling inevitably took precedence. Unfortunately, the longer action on county colleges was postponed, the harder it became to muster the political will to bring these sections of the Act into operation.

HMI – The Roseveare Reorganisation

The decentralised nature of the education system in England and Wales gave special importance to the Inspectorate. Ministers had to rely on HMI for information about what happened in schools. Through HMI, ministers had access to a system-wide network – an intelligence system – and given the limited executive powers vested in the Minister, HMIs were also seen as being in a position to influence as well as to observe.

In 1943, the Norwood Committee had gone beyond its terms of reference to devote a whole chapter to the future of the Inspectorate in the post-war education system. In its view, the Inspectorate would have an essential part to play in the creation of the new secondary education system and in the responsive adaptation of schools and teachers to the needs of a much larger section of the community. In a somewhat perfunctory paragraph, Norwood summarised the functions of the Inspectorate: HMI were 'the eyes and ears of the Board of Education, reporting regularly what is being thought, said and done in the schools' and the public's guarantee that 'the schools are doing their work honestly'. And it was their job to perform these functions while keeping 'the friendship and the willing cooperation of the teaching profession'.

There is something a little coy and tentative about the guarantee which HMI was supposed to offer the public – the work of the schools must be 'honest' but not necessarily effective. Perhaps this was simply a realistic recognition that no one can give cast-iron guarantees about the outcome of teaching and learning. It certainly carried no message of accountability. The third point about 'keeping the friendship of the teachers' sits somewhat oddly with the first two but nevertheless signals the committee's view that good results were only to be obtained by cooperation.

The pretext for the Norwood Committee's observations (the secretary to the committee was an HMI, R. H. Barrow) was the reform of secondary education and the kind of examination regime likely to be appropriate to that reform. Norwood favoured moving away from external examining to a system of internal examinations set by the schools themselves. The role envisaged for HMI was to back this up with a comprehensive inspection programme and with strong professional support for the teachers who, if the members of the Norwood Committee had their way, would have to set their own standards. Hence the recommendation that the Inspectorate should be expanded (with better pay to maintain the quality of recruits), in order to be able to mount full inspections on a five-year cycle.

Later generations have remembered the Norwood Committee for its unflinching advocacy of a segregated secondary school organisation, comprising grammar, modern and technical schools. The argument about school organisation was there, certainly, but it was accompanied by views

Sir Martin Roseveare, Senior Chief Inspector, 1944–57

on secondary school examinations which were liberal in the extreme. HMI shared Norwood's desire to play down external examinations and, as we shall see, spent the first 10 years after the war resisting the attempts to develop an examination for the secondary modern schools.

The Inspectorate was an early Victorian invention[16] dating back to 1839 when the Committee of the Privy Council, having recently begun to make grants for education, ruled that no further such grants should be made 'now or hereafter for the establishment or support of normal schools or any other kind of schools unless the right of inspection is retained'. The first two HMI were appointed – H. S. Tremenheere, a barrister, and the Revd John Allen, a clergyman. Two 'examiners' were appointed by the Committee of Council to read the reports. As the number of schools receiving grants increased, so too did the number of inspectors.

Their early remit, drafted by James Kay (later Kay-Shuttleworth), was modest: they had to be assured that money granted by Parliament was not being misapplied, but they were not to 'interfere with religious instruction or discipline or management of the school, it being their object to collect facts and information and to report the results of the inspections to the Committee of Council'.[17] They would, however, be called on for advice:

> It is of the utmost consequence you should bear in mind that this inspection is not intended as a means of exercising control, but of affording assistance; that it is not to be regarded as operating for the restraint of local efforts, but for their encouragement; and that its chief objects will not be obtained without the cooperation of the school committees; – the Inspector having no power to interfere, and not being instructed to offer any advice or information excepting where it is invited.

Between then and 1944, the Inspectorate had evolved in response to changes in the education system. This has been the essential characteristic of the Inspectorate: it has existed to provide services to and for the education service. As the education service changed and developed, so too has the Inspectorate, in ways directly related to the changing character of public education and ministers' changing needs and expectations.

In the second half of the nineteenth century, working under the Revised Code, the Inspectorate had buckled down to the routine tasks required to operate payment by results. The inspectors organised the examination of the pupils in the six prescribed standards; the pupils' results determined the size of the grant paid to the school managers. The reports of distinguished HMI of whom Matthew Arnold was only one, albeit the most famous, described the evils which flowed from payment by results. They reported what they saw and in so doing were influential in ending the mechanical connection between grant and examination. Their role altered again with the passing of the 1902 Education Act which brought secondary education within the ambit of public provision. Over the next four decades – the years up to 1939 – the modern Inspectorate took shape.

Depleted by war service and the absence of 50 HMIs on loan to other government departments – the Inspectorate struggled to maintain a regular routine of school visits. Full inspections for maintained schools were in abeyance for the duration. Much of the regular work had to be set aside because of the extra administrative tasks assigned by the officials in London who saw HMI as a network of field staff available for immediate troubleshooting and message-bearing. There was a lot of work to do helping to allocate shortage materials and explaining the Board's policies to the local education officers and their staff. It was through them also that chief education officers made their worries known to the Board, invoking the help of HMI as local advocates.

Martin Roseveare was 46 when he returned to the Board of Education as senior chief inspector (SCI) after war service at the Ministry of Food where he had edited ration books and designed the 'points' system. (When bread rationing was introduced in 1946 he went back for a while.) He was a mathematician who had been made a staff inspector in 1939, but had never taken up the job because of the war. He was manifestly inexperienced – a fact which some of his colleagues resented – and owed his promotion, like his knighthood later on, to his war work rather than to his career in the Inspectorate.

Not all his colleagues in the Office were as impressed by him as John Maud, who regarded his appointment as 'another bit of luck' when reviewing his time at the Ministry of Education in his autobiography. He was touchy and given to spraying all and sundry with memos written on a carbon-free pad he carried around with him. He was fit and energetic and a natural organiser: some said, more interested in organising the Inspectorate than advising on the educational issues which the Ministry had to deal with. He was intellectually well able to hold his own with his fellow inspectors and with the Office. He worked himself extremely hard and he was indefatigable in fighting the Inspectorate's corner in the office politics of the Ministry of Education.

His first and toughest task as SCI was to recover control of the Inspectorate. The use of HMI for administrative chores had become an ingrained habit of the Office; it would continue well into the early post-war years. In a long internal memo dated May 14 1944, his exasperation comes across as clearly as the noonday:

> It is just too ridiculous to contemplate that Inspectors out in the country should go on behaving as they have in the past ... At the present moment there is a tendency, not unnatural and difficult to avoid, for all sorts of Branches or Sections in the Office to regard HMI as simply their Outside Man eg Territorial, Meals, Establishment, IPR [Intelligence & Public Relations], Training, Secondary Schools and Primary Schools. This leads to the danger that the wretched Inspector may have anything up to a dozen masters apparently, and to me this is all wrong.

He went on:

> I want us to be quite clear on one point: that the boss of HMIs is SCI together with his CI colleagues. I cannot imagine what SCI's job is meant to be unless it is this.[18]

Sir Maurice Holmes, the then permanent secretary, agreed but complaints that the Office was continuing to use HMI as dogsbodies recurred for many years to come.

Well before the Act itself was passed plans had been laid for the new Ministry which would succeed the Board. For the administrators, the abolition of elementary education led to the creation of a single Schools Branch 'to give policy direction on all matters concerning primary and secondary schools'. A new FE Branch replaced the pre-war Technical Branch. Territorial officers were organised under these two branches to administer the Ministry's policies throughout England and Wales and, to cope with the immediate post-war pressures, a Buildings and Priority Branch was set up. Teachers' Branch was expanded as was the Awards Branch to cover the work arising from the Further Education and Training Scheme (FETS). More staff were also appointed for school meals, teachers' salaries and such external commitments as Unesco.

Roseveare headed a committee which considered what needed to be done to bring the Inspectorate up to date and adapt its structure to the changes brought in by the Act. Reporting in July 1944, the committee listed 15 functions of the Inspectorate. The first two and the last encapsulated the chief duties of HMI:

- 'assessing and reporting on the efficiency of schools by general inspection;
- 'assessing progress in school and offering all possible assistance to teachers in securing and maintaining progress;
- 'generally assisting the Ministry in its development of policy by providing (i) a knowledge of the schools and their potentialities and (ii) expert views on educational matters.'

These remained the main responsibilities of the Inspectorate, being re-stated from time to time over the next 40 years in broadly similar terms.

The pre-war Inspectorate had been rigidly divided into elementary (E), secondary (S) and technical (T). Under the HMI there were assistant inspectors, known as AIs, who were paid on a lower scale and had little chance of advancement to HMI status. The first thing Roseveare had to do was to unify the Inspectorate in line with the unification of the school system brought about by the abolition of elementary education. This meant doing away with the post of senior woman inspector, integrating women fully into the Inspectorate, and abolishing the 'E' designation and the rank of AI. Within the single, unified Inspectorate, there were to be two main sections: primary and secondary (which included special schools) and FE, subdivided into TCA (technical, commerce and art) and OFE (other further education).

At the head of the organisation[19] was a Senior Chief Inspector, who was paid on a scale which equated him, in Civil Service terms, with an undersecretary, the modern rank of Grade 3. Under the SCI there were six chief inspectors (CIs) with responsibility for different aspects of the Inspectorate. The SCI and the CIs constituted the senior management. There was also a cadre of staff inspectors (SIs). Every major subject area or phase (eg primary, secondary) would have an SI who would be the Inspectorate's chief specialist, coordinating relevant HMI activity.

The main body of HMIs formed the territorial force of the Inspectorate, living within the Divisions in which they worked. They were so deployed as to ensure that, for every local or national institution or activity which came under inspection, there was an HMI who was nominated as general inspector (GI). For every LEA area, there were district inspectors for schools and FE, and in the case of larger authorities, OFE (see Chapter 5), who liaised with the chief education officer and his staff. Parallel and overlapping networks led by the SIs were used to focus the specialist resources of the Inspectorate. An SI for a major subject would be assisted by a group or panel of HMIs who would combine a specialist interest in their subject and phase with general inspection duties. The work of the FE branch developed somewhat differently because they acquired some important administrative responsibilities, for example for the approval of buildings and courses and the purchase of equipment (see Chapter 4).

The territorial organisation was headed by 10 divisional inspectors (DIs) each with responsibility for a region. (In the 1970s the number was reduced first to eight and then to seven.) The DIs undertook the personnel management tasks for the Inspectorate in the field, running the divisional office, organising training and staff conferences for the sharing of intelligence, and assigning duties and dealing with administrative matters such as expenses and leave.

Roseveare's reorganisation scheme had been a matter of widespread discussion – and contention – inside the Inspectorate, with a series of papers from the Association of HMI (later part of the First Division Civil Servants Association). Roseveare discussed the proposals at HMI meetings up and down the country and for the most part they were well received – though it is said that in the north-west he got a 'chilly reception', the mildest comment being: 'the goodwill of the Inspectorate is such that even a scheme as bad as yours might be made to work.' This may have said more about the frankness of discussion within the fraternity of the Inspectorate than the merits of the scheme which, in most of its essentials, stood the test of time. There were changes over time in the way the Inspectorate was managed and the priorities which determined its work, but the basic organisation of the Inspectorate established at the end of the Second World War continued without fundamental change till 1992.

The Inspectorate entered the post-war world in a state of rapid expansion and some degree of turmoil. Large numbers of new recruits were taken on while many who had stayed beyond retiring age were leaving. HMIs wished above all to settle down to the regular routines of inspection, reporting and in-service training, which were regarded as the staple of the work of HMI but the pressure of administration continued into peacetime.

Roseveare added his own gloss to the classic *Instructions to Inspectors* issued by the Committee of Council, in 1840. In a letter which he sent to all newly appointed HMIs, he emphasised the independence and impartiality of inspectors appointed by Royal Warrant and the proper limits of what he called 'considerate' inspection:

> *HM Inspector does not give directions, nor does he see that these directions are carried out, and it is important that he should not add to his own responsibilities the duties of others ... HM Inspector wields great influence ... and if he is liked and trusted by his schools, and if he is always honest in his assessments and clear in his advice, it is only on very rare occasions that he needs to speak with unusual emphasis.*

There are obvious echoes of Norwood here: HMIs are to inspect, but in the nicest possible way and without jeopardising good relations with the teachers by whom they are to be 'liked and trusted'. The language in which the SCI expressed himself was no doubt chosen with care: it was surely both important and surprising that he should have gone to such lengths to emphasise the unthreatening nature of the inspection process.

It would have been quite understandable if Roseveare and his ministers had come to quite different conclusions. Inspection was one of the only instruments the 1944 Act gave the Minister as a means of influencing what happened in schools. Confronted by a decentralised system run by powerful local authorities and a teaching profession whose independence was not constrained by any national curriculum, might it not have seemed a good time to reassess the Kay-Shuttleworth tradition and erect a tough inspection regimen in its place?

It is doubtful if the question was ever seriously asked because the consensus on which the new education system was being built was that of partnership, the overworked word which nevertheless expressed the *de facto* power structure within the system. From the Minister's point of view, encouragement and positive reinforcement seemed much more likely to succeed than confrontation – and without a national curriculum there was no prescribed set of approved procedures to police.

It was only much later that it became a universal assumption that all professionals would exploit their clients unless they were monitored and regulated by an external authority. The post-war mind-set was different, less cynical. By common consent there were large no-go areas for politicians in education – it was not for them to decide what should be taught, or even to express their opinions on the subject. They were disposed to trust the professionals and in the case of teachers to believe they would perform better if they were treated more like professionals. This was part and parcel of the optimism of the period and it was rooted in a simple truth – the only people who could deliver the educational revolution were the education professionals.

There was another reason why the Inspectorate wanted to discount its monitorial function. In the interwar period HMI had fairly good relations with the grammar schools but not with the elementary schools. In the case of the grammar schools and independent schools, HMIs were gentlemen dealing with gentlemen. Not so in the case of the elementary schools which had an altogether lower status. Long after the passing of payment by results, the National Union of Teachers (NUT) continued to make capital out of folk memories which cast inspectors and teachers as natural enemies. It was not surprising that relations were poor. HMIs had little first-hand experience of the elementary schools. Most were educated at independent schools or well-established grammar schools. After Oxbridge, their teaching experience had been in similar schools. The divided structure of the pre-war Inspectorate was tailor-made to ensure that HMIs would look down on the elementary schools which were, essentially, schools for other people's children.

What Roseveare was looking for were methods of working which would break down old suspicions and historic antagonisms. Hence the emphasis on politeness and courtesy. Style was important. HMIs were to win respect through their impartiality, fairness and openness. They saw no contradiction between this and making firm and if necessary, critical, judgements. Looking back, HMIs recall the occasional 'sacking' inspection when local authorities made radical changes on the basis of HMI recommendations and adverse comments brought about resignations or retirements. HMIs were not to be seen *primarily* as watchdogs or compliance officers or police officers, but as members of an intelligence service available to the Minister and Ministry and in daily contact with the schools, colleges and the other institutions for which they had responsibility – responsibility without control. Their remit covered the system at all levels (up to but not including the universities); common to all was the expectation that they should use their unique position as *animateurs* at large to identify, encourage and spread (but not impose) good practice.

As important as what they did, therefore, was the way they did it and who they were. They were professional experts mainly drawn from the ranks of practising teachers (augmented as necessary from other backgrounds) and in that sense most of them were insiders. Becoming an inspector did not mean ceasing to be a member of the teaching profession. This was one of the things which gave HMI their strength. But in another sense they were definitely outsiders because they were not part of the line management of the school system, they were independent of the local authorities, and even if they were 'at the disposal of the Minister' and subject to Civil Service discipline this is not how they were perceived. And one independent power of HMI was real enough: it had been established since the middle of the nineteenth century[20] that their reports could not be altered by ministers or officials. The Ministry could decide whether or not to issue an HMI report but could not change what HMI had written.

As we shall see, different roles were emphasised at different times. The formal inspection of individual schools never ceased to be one of the Inspectorate's functions and an essential part of its information gathering. But as time passed, more of its efforts went into surveys – and later, inquiries into specific questions suggested by policy priorities – which would be based on visits to schools but be focused on particular issues. HMIs would occasionally find themselves sent in to report on schools and local authorities which had hit the headlines. Their integrity was on the line when their findings – from routine inspection or from troubleshooting exercises – failed to give political satisfaction. Annual reports on local authority education expenditure would pose yet more quasi-political questions to which the Inspectorate was expected to give professional answers.

Notes

1   Robert Rhodes James (1993) *Chips: The Diaries of Sir Henry Channon*. London: Weidenfeld & Nicholson, 410.
2   Pimlott, B. (1986) *The Political Diary of Hugh Dalton, 1918–40, 1945–60*. London: Jonathan Cape in association with the LSE, 362.
3   Hennessy, P. (1992) *Never Again: Britain 1945–1951*. London: Jonathan Cape.
4   Crosland, S. (1982) *Tony Crosland*. London: Jonathan Cape, 40.
5   Letter from Roseveare to C. C. Clear, 28 July 1944. PRO ED23/714.
6   Marwick, A. (1982) *British Society since 1945*. London: Allen Lane, 22.
7   Timmins, N. (1995) *The Five Giants: A Biography of the Welfare State*. London: HarperCollins, 472.
8   Harris J. (1990) 'Enterprise and welfare states: a comparative perspective'. *Transactions of the Royal Historical Society* **20**: 175–95, 180, 192. See also Middleton, N., Weitzman, S. (1976) *A Place for Everyone: A History of State Education from the End of the Eighteenth Century to the 1970s*. London: Victor Gollancz, 241.
9   See note 8, Harris, 192.
10 Gosden, P. H. J. H. (1976) *Education in the Second World War: A Study in Policy and Administration*. London: Methuen.
11 Butler, R. A. (1971) *The Art of the Possible: The Memoirs of Lord Butler KG CH*. London: Hamish Hamilton.
12 See note 11, Butler, 92.
13 R. A. Butler speaking about the Education Act in a Central Office of Information film, 1944.
14 R. A. Butler speaking in the House of Commons during the Committee Stage of the Education Bill, 8 February 1944. See Hansard, Vol. 396, Col. 1707.
15 See note 11, Butler, 90.
16 Recommendation from the Committee of Council on Education, April 1839.
17 'Instructions to inspectors, Committee of Council on Education, 1840–41', quoted in Stuart Maclure (1986) *Educational Documents: England and Wales 1816 to the Present Day*. 5th edn. London: Methuen, 49.
18 Roseveare to A. J. Finny, Ministry of Education. PRO ED23/714.
19 'Report of Inspectorate Committee B'. PRO ED23/838.
20 In 1863 a row occurred over allegations that an HMI report had been altered by officials of the Committee of Council on Education. In good faith, Robert Lowe, the vice-president, denied that this had taken place but the offending document was produced in the House of Commons and he had to resign. As a historical note in the 1949 edition of the *Inspectors' Handbook* put it: 'The principle of the inviolability of HMI reports was thus established and an important safeguard both of educational and professional freedom set up.'

Part 1: Reconstruction and Reorganisation – 1945–70

Chapter 1   All Things New

Teachers and Schools. The Emergency Training Scheme. Teacher Training – 1945–70. Roofs Over Heads: Emergency Programmes. Seven and a Half Million Places in Thirty Years. Hertfordshire Effect.

The economic news was uniformly bad and austerity was the order of the day, but Labour had been elected to take on the Five Giants[1] which Beveridge had denounced – Want, Disease, Ignorance, Squalor and Idleness – and would not be forgiven if it failed to do so. Aneurin Bevan brought his own brand of Welsh fire, passion and wit to the debates on the National Health Service, using bludgeon and rapier with equal skill to overcome the resolute resistance of the doctors. And heading the Ministry of Education was Ellen Wilkinson, the one-time firebrand from the northeast.

Ellen Wilkinson grew up on Tyneside, went to a higher grade elementary school in Ardwick and thence to the Manchester Day Training College. Like Bevan she was regarded as a left-wing Labour Member of Parliament but she moved towards the centre in her later career, coming under the influence of Herbert Morrison with whom she was extremely close. She was a rousing speaker, whose left-wing credentials had been demonstrated once and for all on the Jarrow march. Now, at the age of 53, and already a sick woman, she became the only female politician in the Attlee Cabinet and had the job of giving practical effect to the educational ideals she had fought for all her life.

Her period in office was brief; she died in February 1947. Her successor, George Tomlinson, a small, humorous, good-natured man from Rishton in Lancashire, had left school at 12, becoming a weaver and a trade union official – president of the Rishton District Weavers Association. He made his way through the ranks of the Labour Party, and local government – one of his claims to fame as an educationist was as an education committee chairman campaigning for the provision of boots for needy schoolchildren in the 1930s. It was these two who had to take the Butler Act and turn it into a working reality in the Labour governments of 1945–51.

The cast of characters who would influence what could and could not be done was interesting and colourful. As her new permanent secretary, Wilkinson had John Maud, probably the most gifted and distinguished civil servant ever to head the Education Department. He was a man of infinite charm – the quintessence of Etonian good manners – a man of whom it was fairly said, 'you have to take the smooth with the smooth.' The son of a Church of England parson, he won scholarships to Eton and New College, Oxford, and became a politics don at University College. He was dashing and versatile, had acted with the OUDS, had become an independent councillor on Oxford Council to learn about politics at first hand, and when war came, he was snapped up as a temporary civil servant, spending much of his time at Lord Woolton's right hand in the Ministry of Reconstruction.

When peace broke out, he was the top civil servant in the Lord President's Office, helping Labour's incoming leader of the House, Morrison, plan its spate of legislation. Having decided to make his career in government rather than academe, he jumped at the offer of the top job at the Ministry of Education which seemed designed for him. Later he went on to be permanent secretary at the Ministry of Power before another change of direction took him to South Africa as high commissioner at the time of Harold Macmillan's 'wind of change' speech.

As his deputies he had Robert Wood, who went on later to become vice-chancellor of the University of Southampton and Gilbert Flemming, a high-flier who was returning to the Ministry of Education after wartime duties in the Cabinet Office and the Ministry of Production. The Minister's private secretary was Antony Part, rejoining the Education Department after a brilliant army career, a man who would hold a series of senior jobs in the Ministry before moving on to head up the Board of Trade. Among those joining the Ministry from other wartime jobs was Toby Weaver, who had been plucked from obscurity as an ordinary seaman, to work with Philip Morris – later vice-chancellor of Bristol University – on developing the army education scheme. Weaver, too, would be another who left his individual mark on the Education Department. He became deputy secretary in 1962, and before he retired in 1973 had served under eight ministers and six permanent secretaries.

Other important players who would have an influence on what happened in the post-war educational world were the leaders of the LEAs and the teachers' unions. Technically it was the County Councils Association and the Association of Municipal Corporations which represented the authorities, but in practice it was the Association of Education Committees (AEC) which spoke directly for education in local government. Each LEA had, by law, to appoint an education committee and a chief education officer. The AEC had established its right to be consulted by the Ministry of Education and its secretary acted as secretary of the authorities' side in the Burnham Committee.

One characteristic of the AEC made it unlike the other local authoritiy associations – its executive committee was formed of elected representatives – committee chairmen – and of an equal number of chief education officers. This gave it a combination of political and professional authority. Sir Percival Sharp, a former director of education for Sheffield, had been secretary of the AEC during the war and involved in the wartime negotiations on the education bill. His successor in Sheffield was also his successor as secretary of the AEC – William Picken Alexander[2]. Alexander was a Scot, a mathematician, a qualified teacher who had done research on psychology and psychometrics at Glasgow.

Alexander was a strong personality who tended to get his way in argument – a cleft appeared in his chin when he became fully engaged and his piercing eyes had an intimidating effect on those who sought to resist him. Though his title was that of secretary of the AEC, Alexander dominated his executive committee by sheer ability and force of character, leading them through his agenda to make his policy, their policy. He was equally forceful in his dealings with the Ministry where he had ready access and was able to bring influence to bear on policy at the formative (assistant secretary) stage before conclusive decisions had been taken.

He developed close relations with Ronald Gould[3], general secretary of the NUT, and with officials in the Ministry who respected his ability to deliver the support of the AEC if he committed it. Alexander's *politique* was based on the principle of partnership between the Ministry, the authorities and the teachers – he believed that any two, in combination, should be able to defeat the third. His good relations with both the other partners enabled him to maximise the influence of his organisation. For the next quarter of a century, Alexander was probably the single most influential figure in English education.

Gould, the leader of the NUT, was a former elementary school head teacher from Shepton Mallet in Somerset, a fine platform speaker and a former NUT president. He and Alexander were frequently to be seen together at the long bar in the National Liberal Club sharing insights and ways of cooperating without frightening their own constituents. Both were totally committed to making the new Education Act work and saw eye to eye on many issues. The NUT had a love-hate relationship with Alexander. They knew he was the bosses' man but also knew he was on their side much of the time.

Gould's long reign as NUT general secretary (1947–70) became increasingly fraught as teacher politics became dominated by the membership struggle between the NUT and the National Association of Schoolmasters, led by a maverick from Northern Ireland, Terry Casey.

Teachers and Schools

Two emergencies commanded everyone's immediate attention – teachers had to be found to teach the extra children who would stay on when the school leaving age went up to 15 on April 1 1947; and school buildings had to be found to teach them in. For Ellen Wilkinson, a threat of a third kind surfaced in the last months of her life when a section of the Cabinet tried to postpone the raising of the age. The economic ministers, Hugh Dalton, the Chancellor, and Stafford Cripps, the President of the Board of Trade, supported by Morrison, had no shortage of grim statistics to back up the case for delay which they brought to Cabinet. What such a postponement might have done to the hopes invested in the Education Act can only be imagined. In the event, Wilkinson won the support of Attlee and a majority round the Cabinet table, and a major political crisis was averted. It must have been a resigning matter for the Minister of Education if this battle had been lost. If the business of implementing the Act had faltered at the first obstacle, the loss of momentum would have been damaging in the extreme. Memories of what happened to the 1918 Act after the First World War were still far from dead. Morale would have plunged if the Government had wavered.

Teacher supply and school building were matters of major concern. For the Ministry which had so few direct responsibilities, these were areas of key importance: it was the duty of the Minister to decide the number of teachers to be trained and the size of the building programme. These were policy matters on which high-fliers cut their teeth and made their names. Both made heavy demands on the services of HMI.

The Emergency Training Scheme

Wartime planning for the first years of peace had included preparations for an emergency training scheme for teachers (ETS) the first details of which appeared in Circular 1652 dated May 15 1944. It envisaged a one-year course for ex-servicemen and women – war service was given a broad interpretation – followed by part-time study over a two-year probationary period.

It was estimated that the raising of the school leaving age would increase the secondary school population by 390,000. The wartime statistics were sketchy but the best guess the planners could make suggested a need for 70,000 teachers 'within a few years of the end of the war' over and above the number who could be expected from the existing universities and training colleges. Nobody knew what proportion of the teachers who had been away on war service would return – as it happened almost all of them did. It only became clear after the scheme was under way that there would also be a sharp increase in the annual number of live births as the war came to an end.

Of the 70,000 extra teachers, some could be found by increasing the number of regular training places in universities and colleges. But in addition there would have to be a crash programme. The original plan was for 10,000 places in 50 emergency training colleges, each with 200 students. In the event there were 55 somewhat larger colleges in the scheme, with numbers in the ETS peaking early in 1948 at about 13,500. Inside the Ministry, the scheme came under Flemming and the Teachers' Branch with Weaver one of those closely concerned. Before he became a civil servant, Weaver had seen more of the education system than most newly appointed principals, having taught (briefly) at Eton, and been an assistant education officer in Wiltshire.

Much of the work of planning and preparation fell to the Inspectorate including the drawing up of a study plan and working on the pilot course at Goldsmiths College, London. The HMI contingent was led by C. A. Richardson, a Chief Inspector whom Martin Roseveare described as 'probably the ablest thinker we possess'. (The story of the ETS was later set out in a Ministry of Education pamphlet – *Challenge and Response* – edited by G. W. Paget a Staff Inspector.[4])

HMIs took part in all the interviewing of candidates at home and abroad. They vetted the buildings which were to be adapted as college premises. They kept an eye on teaching practice – the scheme relied on some 6,000 schools nearly half of which had never before received students in training – and the subsequent supervision of teachers on probation. The Ministry looked to HMI for the professional input into the planning and execution of the scheme which continued to make heavy demands on their time, displacing other necessary work – some HMIs recall spending two or three days a week on ETS-related matters.

Most of the men students – who outnumbered the women by two to one – were aiming to teach children in the secondary age range in the new secondary modern schools. The course of study included most of the regular school subjects, while leaving students some choice. All had to study the principles of education – by which was meant a course designed 'to bring the student to realise the existence of the problems which confront anyone seriously engaged in education, and to encourage him to adopt a method of approach based on first-hand observation, reading and discussion'. Having made out this demanding prescription, it is less than surprising to read in the Ministry's report on the ETS, that: 'it did not prove easy to find competent lecturers in education.'

With next to no labour available for educational building, the emergency training colleges had to be improvised in such other buildings as might be available – country houses were pressed into service but often proved unsatisfactory because of the size of the rooms and the variety of the teaching and living spaces required. Many of the early colleges had to make do with picturesque but substandard facilities. As industrial hostels and hutted hospitals became available, the accommodation became uglier but more nearly matching minimum needs: these became 'the backbone of the scheme'.[5]

The costs were borne centrally but the administrative tasks were shared between central and local government. The local authorities had to find suitable buildings to suggest to the Ministry who made the final selection and arranged through the Ministry of Works for whatever had to be done to adapt and equip them.

The selection of candidates went ahead of the opening of the colleges – by the end of 1945 only six colleges taking 1,000 students had opened while 5,000 accepted candidates clicked their heels waiting for the word 'go'. Twelve months later, 31 colleges had opened and the waiting lists were down to reasonable numbers but 7,500 potential students had withdrawn, unwilling or unable to wait. Three out of four of the applicants for places had some sort of secondary school or FE qualification – half had School Certificate – and the service experience they brought with them was varied and extensive. They were said to have three characteristics: 'their keenness and singleness of purpose; the wide range of their talents and accomplishments; and their powers of initiative and organisation'. Most of the lecturers, too, had served in the forces.

By common consent, the weakest part of the scheme was the optimistic assumption it made about probation and the two years of part-time study. The trouble with part-time study by newly appointed teachers was, as one of them put it, 'there is no part-time.'[6] The course was limited to one year for logistical reasons – a large number had to be trained within five years. But the post-qualification study provisions were always based on hope rather than confidence. All Ellen Wilkinson could do was appeal to LEAs to give as much help as they could. The response was predictably uneven; some authorities tried to organise some support, others did nothing at all. And inside the NUT there was murmuring about 'dilution' and undercutting the union's long-term aim of a graduate profession. It was an episode which demonstrated the limitations of the oft-proclaimed concept of partnership. It was evident that HMIs, who had explicit responsibilities towards probationers, could do little about this failure of the system in its pastoral care of newly trained staff – a failure which in one form or another would persist over time.

The scheme was judged to be a success in that, within a relatively short time, it brought an extra 35,000 teachers into service: by 1951, one in six of all teachers in the maintained schools was emergency-trained. How good were they as teachers? The official verdict was diplomatic:

> In so large a company, drawn from such diverse elements in the community, one would expect a wide variation of professional competence; and it is probably true that between the most promising and the least promising there is a wider gap than is likely to have existed in any previous recruitment to the profession.[7]

There can be little doubt that the breadth of experience which they brought with them enriched the profession and extended its horizons. H. C. Dent concluded that many became above-average teachers – and more than a few first class – but that there was 'possibly a higher proportion of weak teachers than among those produced by permanent training colleges'.[8] In a profession which tends to be overly respectful of paper qualifications, being emergency-trained was not in later years regarded as a powerful recommendation for promotion.

The part played by HMI in the ETS was an illustration of one of the functions of the Inspectorate. They designed the courses in outline and worked closely with the teacher trainers in putting them in place. They helped to select the candidates, chaired selection committees and established in practice the criteria for choice. They oversaw the probationary process. They were on the inside looking out, not on the outside looking in. It would have been unreasonable to expect them to appraise the scheme with a dispassionate eye: they were too close to it, too much part of the team whose job it was to make a success of an exercise in large-scale improvisation. This draws attention to a recurring feature of the Inspectorate and its work. They were expected to be impartial and judicious observers and reporters on the work of others, while at the same time being participants. There was always tension between their functions as Inspectors, in the narrow sense of the word, and their wider functions as *animateurs* and encouragers of good practice. How they handled this tension – how they were expected to handle it – changed over time with changing public expectations and moods. As time went on, the tension caused by these conflicting demands became more acute.

However, the role of HMI, in the post-war period, cannot be understood without appreciating that these were heady and exciting and above all hopeful, times. Whatever its faults and limitations, the exercise they were all engaged in was about making things better; they were making a difference, laying the foundations of a better world, and generating the enthusiasm and optimism which were essential for success. HMI had to be part of this enterprise, they could not masquerade as watchers on the sidelines.

Teacher Training – 1945–70

During this period the foundations were laid for the expansion of teacher training in the two-year colleges, stimulated by central grants and a pooling of costs among LEAs. By 1951, the number of colleges had gone up from 91 to 132 and the balance between the Church-related colleges and the LEA colleges had changed: the voluntary colleges had gone down in number from 63 to 56, while the LEAs had stepped up their efforts under the stimulus of a central government grant and created 38 new institutions (some of them from former emergency training colleges). The result was a doubling of the number of students in training to more than 24,000 with, as intended, less dependence on the Church colleges.

In 1949 a new body, the National Advisory Council on the Training and Supply of Teachers (NACTST) was set up to advise the Minister. Members were drawn from the local authority associations, university departments of education, the representatives of the training college staff and the teachers' unions. It worked through two standing committees. One of these concentrated on supply and recruitment, the other on training and qualifications.

Questions of supply and how to recruit and train enough teachers were a constant preoccupation throughout the first quarter of a century after the end of the war. Because of the boom in the numbers of babies born between 1944 and 1948 pupil–teacher ratios were likely to get worse before they got better. Even so, the Minister decided to end the Pledge – the promise which linked grants to an undertaking to teach for at least two years in a maintained school.[9] Student support was stepped up in other ways but not enough to prevent a short term decline in numbers. (One pre-war teacher who had benefited from a grant when such strings were attached was a future secretary of state for education, Edward Short. The experience left him a strong supporter of unconditional student grants and opponent of loans.) The age profile of the profession was skewed by the large number of teachers retiring in the post-war period and the low recruitment in the 1930s. The complexities of demography made the accurate forecasting of demand notoriously difficult.

Entrants to initial teacher training

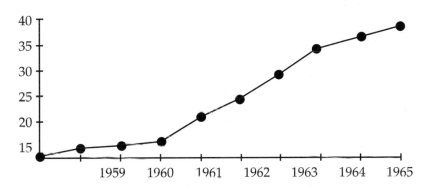

Students admitted to initial teacher training courses at colleges, excluding university departments, 1959 to 1968. From DES Reports of Education No. 49, *Colleges of Education*.

The trend in the annual numbers of live births was one of the variables. Another concerned marriage and family-raising *mores* among teachers: wastage from the profession depended directly on the age at which teachers married and how many children they had. Changes in society at large affected such matters as the length of time mothers took out of their working lives to raise their children. In the early post-war period it was still regarded as usual to expect a gap of 12–15 years. Working out how many teachers had to be trained to maintain a given level of staffing was likened to the proverbial speculation about baths filling or emptying according to the vagaries of the plumbing.

Wastage rates (percentage) of non-graduate women teachers, 1958–62

	1958–9	1959–60	1960–1	1961–2	1962–3
Under 25	9.5	10.1	10.5	12.4	12.3
25–29	16.2	17.1	17.6	18.9	19.7

Source: Department of Education and Science, *Statistics of Education: Teachers, 1962*, Table 40

What nobody disputed was that the schools were seriously short of teachers. The Ministry regulations on class size laid down 40 as the intended maximum for primary classes and 30 for secondary. Throughout the 1950s and well into the 1960s and 1970s there continued to be a large number of classes which exceeded the regulation size. There were arguments about the value of setting maximum class sizes at all because schools needed to be free to have smaller or larger groups in different circumstances. The regular publication of the figures was a standing reproach. In 1956, 27.8 per cent of primary classes had more than 40 children. The figure for secondary classes was even worse – 52 per cent of classes were oversize. By 1965, some improvement had been made as a result of the huge expansion of the teacher training programme: the percentage of primary oversize classes had come down to 12.6 and for secondary, to 39.8. In the same 10 years, pupil–teacher ratios had improved, but only slightly: primary improved from about 30.9:1 to 28.3:1. At the secondary level, the ratio was 20.3:1 in 1955 and 18.7:1 in 1965.

The training colleges continued to expand throughout the 1950s, as new colleges came into operation. Between 1947 and 1960 the annual intake more than doubled to nearly 15,000. By 1957, it looked as if things were easing, annual wastage appeared to have stabilised and the statisticians expected a healthy net increase in the number of teachers coming into service. This seemed to provide the opportunity to extend the training college course from two years to three. (At this point, local authority representatives on NACTST had even become anxious that there would be more trained, would-be teachers than jobs.)

In 1957, on the strength of these forecasts, the Minister, Geoffrey Lloyd, announced the decision to introduce the three-year course and included it in a White Paper announcing a five-year drive to raise standards which would include a five-year school building programme and a programme of improvement for the secondary modern schools (see Chapter 3).

The three-year course was an overdue reform, recommended by the McNair Committee in 1944 and widely welcomed by the teachers and the authorities, but as it happened the demographers had misread the runes; wastage worsened and the rise in the annual number of live births resumed and continued till 1964.

The new arrangements were duly introduced in 1960 with no sign of any let-up in the continuing teacher shortage – the immediate effect of the extra year being to interrupt the flow of new teachers from the colleges for the transition year. During the 1960s, expansion programme followed expansion programme. Sir Edward Boyle used Passchendaele as a simile for the problems of teacher wastage – more and more teachers had to be trained and sent to the front to make good the ever-growing losses. Boyle's expansion was followed by Anthony Crosland's. The colleges were called on to accept overcrowding, doubling up, Box and Cox arrangements – expedients for cramming in more and more students.

In the early 1950s there were complaints about the number of students admitted to the colleges with fewer than the minimum (5 O levels) entrance requirements – 775 in 1952. F. W. Land published a survey of one in five entrants to training college in 1957 – 374 men and 1,880 women.[10] This found that of the men, 194 had no A levels but 114 had more than the minimum five GCE O levels. Of the women, 822 had no A levels and 554 had more than the minimum qualifications. They were also given a maths test which showed shortcomings which would need attention before they were sent out to teach – certainly if they were going to teach in primary schools where they would have to teach the whole curriculum.

All this was taking place against the background of the social revolution of the 'swinging' sixties and the rapid changes in convention and social regulation which were sweeping away many of the features of the traditional training colleges – notably their strict rules about student behaviour in what had for the most part been seminaries for young ladies. Many single-sex colleges became mixed. Rules were relaxed and the colleges reinvented themselves as the numbers multiplied.

Improvisation was the order of the day. When the House of Commons Select Committee questioned Department of Education and Science representatives on these matters in 1969 there was an inevitable question about the cost of adapting toilet facilities for a mixed student body. Hugh Harding, the under secretary to whom in the 1970s would fall the task of cutting back the expansion of the 1960s, said: 'There is a very good system in colleges of education where they have a label which on one side says "Gentlemen" and on the other side says "Ladies", and they hang it on the door knob and turn it round.'[11]

The roller coaster ride of teacher training told its own story. In 1961–62 there were 60,000 teacher training places. Ten years later there were 120,000, which meant a 7 per cent annual growth rate. It was a period of unprecedented expansion and unequalled stress for those responsible. This was also the time when the three-year course was being introduced. It would have been extraordinary if the quality of what was offered did not suffer. Everyone was so fully committed to getting by – to surviving – that this became an end in itself and students had to make the best of their preparation for teaching in the circumstances.

Most graduates who went into teaching did so by way of the postgraduate certificate of education (PGCE). Such certificates were awarded by universities as part of their regular academic provision. University departments of education designed the courses and examined the students. The main outlines of the PGCE arrangements were established well before 1945 as the method of training secondary teachers – secondary then meaning grammar or independent. Training was not a condition of practising as a primary teacher till 1970. Training was required for secondary teachers from 1974, with various exceptions for shortage subjects.

The McNair Report (1944) had emphasised the need to improve the quality of teacher training in the colleges and raise the status of teachers. To this end the members of the McNair Committee had wanted the colleges to be linked to the universities and for the universities to take some responsibility for their activities. They were split down the middle on how to do this: in the event the Government favoured the creation of Area Training Organisations (ATOs) each based on a university and its hinterland. The colleges were divided up among the ATOs, gaining a loose connection with a university. The hope was that the link with universities would help to lever up college standards and expectations; in fact the ATOs were essentially loose federations with very little real power. HMIs, who had acted as external examiners for training college examinations, relinquished this task to the ATOs. HMI continued to visit colleges of education as of right but university departments by invitation only.

After the Robbins Report, the academic links with universities were strengthened. As the shape of higher education changed, some of the rechristened 'colleges of education' established connections with polytechnics and the Council for National Academic Awards (CNAA), and the basis of a graduate profession was laid with the creation of Bachelor of Education (B.Ed.) degrees. The LEAs and the Churches hung on to their colleges and ministers safeguarded their own authority over teacher training in general.

These arrangements still effectively kept decisions about the content of teachers' professional education and training with the ATOs and away from the Minister of Education. Ministers were expected to worry about the size of the profession and the number of qualified entrants to the profession but to leave the content of the courses to the professional teacher trainers. It is true that Ministers were responsible for certifying who was to be recognised as a qualified teacher – 'QT status' was important in terms of getting a job and getting paid – but for many years they were happy for responsibility for the content and process of teacher training to be delegated to the universities and the ATOs. It was not till the 1980s that this was challenged by Keith Joseph.

As colleges began to prepare students for the B.Ed. there were continuing debates about the proper balance between 'education' courses and those studied as main subjects for personal development. This was the time when the sociology of education was 'poised to join educational psychology as a major component in the professional training given to teachers'. [12]

The arrival of the B.Ed. held out the possibility of more challenging intellectual study of one or more academic subjects. For trainee teachers, most of whom would teach in primary schools, the traditional college response had been to focus on child development and the psychology of childhood, on the history, sociology and philosophy of education and on a general introduction to the curriculum.[13] More academic study depended on the more academically qualified teaching staff whom the colleges were hastening to recruit – staff who once they had arrived would fight hard for their share of the timetable.

The new courses put more responsibility on students who had to keep all the different components in their courses going at the same time. The most difficult thing according to Joan Browne, the principal of Coventry College and a leading figure in the teacher training world, was to make the whole course centre directly on professional training or arise directly out of the professional interest in education, given that the student would start with no experience, and yet was expected to make connections at every point.[14]

Peter Gosden attributed the increased fractiousness of the NACTST in the early 1960s to a clash between the professional aims of the teachers (and through them, the teacher trainers) and the needs of the national economy as represented by the non-professional members of the council, who were concerned about value for money and opportunity costs. Teacher preparation was being lengthened and made more expensive while the length of service expected of teachers, married or otherwise, was getting shorter.

How could the most use be made of the scarce resource of highly trained professional manpower? The most controversial suggestion – which hung in the air for several years poisoning relations with the teachers' unions – was for the training of auxiliaries who could work in the classroom under the supervision of qualified teachers. David Eccles aired the idea in a House of Commons debate in May 1962. After 12–16 weeks training, teaching assistants would be available for service. Undeterred by the immediate and unflinching hostility of the NUT, Anthony Crosland included auxiliaries along with ancillaries (outside the classroom) in his 14-point scheme for overcoming the teacher shortage. The NUT welcomed ancillaries – people such as clerical assistants and laboratory technicians who would provide back-up for teachers outside the classroom but not engage in teaching activities inside it – but would have nothing to do with auxiliaries.

The NACTST became increasingly acrimonious. The eighth report in 1962 voted by a majority to press the claim for a four-year course on grounds of general parity with other professions. This produced notes of dissent from some members of the committee who were unconvinced by what they took to be special pleading by the teachers and the teacher trainers. Dissension inside the council got worse in the aftermath of Robbins and the ninth report (1965) split the council into a majority and a minority. Among the matters at issue were the use which might or might not be made of auxiliaries in the classroom and the introduction of a four-term year for the colleges. Alexander's minority report was supported by nine members of the committee. There was also a note of dissent by Eric Robinson of the Association of Teachers in Colleges and Departments of Education and the two economists on the NACTST, John Vaizey and Charles Carter, rejected the majority recommendation. Alan Bullock, the chairman, resigned and the members were not reappointed. Crosland allowed the body to lapse into oblivion, its useful life having ended. It put another question mark alongside the notion of partnership. The council had broken down because it had been impossible to bridge the gap between the teacher training interest as represented by the teachers' unions and the teacher trainers on the one hand, and the local authority nominees and those of the Secretary of State on the other. The council had split according to the vested interests represented and no matter how shrewd or agile the chairman there was no way of papering over the cracks.

HMI continued to visit and watch over the colleges in the upheavals of rapid growth of the student body and teaching staff. The stonewalling tactics of Herbert Andrew and his colleagues in the House of Commons Select Committee on Teacher Training in 1969 were understandable but comprehensive. M. J. G. Hearley, the CI for teacher training, said as little as possible and was not asked for a general appraisal of the events of the previous decade.

Roofs Over Heads

Emergency Programmes

At the same time as tackling the immediate shortage of teachers through an emergency teacher training programme, ministers had to make similar emergency provision for additional classrooms. It was assumed that this could only be done by the extensive use of Ministry of Works huts – 72ft by 18ft 6in structures of the kind provided in large numbers for the Army – which could be put down with the minimum of foundations in school playgrounds.

After the First World War there had been a similar need for extra classrooms and this, too, had been met by huts, many of which had been retained long after they had become obsolete. It was recognised that there was a danger that this would happen all over again, but given the shortage of basic building materials and labour, there seemed to be no alternative to what became known as the HORSA programme – 'Hutted Operation for the Raising of the School-leaving Age'. In all between 1945 and the end of 1956 some 168,000 school places were provided in this way. 'Blot on the countryside'[15] or no, HORSA huts were in truth a great deal better than the premises which housed many of the ex-elementary schools.

Once again it fell to HMI to carry out many of the administrative chores associated with the scheme, explaining to LEAs what was required, approving sites and signing certificates authorising provision. There were constant complaints of delays and difficulties and continued overcrowding. And all at a time when the Inspectorate was in turmoil: attempts to bring numbers up to strength by rapid recruitment was putting induction and training procedures under strain. The continuing influx of new inspectors meant that the assignments of individual HMIs were frequently changing and there was a frustrating lack of continuity. Given that the HMIs' first duty was to visit schools and engage in inspection in all its various forms, overseeing the provision of huts was another major distraction.

What can be said is that the HORSA programme, for all its faults, succeeded in keeping the schools running without having to resort to double shifts and part-time education. And while the huts were going up, plans were going forward for the regular building programme. As early as 1942, consideration had begun on ways of tackling the schools' post-war building needs in a committee of architects and officials chaired by the deputy secretary, Sir Robert Wood, which sought to promote the possibility of standardised school building plans using light construction and prefabricated methods.

Seven and a Half Million Places in Thirty Years

These ideas were circulating among the fairly small circle of architects who were interested in school building. Before the war, many counties and boroughs had no county or borough architect, leaving building matters to the Engineer's Department. One such was Hertfordshire which John Newsom, the chief education officer, was preparing to push to the forefront of education authorities. The population of the county had risen sharply before and during the war and was now set to expand yet more with the construction of new towns and London overspill estates. C. H. Aslin, formerly borough architect for Derby, was recruited to be the county's first architect and he gathered round him a talented team for whom school building would be the first priority.

Hertfordshire was one of the counties which had tried (unsuccessfully) to avoid using Ministry of Works huts and make a start instead on building. Aslin's deputy, Stirrat Johnson-Marshall, set up a development group to design a prefabricated system for building schools rapidly and with a minimum use of scarce materials. They devised a modular system of construction – a Meccano set based on an 8ft 3in module – which they used to build some outstanding primary schools. These were notable not only for the short time they took to erect, but also for their clean lines and brilliant use of colour, creating teaching areas totally different from any others in the county. They raised the spirits of the teachers and children who moved into them. For them it was like coming into a new country – more light, more space, more colour. These in turn made possible more active forms of teaching and learning.

Hertfordshire Effect

Norman Thomas emerged from an emergency teachers training course and began life as a Primary teacher. In due course he would go on to become an HMI and CI for Primary education. After five years teaching at an inner city school in Islington in north London, he moved to Boreham Wood, to join the staff of a new, Hertfordshire, junior school.

Norman Thomas HMI

He found that the fact that the school was new ... allowed more freedom of thought.
There was no established set of practices. Each of us brought some difference of
experience with us. Especially important, the school design was, for the time,
revolutionary. In effect there were four pairs of rooms plus hall, dining space, staff and
headteacher's room and a medical room. The innovation was that the pairs of rooms
included what would have been the corridor to the hall, and off that space were the
lavatories for the children. The interactions between the teachers were much increased
because the outer class of each pair and its teacher necessarily went through the inner
class a number of times each day, though there remained virtually no combined work
between the classes.

There was another factor. The children came from more spacious homes than they had
known in London. The decorative finishes in the school undoubtedly influenced the
ways that houses were decorated. Outside play was much easier in Boreham Wood than
it had been in London and I noticed a softening of the children's voices. The same
children that I knew in London lost the nasal edge. I concluded, perhaps wrongly, that
in London, they pitched their voices partly to overcome the background noise and
partly to sharpen the echo from the surrounding buildings.

The Hertfordshire schools attracted a lot of notice – not least in the
Ministry of Education where Maud was an old friend (and former tutor at
Oxford) of Newsom. Newsom, himself, was no mean lobbyist – he was
reputed to build schools with a trowel in one hand and a trumpet in the
other. By now the man in charge of school building at the Ministry of
Education was Anthony Part. He began to move ahead on the basis of an
annual building programme, backed up with a rolling reserve programme
for each authority, so there was always work in the planning pipeline to
maintain continuity at LEA level. The volume of work had to be geared to
the capacity of the building industry and run in parallel with the housing
programme. While the scheme was getting under way, a team of regional
priority officers were appointed on short-term contracts as progress
chasers – they included a retired air marshal, and a captain RN, and an
assortment of ex-officers of field rank – with the authority and initiative to
solve problems on the spot.

When the chief architect at the Ministry of Education, Frederick Jackman,
retired, the post was upgraded and Johnson-Marshall was persuaded to
apply. His appointment at the age of 35 opened a remarkable chapter in
the history of public sector architectural management and
interdisciplinary cooperation. Part and Johnson-Marshall were a
formidable pair. Part was a forceful and effective administrator, an
assistant secretary in his mid-thirties who was clearly destined for the top.
Johnson-Marshall was quiet and apparently diffident but possessed of a

steely determination; without any outstanding talent as a designer, he had a remarkable gift for getting the best out of others – it was said that if you went to him with a problem, you would come out without a solution but convinced that you were the only person who could find one.

During the war he had been taken prisoner in the Far East, escaped, and on return to England worked in a hush-hush camouflage unit whose job it was to make the Germans think that the D-Day landings would be in the Pas de Calais area. This involved mocking up plywood model landing craft and barges and deploying them at strategic places along the coast. No doubt such models could be made and deployed with the minimum of architectural theory, but for Johnson-Marshall it was a Bauhaus exercise combining the skills of the designer, the constructor and the user to achieve a practical and effective result at reasonable cost. It was also a demonstration of what could be done when experts with varied skills worked together from start to finish in close association with people who were going to use their collective product.

The Architect and Buildings Branch was set up in 1949 with Part and Johnson-Marshall as joint heads. (Part's original plan was for Johnson-Marshall to be head of the branch with himself as deputy but this was scotched by the First Division Association.) Johnson-Marshall had radical ideas about the Ministry's role. He had made it clear before interview that he did not believe it should be confined to vetting plans and implementing building regulations – he wanted to give strong leadership in order to get the best value possible for the millions which were being poured into school building. He was determined to set up a Development Group in the Ministry, like the one in Hertfordshire, only bigger and better, and for this group to be allowed occasionally to build schools for LEAs, acting in the role of private architects.

After some delicate negotiation, this was accepted by the Local Authority Associations and the A and B Branch Development Group was in business. Between 1949 and 1981 the Development Group published 60 building bulletins in which they passed on the fruits of their experience and research. These became standard reading for all concerned with school building. The projects they embarked on were chosen to provide a cross section of architectural and educational problems.

The overarching aim was to carry through a vast building programme at affordable cost – that is, within the limits of materials, labour and money available. Questions of quality, including the quality of schools as places for teaching and learning, had to be fitted into this larger frame of reference. Johnson-Marshall was a realist. He believed in 'schools for the people' – a people's architecture which had to be provided at affordable cost.

When the first post-war schools went up, the cost-per-place for school building – the amount of money spent on building a school divided by the number of pupils – varied hugely. Primary schools in a single region were being priced at from £70 a place (in Doncaster) to £240 (in Leeds). This compared with the Ministry's rough yardstick of £130–50 a place. Amid crisis cuts in 1949, the Ministry issued a Circular which laid down limits of £170 a place for primary and £290 for secondary.

One object of the A and B Branch Development Group was, therefore, to find ways of cutting costs without damaging teaching. They built on the Hertfordshire experience with modular systems to monitor closely the material resources required and limit the construction period. And with the assistance of James Nisbet, a quantity surveyor who had also been part of the Hertfordshire team, they developed techniques of design cost analysis which could be used to pinpoint where savings could be made. The results were duly written up in Building Bulletin (No. 4) *Cost Analysis*. Cost planning quickly became part of the repertoire of the school building architectural fraternity.

Costs were marginally reduced by trimming the building regulations. Some savings (of time and materials) came from modular construction, but the main cost reduction came from cutting circulation space. The early post-war schools (like the last pre-war schools) were single storey structures, based on 'finger plans', with classrooms strung out along lengthy corridors. With the aim of cutting down the size of the building, while retaining as much teaching space as possible, later designs were more compact. In some cases this meant one classroom leading into another which some teachers found unsatisfactory but which also paved the way for the more ambitious forms of open plan which was thought to facilitate team teaching. (Open plans offended Margaret Thatcher when she was Secretary of State.)

The design changes brought about a marked reduction in costs-per-place. Circulation space in primary schools came down from 23 per cent to 7 per cent of the area of the building; in secondary schools, from 27.4 per cent to 12.8 per cent.[16] Teaching spaces, on the other hand, were maintained or increased – in primary schools from 2.50sq. metres per pupil to 2.69; in secondary from 3.78sq. metres to 3.87. By 1952, cost limits had been cut by 43 per cent. Had the limits been reduced arbitrarily, by government fiat, there would have been powerful resistance from the local authorities and their associations. As it was, because the Development Group had proved it was possible to build good schools within these limits and published the details in building bulletins – the early ones were remarkable for their clarity and directness before bureaucracy took its toll – the Ministry was able to retain the respect and confidence of the authorities and their architects and exercise the effective leadership Johnson-Marshall had promised.

These methods made it possible to carry through a programme of unprecedented size. The development of modular building systems was a feature of this programme and was central to the plan devised by A and B Branch for overcoming the material restrictions of the early period. CLASP – the Consortium of Local Authorities' Special Programme – was successfully spun off from the work of the Development Group to extend the use and development of modular building techniques, and this was followed by other local authority consortia. The cost limits regime continued through the 1950s and 1960s, coming to grief in the early 1970s, blown away by the inflation set off by the Middle East oil crisis. But even before the oil crisis there were signs that all was not well: under pressure from the Treasury, cost limits had been held down too tightly and some mean schools resulted.

What might have been done – or failed to be done – if these methods and practices had not been adopted is a matter for speculation. There were those who were never convinced of the need for system building. The modernist theories which provided part of the impetus behind it went out of fashion with the tower blocks of the 1960s. It is true that all schools began to look alike with flat leaking roofs and large expanses of glass. The idiom which produced grammar schools which made architectural statements with Corinthian columns and honours boards, seemed to have been replaced by an architectural language which made non-statements about mass culture and mediocrity. Encouraged by princely promptings in the 1980s, nostalgia demanded pitched roofs which did not leak.

Whatever criticisms might justly be made of the school buildings of this period, it must be acknowledged that there was a scandalous failure to maintain them properly – cutting down on maintenance was a favourite way of saving money in the short term at the cost of piling up trouble later on. Sophisticated discounted cash flow exercises had established that it was cheaper to save on finishes on the initial structure and allocate more for repairs and maintenance later on than to put in expensive and durable materials when a school was first built. Unfortunately only the first half of the equation was applied. It was even cheaper – though short-sighted – to skimp on maintenance and hope to get away with it which is what most LEAs would say they were forced to do.

The economic achievements of A and B Branch were remarkable and widely recognised. No less remarkable was the way in which the Development Group tackled the specifically educational questions which school buildings were intended to answer. Essential to Johnson-Marshall's idea was the bringing together of complementary disciplines and expertise. Beside the architects in the group, there was always an administrator and an HMI among the key members of the team. Leonard Gibbon HMI was a founder member, joined in 1951 by Eric Pearson HMI, who took over when Gibbon retired. Over a period of more than thirty years, two former members of the Hertfordshire architects department, the husband-and-wife team of David Medd and Mary Crowley, became closely identified with the work of the group.

Every project, therefore, began with a study of the particular kind of teaching and learning which the school would embody. Gibbon was the main conduit through which educational information was fed into the design process, gathering from his colleagues in the Inspectorate views and experience, tapping into the regional and national networks of the Inspectorate and the SIs and their specialist panels, to put the group in touch with best practice.

Gibbon also helped to get the ideas which were coming out of the Development Group across to the members of the Inspectorate. A descendant of the historian, he affected a somewhat pompous manner, but quickly struck up good relationships with the other members of the team, and hidden behind his formal manner there was a strong creative streak. Because he did not appear to be a radical, he was all the more effective when he became a spokesman for new ideas.

Every so often, Gibbon, Pearson and the Medds would attend HMI specialist committees as guests to explain the work of the Development Group and encourage closer cooperation. The minutes of the Secondary Panel record meetings to discuss the group's first secondary school (at Wokingham) where there were critical comments on the science laboratories – the SI for science felt he had been left out. On another occasion there was a lively discussion of 'houses' as social groups in large secondary schools – the Development Group had tried various approaches – without satisfying everybody. As Bill Elliott, an SCI in the 1960s, commented: HMIs were 'sympathetic, but perpetually rebellious', about building requirements.

HMI were not, of course, the only source of educational ideas on which the architects drew. Mary Medd spent a lot of her time in and out of schools (many, but not all of them, recommended by HMI) observing what teachers did (and comparing it with what they said they did). There was a conviction in the 1950s and 1960s that the Development Group should be at the leading edge of educational thinking and this was most obvious in relation to primary education where a minor revolution was taking place. Inevitably the Medds linked up with exponents of progressive ideas such as Robin Tanner and Christian Schiller who were making the running in the Inspectorate, and with chief education officers like Alec Clegg in the West Riding and Alan Chorlton in Oxfordshire.

The attitudes were unshakably progressive and assumed an uncompromising commitment to inter-professional collaboration. It was not simply a cooperation between architects and educators: the administrators had a big part in it, too, led by such outstanding officials as Anthony Part, David Nenk and Derek Morrell, who all acknowledged the potency of the experience in their own development. David Medd had no doubt about the value of interdisciplinary cooperation, nor yet about the hard work it entailed:

> The understanding of how to design for education has emerged through close and continuous association between professionals ... An educator's chief responsibility is to guide the designer to significant educational experiences and to share and to discuss them with him ... Learning the job is not a process of rushing to see the latest building ... Neither is learning the job a process of questionnaires ... Design has to evolve continuously as educational, social, and individual aspirations evolve.[17]

The Medds used HMI courses as opportunities to try out ideas, producing innumerable sketch plans to show different layouts incorporating different educational approaches. They were not just concerned with the design of the buildings. David Medd was a skilled cabinetmaker and he (and the Development Group) took a close interest in the design and manufacture of school furniture. Always eager to get teachers to say how they would use the schools which were being created, the Medds would involve them with HMIs in practical exercises, using scale models of tables and chairs to try out different ways of arranging furniture within prescribed teaching spaces. All this was fed into building bulletins.

It was an exciting time when architects thought they were making a real difference – and so they were. What could not be anticipated, however, was that continuing growth in numbers would mean that in many cases schools would be altered and extended several times within a decade of construction. As a result, the original design would soon be overlaid by additions and enlargements and these, along with staff changes, could quickly make nonsense of the most conscientious pedagogic planning.

Gibbon was the SI with A and B Branch from 1949 till 1965. Later on one of those who became involved was Conrad Rainbow, a former grammar school teacher who became an HMI in 1960, and who after 14 years in the Inspectorate, exchanged the job of district inspector for Lancashire for that of chief education officer. Rainbow joined A and B branch in 1967 when Dan Lacey was the chief architect, John Hudson the senior administrator, and Pearson the SI. For a junior member of the team there was a lot to learn. He recalled being on a 'rapid learning curve', going out to visit schools with David and Mary Medd and learning to look at what he saw in quite new ways. The Medds made it clear that they were not looking to HMI or to teachers to be told how to design schools. That was the architects' job. If you asked teachers, they would only ask for more of what they had already.

> 'Tell us,' the Medds would say, 'what you do and want to do. We must then design to make those activities possible and practicable.' They had a vast collection of photographs showing school situations which were good and some which were not so good. One showed a mountain of bags left in the corridor outside a classroom because there was nowhere to store them. We had lockers in some schools too small to take the pupils' belongings which they needed in school every day. David and Mary measured musical instruments so that the storage in music rooms could actually house them. It sounds obvious but had never been done before.
>
> The A and B team spread news of its work through Building Bulletins which had a wide influence throughout the country. Sometimes they dealt with a small infant school. One of the most exciting projects recorded in a Bulletin was the building of what I believe was the first 'sixth form centre' at the Rosebery County School for Girls in Surrey. Sometimes they dealt with subject demands such as music. We were moving away from the old assembly hall and a series of standard size boxes. It was an outstanding team in which I believe HMI made an important contribution.

A and B Branch contracted sharply in the 1970s when school building programmes were cut in the wake of the oil crisis, and in the 1980s

Thatcherite hostility combined with falling school rolls to undermine 'official architecture' at the local authority level. A and B Branch was dissolved and the few remaining architects on the departmental payroll were absorbed into the Schools Directorate as part of the School Organisation and Buildings Group. In the process the accumulated wisdom of a powerful architects department was dissipated. In its heyday it was a unique resource which combined an overview of the school architecture scene with the practical capacity to tackle specific problems and share solutions. It was essentially a collaborative enterprise which drew on collective wisdom rather than the brilliance of individual architects, and it pioneered methods of interdisciplinary cooperation which gave the educators a valued part in the process.

Because it was concerned with translating educational ideas into physical structures the Development Group focused consideration of the curriculum in a highly practical way. Without changing the conventions which excluded the Minister from the curricular debate, A and B Branch moved in, formulating the questions which the Ministry never had occasion to ask, and arrived at the answers they needed to refine an architect's brief. The Ministry did not lack experts – the Inspectorate was staffed with subject specialists – but in the 1950s, it was only in the Development Group that there was a concerted attempt to bring the expertise into focus in a practical and coordinated way.

It is no coincidence that when in 1962 David Eccles set up the short-lived Curriculum Study Group (CSG), it adopted an interdisciplinary format, based on the Development Group model, and Derek Morrell, formerly head of A and B Branch, moved across to take joint charge with Robert Morris, an HMI. Opposition from the teachers and the local authorities blocked the Ministry's first tentative steps to move in on the curriculum and the CSG was replaced by the Schools Council with Morrell and Morris as two of the joint secretaries. (See Chapter 3.)

The part played by HMI in the school building story was not confined to supplying the architects with advice and contacts. District inspectors were concerned when school building programmes were being put together – liaising with chief education officers on priorities – and at the same time, they were in regular touch with the territorial principals in the Office. It is not surprising that sometimes HMIs found it difficult to combine loyalty to the Office and loyalty to 'their' LEAs. An authority with a weak architects department might lean heavily on HMI to the extent that other work might suffer.

Notes

1 Timmins, N. (1995) *The Five Giants: A Biography of the Welfare State*. London: HarperCollins.
2 Alexander was knighted in 1961 and created a life peer in 1974 as Lord Alexander of Potter Hill.
3 Gould was knighted in 1955.
4 SCI Roseveare, Minute to Deputy Secretary, 22 November 1944. PRO ED23/714. See Ministry of Education (1950) *Challenge and Response: An Account of the Emergency Scheme for the Training of Teachers*. Pamphlet 17. London: HMSO, 76.
5 See note 2, Pamphlet 17, 16.
6 See note 2, Pamphlet 17, 119.
7 See note 2, Pamphlet 17, 130.
8 Dent , H. C. (1977) *The Training of Teachers in England and Wales 1800–1975*. London: Hodder & Stoughton, 127.
9 From 1956, Grant regulations for the training of teachers no longer included the 'Pledge'. See Gosden, P. H. J. H. (1972) *The Evolution of a Profession: A Study of the Contribution of Teachers' Associations to the Development of School Teaching as a Professional Occupation*. Oxford: Basil Blackwell.
10 Land, F. W. (1960) *Recruits to Teaching: A Study of the Attainments, Qualifications and Attitudes of Students Entering Training Colleges*. Liverpool: Liverpool University Press.
11 House of Commons, Select Committee on Education and Science (1970) *Teacher Training*, Session 1969–70. HoC 182, 2 vols. London: HMSO. Quote from Vol. 1, para 1441.
12 Shaw, K. E. (1966) 'Why no sociology of schools?'. *Education for Teaching* 69: 61–7, quote on page 61.
13 Browne, J. D. (1969) 'The balance of studies in colleges of education', in Taylor W. (ed.) *Towards a Policy for the Education of Teachers*. London: Butterworths for the Colston Research Society, 99–109. Proceedings of the twentieth symposium of the Colston Research Society, 100.
14 See note 12, Browne, 102.
15 A. R. Maxwell Hyslop to J. H. Burrows, 10 September 1945. PRO ED150/223.
16 For discussion of reduction in circulation space, see Maclure, S. (1984) *Educational Development and School Building: Aspects of Public Policy 1945–73*. London: Longman, 74.
17 Medd, D. (1976) 'Designing buildings as a resource', paper given at a summer school for teachers, Eaton Hall College of Education, Retford, Notts., mimeo.

Chapter 2   Schools for a New Generation

The End of the Elementary School. The New Primary School. New Approaches. Plowden Report. Gittins Report. Basics – Reading. Basics – Mathematics. Middle Schools.

The End of the Elementary School

Chuter Ede, parliamentary secretary to the Board of Education in the wartime coalition Government, was a former elementary schoolmaster. He recorded in his diary how he lay awake till midnight on April 1 1945, to make sure he did not miss the statutory demise of the elementary school.[1] He knew that this was the great structural achievement of the 1944 Education Act.

The elementary school was the symbol of the old regime. It had its origin in the Victorian, class-based, education system: it was the nineteenth-century prescription for a school for working-class children. To describe it as class-based is not a piece of latter-day liberal polemic: the Victorians were quite open about these matters. They had a straightforward understanding of the sociology of education. They would not have been surprised by twentieth-century research indicating a link between social class and educational performance: it is what they would have expected. Where they would have differed from later generations is that they simply accepted social inequality as a fact of life and designed a school system to fit in with it. They took it for granted that schooling should be related to parental socio-economic position – that middle-class children needed schools graded to their parents' upper, middle and lower middle class occupations and, therefore, to the employment expectations of their children.[2] The great majority of children would enter working-class occupations like their parents and it was for them that elementary schools were provided. The elementary school codes existed to make sure such schools did not get ideas above their station.

The 1944 Act ratified – and completed – the retreat from the elementary school which had been taking place since the Hadow Report of 1926 which had recommended that the all-age elementary school be divided into primary and secondary schools for children under and over 11 respectively. This was accepted, but England and Wales being the countries they are, the transition was left to the judgement (and in large measure, the financial resources) of individual LEAs.

The New Primary School [3]

A start had been made but there was a long way to go: by 1945, about two-thirds of the schools had been reorganised – that is, turned into junior and secondary schools or departments. Many others followed in the first years after the war, but it was relatively easy to change a school's name and put up a new sign board – much more difficult to make the psychological changes. The new primary and secondary schools had to find identities for themselves within an education system which aimed to open up equality of opportunity – whatever that meant.

It was at the secondary level that the implications would be most controversial. But for many urban primary schools, the outbreak of peace made little immediate difference. There were still classes of plus-or-minus 50; teachers were coming and going, as those who had postponed retirement went and those released from war service came. The disruption continued as the new emergency-trained teachers took up their jobs and began to learn their craft.

Calling post-Hadow junior schools 'primary' did not change the curriculum – on paper, the subjects were much the same as those outlined 20 years later by the Plowden Committee and 40 years later in the National Curriculum. Practice was different, however. Many junior schools were dominated by textbooks. For the larger schools, arithmetic, English, geography, history and sometimes nature study books were ordered in class lots, 40–50 at a time, many with a teachers' book which was seldom looked at. In schools which were big enough to have several parallel forms of entry, classes would be streamed – in practice, usually on reading ability.

On a typical day, after morning assembly and a Bible story, the standard practice was to dictate and mark 10 (or so) mental arithmetic sums or spend 10 minutes reciting and testing multiplication tables. Then a new aspect of some arithmetical process was demonstrated after which the children worked on examples from the textbook. After play, the younger children would turn to reading, using mainly phonic methods and published reading schemes. There might be some work in smaller groups, for those who found reading difficult, with one of the better readers taking a leading part and the teacher moving from group to group. The second half-hour after the break might include testing the week's spellings, writing the weekly composition or working through exercises from the English workbook: 'Write out the following sentences but make sure you put a comma after each opening "No" – No, tigers do not have trunks. No, ...'

A typical afternoon might be geography and history – the next chapter of the relevant textbook – say 'The Bedouin in his Tent'. The teacher or one of the better readers would read the text to the class and the teacher would ask questions, writing sentences on the blackboard leaving gaps to be filled from a list of suggested words. Then the class might go to the hall for music – singing – while their own teacher took the music teacher's class for poetry. The final hour would be craft – some kind of handicraft for boys and sewing for girls – or physical exercises in the hall or games in the playground (football for boys, netball for girls). Disciplinary measures in most schools would include physical punishment.

This (or something like it) was what getting back to the pre-war norms implied and it would be a mistake to suppose that there were not many schools where this persisted. There were, however, signs that things were changing: activity methods soon began to feature in HMI reports and in the discussions of the HMI Primary Panel. Already before the war, the Hadow Report of 1931[4] had flagged up changes in attitude and approach which were based on a more liberal view of childhood. It may have reflected aspiration more than actuality, but the sentiments are much closer to Plowden than Gradgrind:

> *The primary school has been broadened and humanised. Today it … offers larger, if still inadequate, opportunities for practical activity, and handles the curriculum, not only as consisting of lessons to be mastered, but as providing fields of new and interesting experience to be explored; it appeals less to passive obedience and more to the sympathy, social spirit and imagination of the children, relies less on mass instruction and more on the encouragement of individual and group work, and treats the school, in short, not as the antithesis to life, but as its complement and commentary.*

One of its recommendations has achieved a wider currency by frequent quotation:

> *We are of the opinion that the curriculum of the primary school is to be thought of in terms of activity and experience, rather than of knowledge to be acquired and facts to be stored.*

Needless to say the 'progressive' passages were balanced – more than balanced – by others which make it clear that the liberal-minded authors still wanted children to learn to spell and know their tables. Traditional methods and traditional authority were being challenged by men and women who sensed a new spirit of the age at work, loosening up formal relationships and inviting experiment. But many teachers remained committed to formal methods of instruction through the 1950s and beyond, and they did not need reminding that they had to prepare their pupils for the 11-plus exam.

The pre-war secondary selection procedures were usually based on some combination of attainment and intelligence tests. Primary HMIs discussed the selection mechanisms at length in the specialist primary committee, noting the refinements which the psychologists and statisticians suggested, and commenting on its influence on the schools. Although it was meant to be a value-free allocation process at the end of the primary phase, like other examinations it cast its shadow before it and exercised a form of control on primary education. This was particularly true in middle-class areas where schools were judged by the proportion of their pupils who secured places at the grammar school. Not only did many schools actively prepare pupils for the tests, coaching them and giving them practice so that when it came to the appointed day they would not be taken by surprise, but the looming 'scholarship' also focused attention on the grammar school as a symbol of academic learning and encouraged formal methods at the top of the primary school.

As local authorities introduced comprehensive school plans the situation changed. Schools did not wait for the ending of the selection procedure to introduce more active methods: the softening of subject barriers, changes in the teaching of reading including the development of primary school libraries, the extension of the requirement on children to write and changes in the teaching of mathematics – all these could be found in primary schools which remained under the discipline of the 11-plus. But the passing of secondary selection gave the primary school more freedom. One cause of parental anxiety was removed: primary schools could concentrate on creating happy and industrious school communities to be judged on their own terms and not those of the grammar schools. It was no coincidence that the 'new' primary education took off in places like Leicestershire which were among the first authorities to go comprehensive. But there was an underlying risk attached: the ending of the 11-plus removed the only remaining constraint on the primary curriculum and left the head teachers in complete control of what was to be taught and how. When the reaction came later on, critics – especially those who deplored the passing of the grammar schools – would link what they took to be the 'excesses' of child-centred education to the ending of the 11-plus and question the unfettered curricular discretion that had been handed to the primary school heads.

New Approaches

Teachers who wished to break away from the old routine tended to do so by emphasising the expressive aspects of the curriculum – as, for example, such pioneers as Marion Richardson (who became an LCC inspector) and Robin Tanner, who began teaching in an elementary school in Greenwich and found he could use his skill as an artist to fire the imagination of children.

Tanner was recruited as an AI in 1935. Upgraded to HMI under the post-war reorganisation, he combined the work of an inspector with his personal life as an etcher of distinction.[5] He was a romantic and in many ways a subversive influence. 'I saw,' he wrote, 'how wrong were the generally accepted and lofty aims of education ... the only goal ... material gain ... The great unmeasurable qualities of feeling, of personal creativity, of discrimination, of sensitive awareness of others, and of dedicated service, seemed more and more to be regarded as lesser by-products, commendable but unimportant. The ... academically bright ... [who] ... could regurgitate the factual knowledge poured into them were fostered at the expense of the majority; and schools still tended to be valued according to what are called "results", though everyone knows that the true results of education only show with maturity.' With his intense feeling for the north Wiltshire and Oxfordshire countryside, he believed children's creative powers could be released through art and design, and that by giving rein to these creative activities their wider education could be advanced.

His autobiography entitled *Double Harness* – a reference to his double life as HMI and artist – includes an idyllic account of his daily life as district inspector for Oxfordshire in the late fifties and early sixties, in and out of schools, conspiring with the LEA advisers, encouraging and empowering teachers, 'doing good as he went'. After 30 years in the Inspectorate, he believed his job was

> *inspecting and advising. The two were intermingled. I had never looked upon a Full Inspection Report as a whip with which to lash the schools ... When I had got to know a school well, so that there was complete openness and trust between us, it was often the school that suggested or asked for a full inspection. If the school was large enough I would share the work with one or more colleagues, and I think the event was anticipated with real pleasure all round. The schools felt cared for because of all this meticulous attention and they found satisfaction in having an appraisal from people who had nothing to lose, no local allegiances to consider, but only a desire to share and to help. So I think of these many special occasions as happy and constructive ones; and*

I remember too the dinner parties in country inns or city hotels to which I would invite the head to mark the end of each.

Among his colleagues in the Inspectorate there were other influential exponents of such methods, most notably Christian Schiller, a mathematician[6] – the 'fiery prophet' – as Tanner called him. Schiller gained a national reputation and used it to promote the educational values which he held dear. Through the courses which he ran for primary teachers – in which Tanner regularly took part – and the talks and lectures he was invited to give, he came into contact with a large number of primary teachers, including many who moved into positions of responsibility as heads and advisers. Many of the courses ran for two weeks in which teachers learnt by doing the kinds of practical activities through which children might be encouraged to learn – writing and calligraphy, painting, modelling and design, music and movement. Both he and Tanner had what later generations would have called charisma and were inspirational teachers and powerful communicators.

By the end of the second millennium, progressive primary education and child-centred learning had become bogey words – shorthand for pedagogic child abuse – and it would be easy to forget how widely the new primary education was admired at the time – and not just by 'educationists'. Though it was never by any means universal, this was not a revolution which went unnoticed by ordinary parents. Wise heads would spend time on telling parents what they were doing and try to meet the doubts of middle-class parents who felt their children were not being 'pushed' enough. In practice, children who had plenty of support at home did very well in the child-centred environment. Where there was unease among the parent body it was usually because heads had introduced big changes without taking parents into their confidence. But for most, the proof of the pudding was in the eating – they saw their children eager and enthusiastic to learn and admired teachers who could exploit their natural curiosity. There were, of course, always some who had doubts about the Emperor's tailoring, but their voices were muted.

The lasting legacy of this revolution was what was learnt about children and their development rather than any particular change in teaching practice. It would be a mistake to undervalue the work of men like Schiller and Tanner or to regard them as exponents of a discredited system. To do this would be to ignore the seriousness of their pursuit of excellence and their passionate belief that pupils should have a sense of genuine, not spurious, achievement. The first generation of their disciples were men and women who had experienced the conventional elementary school classroom and acquired the management skills demanded by classes of 40 and 50. They knew about formal instruction and its limitations: they had seen what it could do to children's appetite for learning. Their idealism was tempered by hard lessons of experience. What Schiller did was set teachers free to use their professionalism in new ways – ways which were more congenial to the liberal mind-set of the post-war period and which achieved a ready response from the children. It was clear from the evidence of the classroom that some teachers had the technical resources to embrace this freedom with impressive results. It also became clear – though not immediately – that less experienced and less gifted teachers might not be so successful and children's learning might suffer as a result.

It was men like Tanner and Schiller who made the running on primary education in the Inspectorate. Their views turned as much on a general view of children and childhood as it did on teaching and learning. Just how far the Inspectorate as a whole shared their progressive stance and the psychological theories and social philosophy which underpinned it, is more difficult to establish. Among the hundreds of HMIs who were regularly visiting primary schools, day by day, there was no single opinion. In the Primary Panel – the committee of primary phase HMIs – there were some who took issue with the progressives and many HMIs, reflecting on their earlier experience 40 years later, claimed to have had doubts. But hindsight is a wonderful thing and all in all, there can be little doubt that the progressive influence was strong and that it contributed in practical ways to the indisputable improvement and revitalisation of primary education in the post-war period.

Powerful as these messages were, insofar as there was an official HMI view, it was set out in the 1959 edition of Primary Education in a cautious and balanced manner. This gave due weight to creative work in art, craft and language, and the need to stimulate children's imagination if they were to learn. But it also disputed any suggestion that activity methods could justify a retreat from serious teaching and instruction in the basics. As for the senior officials at the Ministry of Education, they were not required to take a view on the content and practice of primary education. They were aware that the progressives were in the ascendant but few let their regard for individual HMIs overcome the detached scepticism of well-trained bureaucrats.

Ten years earlier (in 1949) there had been a significant indication of official approval in the publication of a Ministry pamphlet entitled *The*

Story of a School which became the Ministry's number one best-seller. The author was A. L. Stone, head of a primary school in inner Birmingham, who described how he had created a curriculum around the expressive arts – music, dance and drama, painting and modelling, and turned an old and inflexible building into a hive of creative activity. The pamphlet still reads as a graphic description of a place where extraordinary things were being achieved against the odds, in an old and inadequate building, by children who came from deprived inner city homes and teachers who had no special qualifications. It was Stone himself who provided the inspiration. His summing up made it clear that he did not regard artistic achievement as a substitute for other kinds of learning but a way of getting to them.

> *I turned to the arts as the basis of the education which should pervade this school. The three Rs, I decided, should become a secondary consideration, for I believed that, if I could get that confidence, that interest, that concentration from each child which arises from creative art, I had the ground well prepared then for the three Rs.*[7]

One of those who saw Stone at work and was deeply impressed was Alec Clegg, then an assistant education officer in Birmingham. After Clegg had moved on to the West Riding of Yorkshire, he recruited Stone as an influential primary adviser.

The West Riding under Clegg, Oxfordshire (where for many years Tanner was district inspector, Edith Moorhouse the local authority adviser, and Alan Chorlton the chief education officer), and Leicestershire (where Stewart C. Mason, a former HMI, was chief education officer), pioneered the primary school revolution. In point of fact, Mason had the reputation of being one county education officer who preferred to keep HMI at arms length. Clegg, on the other hand, worked closely with the Inspectorate throughout his long reign in the West Riding. He was passionately concerned with primary education and with supporting primary teachers and helping them to mastermind school improvement. In-service training – in which successful practising teachers took a leading part – had high priority in the West Riding and many HMIs recall Clegg involving them in this, along with the county's own advisers, at Woolley Hall, the county's residential in-service centre.

This was the picture of English primary education which foreign observers received and popularised. In North America, a much-reprinted series of articles by Joe Featherstone appeared in the *New Republic,*[8] and the schools began to receive a stream of overseas visitors eager to see 'the new English primary school' in action.

Eric Pearson, the SI attached to Architect and Buildings Branch, was blessed with few doubts about where the future lay. In an article[9] aimed at an American audience he stressed the importance of the school as a powerful socialising force. He believed that changes in the quality and character of social relationships had transformed the inner life of primary schools:

> *Education is an active process of learning by exploration and discovery ... Knowledge is only absorbed and interpreted insofar as its relevance is understood. Children also learn as much from each other and from agencies outside the school as they do from teachers in school. Learning is a personal and individual matter. In infant schools, the 'free day' and the 'integrated curriculum' have replaced an organisational structure based on fixed periods of time devoted to specific subjects. Creative synthesis has supplanted the former analytical approach to the curriculum ... What children do should make sense to them through its very wholeness.*

New primary school buildings encouraged more active and less formal methods – witness the impact which the first post-war primary schools had in Hertfordshire. Cutting circulation space while maximising the amount of teaching space, led in time to 'open-plan' designs which were not universally popular. Such designs assumed developments in team teaching, flexible working methods, and activities requiring spaces of varying size in which to pursue them.

Prompted by reports coming in from the field (and narrowly pre-empting an intervention by Margaret Thatcher, who was then the Secretary of State), HMI prepared a survey of how schools were adapting to open-plan designs (1972).[10] It carefully refrained from offering any general opinion on the merits or demerits of open plans, but it set out a long list of recommendations which added up to a formidable brief for teachers confronted with the challenge of working in an open-plan environment. HMIs had found teachers who had gone to inordinate lengths to recreate for themselves the illusion of a classroom by moving furniture and creating areas of self-containment. Not all teachers wanted to adapt the way they worked to the convenience of the building. Open planning was meant to make the building more flexible – but instead could end up placing limitations on teachers trying to use it.

In the course of the open-plan inquiry, one HMI, Tom Marjoram, had spotted a six-year-old girl in an open-plan area who 'neatly packed her books together and moved off into another area when any one of the teaching team approached her. She did about 15 minutes work in a morning.' Marjoram decided to repeat this exercise in another school, following individual children through a whole day, thereby developing a technique known as 'pupil pursuit' which came to be used more widely by HMI.

Plowden Report

The Report of the Central Advisory Council chaired by Lady Plowden came to be regarded as the progressives' charter – the document which gave a seal of approval to the new English primary school. In fact it was a balanced review, though it clearly reflected the progressive ethos of the time. Given its remit by a Conservative secretary of state, Edward Boyle, the council reported in 1967 to one of his Labour successors, Anthony Crosland.

It drew heavily on the services of the Inspectorate. Stella Duncan HMI worked closely with Maurice Kogan who acted as secretary. John Blackie, CI for primary education, E. M. McDougall HMI and M. E. Nicholls HMI, acted as assessors. Initial preparations were made by the primary team in the recently created (and short-lived) CSG, of which Kogan was a member – HMI helped to select schools in all parts of the country to be visited by members.

The Council was heavily influenced by the sociological evidence which showed the extent to which pupils' performance was linked to social background, and its most notable recommendations had to do with the designation of 'Social Priority Areas' where adverse social factors could be directly countered by social, economic and educational measures. This proposal was associated with two members of the Council, David Donnison and Michael Young, and led to an action research programme under the direction of Dr A. H. Halsey,[11] but the full policy was never implemented. Social deprivation refused to be confined to defined geographical areas – in many LEAs there were likely to be as many socially deprived families outside the proposed priority areas as inside them – and it became clear that to be effective positive discrimination would have to be on a far bigger scale than anyone believed was politically feasible.

The most important piece of evidence provided for the Committee by HMI was a comprehensive paper on 20,664 primary schools and departments, ranking them (subjectively and often on flimsy evidence) in nine categories ranging from category 1: 'in most respects of outstanding quality' – 109 schools – to category 9: 'a bad school where pupils suffer from laziness, indifference, gross incompetence or unkindness on the part of the staff' – 28 schools with 4,333 children, 0.1 per cent of the total. (The report was at pains to point out that all the schools in the worst category were followed up by LEAs and HMI, noting with a resigned air that 'there must always be bad appointments of head teachers; and deterioration in health or character may explain schools such as these. We doubt whether any school in this category would be allowed to stay there very long.')

In essence, the conclusion was that about a third of the schools were pretty good, about a half were more or less average, and the remaining sixth were not very good. The categories chosen by HMI recognised that schools might be good in some respects and bad in others – 9 per cent of the children attended 2,022 'curate's egg' schools. There were no objective measures of quality such as achievement in literacy and numeracy – no test scores. Plowden recommended further surveys at 10-year intervals to monitor progress, thereby prefiguring the Primary Survey which followed in the next decade.

The report recommended the banning of the infliction of pain as a punishment in primary schools, while acknowledging that 8 or 9 teachers out of 10 would want to keep the cane 'as a last resort'. It was not till 1986 that the law was changed to outlaw corporal punishment in maintained schools, and then only after Britain had begun to lose cases brought under the Human Rights Convention.

Gittins Report

A similar inquiry to that carried out by the Plowden Committee was undertaken by the CAC for Wales with Professor Charles Gittins in the chair. The report, which appeared in 1967, covered much the same ground as Plowden from a Welsh point of view, paying particular attention to 'the needs of the small primary schools in the Welsh, bilingual, context and to the initial and in-service training needed for teachers in these schools'. Gittins, a former Welsh chief education officer who had become a professor of education at Swansea, had been a member of the Plowden Committee.

The place of Welsh in the primary school is central to the report – and to the developing debates about education in the Principality. Gittins and his colleagues accepted as a matter of basic principle that every child in Wales should have the opportunity to be taught through the medium of Welsh during the infant stage and that the mother tongue should also form a substantial part of the education given through the transition to the secondary stage. It had a lot to say about bilingualism and set out as an aim 'reasonable oral proficiency in Welsh at the end of the primary stage so that the language may be used with confidence in conversational situations within and outside the school . . .'.

> *Our ultimate aim is that this concept of bilingualism would extend to the whole of Wales. We appreciate the very real difficulties which confront some authorities in areas in which anglicization has progressed rapidly or is long established, but we would hope that even these would wish to participate in experiments in bilingualism. We would point out that nearly half of our sample of primary school parents in Monmouthshire had favourable attitudes towards Welsh.*[12]

Peter Wynn, a member of the Welsh Inspectorate, was involved in revising drafts for publication. He recalled the energetic steps taken to disseminate the message of Gittins:

> *HMI were largely committed to the liberal philosophy of primary education expounded in the Gittins Report. As the advisory services in most LEAs in Wales were exiguous, HMI took on a strongly advisory role, organising conferences and courses both locally and nationally that reflected the Gittins philosophy. These were (at national level) very large and very long events – up to 100 members for 10 days in several instances. They were essentially practical in nature and HMI staff were expected to take an active part. They were designed to be inspirational; the freeing of springs of creativity within the teachers themselves was a prime aim – though the practical implications were also considered.*

Within a few years, the Plowden Report and all it stood for was overtaken by a wave of reaction. Inevitably the reaction was more against what they were thought to stand for than what was actually said. It remains an open question how many schools went overboard with the 'new primary education'.

It is extremely difficult to reach any firm conclusions because everything depends on what are to be taken as the yardsticks of progressivism. Child-centred learning meant different things to different people. John Blackie, CI for primary education, from his inside seat at the elbow of the Plowden Council members, reckoned a third of primary schools had adopted methods associated with Plowden, a third had made a start but had only gone part of the way, and another third remained unaffected. Charles Silberman, a distinguished American journalist who included a lengthy and highly favourable account of 'British primary education' in Leicestershire in his Carnegie-funded critique of American education, *Crisis in the Classroom* (1970), chanced his arm with a guess that one school in four might have adopted the new methods. Neville Bennett, whose research obliged him to be more precise about what he took to constitute the adoption of progressive methods, came up with a figure of 9 per cent of the classrooms he studied for *Teaching Styles and Pupil Progress* (1976).

Common sense suggests there were very few schools which introduced every possible progressive practice and even fewer which were totally unaffected by the educational consequences of changes which in other forms were pervading society. Many staffrooms managed to remain relatively unscathed by the excitement of theoreticians and enthusiastic practitioners alike. What were the quintessential characteristics of the 'new' primary education? Sitting children down at grouped tables instead of in rows of desks did not in itself change relationships and attitudes. Nor did devoting a bit more time to painting or having a flexible timetable. Many of these changes were taking place well before the appearance of Plowden, but as teachers lost confidence in the formal methods of an earlier period, they did not necessarily become confident exponents of the newer methods which were edging them out.

Primary school methods became more diverse and more individual to the teacher but no two 'Plowden-type' teachers were the same. They would include the brilliant junior school teacher in one of Clegg's South Yorkshire mining towns who enabled children to do wonderful things with language, bringing treasured words to school to be examined, played with, tried out, appropriated, as others would bring favourite objects to the nature table. In another mode, they would include the head and staff of a primary school in a tiny enclave in the City of London, who ran a warm and friendly, but businesslike place where handicraft and expressive arts provided the stimulus and encouragement for children to learn. What was achieved always depended on the personal qualities and interests of individual teachers. This was one of the limitations to set against the benefits – not all entrants to the profession would have the combination of skill and imagination needed to sustain high levels of activity on the part of all the children all the time.

If there was clearly no single definition of the package of ideas and practices which carried the Plowden label, it was also true that excellence came in many different liveries, as an HMI, Jack Dale, a former secondary school English specialist who joined the Inspectorate in 1970, recalled:

> The best lessons I saw were ones in which children's curiosity and interest had been aroused. One teacher I recall observing was a middle-aged lady who had spent the early part of her life working as a mill girl and, like me, had come to teaching late in life. Her

classroom, in an old building, was a bit cramped partly because she packed so much into it – plants almost growing out of the walls, great tubs of water bubbling with pond life, clay models and paintings everywhere. When I arrived the class of ten-year olds were writing accounts of a recent visit to a local weir. They wrote well about various impressions, the descriptions of flora and fauna were accurate. One boy had brought back a curiously shaped piece of willow branch which he copied in a charcoal drawing. I saw he'd captured the essence of the shape, giving it real life ... All of this was pure Plowden and most impressive. The teacher's record-keeping might not have been perfect but she knew each of her children exactly, their weaknesses and strengths. To me they all seemed bright-eyed and alert, and lucky to have such a marvellous person over them.

On another occasion, at a quite separate school, I observed a very different kind of teacher at work with a similar age-range. She was brisk, efficient and knew exactly what she wanted from the pupils. They sat in rows facing her and she talked to them and they talked to her in a relaxed manner. The classroom displayed plenty of examples of the children's work of all kinds and of generally good quality, just a bit less of the jungle that I'd encountered in the ex-mill girl's teaching area. When I looked at the children's exercise books they contained personal writing of a very high quality, especially some of the girls who wrote like little angels. Again I felt that any child taught by this lady would be very fortunate. Above all, I concluded that teaching style didn't much matter, that what was crucial was high expectations in an orderly and pleasant environment.

This summed up the traditional HMI approach – to look at the quality of learning and the teaching but recognise that there are many ways of skinning a cat. But not all HMIs were as pragmatic all the time. Prue Wallis Myers was another who brought a fresh and ironic eye to the primary scene:

My own lack of primary schooling made me all the more eager to observe it. I was lent out to primary colleagues who kindly took me round on visits and inspections. They gave me tips. If I found the teacher sitting at his/her desk with a queue of children waiting for help, this was bad. If I found the teacher walking round, this was good. If the children were busy, sitting at their desks, quietly doing exercises from work books, copying out the sentence and changing only one word, this was bad. However, if they were talking together actively examining magnets or cleaning out hamster cages, or even outside the classroom measuring the playground with a 'go-wheel', these were good. Creative writing was 'good' even if the children could not form their letters properly or spell words ... These early efforts were displayed with pride in the classroom for the sake of encouragement, but alas for writing skill and accuracy in spelling ... Should all this have been encouraged at the expense of the 'basics'?

Primary schools varied in size from village schools of 20 or even fewer, to schools with more than 700 pupils. The small schools included many where it was necessary to have classes which covered more than one age group. Devising strategies for coping with this was part of the professional challenge facing the village school teacher. It was curious that 'vertical grouping' – deliberate mixing of ages within a single teaching group – should come to be advocated by some of the more extreme exponents of the 'new' primary school. Few schools did more than experiment with vertical grouping.

In larger schools it was possible to have parallel classes of the same age group. Before the war this had led to streaming by ability. This continued after the war but began to break down for various reasons, not least for fear that putting children into different streams should be a form of self-fulfilling prophecy. Critics like Brian Jackson[13] published research which suggested that streaming was too blunt an instrument to deal with the complexities of individual differences. Other forms of grouping within classes – such as setting – seemed more appropriate for subjects like English and mathematics, a view echoed in the Plowden Report. There were hints of the possibility of making better use of teachers with specialist knowledge in Primary schools – John Burrows who was CI for Primary soon after the Plowden Report made its appearance, had observed schools in Great Yarmouth where for a few hours a week, the children had been divided into subject class groups under specialist teachers, instead of staying the whole time with their form teacher, and he had been impressed by the quality of the work. He wrote about it in *Trends* and the idea resurfaced in the Primary Survey in 1978.

Basics – Reading

One of the post-war tasks confronting the primary schools was to look closely at standards of literacy. Wartime disruption had taken its toll. Evacuation, air raids and other interruptions had adversely affected learning and when an interdepartmental committee – Education, Defence, the Prison Commission, Home Office – was set up in 1947 to look into literacy standards, it concluded that 15-year-olds in 1947–8 had the reading ability of children aged about 13 years and 2 months in 1938. For 11-year-olds the drop was 1 year. Behind the apparent precision was a 10-minute test devised by Professor P. E. Vernon and an HMI, Dr A. F. Watts, along with Gilbert Peaker, an HMI who for the next 20 years would advise the Inspectorate on statistical matters. The test consisted of 35 sentences, each with a missing word which had to be filled in from lists supplied.

Testing was repeated in 1952 and 1956. Setting aside some troublesome technical complications about sampling, the 1956 results showed the

11-year olds had made up nine months since 1948 and the 15-year-olds, about five months. The report was received with satisfaction because it suggested a steady improvement which was consistent with the favourable view of primary education which was generally held. Testing, including an additional longer test devised by the NFER, continued in 1960, 1964, 1970 and 1971. The sampling difficulties grew – as might be expected with any attempt to make meaningful comparisons over time – and the 1971 survey,[14] was further impaired by a postal strike which prevented some schools from receiving the NFER tests.

By 1971, too, a significant proportion of the children had learnt English as a second language and for many, English was not the language of the home. The testers were also aware of the 'ceiling effect': a significant proportion of the 15-year-olds would have achieved higher scores if more difficult questions had been added to the test. Not for the first – or the last – time the technical difficulties inherent in trying to answer what seemed to politicians simple questions led to apparently equivocal results. The best interpretation was that reading standards had neither risen nor fallen in the decade of the sixties. It looked, however, as if the post-war improvement had come to an end and that the changing linguistic mix in the school population was throwing up problems which deserved closer attention.

The response of Margaret Thatcher as Secretary of State was to set up the Bullock Committee to look in depth at the teaching of English, including reading, writing and speech. The committee rehearsed the uncertainties surrounding the earlier testing and endorsed the broad conclusions which others had reached about what had happened to reading standards. Bullock came up with 330 recommendations, stressed that there were no simple ways of improving literacy, but pointed to initial and in-service training. An HMI, Ronald Arnold, was secretary to the committee and had the job of presenting its findings in the form of a readable report which thereupon became the basis of many courses and conferences.

Before the publication of the Bullock Report, HMI had begun work on the Primary Survey (see Chapter 7) which was based on the inspection of work by 7, 9 and 11-year-olds in a stratified, random sample of 542 schools. This was linked to NFER testing in the same schools of 11-year olds in mathematics and 9 and 11-year-olds in reading, using the NS6 test which had been included in national surveys since 1955. This provided a 22-year run of figures:

Date of survey	1955	1960	1970	1976–7
Mean score	28.71	29.48	29.38	31.13
Number of schools	na	na	69	343
Number of children	na	na	1470	4955
Response rate	na	na	73%	99%

Increased sophistication on the part of the statisticians had not made it any easier to reach firm conclusions about standards over time, although the inference drawn when the Primary Survey was published in 1978 was that the rising trend which the results indicated was probably valid but could not necessarily be extrapolated because of the 'ceiling effect'. Similar problems, in different form, would later plague the Assessment of Performance Unit. The figures showed the wide variations between the high and low achievers encountered elsewhere in English and Welsh education.

While those who made their living from testing and measurement discovered more reasons to complicate the monitoring process, developments were also taking place in the field of social linguistics. Empirical studies of the way children learn to talk, and social class differences in the ways mothers interact with their children, brought out the importance of the social influences on language acquisition and literacy. The teaching of English became a political hotbed as the National Association of Teachers of English wrangled over Standard English and social control. Passions ran high. And somewhere along the line, reaction against earlier academic aridity had made it a matter of dogmatic conviction that children should not be taught grammar in any systematic way. The ground was prepared for the arguments of the 1980s about whether children needed to learn about the mechanics of the English language and if they did, what grammatical vocabulary they needed for this purpose.

Public concern about reading fluctuated. When the mood changed in the 1970s and after, panic calls for a return to the basics, based on wild generalisations about falling standards, were never far from the headlines. There was no evidence of decline but was it enough to say that things were not actually getting worse? Given the ever-rising education budget, ought not the schools to be able to raise their performance in teaching children to read – giving them the basic tool for future learning?

Was there an element of complacency in the way the pundits handled the conflicting evidence which could have contributed to public scepticism?

There was no lack of good advice. A Ministry pamphlet, written by an HMI after the 1948 tests, had said that 'teachers should not use methods without a personal conviction of their value … The teaching of reading should be seen as part of the general process of educating a child … No single method is applicable to all children … Sometimes a word will be spotted from its context. Other words may be built up phonetically … With very dull children 'look and say' may put a load on the memory which they cannot sustain … A school library can be one of the central agencies in the educational economies of infants' and junior schools as well as of secondary schools.'[15]

It was assumed that HMIs would look at the teaching and learning of literacy on all their school visits. Children were heard reading and their writing seen. A collection of books, known as the Tann[16] collection after the CI who started it, was continuously brought up to date and exhibited on HMI courses, to which reading experts such as Joyce Morris and Vera Southgate contributed. Library provision was constantly stressed, formally in full inspection reports, and informally at meetings with schools and education officers.

Basics – Mathematics

Standards in mathematics were also a matter of general concern but did not seem to induce panic in the way that allegations of illiteracy did. There seemed to be a fatalistic acceptance that some people could and others could not do maths: an attribution to nature of deficiencies which were much more likely to stem from innumerate nurture. In secondary schools there was a perennial shortage of maths specialists, while in primary schools where the foundations had to be laid, few teachers had a firm grounding in the subject: and many had emerged from their own time at school with an aversion to the subject.

By the early 1960s local authority inspectors/advisers like Leonard Sealey (Leicestershire) and Harold Fletcher (Staffordshire) were pressing for improvements in the effectiveness of primary maths teaching, broadening it to include more practical geometry and introducing children to more ways of displaying mathematical information (for example with graphs). (Why people became so dogmatically convinced that learning tables by rote should be outlawed was never clear to non-mathematicians. Later, such questions would be raised in the arguments about pocket calculators which divided the designers of the maths component in the National Curriculum.)

Mathematics became caught up with the curriculum reform movement stimulated on both sides of the Atlantic in the late 1950s. Edith Biggs, an SI, ran a series of courses for teachers and teacher trainers, gaining a national reputation in the process.[17] By 1962 she had run 70 courses. She stressed the importance of combining basic skills with the new methodology and once complained about the 'inordinate attention' being given to maths, but her estimate was (Primary Panel 1966) that one school in four had made substantial changes in the way mathematics was taught – changes which in large measure people attributed to her efforts.

By then the Nuffield Foundation and the Schools Council were actively promoting new maths curricula – Dr Geoffrey Mathews' primary maths project pushed the teaching of what came to be known as 'new' maths. But both Nuffield and the Schools Council ran projects on primary science which had a more limited impact. Given the lack of teachers with any science qualification, more might have been done if the effort had been concentrated on one scheme. But to engineer this might have seemed too much like central intervention in the curriculum and there were widespread doubts – shared by HMIs in the Primary Committee – as to the wisdom of putting all eggs in a single basket. To have made any impact it would have had to be backed up with a large training programme.

The 1960s ended on a sour note with the attacks on primary education in the Black Papers (see Chapter 7). For the primary school teachers it would never be glad confident morning again. Primary schools changed almost overnight from being a source of national pride to one of constant anxiety, and political breast-beating. Not, of course, that the attitudes of the public or the media were wholly consistent: parents continued to answer questions from pollsters with statements like: 'the school our child goes to is wonderful but what a pity all the other schools are so bad.'

Middle Schools

'Middle schools' were a by-product of the move to comprehensive secondary education discussed in the next chapter. For each LEA, going comprehensive meant juggling with a stock of buildings and looking for ways of fitting comprehensive secondary schools into the plant available. One of the options was to go for a two-tier system. Leicestershire pioneered one such, using 11–14 unselective 'high schools' as a means of postponing selection. Other authorities looked at what Leicestershire had done and thought they could do better with their own schemes. Among them was Clegg in the West Riding: his preference was for 'middle' schools for children between 9 and 13. This would give him smaller comprehensives and might make it possible to extend primary school methods into the early years of what was now the secondary stage.

The issue was of considerable interest to ministers, the DES and HMI. Discussion took place among HMI and the Office about the pros and cons. The more prestigious parts of the independent school system had long experience of children transferring from one school to another at 13 years of age. As one of his last projects as Conservative secretary of state, Boyle introduced a bill to allow LEAs more flexibility on the transfer age.[18] His explicit aim was to help Clegg (and any who might follow him) sort out the problem of buildings.

Three years later members of the Plowden Committee preferred a middle school span of 8–12 because they wanted a first school running from 5 to 8. They thought that by the age of 7, many children had reached a critical stage in their achievement of literacy and that it would be to their advantage if they remained in the same school for another year. A middle school starting at 8 would make this possible. (In the circumstances the committee cannot have supposed that many LEAs would find this argument more pressing than one arising from the disposal of bricks and mortar.)

John Burrows, CI for primary, insisted that 8–12 schools would have to match the secondary schools with the 'introduction of disciplined study .. . the systematic and orderly extension of knowledge in a subject field'. The task before the middle school, he thought, would be 'to create teaching and learning situations in which pupils pass gradually and naturally into those more adult stages ... making a bridge between primary and secondary, dominated by neither'.[19]

The raising of the leaving age in 1973 gave an added impetus to the middle school movement. Providing for the extra year-group would require additional school building which could be done more cheaply by extending primary schools to take 12-year-olds than by adding more specialist accommodation in secondary schools. The first purpose-built middle school opened in 1968 in Bradford, soon followed by others, including a 9–13 school in the West Riding which was the subject of an HMI pamphlet, *Launching Middle Schools*. This described the care taken by Clegg and his colleagues on the transition. Another, entitled *Towards the Middle School*, written by Stella Duncan and Norman Thomas, discussed curriculum, internal organisation, training and deployment of staff, buildings and equipment, and continuity and progression for pupils moving from school to school. By this time, 28 LEAs had plans for middle schools.

To complete the story in brief, HMI surveys in the 1980s kept track of the development of the middle school. The education they offered was not markedly different from that provided for the same age groups in primary schools – Clegg's hopes that the middle schools would be a Trojan Horse in his campaign to ginger up the secondary schools were not realised – but nearly all moved towards a sharper definition of the timetable and more specialist teaching, including setting.

There is little doubt that the drive towards middle schools was generated by the structural changes arising from going comprehensive and the raising of the school leaving age. Falling rolls in the 1980s saw pressure build up in the opposite direction. The number of middle schools began to decline from a high point of about 1,800 in 1983 (with 22 per cent of 11-year-olds) to 1,377 by 1990. Whatever the pedagogic virtues claimed for the middle school, the introduction of the National Curriculum and its assessment procedures increased the pressure for uniformity.

Notes

[1] Middleton, N., Weitzman, S. (1976) *A Place for Everyone: A History of State Education from the End of the Eighteenth Century to the 1970s*. London: Victor Gollancz, 312.

[2] Royal Commission (1868) *Report* of the Schools Inquiry Commission. Chairman, Lord Taunton. See Maclure, *Educational Documents*, 92–5.

[3] This chapter draws, with permission, on three papers prepared by Norman Thomas but does not commit him to the views here expressed.

[4] Board of Education (1931) *The Primary School*. Report of the Central Consultative Committee on Education. London: HMSO. Chairman, Sir W. H. Hadow.

[5] Tanner, Robin (1987) *Double Harness*. London: Impact Books, 138–9, 150, 152.

[6] Christian Schiller MC CBE (1895–1976) was SI junior education from 1946 to 1955. He was then senior lecturer on primary education at University of London Institute of Education from 1955 to 1963.

[7] Ministry of Education (1949) *Story of a School: A Headmaster's Experiences with Children Aged Seven to Eleven*. Pamphlet 14. London: HMSO, 8. The school was the Steward Street Junior School in Birmingham.

[8] His articles were later published as *Schools Where Children Learn*. New York: Liveright, 1971.

[9] Pearson, E. (1972) 'Trends in school design'. *British Primary Schools Today*. Vol. 2, Anglo-American Primary Education Project/Ford Foundation. New York: Macmillan, 274.

[10] Department of Education and Science (1972) *Open Plan Primary School*. Education Survey 16.

[11] Halsey, A. H. (ed.) (1972) *Educational Priority, EPA Problems and Policies*. Vol. 1, *Report of a Research Project Sponsored by the DES and the SSRC*. London: HMSO.

[12] Department of Education and Science (1968) *Primary Education in Wales*. Report of the Central Advisory Council for Education (Wales). London: HMSO, 239. Chairman, Professor Charles Gittins.

[13] Jackson, B. (1964) *Streaming: An Education System in Miniature*. London: Routledge & Kegan Paul for the Institute of Community Studies.

[14] Start, K. B., Wells, B. K. (1972) *The Trend of Reading Standards*. Windsor: NFER.

[15] Ministry of Education (1950) *Reading Ability: Some Suggestions for Helping the Backward*. Pamphlet 18. London: HMSO.

[16] The Tann collection of books, set up in 1949 by the then primary CI, F. M. Tann, provided a representative sample of books of quality for children of pre-school age up to the middle years of schooling, on loan for courses and exhibitions arranged by HMI. The collection was reviewed annually. Eventually there were three different, but equally balanced, collections of about 500 books. In 1980 responsibility was transferred to the DES Library.

[17] Schools Council (1965) *Mathematics in Primary Schools*. Curriculum Bulletin 1. Attributed to Edith Biggs in 4th edn., 1972.

[18] Education Act 1964.

[19] Burrows, L. J. (1967) 'What's in store for the children', in *Middle Schools Symposium*. London: The Schoolmaster Publishing Company.

HMI Miscellany

Extracts from HMI personal accounts

John Burrows 1946

My assignment for the next eight years consisted of visiting 100 plus village schools, most of them at the start, all-age. Many had not seen an HMI for years; one's reception ranged from the welcoming to the terrified. The majority were two or three-teacher schools, and it was rare to find the infants in the charge of a trained teacher . . .

The typical practice in elementary schools, except for some of the work of the older children, was for a class to be taught by one teacher for the whole of the school year. A few primary schools during the early post-war years made use of the specialist knowledge of one or more members of staff, perhaps arranging the children into 'subject' classes for an hour or two a week. I had seen examples of this in schools in Great Yarmouth and had been impressed by the quality of the children's work. I wrote an article on the topic in *Trends* . . .

Robert Morris 1947

When he had been HMI for two years his mentor asked him to write a report on a one-teacher primary school in West Sussex. The school had two rooms, one used mainly by the infants and the other by the juniors. For the early part of the morning – after a common period for RI – the headteacher worked with the infants while the juniors got on, industriously, with work based on individual weekly assignments given to them by the headteacher. After the morning break, the head moved into the junior classroom and quizzed the children in turn about what they had been doing and helped them with their difficulties; an older child worked in the infants' room and kept a general eye on them. Everything worked splendidly and R.W.M. wrote a highly favourable report. His mentor told him that to praise the school was a great mistake: the LEA's policy was to close all one-teacher schools, and it would be a great embarrassment if one were to be praised. (*In interview with Norman Thomas*)

David Hopkinson 1952

As time went on I became disenchanted with this somewhat exhausting procedure (secondary school inspection) which seemed to me little different from that of which I retained a memory from my own school days 25 years before . . . Disturbingly poor performance was rare in the primary schools which were allotted to me for visits to be made on my own. When occasionally taking part in the full inspection of an urban primary school, I absorbed what was to be learned from admirable women colleagues, but found the full inspection experience unappetising compared with the relaxed tempo of advisory visits and complete freedom of discussion when I visited a village school by myself.

Lewis Evans 1956

Lack of time prevented our making the impression on teaching that we should have. This lack of time was partially due to lack of numbers, but also to the proliferation of courses and conferences, valuable though those were. The only HMI I knew who had a major effect on the work of the primary schools in his area fell out with the hierarchy early in his career and spent nearly all his time in schools.

Allan Hill 1965

I had started my teaching career in the primary sector before entering industry then returning to teach in FE. [As an FE Inspector] I found the time spent with P&S colleagues interesting and the changes very dramatic. However, I quickly realised that some colleagues were promoting 'fashionable teaching methods' such as ITA, project-directed studies, discovery learning and mixed ability teaching whilst decrying and dismissing formal methods such as streaming and setting, 'chalk and talk', rote learning and competition. It was obvious that the new and progressive methods were being marketed and taught very effectively by the colleges of education and with considerable encouragement from some HMI.

Many people realise that these techniques have some merit, but their wholesale introduction, to the exclusion of conventional methods, proved to be unwise.

Geoffrey Hearnshaw 1967

One visited in a non-specialist capacity up to a couple of hundred schools of all sorts within the areas of one or two LEAs. One disturbing feature was that some teachers obviously felt that HMI were in possession of exclusive inside knowledge. I well remember the end of my first day of solo inspection in a primary school, when the head teacher sat with pen poised and a new exercise book, open at the first page, ready to record all my valuable words of advice. As a former teacher of older pupils I had to ask myself whether I should really be inspecting primary schools, or indeed inspecting in any sort of school subjects of which I had limited knowledge . . . I found myself visiting small, remote country schools, many of which had not had an 'official' visit for a long time. The headteachers who felt isolated and in need of someone to confide in were glad of the opportunity to unburden themselves to someone independent of the LEA who would respect their confidence.

Rosemary Peacocke 1970

My first experiences in visiting schools were a revelation. Inevitably, as a head teacher, I had had little opportunity to spend time in other schools, and I had supposed that all schools were pretty much the same as the one I had just left. My competent mentor quickly devised a very varied programme which showed there can be quality in diversity, which stood me in good stead for the rest of my time in the Inspectorate. It took some time before I was able to make appropriate judgements on the quality of provision I observed, and eventually this was made possible by the wide variety of schools I visited and the help of members of the Inspectorate, other than my mentor, who visited schools with me. It was never easy to distance oneself and take a broad view of provision having been so closely involved as head of a school where so many initiatives had come from myself and an able team of teachers. It was the opportunity to discuss schools in depth with colleagues, whether in routine visits or inspections, which was so valuable in reaching conclusions. The practical, tactful, way in which these visits were organised is fresh in my memory . . .

When I eventually became SI and needed a national view of the quality of provision, the method I used to gather the information was, in the first instance, a verbal one. At every Early Years Committee meeting each colleague described briefly the recent developments in his or her Division. This practice meant that every member of the team had some idea of what was going on nationally and that there was opportunity to discuss matters of import; but also at the end of the meeting there was a written account in the minutes which could be extended, if necessary, by the Divisional representative. In advising the Minister these reports were important; however, they were not enough on their own, and every year I worked one day with each member of the team to have first-hand experience of the provision and have the chance to discuss new development with them.

Peter Armitstead 1971

Particular attention was given to the curriculum of the fourth year of 8 to 12 middle schools. This was a matter of anxiety for many secondary school teachers, since it had been the first year of secondary education. Many secondary teachers, especially scientists, feared that middle schools would not cover enough ground in a primary school pattern of teaching and foresaw a lowering of standards and consequent fall in examination results.

Chapter 3   Secondary Education for All

A Mix of Schools. The Post-war Selective System. Three into One. 1958
White Paper. Circular 10/65. Central Advisory Council Reports.
Curriculum Development. Postscript.

A Mix of Schools

The 1944 Education Act offered no definition of a secondary school.
Before the war everyone knew what a secondary school was: it was a
grammar school. There was some blurring at the edges. Some places like
London had created 'central' schools or 'higher grade' elementary
schools, but though these provided some of the missing rungs on the
ladder of advancement, they were not secondary schools.

Grammar schools had a monopoly, but they too had their gradations.
There were the grant-aided grammar schools, some of them with ancient
foundations and long histories, and there were the county and county
borough grammar schools founded after 1902 when the newly formed
education authorities were allowed to set up secondary schools of their
own. And, of course, there were independent schools, the elite group of
which were known as public schools which, like grammar schools,
offered courses leading to the School Certificate and Higher Certificate,
and prepared pupils for university and entry to the professions.

As we have seen, many elementary schools had already been split into two –
the junior forms became primary schools and the senior forms were waiting to
become secondary modern schools. There were also junior technical schools.
For the most part, these were junior departments of technical colleges, taking
in pupils at the age of 13. In the new age, it was intended that technical schools,
recruiting at 11, should provide the third element in a tripartite system.

The task facing the educational community in the post-war world was to
turn this mix of schools, and the mix of teachers and pupils which went
with it, into a coherent secondary education system in order to make a
reality out of what had till then been no more than a slogan – 'Secondary
Education for All'. Tawney's phrase continued to resonate: it did not lose
its potency even when he himself had begun to qualify its meaning.[1] The
Act itself had nothing to say about how secondary education should be
organised or what should be taught – all it said was that local authorities
must provide sufficient schools to meet the age, ability and aptitude of all
pupils.

The conventional wisdom, however, was that there would need to be different kinds of schools for children of different kinds of ability. This had been the advice of the Spens Committee in 1938, re-echoed in Norwood. The White Paper on *Educational Reconstruction* which preceded the bill recognised the difficulties implicit in 'different but equal', but fought shy of the comprehensive or multilateral school alternative. As for the selection process, it insisted that the methods by which children were to be allocated to different types of school should not be competitive but should be based on an assessment of children's individual aptitudes, 'by such means as school records, supplemented if necessary, by intelligence tests, due regard being had to their parents' wishes, and the careers they have in mind'. It also held out the elusive prospect of transfer between secondary schools for late developers. 'The keynote will be ...' said the White Paper, in a pregnant phrase, 'that the child is the centre of education.'

Ministers were well aware of what they were up against if they wanted new forms of secondary education to stand up against the grammar school. 'Under present conditions the secondary grammar school enjoys a prestige ... which completely overshadows all other types of school ... Inheriting as it does a distinguished tradition ... it offers the advantages of superior premises and staffing, and a longer school life ... But ... an academic training is ill suited for many of the pupils who find themselves moving along a narrow educational path bounded by the School Certificate and leading into a limited field of opportunity.' It went on:

> The senior schools have a recent history ... Their future is their own to make ... They offer a general education for life, closely related to the interests and the environment of the pupils and of a wide range embracing the literary as well as the practical bent ... Junior Technical Schools ... hold out great opportunities for pupils with a practical bent.
> Such then will be the three main types ... grammar, modern and technical schools. It would be wrong to suppose that they will necessarily remain separate and apart. Different types will be combined in one building or on one site ... In any case, free interchange of pupils from one type of education to another must be facilitated. (paragraphs 27–31)

These carefully crafted sentences set out an agenda to be worked through in the succeeding decades – not without pain and anguish. The aim was clear enough even if the words often meant rather different things to different people. The social objective of inclusiveness was part of the post-war heritage, but once the euphoria of wartime idealism faded, it became more problematic in the face of individualistic consumerism.

What the White Paper said about the entrenched position of the grammar schools and their old boy networks was in no way exaggerated. They were institutions with powerful backers in the community; they had potent symbolic significance as the embodiment of a set of traditional academic and cultural values. University education was firmly linked to these values. Most educated people, even if they opposed the tripartite system and were supporters of the common school, were products of a grammar-type education which they equated (consciously or unconsciously) with 'real' education and true standards.

This concept of 'the real stuff' came out quite clearly when Dennis Healey described his time at Bradford Grammar School – a rigorous and rapid learning experience shared with other clever boys. The same impression came out of Richard Hoggart's very different account of life at Cockburn High School, Leeds. It was even implicit in Ellen Wilkinson's reforming zeal. Although she eventually approved the Ministry Circular (73) commending the tripartite secondary organisation to local authorities, she railed against it in her diary. What it meant was: 'give the real stuff to 25 per cent, steer the 75 per cent away from the humanities, pure science, even history.'[2]

Tripartite secondary schemes were what the Ministry expected LEAs to propose in their development plans and what Ministers would be willing to approve. Comprehensive and multilateral suggestions were not ruled out but the inference was that such schools were still experimental and untested. Most, but not all, took the Minister's advice and made their plans on the basis of separate grammar and modern schools. Some like Kent, invested heavily in technical schools but most schemes were bipartite – grammar and modern – rather than tripartite.

The Post-war Selective System
Secondary Modern Schools

In advising in favour of a selective system, Martin Roseveare – who wrote Circular 144 which restated the policy on secondary organisation – was throwing his weight behind the secondary modern school to which 75–80 per cent of pupils would be allocated. (Or rather, to which they would be allocated when Hadow reorganisation was complete, which would not be for another 20 years.) The modern schools were meant to be treated on equal terms with the grammar and technical schools. Ellen Wilkinson promised as much to Labour's 1946 Conference: 'If the teachers get the same pay, if the holidays are the same and if, as far as is possible, the buildings are as good in each case, then you get parity for which the teachers are quite rightly asking.' Of her conditions only the holidays could be readily met. Grammar school teachers were paid more and were five times more likely to be graduates than teachers in the modern schools. More than twice as much was spent on each grammar school pupil as on each modern school pupil.[3]

The modern school was to be given time to shake down and work out its own curricular salvation. This had been the advice of the Norwood Committee and it was the advice of HMI. There was no modern school curriculum, set out in advance by the Ministry or HMI. Roseveare's Inspectorate included many who had inspected elementary schools but few who had taught in a secondary modern school – how could it? – till a trickle of former modern schools heads began to be appointed after 1944. HMI was strong on academic specialists with experience in grammar and independent schools. Secondary education for all was something they had to learn about no less than anyone else.

Giving the modern school breathing space did not mean that there were no reporting inspections, but there was a deliberate policy of waiting and seeing – visiting and getting to know the schools while postponing the point at which they would receive the full treatment. But members of the Secondary Panel were also aware that they had to be in a position to give a convincing answer when the Office asked 'What are these schools teaching?' The schools needed time in which to stabilise their own activities and HMI needed time to get round to as many of them as possible.

It was always a somewhat optimistic notion that the modern schools would conjure up their own concept of secondary education, work it out and build it up, spontaneously, if left alone and given enough elbow room. Some exceptional schools did, but it was never going to happen generally because even if the Minister left them alone, they would have to live with the world around them – pupils, parents and communities – and teachers who were conditioned by their own educational experience which had – on the whole – been satisfactory for them.

Some insight into the developing life of the modern schools can be gleaned from the minutes of the Secondary Panel which collectively kept a watching brief on secondary education as a whole.[4] The panel spent a lot of time on the selection process and how it might be made to work better. There seems to have been a general acceptance that it produced anomalies but that such anomalies were inevitable. This produced suggestions that there should be a common core curriculum for the first two years of both grammar and modern schools, which was widely accepted by the time the Crowther Committee was at work in the mid-1950s, but as the curriculum was not regulated in any way except by external exams, it remained an idea to mull over rather than a plan of action.

The crux of the argument for giving the modern schools time turned on what to do about external exams. Roseveare was adamant that the modern schools should be protected from the examination machine for as long as possible. HMI shared this view which was part of the same tendency which led Norwood to believe that the O level examinations in the General Certificate of Education (GCE) (which came into operation in 1951) should be regarded as a temporary measure, to be replaced in due course by an internal assessment conducted by each school. They underestimated the power of 'credentialism' – the expectation that what pupils learnt at school would be authenticated by some external certification, and that this, whether relevant or not, could then be used as a discriminatory instrument for recruitment.

Heads quickly saw that their schools would benefit if their pupils began to collect certificates to mark them out from those whose education was unattested. So they began to look at the examinations which were available – those of the Royal Society of Arts, the College of Preceptors and, in some cases, the technical examining bodies. They also looked at O levels from which at first they were excluded by rules which set a minimum age of 16 at which candidates could be entered. Modern schools were not meant to have pupils capable of doing O levels, nor yet of entering occupations where O levels might be required.

Eventually in 1958, soon after Roseveare's retirement, the Secondary Schools Examination Council appointed a committee with Robert Beloe, chief education officer for Surrey, in the chair to look at the examination needs of the modern schools which in due course led to the Certificate of Secondary Education (CSE). HMI took part in the exercise. Like GCE it was a single-subject exam. It was designed for the brighter students in the modern schools and the weaker pupils in the grammar schools with an overlap with GCE in that Grade 1 CSE was meant to be equivalent to a pass grade GCE.

The new examination was introduced in 1965. In spite of the overlap, GCE and CSE were two different examinations for two different kinds of school. It would take another 20 years to create a single system of examining which could make some sort of sense of the comprehensive system.

From the heads' point of view, making a success of these new schools depended on exploiting the limitations of the selection apparatus – as Miss Adams HMI had remarked in the Secondary Panel: 'the child of the lower ability levels in the grammar schools would be little different from the child of the higher levels of ability in the modern schools.'[5] In 1955 the minimum age regulations for O level were relaxed – the grammar schools found them no less inconvenient than the modern schools – and an increasing flow of pupils from the modern schools began to climb the academic ladder. A chief inspector, Mr Charles had expressed the view at a 1946 meeting, that LEAs should do more than they were doing to discourage the public from attaching too much importance to the School Certificate. LEAs or no, parents recognised the currency of O levels. Once the gates had been opened, LEAs were delighted to see secondary modern schools enjoying success – by the end of the 1960s in the favoured south-east the numbers of entrants from modern schools – though not the number of subjects entered – was approaching the numbers from the selective schools.

The schools themselves were extremely diverse institutions, if only because LEAs differed enormously in the proportion of children selected for grammar school – from as large a percentage as 64 per cent in Merioneth to 8 per cent in Gateshead. Secondary modern schools were more likely to flourish where the selection rate was at the lower end of the scale than at the higher.

The secondary school population was growing through the 1950s and 1960s without there being any corresponding increase in the number of grammar schools. When this was discussed in the panel, it sparked off a sharp discussion of the selection procedure and the proportion of the age group which should go to the grammar school. A staff inspector, Mr F. T. Arnold said he 'would welcome a general reduction in the grammar-place in-take'. The panel was divided into hawks and doves like any other group of education-watchers: some thought grammar school entry should be limited to give a lift to the modern and technical schools; others held that a more competitive entry might raise standards in the grammar schools. P. A. Browne, the CI in the chair, intervened to say that the CAC inquiry had evidence that the more grammar places there were the greater the number of pupils who stayed on to the sixth form.[6] Such matters were outside the control of the modern schools themselves but they all fed into the wider debate on secondary school organisation.

Different as they were, modern schools shared a common characteristic: the majority of their pupils would leave as soon as they were legally allowed to do so. The leaving age had gone up to 15, but the modern schools lost pupils at Christmas and Easter in the fourth year. The curriculum and the schools' ethos and expectations were based on the fact of life that the very great majority would be thinking about work and a pay packet well before the final day arrived. This was expected to influence the curriculum – that in the last year there should be a bias towards preparation for employment, including visits to offices and factories. Any consideration of the secondary modern school was conditioned by the assumption that most of its alumni would find their way into unskilled or semi-skilled employment. An important minority would reappear in the FE system, as apprentices. The valiant secondary modern heads who struggled to do something for able children whose educational horizons had been foreshortened by the selection process had an uphill struggle to change this.

Technical Schools

The original intention was that there would be three types of school, the third being the secondary technical school. The idea was that the technical school would meet the needs of children of good intelligence with a bent towards practical and technical matters. This was another legacy from the pre-war preparations for educational reform. The Spens Committee had been advised by a number of educational psychologists – one of them was William Alexander, who by now had long forsaken the practice of educational psychology for educational administration – that it was possible to devise tests which would identify technical aptitude, alongside the 'general component' of intelligence. (It so happened that Alexander was one who had designed such a test which remained on the market for some years.) In theory, the technical school would draw on the same selected group as would qualify for the grammar school.

Only a few counties and county boroughs created a network of technical schools: Kent was exceptional in providing selective technical schools alongside its grammar schools. The technical schools were meant to recruit at 11 (not 13, like the junior technical schools attached to technical colleges had done). It was intended that they should have parity with the grammar school in the selection process. In practice where grammar and technical schools existed side-by side the technical schools got the second cut. Unfortunately, as A. G. Gooch, the SI for technical schools put it, 'the theoretical justification for these schools received a mortal blow almost at once':[7] the tests which purported to identify technical aptitude were discredited and this removed the pseudo-scientific basis for selection. Many local authorities continued to operate junior technical schools recruiting at 13, on the basis of a second selection for a two- or three-year course.

Inside the Inspectorate the technical schools had some robust supporters such as Freddie Bray and Gooch who made sure the voice of the technical school was heard in the Office and in the Secondary Panel. Like the secondary moderns, technical schools needed time and space in which to settle down – they had to develop a curriculum much broader than the narrow vocational subject mix which had ruled the junior departments of technical colleges.

But time was not on their side. In his book on the secondary technical school, *The Missing Stratum*,[8] Michael Sanderson describes the 'crucial

Sir David Eccles, Minister of Education 1954–57 and 1959–62.

debate' on the future of the technical school David Eccles staged inside the Ministry early in 1955. He wanted to encourage technical options because he thought they might motivate some who were put off by the grammar school. He noted that the technical schools only took 5 per cent of the age group. Why? He fired off a series of searching questions and asked for answers in time for a meeting of ministers in February.

The senior officials split down the middle: in favour of separate technical schools were Antony Part and from the professional point of view, Freddie Bray HMI (later an under secretary in charge of the FE Branch in the Ministry). Derek Morrell, Toby Weaver and A. R. Maxwell Hyslop doubted their validity and favoured the provision of technical courses within the grammar school.

Morrell pinpointed the confusion over ability and aptitude on which selection for technical schools was based – two pupils might share the same aptitude, but at very different levels of ability. As Sanderson put it, paraphrasing Morrell: 'the technical school had been regarded as an "aptitude school" and the root problem had been that technical aptitude had been regarded as indicative of a lower level of ability than the academic.' If the grammar schools were failing bright pupils with technical aptitude they should be encouraged to mend their ways. By the same token, if technical schools were offering lower-level courses than the grammar schools, the technical courses should be removed to the modern schools.

Gilbert Flemming summed up for the Office against the technical schools and Eccles accepted this view, telling the NUT's Easter Conference: 'My conclusion is . . . we ought now to distribute technical courses over as many schools as possible'.[9] As always, Morrell argued persuasively, but the reasons he gave for dismissing the technical schools were also reasons why technical education would never thrive in the grammar school. He was right: technical aptitude was not as highly valued as academic; this alone would shatter Eccles's hopes that the grammar schools would take technical education *qua* technical education seriously.

Soon after the appearance of the *Technical Education* White Paper in 1956 Gooch wrote a paper reviewing the state of the technical schools and their prospects. He noted that they had not been accepted as selective schools on a par with grammar schools – that they had to take the second choices rather than the first. He also pointed out that ambiguity about the age of transfer meant that the technical schools which most nearly corresponded to the official model were in a minority. Links with industry and commerce were good but the technical schools were still more thought of as a source of trainee craftsmen than student apprentices.

In his capacity as SI technical, Gooch ran annual courses at Cambridge which became an unofficial think tank for the technical subjects, out of which came the Association for Technical Education in Schools. One of those much involved was Don Porter who became SI handicraft in 1959. Porter, himself, had been educated at a central school and come up the hard way, benefiting from opportunities which came his way during the war. He identified with the large number of boys and girls for whom an 'alternative road' was needed.

He and others like him believed that a radical rethink for handicraft was overdue. He thought much more could be done in metalwork and woodwork than most schools were doing – it was time to get away from endless filing and sawing; better materials and small components like electric motors were becoming available, opening up the possibility of new applications of craft skills. He followed up interesting developments in many schools throughout the country, and when in 1964–65, he was awarded a Simon Fellowship at Manchester, and the 'think-time' which went with it, he wrote a seminal paper on *A School Approach to Technology*. It so happened that about this time, the newly created Schools Council was taking over Nuffield's Project Technology. The council adopted Porter's paper which became the council's Curriculum Bulletin No. 2. The essence of the new approach was the enlargement of handicraft to emphasise the interdependence of craft, design and technology. It made rapid ground in the schools. One of Porter's last contributions before his retirement in 1973 was to suggest the adoption of CDT as its official title.

Another paper by Gooch (1961) for the Technical Sub-Panel maintained a defence of the technical schools while pointing out the mounting pressures against their continuing separate identity.[10] In time the technical schools became more and more like grammar schools – some like those in Kent were renamed grammar schools. Pupils who hoped to go on to become engineers and technologists needed to get qualifications in mathematics, physics and chemistry and win places at universities or polytechnics. The technical professions began to look for an all-graduate intake and cut off the entry route via articles and student apprenticeship. All the pressure worked against the technical schools' claim to be a different kind of secondary school. As someone remarked in the Secondary Panel it was difficult to find an important subject taught in the technical school which was not also taught in grammar schools. It was left to the Crowther Report to confirm that what were called 'practical and aesthetic subjects' were dropped too early in most schools. They lacked status and as core subjects in a demanding technical course they were non-starters.

As a postcript to the technical school debate, John Hudson, a former deputy secretary in the DES wrote a piece in *The Times Educational Supplement* (3 October 1986) when Kenneth Baker mooted the idea of city technology colleges. 'Two incidents stick in my mind', he wrote:

> the first, when the responsible Staff Inspector, asked in the course of an internal meeting about his concept of the secondary technical school, replied that it was a grammar school without Latin; and on another occasion when a senior inspector said that the technical school should use its vocational orientation to stimulate the motivation of its pupils to provide them with a good general education.

Grammar Schools

If the secondary moderns and the technical schools needed time to settle down and discover their own educational identity, the grammar schools were the established secondary schools, the sitting tenants, the custodians of the secondary education tradition. They were in a strong position with an assured entry. The standard grammar school curriculum enjoyed the uncritical respect and confidence of the community. Their position was underpinned by the existence of 179 direct grant schools of which Manchester Grammar School was the doyen – quasi-independent grammar schools with many free places paid for by local authorities.

It was true that the uneven nature of the selection process meant that grammar schools came in various shapes and sizes. Some were highly selective, producing results which made them leaders in the field. Others were much less so. In Wales the Welsh Intermediate Education Act of 1889 had increased the number of 'intermediate' (grammar) schools, 13 years before the English counties and county boroughs were allowed to build secondary schools. The result was much wider access to Welsh selective schools, many of which admitted 35–40 per cent of the local population of 11-year-olds.

The passing of the Act meant the grammar schools lost their fee-payers and began to take all their entry from those allocated to them by the 11-plus. This was not seen as an unmixed blessing. When preparing a paper for ministers on the eve of the 1964 general election with the Conservatives with their backs to the wall, Christopher Chataway, a junior minister at the DES, would look back nostalgically to the days when modest fees for grammar school entry provided a safety valve for the system. The 11-plus offered no such middle-class safety valve.

Even at the grammar school in the 1950s, early leaving was regarded as serious enough to provide the CAC with the remit for a report on *Early Leaving*, published in 1954. The figures showed that in 1950–51 nearly a third left before the end of their fifth year. The selection procedure had changed the composition of the grammar school population, but had not changed social expectations. The report – the first of the great CAC reports to hammer at this theme – spelled out the links between performance and social class: admission was heavily skewed in the direction of the middle class, and the middle-class children performed better than the working class. GCE had just come in: more than half the grammar school intake left with fewer than three passes; for the children of unskilled workers, the equivalent figure was two-thirds.

The CAC's recipe was to introduce educational maintenance allowances and higher family allowances. Coming in a period of economic stringency when Florence Horsbrugh had been enforcing the cuts required by R. A. Butler as Chancellor in Churchill's first post-war administration, the suggestions made little impact. There continued to be inconclusive talk in the Secondary Panel about the merits or demerits of making parents sign contracts to keep their sons and daughters on to complete the five-year course, but these were of doubtful legal validity.

In the medium term, early leaving proved to be less serious than had been thought – by the end of the decade the proportion of pupils failing to stay till 16 was steadily reducing and the examination results were on an upward trend. It evidently had taken a few years for the new generation of grammar school entrants to respond and take advantage of their opportunities – and for the grammar school teachers to adjust to the new entry. In 1959, the proportion of those staying on beyond the minimum leaving age in all kinds of school was still only 29.2 per cent – most of them in the grammar schools. By 1964 the corresponding figure was 51.3, and by 1969 61.5, indicating more staying on in the non-selective schools.

The grammar schools also had to get used to the new examination – the GCE O level which was a single subject exam which had a pass level pitched at the credit standard in the old School Certificate. It was aimed at the top 25 per cent of the ability range – which included most of the entrants to the English grammar schools – but even so, most grammar schools had a 'tail' of under-performing pupils in their 'C' streams who performed poorly (and who had formed the bulk of their early leavers). (Even Eric James, the High Master of one of the most selective schools in the country, Manchester Grammar School, was heard to speak of his 'duds'.)

The Secondary Panel returned to grammar school topics again and again. They had their say on early leaving, on inspection priorities – did maintained grammar schools get less attention from HMI than public schools? – on the need to keep a close eye on sixth forms. R. H. Barrow, the SI who, as secretary had drafted most of the Norwood Report, observed that 'it took a long time to get to know a grammar school and the varieties of sixth-form work. The function of the sixth-form master was not always understood and in most schools so much attention was on exam subjects that no one took a synoptic view of the boy as a human being or looked after his total mental growth.' The panel discussed the broadening of the sixth form as more pupils stayed on who were not suited to A levels – the 'general sixth-form' 'the waiting-room sixth' – the first references to what would emerge as the wider 16–19 theme in later decades.

The education of girls was a topic of continuing interest. John Newsom published a book on the subject in 1959 which generated a discussion introduced by Mervyn Pritchard, a staff inspector, which offers a sidelight on the times. There were comments about earlier maturity and 'greater freedom outside school' and about the need for girls' education to reflect the fact that many not least 'those of high intellectual capacity', would continue to work after marriage. The discussion roamed freely: there was a vital need for serenity to combat the dangers to mental health; some thought boys stood up to hard work better than girls; some non-academic courses in girls' schools took up too much time. The minutes record that there was vigorous debate on domestic science and personal hygiene: it was 'generally felt that having a bath or learning how to make currant buns must not be regarded as adequate substitutes for planned reading and intellectual disciplines'.

Three into One

When called on for development plans for secondary education a number of LEAs included one or more comprehensives in their plans. Anglesey – a special case because of its size and isolation – reorganised on comprehensive lines early on without difficulty (though HMI noted sadly that this was followed by a drop in exam results). A few local authorities, the most notable being London and Coventry, based their plans on large, all-through comprehensive schools. Graham Savage, the LCC education officer, was a former SCI who had crossed Westminster Bridge and taken up residence in County Hall. (In London's case, its comprehensive plans were frustrated for many years by the resistance of London's aided grammar schools which were outside the control of the Authority.) Middlesex LEA put up plans (which were turned down) for a comprehensive system based on smaller schools mainly using existing buildings.

The Ministry line was that a grammar school needed two–three forms of entry to support a decent academic sixth form. If a comprehensive school was to develop an adequate sixth form it would need, so the argument ran, two–three forms of entry of clever children. If these were to form 20–5 per cent of the total this would mean there would need to be 9 or 10 forms of 'secondary modern-type' pupils, making 11 or 12 forms of entry in all. The assumption was that few of the 'secondary modern-type' pupils would make the sixth form, and that the size of the academic groups needed to be large enough to provide a critical mass of scholarly endeavour.

Schools which conformed to this specification would need to have 1,700–1,800 places like the first London purpose-built comprehensives, Kidbrooke and Woodberry Down. It was regarded as self-evident that protagonists of the comprehensive school had to be able to show they could offer a better deal to the majority without the minority – the grammar school pupils – losing out. With such a small proportion of pupils staying on beyond 15 in the system as a whole, it seemed self-evident that the size of the initial intake of clever children – and therefore of the whole comprehensive school – was a matter of cardinal importance.

Brian Simon's detailed and informative account of these events[11] shows that in the Labour Party there were many who had long argued for multilateral schools and against the tri- or bipartite model and who were bitterly disappointed by the line adopted by the Attlee government. But it was also true that there was a powerful section of the party which held the grammar school in high esteem as the ladder up which they had climbed. Having abolished fees and (as they supposed) opened these schools to all on merit, they were unwilling to throw away the advantages before their children and grandchildren had a chance to benefit. One who stuck to this view long into retirement was Emmanuel Shinwell, former Labour minister and veteran socialist:[12]

> *We were afraid to tackle the public schools to which wealthy people send their sons, but at the same time are ready to throw overboard the grammar schools which are for many working-class boys the stepping-stone to the universities and a useful career. I would rather abandon Eton, Winchester, Harrow and all the rest of them than sacrifice the advantage of the grammar school.*

When the Norwood Committee pushed for a tripartite system, the psychologists, marshalled by Cyril Burt, were confident that intelligence was a measurable, innate attribute, genetically predetermined. If this were the case, and if the tests could do what they claimed, a selective system promised to be both efficient and fair. But as the 1950s progressed the evidence against these propositions began to build up.

Jean Floud had shown the extent of working-class children's under-performance in the 11-plus.[13] Professor P. E. Vernon had shown that performance in intelligence tests could be improved by coaching[14] which had hitherto been discounted. He went on to edit a volume on *Secondary School Selection*[15] in which various educational psychologists discussed the mechanics of selection and the combination of nature and nurture which explained differences at 11. And in 1957, the NFER published the results of a carefully designed and thorough research project on *Admission to Grammar Schools* by Alfred Yates and Douglas Pidgeon, which concluded that each year at least 10 per cent of children were sent to the 'wrong' school – some to the grammar school who should have been allocated to the modern school, some to the modern school who really belonged in a selective school.

This report had a strong impact – if upwards of 60,000 pupils were wrongly selected each year, the whole system was called in question. In reality a 10 per cent margin of error was relatively small, but this was not how it was interpreted. 'Success' or 'failure' in the selection process had major significance for the life chances of the individuals involved. People would accept this if the selection procedure was scientific and indisputably valid. If it was flawed the 11-plus became indefensible.

This did not, of course, prevent the grammar schools from fighting their corner. The Joint Four Secondary Associations – the teachers' unions representing grammar school heads and assistant teachers – staunchly defended their territory, and there was no more doughty protagonist than James. But this was one occasion when educational research could be credited with a clear policy outcome. The evidence was out in the open: it was only a matter of time before political action followed: the psychologists had supplied the Labour Party with the ammunition it needed to convince its own doubters and to win the backing of the nation.

The Conservatives, too, had become anxious about the 11-plus and had issued a White Paper in 1958 (see box) with the inspiring, if hardly original, title of *Secondary Education for All: A New Drive*. It promised a five-year building programme but did nothing to deal with what it identified as the 'root cause of the concern that is currently felt over what has become known as the 11-plus examination'. Labour went into the general elections of 1959 and 1964 with a manifesto commitment to the comprehensive school. When Harold Wilson replaced Alec Douglas Home in Downing Street the work was put in hand.

Circular 10/65

It was Anthony Crosland in 1965 who sent out the circular calling for comprehensive proposals, authority by authority and school by school. It was to be done by persuasion without primary legislation and within the existing school buildings – new building still had to be justified on the basis of additional pupils. Five approved methods were set out including two-tier arrangements of the kind pioneered in Leicestershire, and middle school schemes. Ministers promised that they would not approve 'botched' jobs, but some unsatisfactory schemes went through: there were split-site schools where teachers would have to dash from one site to another by taxi between lessons. Given the financial constraints the alternative was indefinite delay.

Inside the Department of Education, a secondary reorganisation team of selected officials had the job of vetting the proposals submitted by LEAs – a mammoth task: a large authority with upwards of 50 secondary schools could generate a mountain of paper. Each set of proposals required detailed assessments by the district HMI. When a 'reorganisation principal' paid a visit to an LEA to go over plans, the HMI would brief in advance and attend. In many cases the HMI would have been called in earlier by the local chief education officer as someone whose opinion was valued. From the Office point of view, the contribution of HMI was very variable. For the most part cooperation was good and led to increased mutual respect between HMI and Schools Branch. But when disputes arose (as they were bound to) HMIs found themselves in the eye of the storm – bound to support the policy of the Department, yet jealous of their professional independence and wishing to retain the goodwill of

1958 White Paper

At the end of 1957, the prime minister, Harold Macmillan, sent a note to the minister of education, Geoffrey Lloyd:

> *Would you please send me a note on the 11-plus examination. From what I have heard it seems to be v. unpopular. Is it believed to be the best answer and what is our attitude towards LEAs (and I believe there are some) who have substituted some other system?'16*

The decision to issue the White Paper and initiate a 'drive' to improve the secondary modern schools followed from this. Macmillan warmed to the idea of a drive – it reminded him of the drive to build 300,000 houses with which he made his name in 1952.

Macmillan's inquiry also set off a continuing discussion inside the Government about comprehensive education. Ministers, such as Edward Boyle and Christopher Chataway – and Geoffrey Lloyd (in his reply to Macmillan) – acknowledged the 11-plus touched a very sensitive spot. It was 'politically dangerous'. They must 'take the sting out of the 11-plus'. If not, he said, 'Labour will be able to command support and I am not happy about the political prospect. Can we find enough money quickly enough to improve the s.m.s.?' Boyle and Chataway argued strongly for a pragmatic approach and against the Conservatives adopting an anti-comprehensive dogma. The discussion went on inside the Government right up to the 1964 general election.

When it appeared, a year later, the White Paper slightly softened the Government's attitude to comprehensive education – in sparsely populated rural areas and on new housing estates – but hostility was maintained towards any scheme which adversely affected an established grammar school. It confirmed the decision to extend the teacher training college course to three years. And it announced a £300 million, five-year, building programme to include an improvement package aimed at secondary modern schools.

This was the product of much horse-trading between the Chancellor of the Exchequer, the Minister of Housing and Local Government and the Education Minister, with Butler chairing the relevant Home Affairs Cabinet Committee. The Treasury had pushed through a change in the mechanisms of local government finance to do away with grant-aid for education based on a percentage of approved expenditure. It was this percentage grants system which gave education committees their special status within local government. Ending percentage grants and making the central government contribution in the form of a 'block' or 'general grant' was promoted as a way of imposing limits on central government spending and giving more financial discretion to local authorities within fixed sums.

In a handwritten note to the Prime Minister signed RaB, Butler supported the White Paper as a sweetener for Lloyd. 'Education has already been coerced (partly by me) into accepting the general grant. I feel that the Minister has a strong case'.[17] In competition with hospitals, transport and nuclear power, school building was to be given priority.

Subsequent events showed that the general grant did not bear out the worst fears of the education lobby – money meant for education was not diverted to other services. Nor did local authorities have more freedom to spend their own money. The main loser was the Education Minister who was left with even less leverage over education at the local level. The Education Department's lack of financial muscle became a byword in government. It inhibited ministers' capacity to offer leadership and made them eager to blame everyone else for the shortcomings of the education service but themselves. It was the reason why, later on, money was channelled to favoured projects through the Manpower Services Commission (MSC) instead of the Department of Education.

'their' local authority officers. For some it was a new experience to be involved in contentious policy matters and they saw it as a distraction from their proper job of visiting and reporting on schools. Bob Gunn and Murray White were among the SIs who acted as a link between HMIs in the field and the Office on reorganisation matters; their assessments and occasional mediation with district inspectors, were influential.

Comprehensive reorganisation was accepted by most local authorities whatever their political control. The Conservatives at Westminster were more hostile, but rather than come out firmly for or against, argued that secondary organisation should be left to the discretion of each local authority. This enabled them to snipe against reorganisation without disowning their colleagues in local authorities. As time passed political opinion tended to polarise and acrimony increased. The argument quickly progressed beyond the technical disputation about selection and psychometry and focused on social engineering and the 'use' of the education system to attempt to right wrongs inherent in an unequal society.

For HMIs, pursuing their regular round of pastoral visitation, comprehensive schools presented a new challenge. The first purpose-built comprehensives began to appear in the mid-1950s when the Inspectorate was struggling to meet Roseveare's call for all schools to be reported on by the end of the decade. In the Secondary Panel there were frequent discussions of when and how to inspect comprehensives. There were the usual suggestions that the new institutions required time to settle down – and that HMIs themselves needed to visit them many times informally before they were ready to set up full inspections. Eventually a programme of full inspections by a hand-picked team of specialist HMIs was instituted to get to grips with the logistic problems of inspecting large schools with very wide curricular demands. To employ the traditional grammar school techniques made impossible demands on specialist manpower. This was another of the reasons why, by the mid-1960s, the Inspectorate was cutting back on full inspections and putting more effort into surveys.

The minimum desirable size of comprehensive schools was a recurring topic as ministers tried to accommodate LEAs where the logistics favoured smaller schools – Hertfordshire's plans for five-form entry comprehensives were justified by the exceptionally high rate of staying on beyond the leaving age. Small schools proposed in Oxfordshire sent up alarm signals. Much attention in the panel was directed towards two-tier comprehensive plans: HMIs worried about the effect of separating the teaching of the older children from the younger; how would high-quality staff be recruited to the lower schools without the carrot of sixth-form work?

Crowther Report

The major CAC inquiries offered HMI one of the most important opportunities open to them to bring their knowledge and expertise to bear on policy issues. By convention, HMIs were attached to the inquiries as assessors and members of the secretariat. Many of the resulting reports were drafted by HMI.

The Crowther report was written by David Ayerst HMI[18] who knew how to grab his audience with a snappy opening sentence: 'This report is about the education of English boys and girls aged from 15 to 18. Most of them are not being educated.' Gilbert Peaker was again a major contributor of advice and expertise – among the statistical material the committee used was a survey of 18-year-old recruits to the army and RAF which showed 'that a substantial minority of the ablest 18-year-old recruits had left school at 15'. The sociological evidence was used by Crowther to prove the existence of a large, untapped, pool of ability. Waste of talent was also a theme, five years later, of the Newsom Report on *Half our Future* and the Robbins Report on *Higher Education*.

Geoffrey Crowther was a famous editor of *The Economist* turned businessman. He and his colleagues went along with the then Government's policy of defending the grammar schools – 'we cannot afford to lose any good school, whatever its classification' – but was fatalistically aware that radical change was on the way:

> *Once it is agreed, as more and more people are coming to believe, that it is wrong to label children for all time at 11, the attempt to give mutually exclusive labels to schools to which they go at that age will have to be abandoned ... It is clear ... that the shape of the English school system in 1978 will differ from that of 1958 – perhaps as much as that of 1958 did from 1938. (paragraphs 36 and 40)*

Crowther came down firmly for raising the leaving age by the end of the 1960s – a choice of three years was offered – with a single leaving date each year. It combined this with a reaffirmation of continuing education in county colleges to be introduced more gradually but with no fixed target date. The aim was to raise the participation rate in full-time education to 18 by a factor of 4–50 per cent of the age group by the year 1980. (Before going out in 1964, the Conservatives decreed that the leaving age should be raised in 1970–1. Because of the financial crisis of 1968, the date was delayed for two years. The aim of a 50 per cent retention rate was not achieved until the 1990s.)

Crowther came to be remembered for its sturdy defence of the specialised 'English Sixth Form' and the peculiarly English 'subject-mindedness' it attributed to pupils and used to explain sixth-form specialisation. On the other hand it was against excessively early specialisation and supported better use of time not bespoken for examination subjects. Some of the pressure for early specialisation was put down to a shortage of university places – 15 years on from 1944 the opening up of the grammar schools was paying dividends in the shape of more successful A level candidates and therefore more competition for university places. Its strictures on early specialisation were echoed widely but little was done to mitigate it.

To achieve the four-fold increase in participation, the committee focused on the second quartile – the first quartile being the grammar school intake – for whom they wanted an expansion and strengthening of FE. The picture they painted was bleak: two-thirds of FE enrolments were for evening classes only, with a high drop-out rate. Part-time day release was demand-led in the sense that most was linked to industrial training and apprenticeship (hence many more boys than girls). Crowther and his colleagues wanted a genuine 'Alternative Road' alongside the conventional sixth form – a 'practical' education, not exclusively technical, fitting young people for a wide range of occupations and enabling them to postpone career choice for several years of continued education. They stopped short of recommending a network of technical schools – it was too late for that – but hoped for better technical education provision in secondary moderns and comprehensives.

Newsom Report

Two years after the publication of *15 to 18* the CAC, with John Newsom in the chair, was asked to report on the education of average and below-average pupils aged 13–16. The result appeared in 1963 under the title, *Half Our Future*. Miss M. J. (Peggy) Marshall who was SI for secondary modern schools, acted as secretary and wrote much of the report.

Newsom hedged on secondary organisation, knowing that to have faced the issue head on would have divided the committee before it had begun its work; in any case there were many matters to consider which would be relevant irrespective of what type of secondary organisation was chosen. Though much preoccupied with the background social questions which held back progress, the report was essentially cheerful and optimistic – 'though this is ... about the academically less successful, it is a success story that we have to tell'. The National Service Survey showed that the educational standards of recruits had risen between 1947 and the last intake of conscripts in 1960 and this was borne out by the Ministry's four-yearly reading surveys (see Chapter 2). Newsom and his colleagues strongly endorsed the arguments set out in Crowther for an early date for raising the leaving age.

Boyle's letter to Newsom on receipt of the report was notable for its last, oft-quoted, sentence: 'The essential point is that all children should have an equal opportunity of acquiring intelligence, and of developing their talents and abilities to the full.' The suggestion that intelligence could be acquired signified a deliberate rejection by Boyle of the dogma that IQ was a fixed genetic endowment. The report itself, however, was not an influential document – it was overshadowed by the secondary reorganisation controversy which obscured its evaluation of what was being achieved in the secondary modern schools. It advocated more vocationally oriented courses at the top of the secondary modern and comprehensive schools and dealt in a sensitive manner with the major social problems which the schools faced in deprived areas – areas where, as it pointed out, all social services functioned badly, compounding their mutual deficiencies.

With the encouragement of A and B Branch Development Group Newsom called for some experimental designs incorporating different forms of school organisation and teaching methods and for 'an experimental school run in co-operation with a teacher training college'. HMI were deeply involved in collecting the information base on which Newsom relied for the six portraits of the Brown, Jones and Robinson boys and girls which they drew to serve as imaginary stereotypes for upper, middle and lower ranges of 'Newsom' children.

In parenthesis it should be mentioned that the report – as befitted Newsom's genial and humorous disposition – included a few jokes, some of which have entered into the canon of educational quotations. An epigraph on the first page reads: 'A boy who had just left school was asked by his former headmaster what he thought of the new buildings. 'It could all be marble, Sir,' he said, 'but it would still be a bloody school.' And in an appendix on sex education a comment is attributed to 'Boy – 15 years: "Sex. I have not finished my course as a teenager. And this subject has not really hit me in the eye yet. But it is the subject I shall have to get to think about." '

Curriculum Development
Curriculum Study Group

A landmark decision by David Eccles in 1962 set up the CSG attached to Schools Branch inside the Ministry of Education. One of its tasks was to provide a secretariat for the Secondary Schools Examination Council and work on the introduction of the CSE. As already mentioned, the multidisciplinary model for the CSG was drawn – like Derek Morrell – from the Ministry's A and B Branch Development Group. Eccles, coming to the end of his second stint as Minister of Education had at last questioned the Ministry's exclusion from the curriculum – what he called 'the Secret Garden' – and saw the end of the attempt to keep the modern school an exam-free zone as the opportunity for the Ministry to take a more active part.

The group comprised eight HMIs, one LEA inspector, an examination specialist from an institute of education and four administrators, headed jointly by an SI and an assistant secretary – with supporting executive and clerical staff, numbering about 18. In addition to work on the CSE, in the early years it was to have study teams on primary and secondary education and three subject teams looking at mathematics, science and modern languages. In due course the staff would have expanded and the field of action would have grown – but always, it was emphasised, with the proviso that the new unit would be 'one voice amongst others, invested with no greater authority than is merited by the quality of its contribution'.

The authorities and the teachers' unions immediately ganged up against this Ministry initiative and Boyle, Eccles's successor, backed down. The CSG was replaced by a Schools Council for Curriculum and Examinations – a body in which management (and finance) was shared between the Department and the local authorities, while the teachers, through their unions, had the majority say on curricular matters. As an internal paper for the Secretary of State put it: 'the Department would have preferred a less formal division of function, but the teachers and others were insistent that the Council must be seen to be in operational control of its own work.'[19]

The Schools Council

Under its first chairman, John Maud, the Council was welcomed on the educational scene with some enthusiasm. It came into being at a time when there was a head of steam behind curriculum reform, on both sides of the Atlantic. Panic about the success of Soviet space technology set off a wave of attempts to overhaul science teaching in the United States, and in Britain the Nuffield Foundation embarked on a programme of development across the curriculum. The Schools Council took over and greatly expanded the Nuffield initiative. Robert Morris HMI was one of the first joint secretaries with Morrell. Joslyn Owen, an assistant education officer from Somerset, joined two years later.

Throughout its existence a succession of HMIs worked for the Council, some as members of its staff and others on advisory groups for individual projects. HMI reports on projects in the field helped to keep the HMI assessors informed. A staff inspector, Robert Sibson, did seven years at the council on the examinations side. When Morrell moved on to the Home Office, Geoffrey Caston, another upwardly mobile DES assistant secretary, moved in. For the first decade of its life, the Council was a

powerhouse, generating excitement and expectation. The time was ripe
for a radical review of the traditional curriculum and the Schools Council
set about it with zest and enthusiasm.

Its programme committees backed development projects in the main
subject areas, with participating schools which trialled materials and
provided feedback. HMI participation was of two kinds – some were
seconded to work full-time with the Council; others sat in as assessors on
committees and project groups.

The Council began by looking (with HMI advice) at aspects of the
curriculum where development was particularly needed – such as oracy,
technology and science for the young school-leaver. In primary education
there was work on language, science, mathematics and literacy.

Some projects were better than others – some were highly influential,
others made little impact. One of the most original – and expensive – the
humanities project, did not have a large take-up in the schools but
attracted a disproportionate amount of attention. Major projects were set
up for history and geography, for moral education and mathematics, for
English, science and technology, and for other subject areas. A big effort,
and a great deal of enthusiasm in the schools, went into primary French
whose pilot scheme 10 years later, was evaluated by Clare Burstall of the
NFER and discontinued because of the lack of language teachers in
primary schools and poor articulation between the primary and
secondary stage.

The history 13–16 project, like the Schools Council's mathematics project,
negotiated their own O levels with an examination board – taking
advantage of having examinations and curriculum under the same roof.
This happened in several subjects such as Nuffield science, but
unfortunately there was not as much interchange as many would have
desired. The Council's examination efforts were marked by lengthy
attempts to find a way of putting GCE and CSE together in a single
system, and by repeated abortive attempts to reform the sixth form and
its examinations.

The approach adopted by many projects reflected the earnestly
progressive approach which prevailed at the time, notably the liking
for discovery learning. When she was Secretary of State, Margaret
Thatcher paid a visit to a school to see the Schools Council's
humanities project in action. The aim was to get pupils to take part in

controversial debate, with the teacher remaining a neutral moderator, refusing to say what were right and wrong opinions. The Secretary of State was unimpressed. 'When I was a girl,' she said, 'I was taught the difference between right and wrong.'[20] One thing the Schools Council's teacher politicians were not good at was reading the signs of the times.

Uptake – the use of the materials produced by Schools Council teams – depended on market forces: schools could take them or leave them on what they took to be their merits. On the whole the take-up was disappointing. Implementation was an ongoing weakness. As we shall see (Chapter 7) the Council ran into difficulties when the Department began to articulate views on the curriculum and to regard the Council as an unnecessary complication.

In retrospect, the Schools Council looks like a 20-year diversion. By the time it was done away with by Keith Joseph in 1984 (see Chapter 10) the Department of Education was no longer prepared to entrust the curriculum to the teachers and had begun to take a more direct hand in its content. Had the CSG not been stifled at birth events might have moved faster towards a national curriculum by whatever name. As it was, the Schools Council oversaw the necessary preparatory work on the CSE and the routine work on GCE.

Postscript

Alongside the work going on in the Schools Council interest in the secondary curriculum among senior members of the Inspectorate led, in 1968, to the setting up of an internal SIs' Curriculum Group, led first by Mervyn Pritchard and subsequently by John Morris and Geoffrey Petter. The group consisted of 10 inspectors, with corresponding members. It was a new departure for subject specialist SIs to take an overview of the curriculum.

The Schools Council had launched into a programme of separate subject projects without first considering the curriculum as a whole. There were reasons for this: the Council did not want to give the least impression that it was in the business of prescribing a national curriculum. If it started with a whole curriculum study it might suggest just that. Only after it had become heavily involved with the separate subjects did the Council get round to considering questions of balance and priority – and then only with difficulty and without conviction. Yet without any consideration of the curriculum as a whole there was an inevitable tendency to overload the content of individual subjects.

The SIs group worked to a formal programme, drawing on inspection evidence of what they regarded as most promising practice. Topics included: 16–19 generally, education in the rest of Europe, the evolution of the school curriculum, the purpose of secondary education. It produced papers for internal distribution and discussion – at least two of the papers (on 'balance' and 'problems and objectives') were published in *Trends*. The material was used by the Schools Council when it did eventually get round to whole curriculum issues.

Between 1968 and 1974, the group held 38 meetings, its membership broadened to include fewer SIs and more field HMIs including one from FE. It tried to influence the short-course programme and suggest areas of interest for inspection visits but in the end, other pressures such as coolness on the part of HMI in the divisions, and tensions between DIs and SIs, brought it to an end in 1974. As we shall see, soon after the group disbanded, the Red Books exercise got under way and the curriculum moved up the Office agenda in the wake of James Callaghan's Ruskin College speech.

It was an example of the Inspectorate's capacity for forward thinking but also of its limited effectiveness. It was an intellectual exercise rather than a policy initiative. It ran for seven years and ended with little to show for it. All that can be said is that the work contributed to the Schools Council's belated efforts and fed, eventually, into the constructive work on the curriculum by HMI after Ruskin.

Notes

1 Simon, B. (1965) *Education and the Labour Movement: 1870–1920*. London: Lawrence & Wishart, 362–3.

2 Quoted in Betty Vernon (1982) *Ellen Wilkinson, 1891–1947*. London: Croom Helm, 222–3.

3 Judge, H (1984) *A Generation of Schooling: English Secondary Schools since 1944*. Oxford: Oxford University Press, 20, 22.

4 HMI Secondary Education Panel. PRO ED158/18–22. There were also three sub-panels for secondary modern, technical and grammar schools.

5 Second meeting of the Secondary Panel, 17 January 1946, chaired by CI Mr Charles on 'The content of curriculum in secondary modern schools'. PRO ED158/18.

6 Nineteenth meeting of the Secondary Panel, 27 September 1954. PRO ED158/19.

7 SI A. G. Gooch's paper, 'Secondary technical education', May 1961. PRO ED158/29.

8 Sanderson, M. (1994) *The Missing Stratum: Technical School Education in England 1900–1990s*. London: The Athlone Press, 133–5.

[9] Minute from A. Thompson to A. Part and Sir Martin Roseveare, 4. PRO ED136/86.

[10] See note 9.

[11] Simon, B. (1991) *Education and the Social Order, 1940–1990*. London: Lawrence & Wishart.

[12] Quoted in Harry Judge, note 3, 68.

[13] Floud, J. E. (ed.) with Halsey, A. H. Martin, F. M. (1956) *Social Class and Educational Opportunity*. London: William Heinemann Ltd.

[14] Vernon, P. E. (1952) 'Intelligence Testing'. *The Times Educational Supplement*, 2 January, 1 February 1952.

[15] Vernon, P. E. (ed.) (1958) *Secondary School Selection: A British Psychological Society Inquiry*. London: Methuen & Co. Ltd.

[16] Minute from the Prime Minister, 5 December 1957. PRO ED136/941. See also ED136/942 and PREM 11/2281.

[17] Minute to the Prime Minister from R. A. Butler, 31 May 1957. PRO PREM 11/2281.

[18] David Ayerst had worked for the *Manchester Guardian* before becoming an HMI and wrote the newspaper's history. See Ayerst, D. (1971) *'Guardian': Biography of a Newspaper*. London: Collins.

[19] 'The Curriculum Study Group and the Schools Council', 6 June 1964. PRO ED136/955.

[20] Plaskow, M. (1985) 'A long view from the inside' in Plaskow, M. (ed.) *Life and Death of the Schools Council*. Lewes: The Falmer Press, 1–13, quote on page 13.

HMI Miscellany

Extracts from HMI personal accounts

John Morris 1947

My mentor was a former AI and an effect of this iniquitous system was to place him on virtually an equal footing with newly appointed HMIs like myself. However, his rancour was directed at the system and not at new HMIs ... I built up a picture of contrasting educational philosophies and relationships. At one school in the docks area, the elderly headmaster, at the sound of the mid-morning bell, shouted his excuses, seized a cane and rushed into the corridor to lash about him at the noisiest members of the jostling mob ... He shortly returned, apoplectically rubicund, explaining the need to discipline the ruffians. 'Yes', he replied in answer to my question, 'I always have to do this to get order.' Two years later, under a wise and temperate head, the boys moved about peacefully without supervision; and the members of the virtually unchanged staff said they could scarcely believe that the school had been transformed into a civilised community by a single but determined leader. I learned to look carefully at head teachers ...

Peggy Marshall 1953

On joining the E&W Ridings Division in 1953 M.J.M. recalled an enormous drive to catch up on visits and inspections . . . The full inspection programme was very heavy: one secondary FI or two primary nearly every week was not uncommon and this over a considerable period; the deadlines for clearing the backlog were fairly tight . . . Inspections were undertaken in the context of schools being already well known to the RI; relationships were such that a full programme could have been built up by invitation. This momentum and intensity, though they could not be maintained indefinitely, served to re-establish some base-lines and, for a newcomer, provided a rapid and valuable introduction to all types of schools in many different circumstances, requiring the development of personal relationships and professional techniques . . .

They also sought to find appropriate approaches to these newer types of school – secondary modern, technical and, a little later, comprehensives, which brought new demands. There was concern to avoid undue pressure on schools only just beginning to establish themselves, and at the same time to build up knowledge of new developments, which was even more important. Presumably for these reasons – and manpower? – SCI (Wilson) and CI (P. A. Browne) met a few times with a small group to discuss alternative styles and modes of inspection. The secondary modern panel also embarked on a number of exploratory exercises, largely information gathering. There was certainly some encouragement in the Divisions to experiment locally, within what time there was available. None of this seemed to have resulted in any central policy changes at the time. Probably the ground was changing too fast under our feet before anything could come to fruition . . .

Much of the work of HMI in this period both in school visits and in teachers' short courses was focused on the implications, curricular, pedagogical and organisational, of 'going comprehensive' . . . All of this needed monitoring and writing up in some form, at least for the internal information of the Inspectorate itself, and Ministers. To this extent there was a slowing down of formal full inspections but certainly some programme was maintained.

The longer term consequences of this change became apparent in the mid-70s under Sheila Browne's drive to restore reporting and inspection. There had been a significant loss in the interval: many older HMI who had learned their trade in the 40s, 50s and early 60s had retired and the reduced number of newly recruited HMI lacked that induction. When the policy began to reverse, many 'young' HMI were as disconcerted at the restoration of full inspections and reports, as their predecessors in 1968 had been to see them go. It proved necessary to provide guidance on very basic principles on how to conduct and write up inspections, in addition to the procedures which had to be evolved specifically for the Secondary Survey. (*In interview with Brian Arthur and Roy Wake.*)

Illtyd Lloyd 1964

The in-service training of teachers run by HMI, in particular national and regional courses related to the CSE examinations and the Organisation and Management of Schools – undertaken at the behest of the Secretary of State – made demands on members of the Inspectorate and enhanced their national standing. The secondary team in Wales was at the forefront of O & M developments and ran a number of courses for heads and senior staff – not only in Wales ... These courses soon developed a much stronger curriculum bias and a concern for the monitoring of progress ... They had, I believe, a major influence on the work and management of secondary schools in Wales – and perhaps in England since we accepted on the courses a significant proportion of members from across the border, this in itself being seen as advantageous to our rather traditional heads ... Our series of Secondary Papers (overview documents applying to Wales only) dealing with particular topics, drew heavily on FIs but were topped up with informal survey work, largely targeted pastoral visits. Great emphasis was placed on these, with an attempt to secure some measure of standardisation so as to ensure that basic information was readily available (eg pastoral structure, mixed ability/banding organisation, curriculum) and to ease the work of collating notes.

Jack Featherstone 1968

Having been head of two secondary modern schools, I was loaned out a great deal ... there being nobody in the Division in that field ... The purpose was to visit secondary modern schools, with a different colleague in each school. Of course I enjoyed these experiences; they put *me* in the role of mentor.

I was attending my first HMI meeting and for a few minutes beforehand was chatting with a colleague who joined on the same day as I. The door opened and in came an experienced colleague who came over and said: 'What's your specialism?' My fellow new-boy answered like a shot: 'The vast majority. What's yours?' That answer pinpointed the one weakness of the Inspectorate: an ignorance, in many Divisions, of the needs of those pupils in our schools who were described as 'non-academic'. They were indeed the vast majority and the difficulty most schools had was to interest them in roughly the same subjects as the examination pupils studied. The response was often negative unruliness and absence of learning. And in most Divisions HMI visiting secondary schools were unable to help in that field – they had not worked in it as teachers. I was lucky in that my work as a head-teacher had included developing subjects which non-academic pupils could take as academic subjects.

Don Porter 1946

Specialist work made great progress during my first ten years. I came in half expecting to be one of the link men between science and craft, since (like many teachers) I had spent the best part of six years applying my maths and physics. But priority was given to basic concepts and the idea of 'science and its applications as the core and inspiration' had to wait until later. (The quotation from the Spens report was repeated in one of the first Ministry pamphlets.)

The SI secondary technical (Gooch) ran courses at Cambridge which influenced the technical school ... Reporting on technical schools increased; many were now in new buildings ... As SI Handicraft (1959) I had a team of about 20 main specialists (almost two per Division) though several carried big district loads as well ... I feel that the Inspectorate did well in helping to show that there were intellectually demanding courses other than the established academic ones. The impact of going comprehensive, however, tended to encourage schools to show they were 'as good as' the grammar schools and to neglect the technical aspects. Unfortunately we were left with a system of secondary schools trying to follow the same curriculum with almost all children – so different from what was intended. Whether we could have done more to highlight the dangers is doubtful, but I remain dissatisfied.

Peter Hoy 1952

By the time Peter Hoy became SI for modern languages in 1968 the subject was in a 'ferment'. The Primary French project (Nuffield/NFER) had started, in which HMI were involved as assessors and encouragers ... As schools faced up to the teaching of French to a wide ability range, new methodologies were being developed – audio-visual teaching and language laboratories being widespread examples, and *sections bilingues* an example of a more individual type. Teachers needed professional advice and practical support, some of it of a highly technical nature. These developments – themselves part of the practical expansion of linguistics – were accompanied (even stimulated) by 'new' or renewed emphasis on the spoken language and a rationale of progression based on listening, speaking, reading, writing rather than on the traditional grammatical 'ladder'. These changes and the increase in the teaching of the second foreign language also made organisational demands (not least of timing and selection) on modern language departments. *(Interview with Brian Arthur)*

Tom Marjoram 1966

In those early years I was regarded primarily as a mathematics specialist. As a teacher, I had written mathematics textbooks and served on NUJMB Modern Maths Committee. In the late Sixties the whole field of maths teaching was in a state of flux. In secondary schools there were numerous 'new maths' syllabuses to choose from. Some schools stuck to the traditional syllabuses, others embraced the new with enthusiasm. Between them could be found all shades of opinion – often in the same maths department. Texts by the School Maths Project (SMP) and the Midlands Maths Experiment (MME) became very popular and offered their own syllabuses at O and A level. There were others. Most of these new syllabuses radically altered the algebraic content and introduced set notation, vector algebra, elementary statistics and elementary arithmetic theory of number bases . . . In the primary schools Nuffield maths material also introduced elementary ideas on such topics as sets and binary addition – often to some bewildered teachers who could teach tables and long division to perfection but couldn't quite get the hang or point of empty and disjoint sets, median mode and means etc.

Gordon Hamflett 1962

While on secondment I officially operated outside HM Inspectorate – in fact in late 1970 or early 1971 the four HMI on secondment to the Schools Council collectively and voluntarily agreed not to use our formal title . . . Prior to actual secondment I had mixed feelings about going to the Schools Council – about being away from mainstream HMI work for three years – but in the event I greatly valued the experience and learned a lot from it. Also, after eight years as HMI it was significant to see it essentially from the outside – though continuing to have (and to enjoy) many professional and personal contacts with HMI. Significantly, as with Office colleagues on secondment, HMI at the Schools Council were members of Council staff and not Inspectorate 'spies' or 'Trojan horses' . . . There was great camaraderie, commitment and no little idealism among Council staff, and opportunity to be creative; I learned much about 'professional politics' and I had been able to co-ordinate my own small team of positive, interesting people of professional substance.

Wally Allan 1966

My perception is that senior HMI looked down on the Schools Council. No statement that I saw or heard whilst I was there on secondment was other than patronising and negative . . . I have no doubt that, despite the apparent co-operation, such as secondment, HMI were not as helpful as they could have been and were certainly instrumental in killing it off. The system and attitudes were such that other HMI were not kept properly informed of what was going on at the SC – and of its potential. As a result, misunderstandings and misconceptions among HMI were not uncommon . . . There were many 'products' of the SC which could have been used more effectively by HMI, none more so, in my view, than the knowledge and experience (from many parts of the world) of some of its researchers on the 'dissemination' of curricular change – in simple terms, how to translate new ideas and practices into effective action in schools and colleges.

Jack Earl 1951

Religious instruction was going through a period of radical reconstruction; it was developing into Religious Education. The original notion of RI was instruction in the tenets of one particular creed, and the main interest of the state was to prevent proselytisation in state schools and to establish as wide a measure of common agreement as possible ... The revised Dual System and Agreed Syllabus framework seemed much more sophisticated than any previous arrangements but in fact they still assumed that practically every family in the country would owe allegiance to one church or another and that the study of the Bible would provide an acceptably neutral programme. This was probably an outdated assumption even in 1944, and by 1960 it was obvious that the strains on the system were bringing it near to collapse. The growth of secularism and ecumenism, the spread of non-Christian faiths, and developments in theology and in research into children's understanding of religion, all combined to change the basis of the state's involvement from holding the ring for competing churches to searching for a form of religious education which would be acceptable in an increasingly secular and multi-cultural society and might, hopefully, still promote national unity. No-one had any idea of amending the Act – for which the time certainly was not ripe – and therefore the way forward had to be sought through flexible interpretation of the Act's provisions ... New syllabuses differed from the old ones, not only in their educational approach to Christian themes, but in their treatment of non-Biblical material, such as modern social issues, and then in the introduction, at first very cautious and then more daring, of the study of non-Christian religions and philosophies ... It seemed at the time that all our exploitation of the ambiguities of the Act, though it sometimes verged on the casuistical, was justified by the new life breathed into the subject. Since then it has been further justified by the fact that practically all the developments we encouraged were incorporated in the 1988 Act ... It seems to me that the Inspectorate was more effective than any other body in bridging gaps. ... Perhaps the gap to which we paid too little attention was between the world of education and the outside world of parents, politicians and the general public – and perhaps that has proved more important than we believed.

Chapter 4   The Alternative Road

Culture and Recreation. Bread and Butter. On to Higher Education. Blue
Files. One HMI's Experience of the Development of Further and Higher
Education.

*Section 41. Subject as hereinafter provided it shall be the duty of every local education
authority to secure the provision for their area of adequate facilities for further
education, that is to say:*
(a) full-time and part-time education for persons over compulsory age and
(b) leisure-time occupation, in such organized cultural training and recreative
*activities as are suited to their requirements, for any persons over compulsory school
age who are able and willing to profit by the facilities provided for that purpose.*
Education Act, 1944.

Culture and Recreation

The all-embracing wording of the statute showed the generosity of spirit
abroad when R. A. Butler and Chuter Ede were drafting the bill. It is hard
to imagine what subsidised activity an authority might provide – or a
citizen might ask for – which would be *ultra vires*. In drawing up their
plans, LEAs were to take account of what other facilities for FE might be
provided by other bodies – universities, voluntary organisations,
independent colleges – and consult with them on ways of cooperating, so
the education authority could support many activities it did not itself
provide.

The scope was very wide indeed – as will be seen in Chapter 5 in
connection with what became known as 'other further education', the
catch-all term which included everything from education in prisons and
borstals at one end of the spectrum and Women's Institutes and youth
and community work at the other. All manner of recreational, cultural and
practical courses came within its ambit. Evening work in technical colleges
and evening institutes covered a wide range of courses for adults, some of
immediate vocational usefulness, others for cultural entertainment,
recreation and sport, others which crossed the boundaries between
vocational and recreational interest for people engaged in hobbies with
varying degrees of seriousness. London would publish each year a fat
catalogue called *Floodlight* which would list the extreme diversity of what
was available in all London's evening institutes. Other authorities did the
same. Somewhere or other every taste could be accommodated. In the
early days the fees were nominal. In the 1970s and 1980s they were raised
considerably to meet a high proportion of the teaching costs.

The FE sections of the Act were an attempt to build on the long tradition of educational philanthropy, self-help and self-improvement which had flourished for more than a hundred years – by the mid-nineteenth century, 'more than 600,000 people were in membership of 610 Mechanics Institutes.'[1] Adult education – in its high-culture version – was supported with grants for university extramural departments and the Workers Educational Association (WEA). The WEA had emerged from the war in strength, having proved a powerful lobbying organisation as well as a provider of courses, raising hopes about what adult education might do for cultural enrichment across class barriers. Local authorities bought up country houses and adapted them as adult residential centres where weekend conferences and courses could be held for the subsidised enlightenment of all who cared to attend. As the war receded the residential adult centres began to look like expensive luxuries.

For the post-war policy makers, there were three main lines of development:

- The continuing education and training of young workers (courses leading to City and Guilds certificates and commercial qualifications such as the RSA examinations).
- Education for technicians and technologists, requiring a ladder of courses and institutions leading to degree-level qualifications. (Technicians followed National and Higher National Diploma and Certificate courses with the possibility of external London degrees for the small proportion who went on to professional level.)
- And, by the end of the period, general education for school-leavers and adults. This was not a preoccupation in the early years but became increasingly important later.

Bread and Butter
The Education and Training of Young Workers

Broad as was the definition of FE, the central core of the work of the FE colleges was in technical education, much of it at a modest level, meeting the needs of young workers in industry and commerce, to complement the practical training offered by employers.

The war had seen a large expansion of technical education as part of the war effort – the number of young workers on day release in Britain rose from 42,000 at the beginning of the war to 150,000 by the end[2] – and this continued for some years into the peace: by 1958, according to Crowther, there were about 300,000 employees being released from work for part-time attendance at English colleges.

Apprenticeship provided most of the training opportunities – notably in engineering and the building trades for boys and hairdressing for girls. Commercial courses like shorthand, typing and book-keeping – business studies in embryo – also flourished. Labour's nationalisation programme had contributed to the growth trend – coal and steel, the electricity and gas industries – all were exemplary employers where training was concerned. Inspection of the public and private sectors of FE was included within the remit of HMI. The oversight of apprenticeship itself – negotiations with employers and unions – remained the responsibility of the Ministry of Labour.

The importance of expanding FE in the post-war world was obvious, even to those who were not prepared to give it the absolute priority some latter-day critics would have liked. LEAs set about the task of preparing their development plans but many were never completed and the procedure had lapsed long before it was formally abandoned in 1988. The provisions of the Act which dealt with county colleges would have made day release compulsory but it was acknowledged that this would have to wait till there was more money available – which in fact meant waiting indefinitely.

The FE colleges had, by tradition, been responsive institutions. Their students were voluntary, in the sense that they were not compelled to attend by law, only by the pressures of employment and their own ambitions. The colleges were opportunists in a market place – responding to public demand.

There is a thread of policy which runs from the 1940s to the 1980s which traces national attempts to encourage industrial training with day release or block release for more young workers. The boost for apprenticeship in the immediate post-war period meant a corresponding boost for day release and the colleges' daytime programmes (not that all apprentices got time off by day). But the thorough-going reform of apprenticeship which was needed never occurred. It remained the prerogative of craftsmen (and women) while patterns of employment and skill requirements were changing. The number of apprentices remained static and then began to fall – in 1964, there were still about 250,000 on day release; 10 years later the number was below 200,000. The national need was to extend training across the board and develop a competent workforce at every level. Unfortunately, large sectors of British industry were geared to low levels of skill and little formal training: in many cases these were the sectors of industry which went under when the economic climate became bleaker in the 1970s and 1980s.

Crowther (1959) found about one boy in three among the 15–18-year-olds in employment was getting day release – only one girl in twelve. About a quarter of the boys (rather less for girls) enrolled for evening classes; but, as a Crowther footnote observed acidly: 'the enrolment ... is very much higher than the attendance by the end of the course' – large numbers dropped out. There was a small enrolment of full-time students taking and retaking O levels and on secretarial, commerce and art courses.

In the early 1950s teams of employers and trade unionists were sent (under the Marshall Plan) to the United States to study industrial practices and look for lessons for this country.[3] When these 'productivity teams' returned, conferences were convened where they could tell others what they had seen and learnt. Education and training was high on the list of what impressed them, in particular the seriousness with which top management in the United States approached training matters. The cause was taken up by leading industrialists and commended by Ministers of Labour and trade union leaders but to little avail.

Two stumbling blocks came up again and again: the inflexibility of the craft unions and the economic cost of training which deterred small firms and made the number of training places fluctuate with business confidence. Apprenticeship was tightly controlled by agreements between employers and unions. The number of apprenticeships, the age of entry, and the length of training were fixed by negotiation, and the craft unions regarded their ability to limit the number of apprenticeships as an essential bargaining chip. In spite of the evidence of the shortage of skilled workers and the increasing size of the age groups about to enter the labour market, trade unions stood their ground. By so doing, they not only kept numbers of eligible young people out of training, but also contributed indirectly to early leaving, by forcing some potential sixth-formers to compete for apprenticeships at 15 or 16 – and all this at a time when the unemployment rate overall was only about 4 per cent or less.

As for the economic argument, it was widely noted that under the German apprenticeship system, which more or less guaranteed combined education and training for every 15–16-year-old who completed the equivalent of a secondary modern school course, trainees received a modest subsistence allowance not a salary. The German unions acquiesced in this, whereas the British unions sought steadily to inflate the wages of young workers. (Till the 1970s the unemployment rate among British school-leavers was below the level of adult unemployment. After 1973, the situation rapidly deteriorated.)

It was the job of the colleges to serve the demands of employers as a supermarket serves its customers, so the pace of development in large parts of FE was conditional on the pace of development in training. In 1957, Circular 323 was issued to encourage attempts to introduce the humanities, alongside technical courses for apprentices. For most day release students this was notably unsuccessful – young workers did not want to know and nor did the employers. But this was the beginning of general studies in FE and, as we shall see, paved the way for developments which would change the character of the colleges in the 1960s and after. The response contrasted sharply with what happened in the German *Berufsschule* where the inclusion of some serious general education was established practice.

Organised links between secondary and FE were few and far between. The 'Alternative Road' was not well marked or signposted. There were some good practical courses in the secondary schools, which regularly featured in HMI reports, but these were exceptional and (as events proved) went against the grain. There was not necessarily any progression to FE. There might have been more such courses if the training system had exerted positive pressure on the schools. Had there been a lively industrial training scene, the alternative road would have looked very different. What the employers and colleges were offering – and requiring from the 15–18 age range – might have fed back into schools and nourished the 'practical' courses Crowther (and others before and since) wanted to see. Again, the contrast with Germany, where training and education were integrated in a dual system, was obvious: later the fact that German apprentices were considerably more competent in mathematics than their English counterparts became another stick with which to beat the English school system.[4]

Once the leaving age had been raised to 16, Crowther wanted a three-stage transition from voluntary day release, by way of compulsory schemes in pilot areas, to eventual compulsion everywhere. But the raising of the leaving age was still another 15 years hence and what the Crowther Report did – quite contrary to its intention – was effectively to kick county colleges into touch. The familiar experience of hope deferred

gave another heart-sickening 'no' to the questions posed 40 years earlier
by the Lewis Committee:

> *Can the age of adolescence be brought out of the purview of economic exploitation and
> into that of the social conscience? Can the conception of the juvenile as primarily a
> little wage-earner be replaced by the conception of the juvenile as primarily the
> workman and the citizen in training? Can it be established that the educational
> purpose is to be the dominating one, without as well as within the school doors, during
> those formative years between 12 and 18? If not, clearly no remedies at all are possible
> in the absence of the will by which alone they could be rendered effective.*[5]

The need to do something about training remained. It was about this
time – the late 1950s – that economists of education on both sides of the
Atlantic rediscovered an interest in the economics of education and
training and the returns on investment in human capital. David Eccles
returned from a meeting with other education ministers in Paris
stocked with arguments for justifying educational spending as
investment.

To bring things to a head, the Government set up a review committee
under the parliamentary secretary to the Ministry of Labour, Robert Carr,
to appraise the training situation and find ways of making progress.
Reporting in 1958, the Carr Committee was a last attempt to shore up the
old apprentice system. The birth rate was rising and one of the concerns
of the committee – and of the colleges – was how to increase the provision
of education and training in line with the increase in the teenage
population. The committee was strong on analysis, but weak on action. It
pointed out what the employers and unions should do to remedy the
weaknesses in the apprenticeship system, offered the appropriate
exhortation and left it at that. All the Carr Report could do was urge one
more voluntary effort to put the training house in order. It ruled out any
intervention by the State, reaffirming industry's responsibility for training
and the Government's provision of FE:

> *We feel it would be better to concentrate any additional resources which might be
> available on the building of technical colleges, and to leave to industry the
> responsibility for ensuring that its facilities for industrial training are adequate.*[6]

In affirming strong support for the colleges and day release it offered its
own advice to all concerned: 'It is necessary to ensure, on the one hand,
that the content of further education should be that which industry in fact
requires, and, on the other, that the whole of the apprenticeship period
forms part of a single educational process.' Here again was a noble
aspiration mocked by practical reality.

The report was full of sensible recommendations but left the initiative with industry. Carr's Committee lacked the weight or status to give serious consideration to radical solutions such as a move towards a German or French solution. Ministers were left on the sidelines wringing their hands as industry continued to be guided by short-term economic pressures. It was not difficult to see the financial and political reasons why the Ministry of Labour stuck to its settled departmental position, but relying on exhortation simply ensured an indefinite continuance of the unsatisfactory *status quo*.

The Carr Report marked the end of one phase and the hesitant opening of another. A last warning had been given. From now on there would be hesitant moves toward intervention by the Government, leading via Industrial Training Boards to the Manpower Services Commission (MSC) and the attempts of successive governments to combat youth unemployment by one training scheme after another. In all these developments the colleges had a growing part to play.

In the closing months of the Conservative government (1964) an Industrial Training Act was passed empowering the Ministry of Labour to set up training boards, industry by industry, to promote training, having at their disposal a stick and a carrot – they could make grants towards the cost of training and recoup their costs by levying dues. The Minister of Labour had powers to oversee the process.

It remained public policy to encourage more day release. The Henniker–Heaton Report (1964), aimed directly at industry, called for a doubling of day release in five years, with local targets set by Industrial Training Boards (ITBs) and a 'sustained public relations campaign'. It fell on deaf ears. But, as Percy Wilson, the SCI, observed, apprenticeship seemed 'to be stuck in the past' – caught in a time warp which emphasised its negative characteristics – inflexible conditions on age of entry and duration, no qualifying test of competence. To reinvent it as a quasi-educational rite of passage to adulthood concerned as much with the formation of character and general competence as well as the transmission of narrow craft skill, required imagination and brave leadership: neither quality came from the employers and trade unionists involved.

This was the scheme which operated for the rest of the 1960s. The impact was uneven; some industries had a smoother ride than others but the operation of the Act was generally – and increasingly – unpopular with employers. There were teething troubles as boards worked out how they intended to use their powers. Teething troubles became ongoing conflicts. Like any system of taxation, the levy-grant system became more and more complicated as reluctant employers looked for ways of minimising their liabilities and maximising what they could get out of it. The same company might be eligible for grants in respect of one set of activities and have to pay a levy on others. The more tangled and convoluted the financial transactions became the stronger the opposition from the employers and the more they bent the ear of Conservative MPs in opposition. When the Conservatives returned to office in 1970 preparations began for a new Employment and Training Act (1973) to emasculate the ITBs and set up the MSC.

For the FE Inspectorate, in the 1950s the main-line college work with apprentices and other young school-leavers was relatively humdrum and unexciting but necessary work – an uphill struggle to raise standards and encourage imaginative development. If FE college principals were operating in a market, it was not one in which consumers were particularly interested in innovation. HMIs had their lists of colleges for which they acted as general inspectors and which they visited regularly, and they had their own specialist subjects. Because of the range of skills which were taught in FE colleges, there had to be an equivalent range of skills represented in the FE Inspectorate. This brought into the ranks of HMI a diverse range of technical expertise and a number of inspectors without conventional experience as teachers.

On to Higher Education

Education for Technicians and Technologists: Creating a Structure

Given the narrowness of the English and Welsh educational base in the two decades after 1945, there were limits to the extent to which FE could develop more advanced courses. Advanced courses in FE, like degree courses in universities, depended on being able to recruit students equipped with the necessary preliminary preparation. It came back once again to the narrow secondary education base: in 1960 fewer than 1 in 3 of each age group remained in full-time education beyond 15, only about 10 per cent to 18. University entrance was the prerogative of about 5 per cent of each age group. The age participation rate for all higher education – universities, teacher training colleges and advanced FE – was only 8 per cent.

But as the Robbins Report (1963) was able to show, some of the pieces were beginning to fall into place: the Robbins plans for expansion were based on a reasoned expectation of a rising flow of A levels in the secondary schools: 'our investigations have suggested the existence of large reservoirs of untapped ability in the population, especially among girls.'

Percy Wilson, the SCI, was one of those who saw the inwardness of the changes which were taking place. For him, 18-plus was the new frontier: further and higher education – 'the area where most of our administrative problems, even in schools, will be settled in the next twenty or thirty years: university expansion . . . the expansion and improvement of teacher training, the expansion and integration of FE, both vocational and liberal, part-time FE for all, or at least for all who want it . . . Leave the schools in peace . . . [and] . . . turn our eyes to FHE, including the training of teachers'.[7]

Percy Wilson, Senior Chief Inspector, 1957–65.

There had always been a trickle of upwardly mobile students in FE who battled their way by night school and sheer determination to higher qualifications, but they were the minority who overcame the odds. Post-secondary education was shaped like a pyramid; for expansion there had to be a broadening of the base. FE needed to strengthen its own supply lines if it was to play a full part in the expansion of higher education. Only when the pyramid had been flattened somewhat – four decades later – would the conditions be in place for a move towards mass higher education.

Just as in two world wars Britain's post-war planners had paid Germany the compliment of drawing on the German model for an answer to the educational deficit of the young school-leaver, so too there was a general awareness that Britain was the poorer for having no institution of higher education which performed the functions of the great technical high schools in Germany or the Technical University at Delft in the Netherlands. The need to create a clear and well-marked pathway leading to a graduated set of higher technical qualifications was self-evident; equally obvious was the need to develop institutions where this path could be pursued. The universities were major providers of engineering education and would in due course turn out more technologists. But they were independent institutions which expected to make up their own minds. The major FE colleges represented a valuable resource under public control capable of developing the capacity for advanced work.

A wartime committee chaired by Lord Eustace Percy, a former President of the Board of Education who had by now become rector of the Newcastle division of the University of Durham, had as its remit 'the needs of higher technical education'.[8] It reported in 1945 in favour of designating a limited number of technical colleges as colleges of technology which would be allowed to build up full-time courses of degree standard. They would remain within the local authority sector with enhanced central grant to compensate the LEA for providing what would in effect be a national institution.

Agreed about the main question, the committee fell out (inevitably) on the relatively trivial question of what to call the qualification for high-level work – some wanted successful students to become Bachelors of Technology. The universities jibbed at this. (Later on, Lord Cherwell canvassed the idea of a British version of the Massachusetts Institute of Technology to secure the top-level work for the universities.) Others favoured a state diploma in technology. Percy, himself, wanted to make selected colleges 'Royal' institutions awarding Associateships and Fellowships.

Although much of the attention was focused on the need to provide for top-level technologists – the glamorous end of the market – it was clear that policy had to cover the whole spectrum of further and higher education. What was required was a structure of institutions and courses, broadly based, and providing an ordered framework for the education and training not only of technologists, but also of the much larger numbers of technicians studying part-time, whose work would complement theirs. Other proposals led to the setting up of Regional Advisory Councils composed of representatives of the colleges, the LEAs and industry, to coordinate the programmes of the colleges.

Action on Percy was delayed – partly by continuing argument about what to call the new top qualification, but also by the pressure of all the other developments which were in the pipeline. In 1950, the National Advisory Council on Education for Industry and Commerce came out [9] in favour of a scheme similar to that put forward by Percy, based on a Royal College of Technologists which would be required to approve courses in designated colleges and appoint external examiners. Here was another element in the eventual scheme – an external body to ensure the maintenance of standards. In its last months, Clement Attlee's government accepted these proposals but the general election of 1951 came before they could be acted upon.

Six years had elapsed since the Percy Report. There had already been inexcusable procrastination and delay. The incoming Conservatives sent the designs back to the drawing board. In 1952 a 60 per cent grant was introduced for advanced technical courses and even before the startling evidence of the success of Soviet space scientists hit the headlines, with Churchill's prompting, Anthony Eden, as one of his first policy initiatives on becoming prime minister, announced a five-year investment programme for technical college building and decisions on the future structure of the colleges and advanced qualifications.[10] David Eccles was an enthusiastic supporter, as was Antony Part, deputy secretary with responsibility for further and higher education, who saw the opportunity for a major coup:

> *Nine years ago we fought for a place in the sun for school building. We got off with a bang ... Now we want a place in the sun for a major expansion of further education. This is a much bigger subject so we want a correspondingly bigger bang to begin with. So far FE has been overshadowed by the bulge in schools. Now we must step up its prestige. Prestige comes from what you do at the top. So although the programme of expansion must be balanced, we should do well to place in the forefront our plan for technologists. This emphasis should attract Ministers because developments abroad are much more concerned now with technological education.[11]*

The 1956 *Technical Education* White Paper, drafted by Freddie Bray, a former HMI who had switched across to become an under secretary, envisaged a hierarchy of colleges, headed by colleges of advanced technology – the CATs – which would shed their junior work and focus on degree-level courses for 'technologists and scientists'. Below them regional colleges would also carry work at degree level but not exclusively and would continue to train 'senior technicians and craftsmen'.[12] Next would come area colleges and local colleges. Art colleges would come in time to have their own hierarchy. Many courses within the differentiated college system would continue to be directed towards the national and higher national certificates and diplomas which would two decades later be replaced by awards of the Business and Technician Education Council.

The new qualifications for the CATs were to be supervised by a National Council for Technological Awards (NCTA), led by Lord Hives, chairman of Rolls-Royce. The NCTA was determined to forge close links between the CATs and industry and decided to do this by making the 'sandwich' course the distinguishing characteristic of the Diploma in Technology. Courses would run for four or five years with periods of college study being interspersed with periods of applied learning in industry. Various forms of 'thick' and 'thin' sandwich were devised. Most students were expected to be 'industry-based' with company affiliations arranged before getting college places; others were 'college-based' relying on the college to find them a work placement. Practice differed from course to course and institution to institution. The NCTA insisted on some element of 'liberal studies' in all courses. As time passed it became more difficult to arrange meaningful complementary industrial training to run in parallel with the college courses.

The management of the new regime was overseen by NCTA subject committees. HMI had valuable experience to share from many years of involvement in the national certificate and diploma system. They inspected CATs like the rest of the FE system. Under the so-called FE21 regulations, Regional Staff Inspectors (RSI) had extensive executive powers, unlike schools HMIs. Working closely with the Regional Advisory Councils, they had delegated authority to approve courses and sign proposals for the purchase of expensive equipment (see box).

By 1960 100 courses in 23 colleges had been approved and the Diploma in Technology was gaining wide recognition. As money and resources were pumped into the CATs their status and ambitions rose. The creation of new universities like Sussex, York and Essex, as fully fledged degree-awarding institutions, not required to serve an apprenticeship as university colleges awarding London degrees, like Southampton, Leicester and others, whetted the appetite of the CATs for full self-government. After the Robbins Report, they were duly added to the University Grants Committee list and became 'new' universities. Some like Brunel struggled to keep their sandwich course tradition; more generally they worked hard to shed their image as 'ex-CATs'. With their change of status they moved out of the orbit of HMI inspection.

After Robbins, a new body, the CNAA, replaced the NCTA with a wider remit to oversee the development of higher education in other colleges, and notably in the polytechnics which were to be the flagship colleges of the public sector, still under the aegis of local authorities, though with their own strong governing bodies. The aim of the department – and in particular of Toby Weaver who had succeeded Part as the deputy secretary in charge of higher and further education – was to counter 'academic drift'. Weaver became the man most closely associated with – and blamed for – the 'binary' system. Anthony Crosland, the Secretary of State Weaver persuaded to promulgate the policy, felt for a time that he had been bounced into it. But, as he told Maurice Kogan,[13] 'When I finally mastered the subject I became a passionate believer in binary and polytechnics and I suppose I did as much as anyone else to push the policy through.'

Given the ambitions of governors, urged on by buccaneering principals and staff, the historic trend was for colleges to try to gain respectability and status by becoming more and more like universities and less and less responsive to local and regional demands. Designating the top public sector colleges as polytechnics was an attempt to give them a prestigious role while holding them to their appointed task. In the 1970s, the reorganisation of the teacher training colleges (retitled colleges of education by Robbins) extended the role and the range of the polytechnics.

The binary divide continued till 1992 when it was swept away by the changes in the finance and administration of higher and further education which followed the Education Reform Act and the decision to make the FE colleges into self-governing corporations. The inspection of the colleges passed first to the inspectorate set up by the Further Education Funding Council, and subsequently to the Office of Standards in Education (OFSTED) in 1999.

General Education

Reference has been made to Circular 323 (1957) which signalled an attempt to extend the cultural horizons of FE. It was no longer enough to think of FE colleges as places which were narrowly concerned with skill training. Henceforward they would have general studies departments and build up their capability in general education. Liberal studies courses did not fit in easily with the technical college tradition but by the 1960s things had begun to change. As the FE community expanded, the market altered and new demands appeared. At the upper end there was a recognition that advanced courses needed to be supported by better general

Blue Files
Derek Boulton, 1963

My first TCA meeting was a revelation. The room was blue from cheroot smoke, largely from female colleagues, there were piles of blue files passing from person to person, with RSI trying to keep track. A good deal of bargaining took place while priorities between colleges were sorted out and the secretary tried to write up a record of events. I came to understand later the FE Inspectorate was at the interface between the many interested parties (not least with the setting up of the Industrial Training Boards and the consequent misunderstandings and lack of expertise of the other participants). The system only worked smoothly because of our collective knowledge and communication pathways ... HMI Panels and Committees, together with direct links by phone and contact in the local office.

The expertise of specialist colleagues always amazed me and the answers to the most abstruse questions were frequently available within minutes. The other side of things was the ability to become a specialist when required: for instance, I became the DES specialist in Laundry and Dry Cleaning, Dyeing, Waste Management, Pipework Engineering; and a Governor of the Hamble College of Air Training, with none of which I had previously been acquainted. ...

education as the NCTA made clear. It was more difficult to get acceptance of this idea in courses aimed at young workers.

Hostility to liberal studies among apprentices and students on technician courses persisted. The HMI General Studies Panel reviewed inspection reports and all other available material for a national survey on the subject. As a result of bad tactics – and worse editing – what emerged was a large and unwieldy report for SI Ted Parkinson to present to Margaret Thatcher, who had recently become Secretary of State. Her response was to weigh it in her hands and dismiss it with: 'I'm not going to read that!'

Leaving aside the attempt to broaden what was offered to apprentices and technicians, the main build-up was at what might be called the sixth-form level. One sign of success in the secondary schools was the growth in staying on. It was not only the schools which benefited from this growth – FE colleges, too, began to attract school-leavers on to O and A level courses. Retakes provided one source of students at both O level and A level. There were other students who chose to leave school and move to the FE college for A levels because they wanted the more adult atmosphere of the college. And there were adults who had dropped out and wanted to get back on the academic track. A 'break at 16' became a not uncommon feature of the secondary scene. The FE colleges offered a fresh start for those who had performed indifferently at secondary school and wanted to try again. Already by the mid-1970s there were colleges in London and the south-east with 400 and more A level students. The way was opening up which led to the 'tertiary' college, and the time when schools, sixth-form colleges and FE would compete openly for the 16–19 year-olds – all of them with the capability of preparing students for higher education. FE put its own stamp on subjects like English – not just English literature but also, English as a second language, English as a foreign language, English in business studies and so on.

What was not foreseen was the falling away of candidates for traditional engineering courses. The change of name to colleges of further education did not come any too soon – they were ceasing to be technical colleges in the old sense and were learning how to diversify (in the case of the bigger colleges) into teacher training and in all colleges into 'new' subjects like business studies.

Sir Edward Boyle, Minister of Education, 1963–64 (right) with Henry French, Senior Chief Inspector, 1972–74.

One HMI's Experience of the Development of Higher and Further Education

Harry French was an FE inspector whose career in the 1950s and 1960s neatly shadowed the development of advanced technical education nationally. He became an HMI as a 38-year-old electronics expert and retired in 1974 as SCI.

His experience before he became an HMI had been extremely varied. As a boy of 15 he had joined the Royal Corps of Signals as an instrument mechanic. Five years later he transferred to the Army Education Corps, and took an external London degree in physics and mathematics by evening study while teaching basic literacy to Royal Artillery recruits. At the Military College of Science, he taught artillery officers about radar, at more and more advanced levels, eventually leaving the army to lecture at the college in electrical and radar engineering.

As an HMI his first assignment was in the Midlands, becoming general inspector for Coventry Technical College and colleges at Rugby, Nuneaton and Stratford-on-Avon while having specialist responsibility in electronics. Coventry was one of the colleges capable of undertaking more advanced work to which, as HMI, French gave practical support.

Another side of his job was concerned with national and higher national certificates and diplomas: he sat on specialist panels of HMIs and members of the professional institutions which oversaw examinations in electronics and applied physics. Electronics was a rapidly developing field. The work took him all over the country looking at specialist courses. In helping colleges to take on more demanding work, his job was to suggest how weaknesses could be overcome and deficiencies made good. The constant theme was the increasing capacity of the colleges, especially the major colleges, to set up advanced courses at a level approaching that of first degrees.

His assignments changed as his career developed. The Birmingham Central Technical College – the future University of Aston – was one of his. He strongly supported the case for a new building for the college (nicknamed by Antony Part, 'French's folly'). For another spell he served as Regional SI for the North-West Division at a time of major development for what was then the Manchester CAT (now the Manchester Metropolitan University).

He also doubled as SI for electrical engineering from 1956 – the year Sir David Eccles issued his *Technical Education* White Paper. French played his part in the review which led to the designation of CATs and regional colleges. He sat in on the governing body of the newly formed NCTA, urging them to establish the currency of the Diploma in Technology – the Dip.Tech. – before becoming bogged down in arguments about higher degrees.

After three years of holding down the two jobs, French moved to London to concentrate on the job of SI for electrical engineering with direct responsibility (as specialist or general inspector) for a number of rapidly advancing colleges all of which later went on to become universities. These included the Northampton Polytechnic, Woolwich Polytechnic, Cardiff Technical College, Brighton Technical College and Loughborough (where the ambitions of the great Dr Schofield, the principal, notoriously exceeded the immediately available resources needed to back them up).

The CNAA having succeeded the NCTA, French worked with John Pimlott, the DES official who drew up the CNAA Charter. He sat on its governing body and influenced its specialist panels. But HMI had a less prominent role in CNAA than in the NCTA. He remained a firm believer in the Alternative Route and supported the case for admitting students to university courses on the basis of non-standard qualifications – ONC/OND students were some of the most successful students at the CATs. After serving as CI (FE) for six years, he stayed on beyond retiring age to serve for two and a half years as SCI under Margaret Thatcher. 'My chief inspector', she called him.

Notes

[1] Hall, V. (1990) *Maintained Further Education in the UK*. Bristol: FE Staff College, 3.

[2] See note 1, 3.

[3] The programme was organised by the Anglo-American Council on Productivity.

[4] For a review of research on Germany, France, Japan, USA and Britain, see Green, A., Stedman, H. (1993) *Educational Provision, Educational Achievement and the Needs of Industry*. London: National Institute for Economic and Social Research.

[5] Board of Education (1917) *Juvenile Employment in Relation to Employment after the War*, The Lewis Report. London: HMSO. See Maclure, *Educational Documents*, 168.

6 Ministry of Labour, Joint Consultative Committee (1958) *Training for Skill*, The Carr Report. London: HMSO.
7 Wilson, P. (1961) Snakes and Ladders in English Higher Education, in *Views and Prospects from Curzon Street*. Oxford: Blackwell, 79–87.
8 Ministry of Education (1945) Report of the Special Committee on *Higher Technological Education*, The Percy Report. London: HMSO.
9 National Advisory Council on Education for Industry and Commerce (1950) *The Future of Higher Technological Education*. London: HMSO.
10 Ministry of Education (1956) *Technical Education*, White Paper. London: HMSO.
11 A. Part to the Secretary, 6 December 1955. PRO ED136/86.
12 The quotations are from the 1956 White Paper, see Maclure, *Educational Documents*, 242.
13 Kogan, M. (1971) *The Politics of Education: Edward Boyle and Anthony Crosland in Conversation with Maurice Kogan*. London: Penguin, 194.

HMI Miscellany
Extracts from HMI personal accounts

Mary Johnston 1952

For several years from the early 50s there was tremendous energy and a sense of excitement as FE was developing rapidly . . . It seemed that at last FE was being recognised as an essential provision for the majority of the population who were unwilling or unable to go to university but were anxious to continue in education and gain further qualifications in technology or general education. Both employers and employees in growing numbers realised the growing value and need for a more educated/skilled workshop and both sides were willing to co-operate by means of day release or evening courses. This was the general feeling throughout the North West and it was a wonderful time to be working and helping in that atmosphere . . .

There was a team of what were known as 'T' women but it had little weight in policy matters and administration. There was one in each Division, specialists in their own right (art, housecraft, needlework, cookery etc) responsible for overseeing women's departments in technical colleges. The team met at the Ministry once a month and discussed anything we wanted and planned the courses . . .

As SI for Women's Further and Technical Education, based in London, I spent a large amount of time developing para-medical and nursing and other courses, which entailed meetings with individuals and professional groups, as well as the Office who had to be convinced that the courses should be in the colleges. Although there was a growing desire to be included in the mainstream of education, especially if this would mean eventual degree status, there was considerable anxiety as to the effect such inclusion would have on the carefully guarded courses developed by the professional organisations.

Kay Tobin 1954

In Kay Tobin's specialist areas of women in FE and of food education the pace of change and the volume and direction of the work altered dramatically. In the case of women in FE these changes reflected social, economic and political developments in society, especially in the different expectations and ambitions of women. Other factors were the commercial and industrial acceptance of women at all levels and an increased awareness of their abilities and value to an organisation.

As SI and chairman of the women's sub-panel, she guided the group away from the nursing orientation towards a broader approach to educational opportunities for women across the range of women's subjects and beyond. These included the training of playgroup leaders and the provision of Access courses for post-family women which opened the way to professional courses in HE and employment in non-traditional fields like engineering, architecture and management. (*In interview with Brian Arthur*)

Bill Emery 1957

In the main during my initiation period I accompanied HMI to a large range of schools . . . It would have been a help to new schools colleagues had they had a similar introduction to the FE world. This rarely seemed to be the case . . . When I got my first general inspectorship at a college, Cyril English advised me to get into the college concerned, to go round each department and to learn about subjects and courses which were not my particular specialism . . . One always endeavoured not to act as a specialist in a subject outside one's specialism. Of course the staff soon knew where you stood and many of them had considerable experience in commerce and industry so one had to be very careful.

A number of firms got together to allow their engineering apprentices to get six months training and education in the college on a full-time basis. Antony Part, then an Assistant Secretary, came up to see the work. Having seen what was happening on this apprentice course he casually asked me why the education section was separate from the training. Why not do the work on an umbrella scheme when education is spread through the week as the training progressed and not give it its ritual day a week? . . . The college took it on very successfully and this really became the first modern off-the-job training and education scheme . . . Other more enlightened firms began proper off-the-job schemes with the training element done either at the local colleges or on their own premises . . . In the South West I found there was little co-operation between the colleges: there was a reluctance for staff to visit nearby colleges. As far as I was concerned this inter-visitation became a priority. I began by calling a HoDs' meeting in one college which supported the idea. It soon spread and there were few HoDs unwilling to take part. Thus began quite a revolution in engineering education in the South West.

Harold Taylor 1959

In the job of HMI I tried to fuse together art and technology in order to fill the 'design gap' which then existed and which has not yet been filled. I preached this fusion and ran annual design courses to spread the gospel – and we got results. In due course I found that I had been given management education in a Division, so, as well as a district inspectorship, I had specialist responsibility for engineering, construction and management (a three-man load), to which was added national responsibility for education in the gas industry. One further step was to suggest a complete re-design of the construction courses, for example, builders, surveyors, quantity surveyors all combining their separate ideas into root subjects common to all, such as maths, science and even general studies. The ideas were accepted by my HMI colleagues and by the Chartered Institutions concerned with the administration of separate qualifications.

Allan Hill 1965

Link courses were a particularly interesting development of the 60s and 70s. They were organised, run and financed by many colleges of FE for schools in their locality, and provided 14–16 year olds with the opportunity to gain simulated experience of the working world for one day a week over one term, with the opportunity to sample a different course each term ... Unfortunately the colleges were never funded for this work but, as there was usually a little surplus from the ITB funded work, many college principals saw this sprat as a means of catching many mackerel. Equally, schools retained full funding but had the pupils for four days only. Some used it as a means of broadening the curriculum whilst others saw it as a way of removing those who lacked motivation in academic studies. Some but not all local industrialists co-operated with and serviced local schools to provide simulated and real experience of the 'world of work'. I recall some interesting and enterprising schemes when pupils even attended college for one day when their school was closed for half-term. . .

James Edwards 1948

Pretty soon the Government decided it could not afford County Colleges, had little to spare for the Youth Service and Community Centres quietly withered away. This left OFE Inspectors without any backbone to their work. Instead they had a baffling assignment of bits and pieces, mostly evening work and none of it regarded as being of any importance by the main body of mainstream P&S and FE Inspectors. . .

When the Home Office decided to improve the educational facilities available to inmates of prisons and borstals, it was agreed HMI should inspect the work. As a result I suddenly found myself made the general inspector for about 18 prisons and Borstals in the South of England and the Isle of Wight and the secretary of the new Prisons and Borstals Panel. To understand what could and could not be done in these unusual circumstances called for much hard thinking about education and training. It also enabled me to meet an amazing group of teachers, governors and Home Office officials and appreciate their work.

Harold Marks 1950

Though the proportionate claim of expenditure on adult, youth social and cultural was always very small, dominant Office opinion was generally hostile . . . Great efforts were made to stop publications – and even HMI reports – from encouraging increased OFE expenditure by LEAs . . . Roseveare fought hard when OFE fell under heavy attack, especially with Eccles who deplored the expenditure as unnecessary and wasteful . . . Many more field OFE practitioners were brought in as HMI to support and strengthen OFE opinion. The OFE body as a whole, with Salter Davies' support and leadership, skilfully exercised and characterised by the Salisbury courses, managed to retain its supportive identity . . . It sustained morale among field practitioners, and provided invaluable support when LEAs wanted to make progress. HMI independence enabled the OFE Inspectorate to work in directions in conformity with the intentions of the 1944 Act, relatively unimpeded by immediate Government and Office priorities . . . But OFE was on the way out. General studies in FE still retained some official support, in a progressively less liberal style, but OFE Inspectors in the new set-up were able to influence its development. Similarly there was continuing support for careers work in schools, after 1977 rightly a secondary phase HMI concern. HMI concern for community centre and playing field provision had been passed to the LEAs in 1975. Adult Education continued to receive diminishing inspectoral attention both in general and in the prisons area in which it had made so remarkable a contribution.

Chapter 5 The Working of the Inspectorate

Roseveare's Inspectorate. FE Inspectorate. Other Further Education. Independent Schools. HMI Publications Series.

Roseveare's Inspectorate

The basic organisation of the Inspectorate established at the end of the Second World War continued without fundamental change till the creation of OFSTED in 1992. That is not to say that there were no changes over time in the way the Inspectorate was managed and the priorities which determined its work, but its shape remained essentially the same.

Between 1945 and 1984 it was subject to at least 13 separate internal and external inquiries. One reason for this was that inside the Ministry, the Inspectorate represented a clearly defined, and relatively large, group of expensive staff whose costly activities were always open to debate and whose numbers always appeared to be capable of being trimmed.

The Inspectorate was not like the rest of the Ministry. It was not neat and tidy. HMIs were a disparate group of talented individuals. For much of their time they acted as such, dependent on their own professional initiative and controlling their own time. How to get the best value for money from the resources invested in the Inspectorate was a continuing concern – not because people thought HMIs were falling down on the job, but because no one outside the Inspectorate – and not every one inside – was quite sure what the job was or how it was developing.

High quality leadership was essential if they were to make an impact as a corporate whole. Not all SCIs could provide this sense of direction in equal measure. Martin Roseveare gave strong leadership but his relations with the Office deteriorated and eventually he was retired early, having failed to see eye to eye with his Minister, David Eccles. A lack of dynamic leadership left the Inspectorate drifting through the 1960s. It was not, of course, a matter of robust leadership alone: till there was more clarity on where the Inspectorate was heading and how to get there, no SCI could lead effectively.

For our purposes, the history of the Inspectorate divides into two periods with a break around the end of the 1960s and the early 1970s when, for a variety of reasons discussed later on, major social, economic and political changes had a direct impact on the educational system. In due course these changes had a profound effect on the department. It was then that shrewd leadership was called for from the then SCI to overhaul the Inspectorate's methods of working and equip HMI to play a central part in a new era of policy making.

Roseveare's plans were for an Inspectorate of 600 HMIs – getting on for double the number at the end of the war – but this was never achieved. Numbers peaked in 1950–1 at about 570, coming down, in time, to hover around the 450 mark. There were six CIs (or, at certain times one deputy SCI and five CIs). During the 1950s and 1960s, there were ten divisions (and DIs); the number of divisions was reduced to eight in 1970 and seven in 1977. The number of SIs increased as the education system expanded and diversified. List 6, the annual publication which recorded the membership and central and field duties of the Inspectorate, shows 41 SIs in 1947, rising to 57 in 1967.

The Organisation of the Inspectorate

This account is taken from the 1954 HM Inspectors' Handbook. In accordance with the usage of the time, both men and women inspectors are assumed to be masculine in gender.

The Inspectorate consists of: a Senior Chief Inspector (SCI), Chief Inspectors (CIs), Divisional Inspectors (DIs), Staff Inspectors (SIs), and Inspectors. Also, Occasional Inspectors, brought in from time to time for specific purposes, who are not on the permanent staff.

General Policy

- The education system ... must be regarded as a single unified system. The Inspectorate is a single body under the control of and responsible to the SCI.

- Every Inspector in his first few months will be allotted specific responsibilities ... [covering] as wide a field as is feasible ... designed to make the utmost use of his knowledge and powers.

- Only rarely will an Inspector be an expert in all matters arising within his sphere of responsibility. He will be expected to call in colleagues when he needs their help.

Chief Inspectors

... Each CI is responsible for a ... block of work and for ... blocks of work done by other Inspectors. This ... implies knowing and guiding the work of the Inspectors, ensuring close cooperation between the Office and the Inspectorate and advising the Ministry on matters of general policy and practice in their respective spheres of responsibility. Alongside these ... responsibilities, the CIs form a unified body with the SCI for knowing and directing the whole work of the Inspectorate; and for maintaining a general oversight over the whole educational system, collaborating closely with each other and with Administrative officers.

Every Inspector has the right of direct access to the CIs and to the SCI.

Divisional Inspectors

The Division is ... the effective unit of organisation ... The main function of the DI is to take general responsibility for the Inspection arrangements and the Inspectors in the Division. He is the chief representative of the Ministry in regional contacts with other Government Departments.

Staff Inspectors

An SI is primarily concerned with a particular subject, phase, or aspect of education; ... a leader among and spokesman for colleagues, and an adviser to the Ministry ... He is required to keep abreast of developments in thought and practice at all stages inside and outside the State system ... He is directly responsible to the SCI . .. but refers to the CIs ... and DIs on matters within their jurisdiction.

Inspectors

Every Inspector working within a Division, ie every Inspector except SIs or others whose work is on a national basis, is directly responsible to the DI and submits his diaries to him.

Every Inspector ... may be detailed to act in any or all of the following capacities: General Inspector ... District Inspector ... Divisional Specialist Adviser ... Divisional Adviser. He may also be called upon to take part in special activities, eg short courses, committee work, panel work, examination work, research.

Every Inspector's programme is designed to keep him in direct and adequate touch with schools, teachers and pupils in more than one field of education, and this constitutes his basic work, on which the value of any other work assigned to him will depend. Narrow specialisation is avoided as far as possible.

General Inspectors

The General Inspector is personally responsible for inspecting and reporting on his schools and for seeing ... [they] ... are visited ... (not necessarily for report purposes) by ... [expert] ... colleagues ... [whom] ... he can call upon ... within the Division ... He will ... [alert] ... the District Inspector ... [to] ... any circumstance in any of his schools which impinges or might impinge on general matters of policy or seriously affect the state of the school ...

District Inspectors

There are three District Inspector fields

- Technical, Commercial and Art (TCA)
- Other Further Education (OFE)
- Primary and Secondary Education (P and S)

For every Authority that handles Further Education, ie every Local Education Authority as distinct from an Excepted District or Divisional Executive, there are three District Inspectors acting as liaison officers between the Ministry and the Authority. Sometimes, however, one Inspector combines two of these appointments ...

References from the Office on administrative matters are in the first place sent to the District Inspector for the Local Education Authority, who needs to be aware of all negotiations between the Ministry and the ... Authority ... Subject to the agreement of the District Inspector and the Authority, direct contact is to be encouraged between an Authority and any Inspector operating in its area ...

Divisional Specialist Inspectors

Specialist Inspectors are responsible for supervision of their subjects at all stages of the education system. They have the right of entry to any school in which their subject is taught in the area allotted to them though they do not visit schools without full collaboration with the General Inspectors concerned ... Their visits to schools should not be restricted to the specific subjects in which they are specialists but should embrace the influence, actual and potential, of those subjects on the school as a whole ... They are *ex officio* members of the appropriate panels.[that is, the specialist committees at national level led by the relevant subject SIs].

Divisional Advisers

They keep abreast of developments in their subjects and form a link between subject panels and the Inspectors of the Division. Their services and advice are available to colleagues as required ... They are *ex officio* corresponding members of the respective panel.

[By the 1960s the distinction between Divisional Specialist Inspectors and Divisional Advisers had been ended – all General Inspectors, depending on their qualifications, were also available as specialists.]

Co-ordination

Many problems of an administrative and policy nature require joint handling by at least two District inspectors (sometimes together with specialists) eg in connection with Evening Institutes, Colleges of Further Education, County Colleges, Secondary Technical Schools, part-time day courses, Juvenile Employment. District Inspectors for a single area and for neighbouring areas must collaborate closely, and the Inspector primarily concerned will be responsible for bringing colleagues into consultation. For general inspection purposes a single unit under one Head or Principal will normally be allotted to a single Inspector...

Special Educational Treatment

The District Inspector (P and S) is responsible for contacts with the Local Education Authority concerning ... [such treatment] ... in ordinary schools or in special schools. Questions involving the extent and type of provision and any doubtful points should be referred to the Divisional Specialist Inspector. Questions concerning the classification of children ... and about schools for the blind and deaf, and hospital schools, should be referred to the Staff Inspector for Special Educational Treatment.

WALES

The Inspectorate consists of the Chief Inspector, Staff Inspectors, Inspectors ... Where in this Handbook a reference is made to the SCI or to the DI in England, it should be understood as meaning the Chief Inspector in Wales.

Recruitment and Probation

Recruitment to the Inspectorate was by public advertisement and interview but many candidates, especially in the early years 'had their shoulder tapped' by an HMI who spotted them at work as heads or heads of department and saw them as good potential HMIs. Robin Tanner wrote of how while teaching in an elementary school in a Wiltshire village he got to know an HMI – or rather, an HMI got to know him and enlisted his talent as a teacher and an artist in the Inspectorate. HMIs looking back frequently describe how their interest in the Inspectorate as a possible career move arose from an encounter with an HMI on a course or during an inspection. The Inspectorate needed to draw on the ablest teachers of their generation – where better to identify them than during a full inspection? This kind of personal recruitment came to be deprecated later because it conflicted with the best personnel management theories and carried a risk that HMIs would simply reproduce themselves in those whose shoulders they tapped. But no doubt it continued in many cases and led to many good appointments.

Most were recruited between the ages of 35 and 45. HMI was regarded as a career grade – some would be promoted to the hierarchy, but this was not to be counted on: new HMIs were told they had had their promotion. In Roseveare's time, there were relatively few HMIs who had had teaching experience in primary schools or secondary modern schools; when comprehensive schools appeared on the scene it was some time before there were any HMIs with personal experience to bring to their inspection.

On receiving the Royal Warrant, a new HMI would be appointed to a division and begin a two-year probation (one year after 1970). HMIs were not meant to inspect schools in an area where they had worked as teachers, so joining the Inspectorate usually meant moving house. New HMIs would be given mentors to initiate them into the customs and procedures of the Inspectorate and it would be for the DI to arrange a training programme. The experience varied enormously. Many HMIs write of the care their mentors took to show them how to conduct themselves when visiting schools and writing reports and the etiquette to be observed. (HMIs addressed each other by their surnames irrespective of rank, did not shake hands after the first introduction, ladies wore hats, men wore suits to secondary schools. Some daring radicals held that sports jackets might be in order for a primary visit.)

Some felt they were thrown in at the deep end. According to C. H. Barry, a DI, mentorship almost broke down in the immediate post-war period when there was rapid recruitment and some new HMIs were left to sink or swim. But some ex-officers returned from the war with strong ideas about the responsibilities of man-management. A number of former HMIs recall the priority Colonel Ames, the district inspector in Southend, gave to training new entrants. AIs had been promoted to the rank of HMI but grudgingly and with bad grace – they did not automatically move onto the HMI pay scale and continued to receive lower travelling and hotel expenses. This made for ill feeling when former AIs acted as mentors to newly appointed HMIs and found they were paid less than the probationers they were meant to help. Human nature being what it is, former AIs were liable to be treated as former AIs till they retired – some teachers and chief education officers had long memories – but others, like Tanner and Leonard Clark, went on to have long and distinguished careers in the Inspectorate.

Subject and Phase Specialisms

HMIs' general duties and the regular attention they were expected to give as GI to the schools on their list were only part of the job because by the 1960s every HMI was also a specialist in a phase – primary or secondary, or some aspect of activity such as school meals or educational technology – or in a subject like English or history or a branch of engineering. There was always a certain tension between the growing claims of specialism and the claims of general inspecting. This tension tended to grow over the years – HMIs were often recruited to fill a specialist vacancy and some thought of themselves as first and foremost a modern linguist or a geographer rather than a general inspector of schools. It was important, though difficult, to maintain the generalist principle. Specialists were brought in from outside their immediate area to take part in full inspections, not necessarily for the whole time, to look at a particular department.

The interests of specialists were focused on the panels and committees, chaired by the relevant SI. It would be for the SI to give leadership to his/her group of specialists and give direction to their work on matters related to its development. They were not specifically responsible for curriculum development but they were expected to know what was going on and where the most interesting work was being done.

In the 1960s the creation first of the CSG (1962) and then of the Schools Council (1965) signalled the beginning of a period in which all the major subjects would come under review, both inside the Schools Council and outside. Later, when the Secretary of State and the Department began to take a more direct interest in curricular matters they depended on specialists in the Inspectorate to show the way.

The increased emphasis on HMIs' specialist interests competed for time with the routine inspection on which the Inspectorate's claim to authoritative judgement was based. As we shall see, the demands of the 1970s brought about changes in the balance of the activities undertaken by HMI and the relationships between the field force of HMI in both their general and their specialist roles, the DIs and the central leadership of the inspector headed by the SCI and the CIs.

The Drive to Inspect All Schools by the End of the 1950s

For Roseveare, the first priority of the unified and reorganised Inspectorate was to reinstate the programme of regular reporting inspections which had been interrupted by the war. Barry writes of 'a ruthless campaign'[1] – HMIs running down their lists, carrying out inspections and striking schools off, 'almost as if they were items on a stock list . . .'. Full inspection reports were 'churned out at such a rate that they became almost indistinguishable from one another and their currency became debased'. Primary reports could be indecently brief – from half to two and a half foolscap pages. Not surprisingly, with such a spate of inspection reports there were recurring complaints of delays in completing them and getting them through the machine. All the reports had to be read by a territorial principal in Schools Branch before being printed and issued by order of the Minister to the LEA, the governors and to the head. They were not public documents till Keith Joseph relaxed the restrictions in 1983: till then, they had to be published in their entirety or not at all.

While, in theory, peacetime was meant to enable HMIs to resume the even tenor of their ways – in Barry's words: 'pastoral visit, Full Inspection, panel meeting, course or conference (if we were lucky), and the annual Divisional Conference' – in the 1950s full inspections occupied an altogether disproportionate amount of time. In 3 districts of Glamorgan alone there were 29 in 1950 and 25 in 1951. John Morris recalls acting as reporting inspector for 3 grammar, 4 or 5 secondary modern, and 15 primary inspections, as well as acting as a geography specialist in inspections of another 13 or 14 schools. Even so, Roseveare kept up the pressure – his aim was to be assured every school had been covered by the end of the 1950s.

One consequence of the heavy programme of inspection was to strengthen the divisional organisation. The DIs became more powerful figures – HMIs write of the close attention some took to the drafting of full inspection reports. They were concerned with the management and administration of the HMIs within their division; they organised HMIs' individual assignments, monitored their fortnightly diaries, and were responsible for the divisional inspection programme. They also maintained links with industry, with the Ministry, and with other government departments in the regions (where DIs were the official representatives of the Minister).

Inspection Routines

'Inspection' included both the daily round of pastoral visiting and the programme of more formal inspection. It was these activities, taken together, which gave credibility to HMIs' judgements and authenticity to their counsel. It was an uphill struggle to maintain routine visiting in the face of all the other demands on their time. What was called 'pastoral' visiting diminished during the 1960s and HMIs complained that they were losing touch. In the 1970s and 1980s changes inside the Department led the Inspectorate to focus on specific policy-related tasks rather than the daily routine of visiting and observing schools.

Long before the completion of the two-year probationary period, a new HMI was likely to be given a list of the schools, colleges and other activities for which he or she would be the GI. Each school would have a file; a 'Note of Visit' was meant to be added to the file after each occasion when the inspector called, and circulated to others concerned. Norman Thomas, for example, had 130 Lincolnshire schools, mostly village primary and all-age schools, on his list when he started in 1962. In later years many lists ran to 150 or more schools. The Handbook advice was that every school on the list should be visited once every five terms, it being 'especially necessary for HMI to know his schools and to be known by them. His continuing relationship with them must be the foundation of his work; only so can he understand and assess justly the schools' purposes and achievements.' Five terms stretched to six and longer as other tasks intruded.

Full Inspection

As Barry pointed out,[2] full inspections were regarded, in the public mind – then and later – as 'the hall-mark of Inspectorial quality and the yard-stick of Inspectorial productivity'. Each year some schools would be selected for full inspection. The rubric laid down that 'the normal interval between reports is seven years for Grant-Aided and ten years for Independent Schools', but though this was a pre-war ideal, restated in pre-war terms, it was one which had probably never been achieved. After the initial drive, the momentum was lost because of other commitments and during the 1960s the number of full inspections was severely cut back. By the time a House of Commons Select Committee came to take evidence in 1968, full inspections were being used more selectively – that is, when they could serve 'some useful purpose'. The fact of the matter was that the manpower of the Inspectorate did not run to reporting inspections on a seven-year cycle, and surveys, using a sample of schools and looking at specific questions, came to be seen as a more productive way of collecting information.

The conventional full inspection was based on a model devised for grammar schools and independent schools. It was developed after 1902 when local authorities became involved in secondary education and a new generation of LEA grammar schools came into existence. It was this model which was applied with modifications to the post-war mix of primary and secondary schools.

List 55A schools – the grammar schools and recognised independent schools – were inspected by teams of specialist inspectors. The programme of inspections was planned centrally and the HMIs were drawn from a national list of HMIs highly qualified in their subjects. Roy Wake, SI for history and then for secondary, describes how later on when List 55A was no more, the Headmaster of Eton had pressed him to arrange a full inspection. ' "By the way," he said, "I should, of course, expect to be inspected by our intellectual equals." – meaning people with Firsts. He got highly competent professionals some of whom were not academic.' Wake was at pains to insist that the top independent schools were treated like everybody else, and so they were – up to a point. The top public schools were on a list of their own – the A list – and known as 'lettered schools'. Prudence, if nothing else, made sure that only HMI who could hold their own with high-powered common rooms, were assigned to inspect these schools.

Other large schools were similarly inspected by teams of HMIs, but these visitations were planned at divisional level and drew on divisional subject and phase specialists. The reporting inspector was usually the general inspector for the school. He or she would collect preliminary information on the school to circulate to the team – there was a tendency for the amount of advance information required to increase over the years. Schools were given advance notice of a full inspection and the timing was, if necessary, negotiated to avoid clashing with pre-arranged school events. For routine visiting, it was quite usual to arrive without warning at a primary school but let the head know in advance in the case of secondary schools.

The typical secondary school full inspection would last four or five days – say, Monday or Tuesday to Friday. There would have to be a series of meetings with heads of department and their staffs. The team would confer on the Thursday evening, sharing their conclusions, and spend the Friday morning going over their findings with the head and senior management. It was a point of principle that any criticism which was to be included in the report should be discussed with the head and others concerned during the inspection visit. The rule was that when the report eventually was forwarded it would contain 'No Surprises'.

There would remain to be arranged – ideally on the Friday afternoon but usually at a later date – an invitation to meet the governors, when the reporting inspector would discuss the findings. The head might be present for the whole of the meeting, or be invited to join it after a while – it would be for the governors to decide, but HMI was against anything which suggested there might be a secret report behind the written one. The reporting inspector would state, in terms, that his oral summary was *not* the report. The atmosphere to strive for was one of 'mutual confidence, respect and cooperation'. It would be usual for the LEA adviser and a representative of the chief education officer to attend.

Primary schools were for the most part visited by three or fewer HMIs for a full inspection. It was well understood that there was a risk that the prospect of inspection might give rise to unnecessary anxiety. One way to minimise this risk was to cut down the waiting time – it was left to the general inspector to decide how much notice to give, with a view to keeping 'an easy, informal, atmosphere' and to avoid giving 'undue prominence to the Report'. It was drilled into HMIs that in all schools and colleges, 'it is the work being done which should be appraised, not the individual teacher.' And there was an insistence on the elementary principle that 'things not seen should not be appraised.'

In the successive editions of the *Inspectors' Handbook* the SCI gave instructions on the conduct of inspection, including full inspections, but schools were never issued with any detailed explanation of what the inspectors would be looking for. They were asked for some basic information which they could present in whatever form they found convenient. Roseveare's 1955 edition asks HMI for reports which provide an 'accurate, coherent, well-balanced, and unbiased survey of what has been seen, in plain standard English, readily intelligible ... [with] ... no expression of educational doctrine and no hint of dogmatism or prescription'. This, of course, sounds very much like the counsel of perfection: HMIs became masters of interlinear writing and coded messages.

The section on primary schools is brief and written in general terms about what HMIs should look for. The secondary section is much more extensive and provides headings and questions for an inspector's guidance, in relation to both the inspection as a whole and the examination of individual subjects. As for the report,

> No pattern is necessarily desirable but no report is complete without:
> (i) some general picture of the school or establishment as a whole, its aims and achievements, its corporate life, and when appropriate its place and effectiveness in the educational life of the locality;
> (ii) an adequate and relevant analysis of numbers, age-range, organisation and significant changes in premises or catchment area – sometimes this material is best given in tabular form and consigned to an appendix.
> ... A final note of encouragement may well be appreciated, provided that it does not go beyond the evidence.

What could better convey the culture of the post-war Inspectorate than the last sentence quoted here – benign, optimistic, supportive – determined to ensure that the process of inspection was valuable for the school as well as for the Minister whom HMI served? For many HMIs the process was all. They filed their reports without much idea what happened to the reports when filed. They were duly read by long-suffering officials in the Office – representatives of the Minister to whom the reports were addressed – and that almost invariably was that. There are examples of a follow-up report being called for but this was unlikely: a copy would go into the school's file and the next time the general inspector paid a visit he would have an eye to any suggestions or comments which had been made. A copy of the report would also go to the chief education officer whose attention (and that of the LEA adviser) would be drawn to matters of concern. After that something might happen – exactly what, would be up to the LEA.

FE Inspectorate

HMIs in the technical, commerce and art section were disposed territorially like those designated primary and secondary; all had a list of colleges and activities for which they were responsible. Their lists were shorter than the lists of schools given to primary and secondary inspectors but the institutions were usually larger and the range of activities wider. HMIs recall the emphasis put on getting to know college principals and heads of department.

Further education had not been the most glamorous part of the education system in the pre-war period. Many technical colleges had limited horizons; it was their job to provide a down-to-earth service of vocational evening classes. Looking back, HMIs write of the effort needed to galvanise colleges to make the most of post-war opportunities for development, accustomed as they were to hard times and tight budgets. Each LEA would have an FE district inspector working alongside the district inspector for schools. In large districts there might also be an OFE district inspector. As in the case of the schools, the HMI who acted as general inspector for an FE college would need to draw on the expertise of specialist colleagues and keep them in touch with what was going on at colleges on his/her list.

Technical HMIs had to be versatile enough to inspect a wide range of work, but as well as inspecting generally, they would also have their own specialist interests. The post-war Inspectorate had to recruit men and women with many forms of industrial experience in craft and technical subjects and more advanced technological applications – the FE Inspectorate was always a more varied and less homogeneous professional group than the primary and secondary inspectors. If necessary the collective wisdom of the FE Inspectorate could be augmented for particular purposes with experts brought in on a temporary basis.

Most HMIs working in FE soon found themselves appointed as district inspectors with responsibility for one or more LEAs. Full inspections followed the same general pattern in colleges as in schools, with a team of inspectors, covering a variety of specialisms spending some days at a college, the same formal procedures for reporting to governing bodies and the same courtesies which required any adverse comment in the final report to be flagged up in advance with the principal and individual members of the staff. There was no fixed programme or prescribed cycle for full inspections – regular national surveys being a preferred option as the size of colleges grew and became too large for a conventional full inspection. Often HMI would inspect a group of departments rather than try to tackle a whole college.

Within Roseveare's unified Inspectorate, FE inspectors did not confine their activities entirely to FE institutions, but their experience and much of their work set them apart from the HMIs who worked in schools. The two sections of the Inspectorate remained separate in ethos and temperament, even if they were recognisably part of a single organisation. When Cyril English succeeded Percy Wilson as SCI he was the first FE inspector to be appointed to the top job. This was not to everyone's liking – Wilson, himself, did not approve and there was murmuring among the rank and file primary and secondary HMIs. The objections were not personal – English was a man of ability, a former naval man with a bluff quarter-deck manner – more a matter of tradition and expectation. As it was, English never made the impact he might have made because after two years in post, he left to become director-general of the City and Guilds of London Institute where he earned a knighthood and was able to continue to draw a salary till he was 65, instead of being required to retire at 60 as in the Inspectorate.

Cyril English, Senior Chief Inspector, 1965–67.

During the period of rapid expansion and the build-up of the advanced work in the colleges, the FE Inspectorate was much involved in the administration of the system of approvals for courses and for the purchase of major items of equipment. Advanced work in the colleges was financed nationally – shared in a way to prevent an undue proportion of the extra expense falling on the towns and cities where the larger colleges happened to be located. This made it necessary for the Education Department to have some control of where courses were being offered and, in conjunction with the Regional Advisory Councils, to prevent overlap and empire-building. Regional SIs were given the job of approving or not approving proposals for new advanced courses – that is courses, of a standard above A level and the Ordinary National Certificate (ONC) – and all FE inspectors were dogged at some time or other by 21FEs or 'blue files' which had to be turned round quickly.

Other Further Education

For an HMI in a unified Inspectorate duties were many and varied. Beside the schools and FE colleges there were other diverse grant-receiving activities to keep under review. OFE was a residuum: there was 'FE in connection with industry' and 'all other FE'. The activities which came under the OFE heading included: youth, youth employment, evening institutes, community centres, village halls and playing fields, part-time day work, adult education (RB), field study centres, residential colleges, voluntary organisations, HM Forces, prisons and borstals, museums and camping (outdoor pursuits). HMI inspection was extended to the Armed Forces 'to oblige another Department' and museums crept in because they were used for educational purposes.

The OFE work was initially supported by a CI and four SIs – 2 for adult education and one each for youth, and county colleges/juvenile employment. Increasingly specialists with knowledge and experience of particular OFE areas of activity were recruited to the Inspectorate. It was Roseveare who established OFE as a section of the Inspectorate and fought hard in its defence: Eccles, in particular, regarded many OFE activities as unnecessary.

(In 1967, OFE and TCA HMI were merged in a single FE section under a single CI but the activities which the term covered continued and the inspection duties were shared throughout the unified Inspectorate. FE in time became further and higher education as the size of the higher education component increased – see Chapter 10.)

About half the OFE members of the Inspectorate were concerned with the vast area of activity known as *Youth* – two unmanageable empires run by local authorities and voluntary organisations. Much of it had a strong social dimension – keeping young people off the streets and out of trouble. As Salter Davies, CI for OFE, put it: 'England is frightened of its young people.' Support for youth work increased in the 1960s after the Albemarle Report. Capital grants were provided for youth provision: each proposal had to be vetted by HMI. Some authorities based youth provision on their secondary schools or colleges – terms like 'community school' and 'community college' came into use. Leicestershire, Cumbria and Nottinghamshire were among the LEAs which added youth and community facilities to secondary schools.

As society changed, so too did provision for young people. Youth organisations began to look more towards community service and forms of social action. Rising youth unemployment brought youth opportunity programmes and money from the MSC. Inner city riots stimulated government interest in youth. HMI, under Eric Bolton's leadership, took part in abortive attempts to put together a package for Liverpool 8 – Toxteth – in the face of opposition from local politicians. There were continuing political difficulties which HMI had to deal with arising from the mutual antipathy between the youth service community and the Thatcher–Major governments. Youth matters linked up with poverty, unemployment and ethnic diversity to form a minefield through which HMI had to thread their way, reporting honestly but often saying what the Office and ministers did not want to hear.

Youth Employment in due course became *Careers Education and Guidance*. The Juvenile (later Youth) Employment Service came under the aegis of the Ministry of Labour but was mainly administered by LEAs. In the immediate post-war period its primary concern was placing 15-year-old school-leavers in jobs. An inter-departmental unit, the Central Youth Employment Executive (CYEE) was set up by the Ministries of Labour and Education to give direction to the service. Davies and his successors were members. HMI inspected LEA youth employment departments with CYEE inspectors.

As the youth employment service developed it became as much a matter for secondary phase HMI as for OFE inspectors because in addition to placing young school-leavers, youth employment officers were working closely with teachers to promote careers education. For older school-leavers, it made no sense to separate guidance on jobs from educational guidance. Careers education was boosted by the Newsom Report in the 1960s and HMI published a survey under the title *Careers Education in Secondary Schools* in 1973. After the Education and Training Act of 1975, careers education and guidance became the responsibility of the secondary schools Inspectorate, under a secondary phase SI.

Adult Education with a capital A and a capital E usually meant the courses provided by the university extramural departments and the Workers Educational Association, known as the RBs – responsible bodies – which received grants from the Ministry. Local authority adult education was less prestigious but more extensive and more popular. What began as 'night school' and flourished in the evening institutes of great cities like Birmingham, extended to day classes in FE colleges as recreational further education took off, curbed only by rising fees.

OFE also included *General Education in FE Colleges* which began to augment the provision for the 16 to 19s and eventually offer an alternative to the conventional sixth form. This brought in schools HMI and occasional turf wars between them and the FE Inspectorate. For example, SIs for history insisted on looking at history when FE colleges began to offer humanities courses.

HMI involvement in *Prisons and Borstals* developed strongly after the war. The Prison Commission appointed a recently retired HMI as director of education and asked Roseveare to act as education adviser. A large-scale inspection programme was initiated in the mid-1950s – 62 in 6 years – which was followed up in the 1960s and 1970s by a series of surveys. In due course the prisons education service developed its own Inspectorate and HMI involvement in penal education was cut back. Work in prisons had included remedial literacy programmes. When the DES set up the Adult Literacy and Basic Skills Unit, they were able to draw on this experience.

Services Education

After the war Roseveare agreed that HMI should inspect the education of service families in Germany and elsewhere – among the countries visited by HMI were Cyprus, Gibraltar, Malaya, Singapore, the Maldives and Hong Kong. The FE involvement drew also on HMI for reporting on the education and training – mainly at home – of junior soldiers, junior leaders and services apprentices schools including the Army School of Music.

Independent Schools

HMIs had independent schools on their lists along with maintained schools. In pre-war days about 750 public and preparatory schools were among those who had applied under 'Rule 16' to be inspected and 'recognised as efficient'. HMI kept in touch with the independent schools, visiting them and occasionally carrying out full inspections. But the old Board of Education did not have supervisory powers over schools which were not grant-aided.

Part III of the 1944 Act extended the Minister's responsibilities by obliging him to appoint a registrar of independent schools whose job it would be to compile a register of such schools, open to public view. Anyone or any board of governors wishing to run an independent school had to secure its registration and for this there had to be an inspection by HMI.

In 1959, Part III of the Act was brought into force. Thereafter, HMI contacts with the independent sector were of two kinds: they continued to visit and inspect established independent secondary and preparatory schools in the ordinary way, and they acted as gate-keepers to the register. HMI had already begun a major exercise visiting and inspecting candidates for registration. It was the beginning of a 'short hectic period'. By all accounts, HMIs were appalled by many of the schools which applied to be registered. The worst schools closed almost at once 'when they had been apprised of the standards of premises, equipment, and teaching that was required'. Others leant heavily on HMI for advice in putting their houses in order. Only three or four a year appeared in the Ministry's annual report as having been closed down. (One HMI discovered a case of whisky in the boot of his car – which he duly returned – after one such inspection. The donor's bottled admiration for the Inspectorate did not win his school a reprieve.)

Being put on the register was not like joining an exclusive club. The register was a very broad church, comprising schools which varied from those of the highest quality to others of a much more modest, but not 'objectionable', standard. 'Objectionable' schools were those which failed to meet threshold standards on premises, accommodation, instruction or personnel. Shortcomings on any of these counts were a cause for denying schools registration. HMI reports had to be composed with a careful eye to a possible appeal but there were not many appeals: the rise in property values led many proprietors to realise the development value of school sites rather than invest heavily in bringing their schools up to standard.

Two commissions on the independent schools in the 1960s – chaired by John Newsom and David Donnison – failed to forge closer links between the independent and the maintained systems. Both had HMIs as assessors. The topic was regarded as highly controversial and sharply political and HMI were extremely discreet. Formal inspections of independent schools were suspended while the commissions were sitting. Direct grant schools were phased out in the 1970s, assisted places phased in during the 1980s and out in the 1990s. What, if anything, to do about the distorting effect of a powerful independent sector on the rest of the education system, remained a rhetorical question for radicals like George Walden, a disillusioned one-time Conservative junior minister and self-styled 'anti-politician'.[3] HMIs continued as before to inspect both sectors with independent school reports being printed (for some reason) on blue paper. In their way HMIs provided a bridge between the two systems, finding evidence of good practice to share, on both sides of the divide.

After 1967, independent boarding schools were required to meet a higher standard than that needed for registration. They had to be 'Recognised as Efficient' and a special team of HMI was assembled to carry out the necessary inspections. It had been intended to extend this quality requirement to all independent day schools but this expensive ambition was never achieved and 'Recognition' was ended in 1978. In its place a self-regulatory accreditation scheme was set up, run by the Independent Schools Joint Council, relying heavily on the help of retired HMIs and independent school heads. As late as 1985 there were still 24 HMIs in the Inspectorate's independent schools team. The creation of the city technical colleges in the years immediately before the beginning of the OFSTED era gave HMI a chance to contribute to the curriculum planning of these new independent schools.

European Schools

Mention should also be made of the role of HMI in the development of the schools set up by the European Community for the children of *fonctionnaires*. Two HMIs – one primary, one secondary – worked half-time on European school matters introducing many elements of English and Welsh practice into the inspection of these schools.

Channel Islands

Schools in the Channel Islands enjoyed the services of HMI through an arrangement with the Department. Each year there would be a request for HMI to inspect Channel Island schools. While on such missions, HMI were enrolled as temporary Channel Island civil servants. One HMI was designated as, in effect, district inspector; latterly this became the responsibility of the SI for independent schools.

Overseas Activities

At any given time there were likely to be two or three HMIs on overseas assignments. There was a steady demand for HMIs to go out to Commonwealth and other countries to advise on behalf of the British Council or the Foreign Office. In addition to visits which came under the

Overseas Aid heading, there was a travel programme for fact-finding – HMIs had been on such visits from the time of Matthew Arnold. Later on this changed – by Joseph's time in the 1980s disturbing comparisons from international surveys took HMIs on evidence-gathering visits to countries such as Germany and France, as well as to the United States and Canada and Japan. In the early post-war years, John Maud was much involved with Unesco. HMIs regularly contributed to the professional activities of such bodies as the Council of Europe and the Organisation for Economic Cooperation and Development (OECD).

Sharing Knowledge – Publications

A constant concern of senior HMI was how to bring together the concerted knowledge and experience gathered in the course of routine inspection. Collectively HMI was extremely well informed, but how was this information to be brought to bear on policy matters – the concerns of the Office – and where appropriate, shared with the teachers in the schools?

One obvious way of sharing HMI's knowledge has been by publishing reports and studies in a form which is accessible to a wide professional audience (see box).

HMI Publications Series

Apart from the flow of occasional papers and reports which increased from the 1970s, there were a number of HMI publications series. Many are included in the bibliography at the back of this book.

The *Inspectors' Bulletin*, an HMI house journal, appeared three times a year from 1948 to 1973. It was written mainly by HMI with occasional contributions from outside; articles covered matters of general and particular HMI interest and included historical items, poetry and humour. Curiously, it retained a strictly confidential classification. Another periodical, however, *Trends* (1965–80), was a quarterly open forum for the dissemination of information and ideas. It accepted contributions from outside as well as from civil servants and HMI. The articles were wide-ranging and related to work in progress – HMI surveys, the new Planning Branch, Robbins, research, reviews, statistics, developments at home and abroad. Its attempts to discuss contentious ideas led to trouble when an item on religious education in multi-faith Britain angered Thatcher. Thereafter all contributions had to go through her Private Office.

Between 1967 and 1976 22 Education Surveys were published based on the observation of practice in such areas as drama and the curricular differences for boys and girls. From the seventies, HMI series multiplied and got more glossy. 'Matters for Discussion', 'based on HMI observation ... and their thoughts (not necessarily of HMI as a whole) on some of the issues involved', was a series of 15 publications which included *Ten Good Schools, Mixed Ability Work in Comprehensive Schools* and *The New Teacher in School* – all based on specific inspections or surveys. *A View of the Curriculum* (1980) was important as a first attempt to draw together HMI thinking on the curriculum from 5 to 16. (The important 'Curriculum Matters' series is described in Chapter 9.)

After it was decided that HMI school reports should be published, periodic reviews of what they revealed were published in a series of free booklets entitled 'Education Observed'. The series ran from 1983 to 1992, covering 16 topics, among them *Good Teachers, Effective Youth Work, Special Needs, Attendance at School* and *Homework*.

Joseph's interest in education in other countries led to a paper on West Germany and subsequently papers were published as a result of one or more visits to the United States, the Netherlands, Denmark, France and Japan.

FE publications gathered pace in the eighties – after *Education for Employment* and *Part-Time Advanced Further Education*, a series began in 1987, following the inspection of 34 colleges of FE two years earlier. These included *NAFE: Non-Advanced Further Education*, and 10 survey reports on vocational courses. A similar series on higher education began in 1989 with *The English Polytechnics* and *Education in the Polytechnics and Colleges* describing practice in 11 subject areas.

At the other end of the age range, between 1988 and 1991, there was a series on primary education to illustrate good practice in the curriculum – a last throw by HMI before the launch of the National Curriculum.

Panels and Committees

The national and divisional panels and committees, already referred to, brought together specialist HMIs by subject, phase and aspect. For example, there was a national Secondary Committee which discussed and shared information on all aspects of the secondary phase and to which reports passed from subject committees or panels. The committee structure was the chief mechanism by which the collective knowledge and views of HMI were focused. Getting on to the relevant committee was a mark of progress for an ambitious HMI – a point made by correspondents to the *Survey of Communications* in 1966.[4] How effective they were depended on the SI in the chair. An outer circle of corresponding members received the papers without attending the meetings. Much of the discussion was best described as high quality, but inconclusive, chat. But the annual or biannual meetings provided an essential link between colleagues and a sharing of experience which helped to form a common professional experience. Many HMI publications sprang from the work of the committees.

In-service Training Courses

In-service training courses for teachers were another way in which the knowledge and experience of the Inspectorate could be garnered and brought to bear on the work of the schools. The teachers' short-course programme, a central feature of the HMI calendar, formed a major part of the Inspectorate's work on the curriculum in the 1950s and 1960s. SIs ran regular national courses in their specialist subjects, sometimes in conjunction with national subject associations. HMI also took part in courses run by LEAs and others. An important benefit HMIs derived from the programme of courses was the chance to engage with teachers and the two-way communication which resulted.

In the early post-war years, courses were held at weekends and in school holidays; later they came to be held in term time, lasting one or two weeks, and in some cases (as for modern languages) involved travel abroad. The number of in-service courses increased during the 1960s. By 1968–9 the number of courses had reached 175 and the number of teachers taking part had risen to 9,200.

Some of the earlier generation of SIs had used their courses for what some saw as self-indulgent academic refreshment for a regular clientele of teachers who would come year after year for an intellectual treat. Teddy Hales, who was SI for history in the 1960s and one of the finest scholars in the Inspectorate, was much more interested in his subject *per se* than in exploring how best to teach it. His successor broke with tradition and began to focus more on the teaching of history than on the latest developments in historical research. Over the course of time the approach became more practical and more devoted to the improvement of teachers' technical effectiveness. The claims of scholarship remained but pitched at a lower key.

Assessorships

One of the most time-consuming of the responsibilities loaded on HMI – both for the sharing and gathering of information – was representational: the work they undertook as assessors and observers on major and minor government committees, and keeping a watching brief on the activities of many other bodies as a representative of the Department. Specialist HMIs were expected to keep an eye on the professional organisations in their field. HMIs with responsibility for a phase had commitments to a range of organisations where they were expected to tread a narrow line between saying nothing at all and making intelligent but non-committal comments. HMIs were not in a position to take issue with settled matters of government policy, but provided they made it clear they spoke as individuals they could draw on their own experience and the experience of their colleagues to express opinions. Some of the bodies they attended were more important than others. A seasoned HMI became skilled in deciding how to use his time to the best advantage – when to attend and when to stay away.

Notes

[1] Barry, C. H. (1967) 'Twenty one years hard labour'. *Inspectors' Bulletin 53*: December 1967.
[2] See Barry, note 1.
[3] Walden, G. (1999) *Lucky George: Memoirs of an Anti-Politician*. London: Allen Lane.
[4] Survey of Communications in the Inspectorate 1965–69, report dated 1966. AHMI Jack Kitching Archive 2a/40.

HMI Miscellany

Extracts from HMI personal accounts

George Allen 1937

The new SCI gave us a real framework such as we had not enjoyed before. As time went on, it proved somewhat rigid and over-elaborate, an impressive machine which, with effort, ground out valuable and well-produced reports by the score. But, of course, pastoral visits as we called them, became fewer and fewer and more scattered. More serious still, it became clear that within the Inspectorate as a whole leadership was able but uninspired; all the reports led nowhere ... Reports drove out argument and there was a failure to deal with issues ... The first fine rapture of what had seemed really new and promising gradually turned disillusioned and often sour. The Inspectorate seemed to be getting tired... It showed signs of repetitious fatigue with its endless inspections.

Don Porter 1946

In retrospect there were serious shortcomings on the management side, especially in regard to training, assignments of work, future reporting requirements and the provision of resources for HMI in the field ... My main task was to visit the schools that my 'mentor' listed for me on one sheet of foolscap, primary on one side and secondary on the other. I was to write some notes on what I did and to come back a fortnight later to learn how to make out my expenses claim.

There was no precedent for handling the sudden recruitment of numbers of new Inspectors, who in some areas soon outnumbered the incumbents ... Another problem arising from rapid change – of HMI as well as school populations – was the allocation of work. After a short introduction one was given a group of schools, then a small area of responsibility. But, as more arrived, assignments were changed so that, after an initial visit, a school might be handed on before a second, probably more productive, visit was made. Not only was time wasted but one could never rely upon HMI 'knowing his schools' well enough to make reporting simple.

Tim Fenn 1947

The writer, an HMI for 27 years (including ten as DI), was never at the centre of discussion of educational matters as were CIs and many SIs who often served on Departmental Committees and on Committees appointed to produce reports on education. Although he may have been the 'ears and eyes', whose reports helped the decision makers at the centre, he himself did not make any decisions which determined policy ... His short teaching experience made him keen to study the methods of the teachers he visited in many types of schools and colleges. This taught him that there are many ways and techniques in which to teach students to learn and think.

Frank Arrowsmith 1949

Laboriously HMI kept in touch with schools ... observing, encouraging, recording ... Roseveare advised 10 sessions work in schools and keep Saturday mornings for office work but in fact over time there was a wider range of activity ... All schools to have a post-war report ... independent source of information not for policy decisions 'for which priorities came from outside'. There was no sense of sharing or generalising opinions.

Roy Wake 1960

Induction: the greatest stress was on courtesy to everyone: never making notes in public if possible; never discussing a class or the teaching in front of that class or the teacher; never saying anything to the head not already said to the teacher; never calling on a [secondary] school without prior arrangement; never writing on work seen that had not already been said; looking at teaching not the teachers ... There were clubs within the club. On the schools side List 55A was seen as divisive – and there was a club within 55A, really the last of the old S Branch.

Gordon Hamflett 1962

Great emphasis was on the art of inspection:– the disciplines and boundaries of HMI's role, development of empathy in schools, ability to generalise from scattered evidence and make judgements, skills in note writing (*de rigueur* after every visit), the development of 'standards' (central was the work of pupils not the teaching process as an entity in itself), and an ability outside one's own specialisms to ask appropriate questions and to judge whether what one observed may be of special interest or concern ...

Right from the start one learned the privileges and disciplines of work as HMI:– not 'our' schools; the priority was time in schools and in the classroom itself ... half a day was the appropriate amount of official (as distinct from personal) time to spend on note writing and correspondence; judgements were based on evidence not hearsay; prompt distribution of Notes of Visit and submission of reports; concluding comments to the head to be well judged in quantity, delivery and clarity; remember that an ordinary day for HMI was an extraordinary day for the school.

Joe Wiles 1964

The Inspectorate that I joined in 1964 was a very different organisation from that I left in 1984. People were much freer to plan their own work in their personal patches. There might be two or three weeks in a term when they were involved in full inspections. Otherwise there was freedom to go from school to school offering advice and gaining impressions that were recorded in notes of visit and probably never read by anyone. It was hard to see how anything of what we were doing was passed on to anyone in Curzon Street. This system had disadvantages, in that it allowed some colleagues, a minority I believe, an easy life in which little was done either for the schools or the Ministry. But, on the positive side, it allowed full scope for the conscientious and inspiring maverick. Perhaps the greatest of these was Robin Tanner ... For years after he retired I would meet individuals who told me that he had changed their lives, or visit schools where his influence was apparent in all the work. This he achieved by devoting all his time to teachers or schools on whom he knew he would have some effect, while ignoring the others.

Margaret Brogden 1967

My naive idealism failed to grasp HMI's limitations with regard to central government. I had assumed unthinkingly that their professional expertise would be readily accepted and used to modify educational policy for the benefit of the pupils. In this I assumed a style of function more akin to that of other European inspectors and failed to understand HMI's more generalist and advisory role in relation to political decision-makers ... Later HMI gave much time to the primary and secondary surveys of maintained schools which were presumably of value to the civil servants and politicians. It was difficult to discern much direct benefit to the schools.

Sam Adams 1974

During the 60s the inspectorial role of HMI changed. This was in large part due to the view (probably mistaken) that there was little to be gained from inspecting the system while it was in a state of flux ... There were occasional full inspections but they, like the visits, were advisory in character and rarely led to a formally issued report. A flirtation with a form of reporting that would be agreed between the HMI team and the school came to nothing ... (Later) the underlining of phase and subject specialisms following the Fulton Committee did not, as in England, lead to the formation of discrete phase teams and, with few exceptions, individual HMI in Wales have continued to inspect in primary, secondary and FHE (initial teacher training) ... (From the *Welsh Journal of Education* – 5 February 1996)

Chapter 6   The Winds of Change

House of Commons Select Committee

By 1955, Gilbert Flemming, the permanent secretary, and David Leadbetter, the establishment officer, were pushing for a review of HMI and (in particular) a cut in numbers. Roseveare had never achieved the target of 600 HMIs agreed in 1944. In the mid-1950s the numbers hovered around 500 for England and 50 for Wales. It is not clear why Flemming supposed that an expanding education system needed a smaller Inspectorate, but it seems that neither he, nor Leadbetter, were unqualified admirers of Roseveare. It was said that Roseveare did not carry his senior colleagues with him and according to Leadbetter, he was not able to give the quality of professional advice which Flemming wanted. It is also true that he was the driving force behind the post-war Inspectorate and if he had not been a 'genial autocrat' he could never have given it the strong direction it needed.

The Working Party which followed was an internal inquiry, chaired by Roseveare, which did not canvass local authority opinion or that of the teachers.[1] It moved at a leisurely pace and took two years to produce a modest report. It having been made very clear to him that there would have to be cuts, Roseveare traded cuts in duties for a small proposed reduction in numbers – for England, down from 500 to 470 over three years. In the event the cut failed to materialise. Roseveare used the report to press once again for HMIs to be relieved of the 'chores' and 'errands' they were asked to perform for the Office and suggested there should be briefer and less frequent reporting visits. 'HMIs would spend more time in schools and colleges and divide their time differently between the formal and informal sides of their work.' The report also said that there was need for more continuous professional advice on matters of policy and it broached (inconclusively) the question of finding better ways of translating field experience into useful advice for policy makers.

The Minister, Eccles, was deeply unimpressed. 'I feel' he wrote,[2] 'as if we had asked the Admiralty to redesign submarines and they had replied "we found so many jobs to be done on the surface our new model will dive much less".' He strongly supported the idea that HMIs should be relieved of minor administrative jobs but the logic of his minute was that there should more HMIs and more not fewer full inspections.

The report was adopted and Roseveare retired, ostensibly in order that his successor, PercyWilson, should provide the continuity needed to introduce and carry through the changes. It was a strange episode. Wilson had recovered from a breakdown but there was no reason to suppose he would offer more energetic leadership than Roseveare. It may be that the replacement of Roseveare was a reflection of Eccles's poor opinion of the report. Eccles moved to the Board of Trade soon after and the changes went forward under Lord Hailsham. Roseveare retired in the summer of 1957. When it became public knowledge that he was leaving early against his will, conspiracy theories abounded inside the Inspectorate and the Association of HMI sent deputations to see the Permanent Secretary who patiently repeated the official line.

As planned, Wilson's tenure as SCI saw a marked reduction in the number of full inspections. But HMIs' lists of schools got longer, some running to as many as 300–350 schools. Each HMI continued to programme his or her own work – except when brought in on full inspections which were nationally or divisionally planned.

Former HMIs look back on 'assiduous' pastoral visiting, 'day after day' ... 'extensive'. Such a routine was in itself an invaluable form of training for HMIs whose experience before entering the Inspectorate might have been confined to grammar schools. HMIs would make a point of visiting a succession of primary schools to build up their knowledge and confidence. The same applied when the first comprehensive schools appeared on the scene and presented the Inspectorate with problems outside their collective experience.

By the end of Wilson's time it was clear that there was still an imbalance between the resources at the disposal of the Inspectorate and the tasks which HMI were expected to undertake. Such time as had been saved by scaling down the number and size of reporting inspections had been absorbed by other demands such as pastoral visits, specialist inquiries, in-service training of teachers, and the work generated by the major CAC reports and their supporting volumes of statistics and surveys.

As one year gave way to another it became more and more difficult to fit the quart into the pint bottle. It was impossible to write a brief for HMI which laid down a clearly defined set of essential duties which could be used to calculate the number of inspectors required to fulfil the Inspectorate's obligations. The duties for which the Inspectorate was responsible were – and would always be – open-ended. As Sir Herbert Andrew would tell the House of Commons Select Committee in 1968,[3] when he was asked about the number of HMI:

> *If I was asked whether we could use an Inspectorate of 1,000 instead of 500 I would say*

Yes; on the other hand we could get by on 250 but 500 seems a reasonable figure in present circumstances.

Andrew, who made his name working with Edward Heath in Brussels on Harold Macmillan's bid to join the Common Market, was regarded as the most laid-back permanent secretary in living memory. His aims for public administration were said to be summed up in the successful negotiation of the next seven days. He was accustomed to a world where there was a glaring gap between demand and supply in the service and he saw nothing remarkable in the situation HMI found themselves in.

What he did do (in 1966) was to suggest another HMI review, to be conducted by a team which included an HMI (Peter Dudley) and two members of the department's O and M staff. The oddly-titled 'Survey of Communications' focused on the operational pattern of the work of the Inspectorate – how HMIs spent their time and how they might be helped to carry out their functions better. It put forward a hard-hitting critique which said the Inspectorate lacked any effective structure for 'improving standards and stimulating, enriching thoughts or providing the Department with cogent and well-founded advice'. The picture revealed by a questionnaire sent to all HMIs showed a worrying lack of coordination and purpose. HMIs complained their time for visiting schools was crowded out by committees, conferences, working parties and outside bodies to the extent that their 'knowledge of what was happening at ground level may become superficial'. The criticism raked the committee and panel system, training ('a hit or miss affair') and the abysmal lack of office support.

Select Committee – 1968

Hearings began in February 1968. Select Committee inquiries were a new idea which had been devised by Richard Crossman when he was leader of the House to give back-bench MPs something to do. It was slow getting off the ground because many departmental ministers were reluctant to cooperate, but the Department of Education was willing to be a guinea pig. Fred Willey MP was in the chair and among the members was Christopher Price, who was chairman 10 years later when the committee had become more active.

It had been Willey's intention to take first the topical subject of student unrest but there were delays in getting started and this was put off till the autumn of 1968. In the meantime, at Price's suggestion they decided to take a quick look at HMI. Price had recently ceased to be parliamentary private secretary to Anthony Crosland and was also a former deputy chair of the Sheffield Education Committee. (He was an ex-teacher of the classics, who had been inspected – and encouraged – early in his first job by Bill Elliott, who was now about to give evidence as SCI.)

Christopher Price had been taken on one side by Sir William Alexander, the secretary of the Association of Education Committees, who put his arm around him and explained confidentially that the LEAs ought to take over formal inspection from HMI. Alexander was keen to see LEAs appoint more and better inspectors: if the Select Committee backed them it would be easier for him to persuade education committees that they should appoint the necessary staff. Price took the Alexander line (which was also supported by the NUT).

The committee duly recommended that full inspections should be phased out as soon as LEA inspectorates became 'adequate'. It reckoned the major responsibility for inspection should lie with the LEA and that the Secretary of State's legal 'duty' to 'cause inspections to be made' should be reduced to a 'right'. It urged HMI to work closely with the local inspectors and advisers. In noting that HMI were widely appreciated, the committee singled out HMIs' advisory functions for commendation rather than their 'inquisitorial' role. The report noted that 'LEAs have become increasingly jealous of their authority and the teachers increasingly conscious of their professional status.'

Two months into a new job, English, the ex-SCI – he had left early to become director-general of the City and Guilds of London Institute – gave trenchant evidence about the way in which the Office made use of HMI and the status accorded to the SCI. Here was the same campaign which Roseveare had fought for long years. The committee took the point – it recommended that the SCI should be given deputy secretary status and direct access to the Secretary of State. This was accepted and Elliott, English's successor, was duly elevated.

It has to be said that the Department, represented by Andrew and Elliott, and the establishment officer (Ralph Fletcher) provided unconvincing witnesses before the committee. Andrew's juggling with the HMI numbers was picked up by the MPs who noted the department's belief that: 'now as in 1956, 500 seems about the right number and with difficulty the work has been made to fit it.' The committee on the other hand thought 'the number should be made to fit the work.' In the end, the

Select Committee did not recommend any figure for the Inspectorate's complement but confined itself to observing that if the committee's proposals for less inspecting by HMI and more by LEA staff were adopted, fewer HMIs would be required.

Bill Elliott, Senior Chief Inspector, 1968–72.

Elliott thought the report 'slight', which indeed it was – the result of a far from exhaustive study by a job lot of back-bench MPs, few of whom were education specialists. There was a natural disposition in the Department to conclude that the Select Committee had been taken in by the LEAs and the teacher unions. Most of the witnesses were drawn from what had become known as the stage army. Alexander's hand showed through – from the time of Roseveare and the Local Government Manpower Committee, Alexander was seen as someone who wanted to move HMI to the margins.

After the report had been adopted there was a final meeting with Andrew and Elliott who took on board a number of the committee's recommendations – Elliott was made a deputy secretary on the day of the meeting – and it became departmental policy that there should be cooperation with the LEA inspectors and advisers. But on the main proposal, the Secretary of State had no intention of giving up his own inspection duties.

This reaction, if understandable, should not obscure the fact that the Select Committee had correctly sensed that there was a lot wrong with the Inspectorate without being altogether sure what to do about it. Had the *Survey of Communications* been published they would have been even more concerned. The Inspectorate was clearly overstretched and trying to do too many things without enough HMIs and without adequate back-up. It had tried to establish priorities but been unable to find the management steel to make them work. The Inspectorate's strength – the varied professional talent and the independent, self-motivating energies of its members – had become its weakness because of a lack of focus and direction.

It was more comfortable, no doubt, for Elliott and his senior colleagues to dismiss the Select Committee's conclusions as of no consequence than to take them seriously. The instinct of senior civil servants, at this time, was to keep Select Committees at arms length and give minimal answers to their questions, so the Department's response was predictable. But it is not without a certain irony that 20 years later, when the Department was casting around desperately to fend off what became OFSTED, turf wars were forgotten and the solution which they offered instead was one based on a small central Inspectorate, operating a system of inspection with and through the local authority inspectors.

Notes

[1] Ministry Working Party to review the functions and organisation of HMI, 1956. AHMI Jack Kitching Archive 2a/24.

[2] Minute to the Secretary and to SCI (Sir Martin Roseveare) from DE, 23 July 1956, 'Inspectorate Working Party'. PRO ED136/949.

[3] House of Commons, Select Committee on Education and Science (1968) *Report, Session 1967–68, Her Majesty's Inspectorate (England and Wales)* 2 vols. Minutes of Evidence, para 54, 18.

Part 2:   Reaction – 1968–76

Introduction

No bells rang when the 'post-war' period ended. The 1960s were the years in which the boom generation, born in the last years of the war and the first years of peace, grew up and spread its wings. Memories of wartime discipline were fading. Child-rearing methods and relations within the family became more relaxed. Whatever was left of the age of deference petered out as social conventions and definitions of good behaviour changed.

Though full employment and the welfare state were still taken for granted, in the background there was insecurity at home and abroad – the Cold War relied on a balance of terror, and prosperity remained fragile as the economy continued to lurch from crisis to crisis. Wages policies in one shape or another had become a regular feature of domestic politics, souring industrial relations and promoting militancy. Devaluation in 1967 was seen as a form of national humiliation.

In the late 1960s–early 1970s, various social developments brought about a sea change in the way people thought about education. Some of these developments were directly related to what was going on in schools, colleges and universities. Others reflected changes in society, the economy and politics which had an indirect bearing on education policy. Exactly how events and perceptions came together to change the climate of opinion and politics is a matter for endless speculation. It is enough to say that the world changed in a variety of ways which only became fully evident later, affecting the education system at every level.

Manners and Morals

The 1960s had ushered in a brief period of sexual freedom between the arrival of the contraceptive pill and the onset of AIDS. Roy Jenkins made his reputation as a reforming Home Secretary, liberalising the law on obscenity and lifting criminal sanctions against homosexual activity between consenting adults in private. Theatre censorship was ended and actors were allowed to use the profanities playwrights hastened to put into their mouths.

Student Revolt

The so-called permissive society brought about consequential changes in higher education – and notably in residential colleges of education which were bursting at the seams. There was an easing of strict rules of behaviour and single-sex institutions gave way to mixed colleges. Universities,[1] too, saw a relaxation of the undergraduate regimen. Student activists demanded a say in how universities were run – part of a worldwide awakening by the student body from Tokyo to Paris and London. Demonstrations resulted in more or less violence according to local circumstances. *Les evenements de mai* in 1968 threatened to bring down the French government. A succession of American university presidents from California in the west to Yale in the east, were toppled. The relatively peaceful English university scene was enlivened by student action at the London School of Economics, Essex and Oxford to name but three.

Universities negotiated at length with student leaders whose members were largely uninterested in the handful of hard-won seats on boring committees which was all their militancy was likely to win them. Some were quick to complain of 'repressive tolerance' when universities were excessively reasonable.

Revolting students made the headlines and confirmed the generally low opinion in which ordinary people held them. How far the demeanour and appearance of the students ('long-haired lay-abouts') contributed to the reaction which followed is anybody's guess. It was, however, notable that student militancy soon fizzled out in the face of public hostility, and by the early 1970s university dons had begun to complain of student docility and conformism; as jobs became more problematic, students lost their appetite for revolt.

Black Reaction

Mention has already been made of the Black Papers[2] and the significant response which they evoked in public opinion and the media. Plowden-type primary education came under scathing attack, along with poor standards and discipline in comprehensive schools. There were calls for a return to traditional teaching methods in both primary and secondary education. The Black Papers were picked up by tabloids and broadsheets alike who sensed they had struck a nerve. The schools were readily available as lightning conductors for the sudden upsurge of public frustration, the origins of which went far beyond education. The media picked up the public mood and orchestrated it. Within a few months, Ted Heath had become the latest prime minister to turn his hand to the modernisation of Britain.

The Black Papers prompted people to ask: 'what is the Government going to do about education'? – a question pregnant with political implications for the Government, the local authorities and the teachers. The media seized on every potential horror story about schools and colleges – especially schools. When headlines turned a storm in a teacup into a scandal of national proportions, the Education Department's conventional answer was to upbraid the LEA whose responsibility it was. The Secretary of State's powers were limited. Edward Short, Secretary of State from 1968 to 1970, reckoned the only power he could exercise directly was to order the removal of air-raid shelters in school playgrounds. Fred Mulley, Secretary of State in 1975, had a favourite joke about the decentralised nature of the English education system. If you were to ask a civil servant in the Department of Education the time, he would tell you it was a matter for the LEA. By 1970 conventional answers had ceased to be acceptable.

Optimism to Pessimism

The public mood swing was obvious – from a prevailing optimism which hailed new school buildings, improving pupil–teacher ratios and better examination results as evidence of success, to a pervasive pessimism about value for money and standards of learning and behaviour. Public opinion changed, but educational opinion remained caught in the time warp of the optimistic 1960s. Past practice had been to measure educational advance by the increased resources being ploughed into schools, colleges and universities. Now this changed and educators began to be asked more searching questions about the learning which these inputs were supposed to achieve. And just as the optimism had been largely emotional, so too the pessimism owed more to the anxieties and neuroses of the time than to any objective evidence of failure.

Public disquiet meant political concern. National politicians had to respond even if the strict letter of the law laid responsibility on local authorities. One era of policy and practice was coming to an end and another was opening. In future the central Government would expect to take the praise or blame (but mostly blame) for what happened in schools. They would therefore need to develop policies on matters (such as the curriculum) which had till then been out of bounds. This would have direct implications for HMI as the Department of Education's professional advisers.

Central Advisory Council

One incidental consequence of this was the effective end of the CAC set up under the 1944 Act to provide for the collective consideration of major policy questions. The Act reaffirmed the assumption that in a decentralised education system, it was unsafe and unrealistic to let policy be the sole prerogative of ministers: rather it required the collective wisdom and professional experience of schools, colleges and local government, seasoned by a sprinkling of great and good laymen and women. The history of education for more than a hundred years had been punctuated by large-scale inquiries and influential reports. The existence of the CAC helped to keep the tone of political debate on educational issues low-key. The Ministry (and later Department) of Education could readily take the political sting out of major issues – such as whether to give priority to the introduction of county colleges or to raising the school leaving age – by passing them on for measured consideration by the Central Advisory Council. The Newsom and Plowden Committees (like the Schools Council, another arms-length body invented to keep the State out of curricular matters) similarly discouraged the Department of Education from having a view on the content of primary and secondary schooling. A major responsibility of the Inspectorate was to service these bodies with information and advice.

But many of the issues which arose under the heading of educational policy had political overtones. Professionalising matters on the borderline between education and politics was not healthy and could not be sustained much longer. In reality, of course, the CAC, as its name implied, was never more than advisory. As the cost of education rose, education policy became a matter of major importance for the Government as a whole, and the Treasury certainly did not expect to be bounced into costly development by a body of non-politicians, however great or good. By the end of the 1960s, both Labour and the Conservatives lost patience with the CAC model. It suited both the major parties to stop striving for a consensus on education and treat it like any other topic of political disputation. They were impatient with the lengthy deliberations of departmental committees and preferred to strengthen the managerial expertise of departmental officials – a wish which was endorsed by the Fulton Report on the Civil Service in 1968. Plowden (1967) and Grittins (1968) were destined to be the last of the CAC reports.[3]

When Margaret Thatcher wanted a review of teacher training in 1970 she set up a different kind of group – an *ad hoc* committee under the chairmanship of Eric James, by now Lord James Rusholme consisting of seven men and women, working full- or part-time, and given a year to complete their work. High hopes were held out. If this could be made to work it could be the shape of things to come. Unfortunately the result gave little satisfaction to the Department which by then had developed its own pragmatic answers to the complex questions arising from a declining school population and the need for colleges of education to diversify and merge. For the Department, the emphasis in the James Report[4] on the importance of in-service training was timely but in other respects it was seen as a largely irrelevant diversion – what would you expect if you turn important and difficult administrative questions over to a handful of well-meaning educationists who, though expert in their own fields, were amateurs in policy analysis?

Local Government Reorganisation

There were also important developments in local government. John Maud – by now, Lord Redcliffe-Maud – had presided over a Royal Commission which had advocated the creation of large unitary authorities for most of the country, with metropolitan counties and boroughs in a few large conurbations. The reforms took nearly 10 years to finalise and carry through, reaching Parliament in 1972. After much political horse-trading, new boundaries had been drawn and education had been located at the county and metropolitan borough level. Jack Longland, for many years director of education for Derbyshire, was a member of the commission and, as Redcliffe-Maud noted,[5] he fought hard (backed up by the evidence presented by HMI) for authorities large enough to handle all aspects of education including further and higher.

A concurrent review of local government management practice in the Bains Report[6] pressed the principle of corporate management on county and metropolitan borough councils. The aim was to make the local authority think and act as a corporate whole instead of as a series of competing services. One inevitable consequence was the downgrading of education committees and increased power for the majority party management groups. Education committees lost their distinctive right to have a national organisation – William Alexander's Association of Education Committees – and their direct voice in discussions between the DES and the local authorities. It was widely noted that the new regime had the entirely predictable effect of turning up the political heat. It intensified party politics at local level and made the confrontation between central and local government which was a feature of the decade which followed, sharper and more damaging.

Economic Crises

The economy had deteriorated in the later years of the second Wilson government. The Callaghan devaluation in 1967 was followed by cuts and austerity measures introduced by a new Chancellor, Roy Jenkins, which included a two-year postponement of the raising of the school leaving age. These restored stability but cost Labour the 1970 election. The story of the Heath government was of renewed struggles with the unions, and eventual defeat at the hands of the miners. War in the Middle East prompted a four-fold increase in the oil price which sent inflation soaring still higher. After three and a half years, Edward Heath went to the country for a vote of confidence in his fight with the miners and lost. Labour returned to power, a hostage to the unions, to face the economic devastation which the Conservatives and the oil sheiks had left behind them. Unemployment had begun to rise among younger age groups.

The effect of all this bad news was to reinforce the mood changes of the late 1960s. Pessimism and defeatism deepened in the seventies, not least among Cabinet ministers and top civil servants. There was talk of a nation in decline – Portugal and Spain were examples of once great nations which came down in the world. Was the same fate ahead for Britain? The eighth decade of the twentieth century was set to be one of the worst for Britain and mark a turning point for education.

Notes

[1] Neave, G. (1977) *Equality, Ideology and Educational Policy: An Essay in the History of Ideas*. Occasional Paper 4, Institut d'Education, Fondation Europeene de la Culture.

[2] Cox, C. B., Dyson, A. E. (eds.) (1977) *Black Papers 1969–77*. London: Maurice Temple.

[3] Section 4 of the 1944 Act concerned the appointment of the Central Advisory Councils, which was repealed by the 1986 Education (No. 2) Act, ss. 59 and 60. The requirement on the Secretary of State to make an annual report to Parliament was also repealed. The *Annual Report* was replaced in 1986 by an annual listing of publications.

[4] Department of Education and Science (1972) *Report of a Committee of Enquiry into Teacher Education and Training*. London: HMSO. Chairman, Lord James of Rusholme. Mr A. G. J. Luffman HMI was assessor. See also Hencke (1978), pp. 39–64.

[5] Redcliffe-Maud, J. (1981) *Experiences of an Optimist: The Memoirs of John Redcliffe-Maud*. London: Hamish Hamilton, 127.

[6] Department of the Environment (1972) *The New Local Authorities: Management and Structure*. London: HMSO. The Bains Report, named after the chairman of the committee of senior local government officers, M. C. Bains, clerk of the Kent County Council.

Chapter 7 Margaret Thatcher at the DES

Hopes Frustrated. A Framework for Expansion. Schools Council at Mid-point. Repositioning HMI. Other HMI Responses: Primary and Secondary Surveys, Red Books, COSMOS, Assessment of Performance Unit.

Margaret Thatcher, Secretary of State for Education and Science, 1970–74.

Hopes Frustrated

Margaret Thatcher had replaced Edward Boyle as Conservative shadow education secretary in 1969 when Boyle abandoned politics to become vice-chancellor of the University of Leeds. Boyle was not happy in opposition. He was too reasonable to be an enthusiastic party man and found it difficult to mount an uncompromising attack on Anthony Crosland's comprehensive school policy because he (Boyle) had also begun to lose faith in the selective system. Thatcher, on the other hand, had no such doubts. It was she whom Edward Heath appointed to be secretary of state for Education in June, 1970.

Shortly before she arrived, Sir William Pile became permanent secretary. Pile had been a high-flier at the Ministry of Education following a regular *cursus honorum*, through the joint headship of Architects and Building Branch, to Teachers' Branch where he masterminded the rapid expansion

143

of teacher training. After a spell at the Home Office he returned to the DES well qualified to take charge of the department where he had spent so much of his professional life. He and Margaret Thatcher made an unfortunate pairing.

The DES was her first Cabinet post and her strength of character and intellect made her a formidable departmental head. But she was intensely irritated by what she found at the DES. She wanted to stamp her own personality and her party's policies on education but could not find the levers of power. To reverse the direction of policy she would have needed to be a lot clearer in her own mind about what it was she wanted to do. In her frustration she came to believe there were two Education Departments – hers and Pile's – and for much of the time she found herself endorsing policies she did not believe in.

Most notably this was true of comprehensive schools. Her first act as Secretary of State was to withdraw the Labour circular calling on LEAs to submit comprehensive plans. The Conservative line was that each authority should decide for itself how to organise secondary education, as was permissible under the 1944 Act. But this did not remove the Secretary of State's ultimate responsibility. Thatcher was a lawyer. Her immediate reaction to any new set of circumstances was to ask what her precise legal responsibilities were, and to limit her actions to what she was legally obliged to do. She could only step in to stop comprehensive proposals if, acting in a quasi-judicial capacity, she found them flawed in some particular respect. For example, some plans were turned down because they involved the closure of (grammar) schools which the Secretary of State believed should be retained, or because they did not provide a proper balance between mixed and single-sex schools, or because they were 'botched up' schemes creating unworkable schools on split sites. A team of civil servants led by an under secretary, Wilma Harte, made the preliminary assessment of each scheme. The final decision lay with the Secretary of State.

'Quasi-judicial' is a flexible term, and no doubt different ministers from different political parties would exercise their judgement in different ways. But by the time Margaret Thatcher arrived at the DES, the comprehensive policy had been in place for the best part of five years and many precedents had been set. Many schemes which passed across her desk had been several years in preparation and negotiated with the DES at various points along the line. Many had been subject to extensive local consultation. If when the proper notice had been given, few electors had written to object, it was agreed that she could not simply substitute her own judgement for that of the local authority.

The result was that she found herself routinely approving comprehensive schemes while remaining fiercely opposed to the extension of comprehensive education. Long after she had moved on to higher things she was regularly reminded that no other Secretary of State approved as many comprehensive plans as she did. It certainly did nothing to endear the DES to her. In her autobiography she described the ethos of the DES as 'self righteously socialist'. Equality in education had become the supreme good and a stepping stone to equality in society. 'It was soon clear to me', she wrote, 'that on the whole I was not among friends.'[1] She took away with her a deep hostility to the Department and many (but not all) of its senior officials – a hostility she later passed on to Kenneth Baker when she made him Secretary of State in 1986.

A Framework for Expansion

Margaret Thatcher came to the DES at a critical time. The Department was about to start work on a White Paper intended to be, as Sheila Browne put it, 'a once in a lifetime' document staking out education's claim on national resources for the next ten years'. It was to be a first test for the Department's newly reorganised Planning Organisation. This consisted of a Policy Steering Group comprising the permanent secretary, the deputy secretaries, the establishment officer and the accountant general. Under this came the policy groups A and B, for higher education and schools respectively, and an unlettered group on examinations.

From the point of view of the Inspectorate, the revision of the Planning Organisation[2] was of great importance. The SCI now held the rank of deputy secretary which carried with it the right of access directly to the Secretary of State, and a seat on the Policy Steering Group. CIs sat on the planning groups. The Inspectorate had achieved a seat at the High Table – the inner circle of policy-making at the upper levels of the Department.

If there was any single change which signalled the altered role and function of the Inspectorate for the next 20 years, this was it. It marked a stage in the evolution of the Department which was gearing itself up to play a more active part in the making of education policy. The Office needed to know more about what was going on in the schools and local authorities. They would need, therefore, to rely on HMI, their eyes and ears and in-house professional advisers. Pile called the Inspectorate 'the dispersed educational intelligence system essential to a Department which operated from the centre without any specific regional contacts'. They were represented in the Departmental Planning Organisations, Pile said, so that 'information from the grass roots was fed into policy-planning and recommendations to Ministers.'[3]

The starting point for the White Paper and its concomitant planning exercise was – as always – pupil and teacher numbers. Demography had been the dominating factor in educational planning since the end of the Second World War. After the post-war baby boom had briefly subsided, there was a further period of sustained growth which continued to 1964 when 876,000 babies were born – the second largest birth group since the war.[4] Then the trend turned down and went on going down till 1977. But to make forecasting more difficult for the planning exercise, the downward trend line hesitated in 1970–71 and for a time it looked as if it might have levelled off.

Demography is a notoriously difficult business – part science, part sociology, part intuition, part crystal-ball gazing. It involves making a lot of projections based on previous figures, yet the one thing which is certain is that any given trend will not continue indefinitely – as the Treasury poet observed: 'A trend is a trend is a trend/the question is when will it bend?'[5] It was exactly this question which the DES had to ask and answer in making their plans for the 1970s.

The prospect of a somewhat smaller school population held out the possibility of curbing the rate of growth of education spending while at the same time budgeting for higher standards. After the massive expansion of the 1960s, the number of new teachers emerging from colleges and universities was rising fast while pupil numbers in the schools were falling. The result was a rapidly improving teacher–pupil ratio.

For decades, the official maxima of 40 children in primary classes and 30 in secondary had been no more than a pious aspiration. There was now the expectation that teacher supply would outstrip demand. There would be more teachers than the LEAs would be able to employ unless the colleges of education were forced to take one more turn on the roller coaster and shed a lot of the places they had just added. If this were done it would provide a way of keeping the rise in the education budget within the 3–4 per cent annual growth rate which was taken as a planning target.

The overall teacher–pupil ratio was about 22.5:1 in 1970. By the mid-1970s it would be about 20:1. If that were taken to be the long-term ratio – and teacher supply were reduced to hold it there – it was postulated that some £80 million a year of the savings which would accrue in 1980–81 could be used for other improvements. Thatcher was determined that the first priority should be the raising of standards. There were long discussions in Planning Group B, of how standards should be interpreted and about the priorities which should apply in achieving the Secretary of State's aim.

Some insight into the way in which the components of the White Paper were assembled was given by Sheila Browne, the Deputy SCI, in a talk to an HMI course in 1973.[6] She and one of the CIs, Norman Thomas, were members of the Planning Group and put in hand widespread consultations with CIs, SIs and others, from which came an HMI recommendation that some of the notional £80 million should be spent on achieving a teacher–pupil ratio of 19:1 instead of the 20:1 which was postulated. This would head their shopping list.

A wider consultation with the Inspectorate produced a longer list of priorities running from measures to counter early leaving to ancillary staff. The White Paper concentrated on the major items – a 10-year nursery education programme aiming to offer 90 per cent of four-year-olds and 50 per cent of three-year-olds places by 1981, renewal and replacement of old schools, more in-service teacher training and better induction, more places in polytechnics. With this would go a cut in numbers at colleges of education of the order of a third.

Sir Toby Weaver, Deputy Secretary, Department of Education and Science from 1962 till his retirement ten years later.

For Toby Weaver, the White Paper was the culmination of a professional life spent in the Education Department, the last 10 years as deputy secretary responsible for higher and further education; he had provided continuity in a time of rapid and far-reaching change. Although closely associated with the Department's past and present, he was one top civil servant in the Department who escaped Margaret Thatcher's contemptuous disapproval. (Harry French – 'my Chief Inspector' – was another.) Weaver was uniquely qualified to preside over the White Paper's preparation. She recognised this and Weaver retired with a knighthood – a mark of personal distinction.

The White Paper was called *A Framework for Expansion*. Within months of its appearance, war in the Middle East and the oil crisis had put paid to any talk of educational expansion. Priorities worked out in the planning exercise survived even though the actual proposals were swept away, but little beyond the cuts in teacher training materialised – there was redundancy on a large scale for staff in colleges of education and mergers, closures and disruption which inevitably affected students as well as staff. The Chancellor's crisis budget in October left all other plans in disarray. The hope of universal pre-school provision was dashed for another quarter of a century. The bottom fell out of school building – inflation wrecked the cost-per-place arrangements and new building (which would have been sharply reduced in any case) was not replaced, as hoped, with programmes of upgrading and renewal.

The hubristic title chosen for the White Paper only served to underline the dramatic irony. The sense of anticlimax presaged the on-set of the bad times of the 1970s. In teacher training, careers were blighted and prospects slumped. But not all the consequences were bad. The brutal process of contraction encouraged the diversification of higher education and a reduction in the number of small, single-purpose, colleges devoted to the training of teachers.

The reorganisation made heavy demands on the Inspectorate. The teacher-training HMIs knew the colleges at first hand and the Office, in the shape of Hugh Harding, the tough and abrasive under secretary who managed the reorganisation with ruthless skill, relied heavily on HMI for judgements about the quality of individual institutions.[7]

There was a sequel to the White Paper three years later (1975) when a team from the OECD carried out an appraisal of the planning exercise published under the title *Educational Development Strategy in England and*

Wales. The OECD 'examiners', an American professor, a French inspector general and a senior German civil servant, had three main criticisms: the White Paper was not comprehensive – it left out 16–19 and comprehensive secondary education; it was secretive; and it favoured incremental reform rather than raising fundamental questions.

When the examiners discussed their findings with Pile in what was called the 'confrontation meeting', he met their criticisms head on: the avoidance of comprehensive school questions was, quite simply, political. If fundamental questions were avoided this was because English civil servants did not waste their time asking questions which did not have to be answered within the terms and time frame of the exercise in hand. And as for the charge of secrecy, he described the lengthy consultations which preceded the writing of the White Paper, but insisted that when the consultations were complete the Government had to take decisions.

One of Pile's *obiter dicta* went beyond the committee room – and was intended to do so. The record states that Pile allowed himself to think aloud: 'He did wonder whether the Government could continue to debar itself from what had been described as the "Secret Garden" of the curriculum.' This was the first hint that the Department was preparing the ground for a more active role. A few months later Pile met a House of Commons Select Committee chaired by Janet Fookes MP.[8] He was asked if he would 'see advantage in having a clarification' of the Minister's role. He replied: 'Yes, I think I would. I think that a situation is developing about which, if the Committee had any views on this, I am sure that they would be listened to. I think that they should take the form of saying ... that the ambiguities that attach to the Secretary of State's position in relation to the curriculum should, perhaps, be clarified'.

Schools Council at Mid-point

When the 1970s opened, the Schools Council was riding high and still enjoyed the support and encouragement of the Department. One way in which this was signified was by the secondment of another high-flier, Geoffery Cockerill, as one of the joint secretaries (1970–73). The joint secretaryship had been established as a 'plum' job carrying with it the expectation that whoever was appointed might look forward to further promotion if he or she made a success of it. Cockerill's HMI opposite number at the council was Robert Sibson who concentrated on examinations.

Margaret Thatcher was the first Secretary of State to accept an invitation to visit the council. A pictorial display of work on projects supported by the Schools Council was prepared. Her only reported comment was to point to one picture of a young male teacher taking a class and ask: 'Why is he not wearing a collar and tie?' The Council continued to commission new curriculum projects which reflected the progressive preferences of the academics who put them forward.

The take-up by the schools of what the Council produced continued to be very uneven and more and more time within the Council was given to discussing ways of making the work better known. One way to improve dissemination was to appoint field officers who would work with local authority advisers and others to bring Schools Council projects to the notice of teachers. As Roy Wake has pointed out, there was an overlap between the work of the Schools Council field officers and HMI – both were in and out of schools offering advice but not necessarily the same advice. The scope for friction was obvious.

Some of the tension arose from ambiguities about the Inspectorate in relation to the curriculum. Though Sheila Browne insisted that curriculum development was not part of the HMI remit, specialist SIs had long been expected to give a lead in their subjects through courses and pamphlets. At a time when there were a lot of new ideas in the air, this inevitably involved the Inspectorate with development questions. Their attitude had to be one of 'discriminating encouragement'; it was not their job to push Schools Council materials; they would form their own judgements of particular projects on the basis of what they saw in practice.

As already mentioned, HMIs worked closely with many Schools Council projects as members of advisory groups and assessors without any obvious friction, especially during the first decade of the Council's life. It would be wrong to exaggerate such difficulties as there were, but Cockerill,[9] who had worked closely with HMIs inside and outside the Council, noted that, though individual HMIs were accepted as loyal colleagues, the Inspectorate as a body (and as representatives of the DES, sitting on Council committees) were viewed with suspicion.

The limited attention paid to HMI in the Council is confirmed by the recollections of some HMIs. In the deliberations of the Council what HMI said cut no more ice than the comments of a union representative – often less. This contrasted with the serious regard paid to HMI in the Department where they were listened to as the main in-house source of informed advice about what was happening at ground level.

Maurice Plaskow, the Schools Council Curriculum Officer who edited the book published after its demise, claimed there were undertakings of closer cooperation given on behalf of HMI which were never fulfilled. The Council gave full access to HMI who sat in on key committees. Why, he wondered, should not the Council's officers have reciprocal rights in the counsels of HMI? He thought that some such agreement as this had been reached soon after Sheila Browne became SCI. There must have been some serious misunderstanding because it would have been unthinkable – and as HMI would have seen it, unconstitutional – to have agreed to anything of the kind. But Plaskow may not have been the only one to be left with a bad taste in his mouth.

Some suspicion of HMI was quite understandable if misplaced. HMIs who sat on committees representing the DES were thought to be unduly reserved and not free in sharing their inside knowledge and experience. There was a certain caution which stemmed from the awareness that what an HMI said in such circumstances might be interpreted as the policy of the Secretary of State or a critical comment on it. The Department, generally, was not particularly forthcoming with the Council: its senior official representatives were reluctant to show their hand – usually because they had no hand to show – and when the time came for the DES to put the boot in there was deep resentment among the Council staff that, when they had had the chance to do so, the DES mandarins had done nothing to point the Council in a different direction. But by then the Schools Council was being wound up, not for any specific failure to do this or that, but because the Secretary of State wanted a new system under his control.

Cockerill reckoned that he was at the Council when it was 'at its zenith' of optimism and enthusiasm. Teachers' centres were spreading rapidly and an exhibition was touring the land. This said, he also noted that the budget was coming in for more careful examination. His conclusion was guarded: 'the honeymoon was almost over ... but any thunder was still a distant murmur'.

Sooner or later there was bound to be a falling out because of the constitution of the Council, which put the teachers' unions in the driving seat. The corporaratist 'partnership' between the Department, the local authorities and the teachers' unions had begun to creak. A powerful professional influence on the curriculum was one thing: union control was another – an aberration of the early 1960s. Looking back Cockerill was aware that there had been a lack of strategy – that there should have been 'more systematic analysis ... and less reliance on the faith that a scatter of good seed would take root'.[10]

But in a sense, the Council had been set up to head off an attempt by the Ministry to develop a systematic strategic capability, not to develop one of its own – neither the teachers nor the LEAs were eager to see the Council take on responsibility for guidance on the whole curriculum. The same inhibitions prevented any serious discussion of performance levels and what kind of achievement parents had a right to expect from their children.

Professor Jack Wrigley, an original member of the CSG who later spent 10 years with the Council providing in-house expertise on research methods, offered a percipient analysis[11] of the strengths and weaknesses of the Council – and why the large sums of money it devoted to curriculum development made relatively little difference in the schools. The plan had been to avoid mistakes made in the United States

> *where a failure of large-scale curriculum development became evident at an early stage. We felt that by keeping our feet on the ground, by organising feedback, by using formative evaluation, by making sure that the work was done throughout the country ... that we should avoid the airy-fairy nature of certain kinds of innovation ... We felt that by having teacher control of the Schools Council committees we had solved the question of participation. This is, of course, not so. A teacher is likely to be more sympathetic to an innovation if he or she participates ... So the question of the dissemination and implementation of the large curriculum development projects was recognised rather slowly and even when the problems were recognised the solutions have proved to be difficult. It has become clear that before innovations will be accepted in practice in the schools, the teachers concerned will need to be involved, will need to have the support of their colleagues, and will need to feel they have adequate resources. The research and development movement took some time before it became the research, development and dissemination movement.*

Behind the setting up of the Schools Council was the idealistic conviction that if good ideas were put into the public domain, other schools and other teachers would hasten to adopt them of their own accord. In this way the quality of education would improve. A study in 1978 showed that a few programmes such as *Science 5 to 13* and *Breakthrough to Literacy* were widely to be found in schools, while some others made very little impact. The emphasis on 'dissemination' was taken as another excuse not to question the basic hypothesis that innovation could be a self-implementing process once people had been told about it. But given the inertia within the system, it was probably unreasonable to expect this to happen. It was an unexamined belief, rooted in the power structure which had given the teachers *de facto* control over the curriculum.

It is not clear that even if the innovation model had worked as its inventors hoped, it would necessarily have been appropriate to the English and Welsh education system, given that one of the most serious deficiencies within the system was the uneven nature of what was being offered to pupils – its patchiness. It is not obvious that scattering seeds indiscriminately and watching some grow and others fail to grow was going to make things better – it might as easily have made them worse.

Repositioning HMI

Meanwhile, the Inspectorate continued to look inwards at its own methods of working and organisation. In the wake of the Select Committee, Bill Elliott set up a study of HMI working methods and collected views from all the divisions.[12] The outcome was to be *HMI Today and Tomorrow* – an official account of the work of the Inspectorate which was published in 1970. Elliott's questionnaire to HMIs strangely downplayed the responsibilities of the Inspectorate to ministers and DES officials, something which was quickly pointed out in replies from the field. The Metropolitan Division noted with admirable brevity: 'the problem is the familiar one: how best to deploy a small – and possibly smaller – force, and how best to limit individual HMI's contribution so that each operates efficiently and the sum of our contributions is as great as possible.' The Inspectorate was manifestly too small to do all that was being demanded of it. But nobody supposed that a substantial increase in numbers was remotely likely, nor did the possibility of such an increase figure in the debate.

Most of the speculation in this and subsequent discussions revolved round the use of HMIs' time. How should HMIs divide their time between territorial duties, duties relating to their specialisms, and tasks which they could plan for themselves? And how much of their time was not being used effectively? Could better central planning improve the supply of information to the SCI and the CIs and advice to ministers and officials? How much should be planned at national level and divisional level, and how much left to individual district and general inspectors?

By now the broad facts of the situation were already well known and the discussions soon became tediously repetitive. The job of an HMI was changing fast but was still based on the regular visiting of schools and colleges to observe trends and assess standards. This had become imbued with significance of its own as a 'pastoral' activity of giving support to client schools. It was at the heart of the traditional idea of inspection because it provided the background of knowledge and understanding on which to base more formal kinds of investigation – be they full inspections or surveys or specialist studies. But it was hugely time-consuming.

There was continuing support for a modified programme of full inspections which, apart from anything else, formed an important part of HMIs' training on the job, but it having long since ceased to be possible to staff full inspections of all schools on a regular cycle, other forms of inspection had to be thought out. The traditional secondary inspection model had never been suitable for primary schools. Large comprehensive schools presented problems of their own in terms of specialist staff. If all schools were not to have full inspections, there would have to be criteria for deciding which schools should be given the full treatment. It was generally agreed that it would not be satisfactory to confine full inspection to schools which were in difficulties.

There would have to be what the Metropolitan Division called 'a considerable trimming of present HMI loads and more opportunities for the contemplative life than the present dissipated scurry permits'. 'Dissipated scurry' is a phrase which conjures up a picture of a less than contented Inspectorate, but nothing is more difficult to recover than time for the contemplative life. What was in question was the time available for HMIs to follow up their own ideas, carry out their own studies and keep up with their specialisms. HMIs were appointed as independent professionals: at issue here was the degree to which they could be allowed to exercise an independent professional judgement on how to do their job. HMIs in the field valued this personal 'space' and resented the way it was being gradually squeezed out.

HMI Today and Tomorrow was the first official attempt to describe the work of the Inspectorate since the full inspection had ceased to be regarded as its defining function. After a short historical introduction, it presented the conventional picture of the HMIs' routine of visiting schools, observing and assessing what they saw, maintaining good relations with teachers – being there 'neither to record weakness nor to reprimand but to advise and to encourage'.

Another chapter dealt with other aspects of the work of the Inspectorate. HMI reported to the Secretary of State; they were available to the Department as a source of information and advice, and acted as a link between the DES and LEAs. It described the role of HMI in further education where 'rapid and diversified development' made it necessary for the DES to rely heavily on HMI for course approval and the control of resources.

A last chapter, written by Elliott himself, touched in guarded terms on the future. It retained a residual commitment to full inspections in modified forms and exceptional circumstances, but made it clear it was no longer practical to work to a regular cycle for all schools. The emphasis had already shifted to surveys and reports on particular aspects, areas and specialist concerns, geared to the needs of policy and current priorities. The key role of the field force was re-emphasised. Visiting schools regularly would continue to be at the centre of the work of the Inspectorate.

Elliott recognised that a new era had opened but the vision of the future which he presented was in soft focus and imprecise. It was not going to do much to raise morale in the Inspectorate. Why did he adopt such a low-key approach? Because he was writing at a time when the Inspectorate was still in a state of flux and self-examination, and would remain so through French's period as SCI until Sheila Browne had settled in as French's successor.

Following the Fulton Report on the Civil Service a succession of internal reviews was being conducted in government departments. One of these concerned HMI. It was conducted by a working party led by Elliott and an Assistant Secretary from the Establishment Branch.[13] What emerged was a discursive document, issued for wider consideration with no assurance that any action would result. Once again the focus was on the use of HMIs' time. This time, the report emphasised the Inspectorate's duties to the Secretary of State – duties which were interdependent with those which took the inspectors into schools; HMIs could only report to, and advise, the Secretary of State on what was going on in the schools if they had an ongoing and confident relationship with teachers and LEAs. If the Inspectorate were to be required to adapt in order better to provide the service which Ministers and the Department required, something would have to give. It was clear that they would have to face the fact that the level of service offered to individual institutions had been reduced and that more of their visits would have to be linked to specified national needs.

Ideally, it was suggested, every HMI should have only one specialism alongside his/her territorial responsibilities – it was not uncommon for HMIs to wear two or three specialist hats – and an Inspector's time should be divided into thirds: one-third for work in connection with his/her specialism; one-third for assigned territorial tasks; one-third at the HMI's 'own disposal'. This expression of the ideal was put in perspective by a diary study (1972) of what HMIs actually did with their time, with questionnaires to all 443 HMIs. HMIs spent

> *41.4 per cent of their time visiting schools and colleges*
>
> *19.4 per cent of their time in meetings etc*
>
> *20.0 per cent of their time in office work*
>
> *11.8 per cent of their time in in-service training*
>
> *0.6 per cent of their time in foreign travel*
>
> *6.8 per cent of their time was available for other purposes (including meetings with LEA officers, consultations with other HMI, consultations with the Office, reception of visitors and travel).*[14]

The survey looked for ways of increasing the fraction of time which HMIs spent visiting schools to around 50–55 per cent, by clawing back some of the time spent on meetings and in-service training. At the same time there was discussion of a nationally planned programme of inspections which would occupy about a third of the time HMIs would have available for visits.

Salary matters also came into the discussion with proposals for an 'intercalary grade' which HMIs had been pressing for through their section of the First Division Association, as a means of creating a more clearly defined career structure. The proposal was to provide more promoted posts to give recognition to, among others, district inspectors. Discussions dragged on through French's period in office as SCI (1972–74) but eventually no new grade was introduced because of the overriding need to preserve flexibility so that HMIs could be moved from post to post – flexibility which would be lost if, having been promoted to a higher grade, an HMI could then only be posted to another job with the same grading. Instead there was an increase in the number of SIs and some additional responsibility allowances.

French was already over retiring age when he became SCI and saw it as his task to bolster the morale of the Inspectorate by going round the country, visiting the divisions in a time of uncertainty about the future.

Sheila Browne succeeded him in 1974. She soon set up yet another working party, known as the Fulton Review Group, chaired by Jean Deas, a staff inspector. This was to look at the 'Fulton arithmetic' – an attempt to pull together all the earlier attempts to get a quart of HMI activity out of the pint of time available. It was intended to lead to decisive action. As

Sheila Browne, Senior Chief Inspector 1974–83.

the new SCI put it, the Inspectorate was 'very expensive and therefore vulnerable, particularly at present; not yet sufficiently accountability-minded ... Its future turns on its ability to discharge a national role'.

Once again attention turned to the competition for time between the demands of the centre and the interests of division and district. The Inspectorate was well below complement and there were difficulties in recruiting enough good candidates to fill all vacancies caused by retirement, even if financial stringency allowed.

'Area Team Weeks' had been introduced in 1972 – time to be protected for district work. The HMIs for a district or group of districts would meet and choose a topic to be studied. The main purpose was to carry out area-based exercises concentrating on particular topics of national interest, using the combined resources of schools HMI and FE inspectors. It was a way of focusing activity more effectively by taking a coordinated look at selected issues, while protecting time for district use. Many surveys and reports were issued, often on subjects which benefited from combined study from different specialist and phase viewpoints – non-A level post-16 students' needs, for example. Area team weeks also provided valuable training for HMIs and were generally welcomed on the ground, though they still managed to attract snide comment from some older HMI who preferred individual visits to schools on their own patch.

One of the 'patterns of availability' examined by the Deas working party, envisaged putting HMI on first call to the CIs, for national tasks for up to half of their time. A scheme on these lines – known as First Call Centre (FCC): First Call Territorial (FCT) – was developed during 1976 and launched in January 1977. A third of all HMIs, at any time, were to be available for work programmed from the centre. This work could include inspection and had priority over divisional and local programmes. The priorities for the central programme were in part determined by what came out of the Departmental Planning Organisation – Norman Thomas, who was in charge of the inspection programme, and Peggy Marshall, were the current members of Committee B – and partly by the Inspectorate's own reading of future trends and demands.

The new set-up became the central organisational feature of Sheila Browne's regime as SCI. It grew out of her hard thinking about, and intuitive understanding of, the ways in which the DES was changing and the effect those changes would have on the relations between the Office and the Inspectorate. Looking back to the origin of the idea, she recalled a meeting when Margaret Thatcher was Secretary of State. A deputation from the NUT came to protest about cuts. Sheila Browne became involved in answering questions about the consequences of the cuts for schools. After the meeting Margaret Thatcher had commented on the need for HMI to be ready with the evidence when these matters arose. The SCI drew the inference then that the resources of the Inspectorate would have to be deployed more effectively if they were to assemble the essential information needed, in a balanced way, and in a form which she and her colleagues could use in their dealings with ministers and the Office.

The new set-up made clear the Inspectorate's first responsibility was to provide the Secretary of State with the information and evidence-based advice required for a more active role in the making of policy and oversight of the system. It was a way of bespeaking the resources in personnel and expertise for the senior management of the Inspectorate, to enable them to respond quickly and pertinently to the unfolding of events. It enabled the Inspectorate to anticipate the future demands revealed by the intelligence collected by HMI in the field. As Thomas, who was closely involved as a CI in managing the new arrangements, put it: 'the process was one of a shift in the control systems of HMI ... The change to FCC programming undoubtedly reduced the powers of DIs ... [and] ... even the extent to which individual HMIs and especially district inspectors worked closely with the LEA'. And hiccups could occur. One

brand-new district inspector for a large county found himself temporarily
with no team of HMI to help him – all were on FCC.

It was a major break with the past, the significance of which was plain for
all to see. It was a necessary change of orientation: the outcome was seen
in the increased policy-related activity of HMI over the next 15 years.
Many HMIs welcomed the greater involvement with policy and the sense
of helping to shape events. But there were also many who felt themselves
ill-prepared for the tasks they were given. It was not always possible to
match HMIs to the particular inquiry which had to be undertaken; FCC
magnified problems of people management and career planning. Sheila
Browne's own comments at the time reflected her ongoing concern for the
Inspectorate's reputation and usefulness. 'The arrangement has made us
less vulnerable,' she observed. 'The size of HMI's contribution as well as
its importance is regularly and explicitly recognised at the top of the
Office ... Past methods of working have not made for a coherent basis of
territorial knowledge ...'

Of course there were costs attached, some real, some sentimental.
Conscientious inspectors could feel themselves pulled in different
directions by overlapping demands on their time. There was less
stability, more nights away from home, more stress. It marked the end of
the myth of the Inspectorate as a loose-linked group of like-minded
independent professional ladies and gentlemen. This appealing idea of
the HMI as an expression of English eccentricity had always been more of
a caricature than a reality but what was real enough was the large
measure of control HMIs had over how they organised their work. This
was much valued but could easily become self-indulgent and had been
under attack for a decade before the introduction of FCC. The new
arrangements formalised the new dispensation. Henceforward the work
of most ordinary HMIs would be increasingly programmed by members
of the Inspectorate central hierarchy. The stress was felt among the DIs
who found their authority curtailed and at district level, where the
routine visiting of schools was affected. HMIs looking back bear
testimony to the resentment many felt when the new arrangements came
into force.

There was a tendency to regard being chosen for FCC as a recognition of
merit which, as Sheila Browne made clear, was not the intention. The
original idea was to work to a rota which would include all HMIs, but
inevitably HMIs accumulated experience when they were working on
national projects, which was there to be drawn upon when other

demands arose. Some HMIs were used more than others. There were always more demands on the programme than HMIs available.

Repositioning the Inspectorate for a new era had been a long-drawn out process, requiring strong leadership and firmness of purpose. Sheila Browne had been Deputy SCI with day-to-day responsibility for running the Inspectorate for two years before she took over from French. She knew where she was going: when she became SCI things began to fall into place and the work of HMI was given a 'coherent and self-conscious structure'. 'Slowly but surely', she wrote a year later,

> *the necessary mechanisms for this have been established. Attitudes are a different matter. There are still some HMI who believe strongly that they should be ends in themselves and that the true inspectorial life comprehends only HMI and the institutions he visits. There are still some second-tier members of the hierarchy who reflect this attitude and believe in their bones that they ought not to be asked to plan the work of a team and therefore restrict the professional liberty of others.*

What remained essential was to demonstrate that the Inspectorate had not lost its professional independence:

> *The system will clearly not accept HMI even in the traditional aspects of inspection, if it believes that the reality of independent reporting and professional opinion has been in any way diminished. Nor, of course, would HMI accept it and it is no good pretending otherwise.*

A final verdict came in 1982 after yet another review of the working of the Inspectorate, the eighth since the Report of the Select Committee in 1968. This was a 'Rayner' inquiry – a review in the series of studies of government institutions carried out under the aegis of Sir Derek Rayner, the director of Marks and Spencer, who headed Margaret Thatcher's efficiency drive from a desk in the Cabinet Office. The inquiry was headed by Nick Stuart, an under secretary in the DES (the man who would in due course play a key part in work on the Education Reform Bill).

Though the report had many minor improvements to suggest, its wholehearted support for the Inspectorate and for the SCI's operational methods was one reason why it took many months to clear with Rayner and the Prime Minister. The first battle was fought to make sure that the tests of efficiency applied would do justice to the breadth of the Inspectorate's functions – the Rayner demand was always for evidence of what good HMI did for individual children's learning in individual schools. The Office – and HMI – were determined to stress the responsibilities to the Secretary of State and the Department for policy-making and intelligence.

After many skirmishes the report went through unchanged in the uncompromising terms in which Stuart had drafted it: 'Our conclusion is that the advice of HM Inspectorate represents a crucial contribution to the development of policies for the education service by central government ...' (paragraph 5.11). 'Our clear conclusion is that HMI advice is an integral and indispensable part of the Department's operations, both within and in support of policy branches and in the strategic work of the departmental planning organisation ... We would point to the overwhelming evidence within the education service, that HMI is trusted to provide authoritative and accurate information, useful advice and sound judgement. As a professional body their professional competence is highly regarded and their advice is widely respected.' (paragraph 9.3–5).

The FCC arrangements extended and made formal, ways of working which were not entirely new – there had always been centrally initiated projects: for example the work done for Crowther, Newsom and Plowden. Now there were to be rather more, and the reliance placed on HMI by the upper echelons of the Department would increase. Annual reports were now demanded from district inspectors creating another organised data flow.

Other HMI Responses

Primary and Secondary Surveys

These should be mentioned at this point because they, too, were part of the process by which the Inspectorate geared itself up to meet more exacting policy demands. Ministers would want to know a lot more about primary education, which had become controversial, and the same was true of secondary schools.

The Primary Survey – *Primary Education in England* – was put in hand before the Ruskin Speech and was published in 1978. It was a sequel to the survey which HMI did for the Plowden Report which had recommended a follow-up at 10-yearly intervals. Planning Group B backed the idea on the advice of Thomas, the CI for primary education. It broke new ground by combining the outcome of an HMI inspection programme (using a carefully constructed sample of 500 schools) with a parallel testing programme by the NFER, using standardised tests. The decision to bring in the NFER was a recognition of the growing need to provide quantitative evidence as well as the assessments of HMI. Had there been gross disparities between the judgements of the Inspectorate and the results thrown up by the tests it would have been acutely embarrassing. In the event the joint design was successful in presenting a complementary database from which to assemble a balanced assessment.

The survey provided a baseline appraisal of the primary scene, assembling a battery of information about the buildings, the teachers, the children's behaviour and schooling, focusing on five areas of learning: aesthetic education – including arts and crafts, music and physical education; language and literacy; maths; science; social abilities, including history, geography and religious education. To enable HMI assessments and observations to be quantified, inspectors were asked to award grades to what they saw: for instance, in mathematics they had to rate the emphasis given to practical activities involving addition, subtraction, multiplication and division, on a five-point scale running from 'over-emphasis' through appropriate level of emphasis, under emphasis, no evidence, to 'not given attention'. (The use of numerical grades came to prominence in the 1980s as a means of giving greater consistency and comparability to inspection reports, but were already being used much earlier.)

The survey found that the three 'Rs' were well taught and progressive methods had not run riot – improvement in language was continuing but further progress would depend on 'developing a more systematic approach'. Science was 'disappointing' in many schools.

More subject-based than the Plowden survey, it looked at the match between the tasks which children were being given and their abilities and found that only half of the pupils regarded by their teachers as 'able', were being reasonably 'matched' in language, maths and PE.15 Failure to provide an appropriate match reflected low expectations on the part of the teachers – this became a regular refrain in HMI reports. They also found that the topic approach was too often conducted with little or no connection and progression between successive topics. The conclusion was that 75 per cent of primary teachers used 'mainly didactic' methods while less than 5 per cent used 'mainly exploratory'. Some 20 per cent were found to employ a combination of didactic and exploratory methods. HMI recognised the benefit which could come from more direct specialist teaching.

The Secondary Survey – *Aspects of Secondary Education* – appeared in 1979. It, too, was a major study, which had taken four years to complete. It focused on four cross-curricular areas in the later years of the compulsory school period and the variety of programmes which were offered to students – 'a number of building blocks ... with very few rules governing their selection and assembly'. The consequences were: premature choices which foreclosed career decisions, and too many soft options.

The schools were committed to secondary education for all but 'there are no once-for-all prescriptions to be sought or found' by which this could be assured. The survey discussed the way teaching groups were formed and the teaching styles which resulted, with particular reference to mixed-ability classes. It found a lack of differentiation in reading and on over-reliance on worksheets. There was a 'marked disparity' between the apparent 'broad simplicity' of a school's curriculum and the range and quality of what each individual pupil received, partly because of the 'a la carte' curriculum which reflected the influence of an over-dominant 'a la carte' examination system.

By way of conclusion, it called for change: 'It may be time to think again. Particularly, it may be necessary to develop a more explicit rationale of the curriculum as a whole ... [and] ... criteria whereby to assess curricular provision and the resources needed to sustain it'. This would include staffing, qualifications and styles of teaching and learning; 'some teachers were operating at or beyond the limits of their knowledge or of their professional confidence.'

Red Books

Over the decade, the views of HMI on the 'curriculum as a whole' were complementing those of the Office, but from a somewhat different perspective. It was important to the Inspectorate to maintain a separate voice and it was a matter of principle that everything HMI might wish to say had to be based on the evidence of inspection.

HMI's developing view was shaped by a long-term study begun in 1975 when Sheila Browne told Wake, until then SI for history, to 'bring together twelve colleagues, six reasonably senior, all able to write, to answer, for publication, the following question: if all children are required to go to school at five and stay until they are sixteen, what should happen while they are there? To what education, at different levels of ability, are they entitled?' A second question went to Brian Kay, starting up the Assessment of Performance Unit: 'How should pupils' achievements be assessed by a nationally valid methodology?'

The phrasing of the questions was interesting – as was the insistence from the start that they were to publish an account of their work. The remit introduced the idea of 'entitlement', which implied that the pupil had moral (if not legal) rights which must be respected. It was another example of her shrewd ability to read the signs of the times, her awareness that accountability would soon become a key concept for politicians and educators.

The idea was to confront the 'whole curriculum' which the now disbanded SIs Curriculum Group had been looking at but in a more practical way. It involved considering some of the issues which would later surface in connection with a national curriculum but its approach contrasts sharply, in methods and timescale, with what would come a decade later. It provides an interesting sidelight on aspects of the Inspectorate's ways of working.

Wake and his colleagues began by looking at the curriculum for pupils aged 11–16. Preliminary research revealed the extent of the variation in what was provided – what one of their number, Frank Makin, called 'legalised chaos': eight examining boards for GCE, 13 for CSE each of which operated examinations in three modes which could produce a crazy 19,000 different syllabuses. Pupils could find themselves transferring from one type of school to another – according to where they lived – at 7, 8, 9, 10, 11, 12, 13 or 14. The system made it absurdly difficult for students moving from one part of the country to another, or even in some places, from primary to secondary education. Instead of simply taking 'subjects' as the unchallenged components of the curriculum, the exercise examined the areas of experience – eg linguistic, aesthetic, mathematical – which the curriculum had to explore and how conventional subjects could be related to these. As Roy Wake put it:

> *Without any doubt, the work of the new curriculum group was viewed with some suspicion by many colleagues – in whose name did it speak and by what authority? When Red Book One was published in 1977, I was asked by SCI 'to find, say, half a dozen LEAs willing to work with us to explore what would happen if its ideas were introduced into schools'. I found five: Hampshire, Nottinghamshire, Cheshire, Lancashire, Wigan. Each LEA delegated advisers to work with us, and their schools either volunteered or 'volunteered'. We worked with 70 comprehensive schools, with another Lancashire group added on by Arthur Clegg. Much was learnt. The basic thinking was done by HMI – for example on 'the definitions of the eight adjectives used to describe the areas of experience: linguistic, aesthetic, mathematical, scientific, physical, moral/ethical, spiritual, socio/political'. The argument to define spiritual was*

the fiercest, and it was frequently impossible to convince schools of its necessity or even of its existence.

Each HMI subject panel was asked to write how it could contribute under these headings to the whole curriculum 11 to 16. (The age range will be noticed: 5 to 16 came later.) Many over-reached themselves in their claims; it was the first time they had been asked to see themselves in relationship to the whole curriculum for all pupils to 16. Red Book Two was a report on work in progress. Red Book Three was an answer to the question about pupil entitlement in the curriculum.

There were many difficulties along the way. The Inspectorate was not organised for this kind of work. After the introduction of First-Call Centre some colleagues were detached from at least half their ordinary work, and some entirely, to join the team and to be attached to particular LEAs. Not all saw themselves as curriculum thinkers, and not all were happy to be so posted. We all saw ourselves as learners; I had had no more preparation for this work than anyone else. Commitment by HMI, LEAs and teachers was uneven.

What was underlined, if anyone needed it to be, was that our school system depends on headship, and that some heads were far more effective than others. The co-operation with LEA advisers was friendly and fruitful, though each LEA always insisted on its own interpretation of the 'philosophy' of Red Book One, notably Wigan. I knew at the time, and I spent a lot of time telling people, that this was the last chance the schools would have of voluntarily organising their curricula: 'Coercion was waiting in the wings.'

Confirmation that Wake and his colleagues aroused suspicion in some quarters came early in the project, about the time of the Callaghan speech when an invitation conference was held at Oxford, through the good offices of Dr Harry Judge, director of the Oxford University Department of Educational Studies. Professor Jerry Bruner and Dr A. H. Halsey were among the Oxford heavyweights who took part.

Judge, who had been head of Banbury School (and a member of the James and Donnison Committees) found the project disconcerting because he thought that HMI was being managerial and trying to prepare the ground for some sort of central intervention. While he found it difficult to disagree with any of the general propositions which were being put forward (about, for instance, the inconvenience caused by extreme differences from school to school and place to place) Judge scented a manoeuvre to promote a centrally defined common curriculum – a suspicion which he found duly confirmed in the Yellow Book and the Ruskin speech. One of those who attended the conference was Auriol Stevens of The Times Educational Supplement who picked up these anxieties and gave them an airing in a feature article.

Wake had, thereafter, to work hard to dispel suspicion and disavow any intention of invading anybody else's territory. He was, as he said, trying to head off the intervention of the politicians but the more often he warned of the wrath to come, the more he was likely to raise the eyebrows of people like Judge.

The Red Books exercise was a major investment of HMI time and effort. It was an extended piece of work undertaken in close conjunction with the schools and in cooperation with LEAs and local advisers; HMIs were the facilitators, the actual curriculum development was controlled by the participating schools and their heads. This was its strength and its weakness. According to Wake, when Keith Joseph received the third Red Book, he commented on the eight years it had taken to bring 70 schools to a consensus about what they should do. He could not afford to be so patient.

COSMOS

Another ongoing HMI activity which had a bearing on school leadership and the curriculum, was the work on school management undertaken by what became known in England as the COSMOS group. It was developed out of work on organisation and methods started in Wales by an SI, T. I. Davies. The group came into being in the mid-1960s after Anthony Crosland had rejected proposals to set up a heads' staff college. Michael Birchenough, its first head, soon moved on, to be replaced by Murray White, a secondary SI and a man who had the inspirational qualities necessary to make the three COSMOS national residential courses held each year, influential and memorable for all who took part.

LEAs were invited to nominate participants, normally two heads or a head and a deputy, plus one participant from the education office, usually an assistant education officer. In the days before local management of schools it gave secondary heads the tools with which to analyse how the resources of the teaching staff were being used and how to balance the claims of each age group and all subjects against one another. Many of these activities were relevant and complementary to the studies initiated by the Red Books team. (Sheila Browne, who had a brief and less than satisfying experience as a member of the COSMOS team in its early days, was one who had doubts about the venture; she thought it relied too much on management theory rather than empirical evidence.)

Assessment of Performance Unit

The Assessment of Performance Unit (APU) was set up under the joint headship of an HMI and an assistant secretary. One of its aims was to look at under-achievement and the way children learnt (or failed to learn). It was announced in the 1974 White Paper on *Educational Disadvantage* along with a new Centre for Information and Advice on Educational Disadvantage.

It adopted a strategy based on 'matrix sampling' – for a study of, say, maths among 13-year-olds, a composite sample of 2 per cent of the age group in randomly chosen schools would be drawn. A comprehensive test would then be prepared, but instead of giving the whole test to all the 10–15,000 in the sample, it would be split among them so that no individual did more than a fraction of the whole test. As with a series of overlapping photographs used for aerial mapping, the composite result would provide an accurate national picture. Some 43 such surveys were undertaken between 1978 and 1988 of maths, English, science, foreign languages, and design and technology.

Reporting the results was a highly technical and lengthy process. But not only did the APU measure performance, it also brought out much valuable information about how children learn and where they go wrong in particular operations. Inevitably it made its own task more difficult by also finding out more about pitfalls in the testing process – for example the subtle changes in wording which can make questions more or less difficult. The APU began to develop an important in-service training function with courses and conferences and published monographs, occasional papers and booklets on aspects of its work.

Its full potential was just becoming apparent when, in 1988, it was merged with the Schools Examination and Assessment Council and the surveys were discontinued. The introduction of the National Curriculum switched the focus of national monitoring to individual achievement.

Notes

1 Thatcher, M. (1995) *The Path to Power*. London: HarperCollins, 166.
2 For a detailed description of the planning organisation, see Sir William Pile's evidence to the House of Commons Expenditure Committee (1976) *Tenth Report, 1975–76 Session, Policy Making in the Department of Education and Science*. HoC 621. 2 vols. London: HMSO.
3 Organisation for Economic Cooperation and Development (1975) *Educational Development Strategy in England and Wales*. Review of national policies for education. Paris: OECD, 58.
4 Live births in 1964 in England and Wales were 875,975, third highest since the First World War, following 1920 (957,413) and 1947 (881,026).

5 'A trend is a trend is a trend. But the question is, when will it bend? Will it alter its course through some unforeseen force and come to a premature end? – attributed to Alec Cairncross. See Bruce, M. G. (1985) 'Teacher education since 1944: providing the teachers and controlling the providers'. *British Journal of Educational Studies* 33: 164–72, especially Figure 1, page 165, showing the birth rates in England and Wales, 1944–83.

6 DSCI's speech to FE HMIs in Bournemouth on 27 February 1973, entitled 'Educational Priorities'.

7 Hencke, D. (1978) Colleges in Crisis: *The Reorganization of Teacher Training 1971–1977*. Harmondsworth: Penguin. See also a review of Hencke's book by Hugh Harding in *Education* on 29 December 1978 (pp 631–33) and 5 January 1979 (pp 11–12).

8 See Sir William Pile's evidence, note 2, 94–5.

9 Cockerill, G. (1985) 'The middle years', in Plaskow, M. (ed.) *Life and Death of the Schools Council*. London: Falmer Press, 85–92.

10 Cockerill, in Plaskow (1985), 88, 89.

11 Wrigley, J. (1985) 'Confessions of a curriculum man', in Plaskow, M. (ed.) *Life and Death of the Schools Council*. Lewes: The Falmer Press, 41–53, quote on pages 45–6.

12 Elliot ,W. R. (1969) *Evaluation of Various Types of Inspection and of Resultant Documents*. (Information Series 10/69).

13 Fulton Review Group (1976) *Report*. AHMI Jack Kitching Archive 2a/44a.

14 *HMI Use of Time*. 1972 diary study. AHMI Jack Kitching Archive 2a/43.

15 Gray, J. (1997) 'A bit of a curate's egg? Three decades of official thinking about the quality of schools'. *British Journal of Educational Studies* 45(1): 4–21.

HMI Miscellany
Extracts from HMI personal accounts

Trevor Fletcher 1963

In Elizabeth House one heard leaders of the Inspectorate saying 'pastorality is OUT'! . . . A phrase often heard from Sheila Browne when she became SCI was that HMI 'should face the centre'. This new view of HMI ran counter to much that I had been taught as a new entrant. Some colleagues were sure that the old priorities should continue and continued to regard pastoral work as the most rewarding aspect of the job, indeed as its essential component . . . There is a place for reports on individual schools and a place for reports on national aspects as well . . . However, as SI in a major subject area (maths) I regarded the national surveys as justifying my job more than did the accumulation of reports on individual schools, important as this was . . . One difficulty in making the change concerns the number of HMI who can play a national role. It was my view at the time that not all members of a force the size we had could do so and it was inevitable that they should seek job satisfaction in rather free-lance pastoral activities.

Jack Dalglish 1963

It was characteristic of the Inspectorate at that time (mid-60s) that individuals to a considerable extent determined their own work patterns. Most worked hard and some overworked. However, a very few took advantage of their relative autonomy and led lives of comparative leisure. There were also colleagues who were, or had become, temperamentally unsuited to the work . . . The work of the Inspectorate was changing radically. Full inspections were being largely phased out and replaced by centrally programmed national surveys. There was considerable justification for this: the system of periodic FIs could be valuable for the schools concerned and for their LEAs, but it did little to produce information useful to the Office and Ministers.

On the other hand, surveys concentrating on specific issues could give a partial and distorted picture. Their results needed to be related to a broader context of awareness that could come only from looking at whole schools, by pastoral visits and full inspections. This was particularly limiting to the insights of newer colleagues who had no experience of FIs and no time for pastoral visiting. This was exemplified when a limited programme of FIs was resumed in about 1978.

Wally Allan 1966

Things improved markedly towards the end of my time, but for many years I tried without success to convince others that this was not a national Inspectorate. General Inspectors followed their own noses and personal inclinations. DIs tried hard to hold together the many resultant bits and pieces; and at the centre there was some synthesis of the evidence which arose from most HMIs going their own way . . . In my early days I was never aware of anyone saying: 'These are the national priorities; these are the national questions we need evidence about; and this is the co-ordinated national planning and system HMI will follow to produce the best possible (and most accurate?) national picture . . .'

Bill Francis 1968

There was less unanimity in judgement of educational quality than we claimed. In the retrieval work on the effects of expenditure cuts . . . I became aware that District Inspectors' judgements varied from one to another and numbers in boxes were suspect . . . No attempt was made to establish norms or priorities; for example, I would put up with a little peeling paint if key staff were retained, but would others? Likewise the numbers assigned to lesson quality, which became a feature of later work, depended more on the observer's priorities than on the lessons themselves . . . What constituted a good lesson was very much an individual judgement on our part. It was assumed we all thought alike. For example, the conventional wisdom in science was that work had to spring from practical applications, but some lesson notes sent in seemed to assume that this was the sole requirement. I don't remember many, if any, returns which included material less obviously practical but taught with inspiration – yet I saw some ... I thought the idea of 'too academic for them' coloured too many perceptions ... More positively, one of the most striking features of HMI was the quality of discussion, which at the best (and I would say most) meetings, was high – usually objective, vigorous, without rancour and honest.

Alan Turberfield 1968

Owing to increasing pressure on HMI, induction was too rapid; for entrants undertaking primary inspection for the first time it was unsatisfactory. District inspectorship after one year was too soon. The earlier two years probation became one. 'Old hands' used to a leisurely pace, found it had begun to quicken sharply as HMI were being called upon to accept more and more national tasks, secondments, roles as observers on committees etc ... Without any real increase in manpower, HMI had to change from thorough visiting and close relationships with their own 'patch' to 'sampling' and much more general supervision of their districts ... The demands to 'discern the universe in a grain of sand' worried all new recruits: though confidence grew with experience, anxiety remained about the extent and depth of evidence which HMI had the time to obtain, even though they were better placed than anyone else to comment across the national scene.

John Slater 1968

It was suggested that in addition to a 'Red Book' paper on history we should also submit one on political education. The result was *Political Competence*. Crucially, Sheila Browne supported us. When the *TES* sought permission to quote from it, her response was: 'Tell them they can print the whole document', which they did, thus avoiding the danger of selective quotation. The publication immediately gave an HMI imprimatur to political education – an encouragement to those teachers already engaged in it but, to those already suspicious of the idea, a focus for their disapproval ...

HMI was emphatically not urging schools to adopt political education. However, based on observed evidence, we knew that much was already there, not just in civics classes, but within, sometimes unwittingly, the teaching of history, geography, religious education, literature – particularly drama – and occasionally, science. As we wrote, 'Everything that is intended in a school is part of its curriculum. Schools are themselves political institutions in that they involve power and authority, participation, and the resolution of different opinions.'

Our 'imprimatur' was soon backed by SCI establishing an interdisciplinary HMI working party which I chaired, with a programme of specialist school and FE visits. Our task was, primarily, to map, and evaluate the effectiveness of, what was happening in schools, not just to educate ourselves but to identify effective practice. Above all, we had to acquire as much evidence as possible to reassure Ministers, which generally we could, on the absence of unacceptable bias or indoctrination. (The rare occasions when we identified indoctrination, our core concern was less that it subverted pupils but bored the pants off them and wasted public money.) Inevitably the involvement of HMI in political education and their assumed support for Peace Education, particularly our supposed inability or unwillingness to ban it, and our refusal to discourage the teaching of controversial and sometimes politically sensitive issues, confirmed the suspicion of the educational right wing that HMI was unwilling to support their anxieties.

Rosemary Peacocke 1970

When Mrs Thatcher announced her firm belief in nursery education, and the importance of this provision for every parent who wished it – there was money for expansion – the CI for primary education, John Burrows, threw a party in Elizabeth House and congratulated SI Elma McDougell for 'keeping the faith during the dark days'. The expansion was small and priority was given, rightly, to inner city areas. Those of us who were optimists, like myself, thought this was the beginning of a new age ... We were to be disappointed. The commitment ... evaporated as soon as the pocket of money had disappeared. My first and important lesson was learnt: most government decisions are finance-led, and however committted the politicians sound ... the over-riding factor is hard cash ...

Visitors came flocking to see UK nursery practice and at its best there was clear evidence that children were involved in their own learning, they were articulate and motivated to ask questions, they experimented with materials and ideas reaching peaks of knowledge and understanding of their own volition which no teacher could have asked of them. There was creativity which extended beyond two-dimensional work, and there was time and opportunity to carry out the work in hand.

Jack Dale 1970

I recall vividly the programmes specially prepared for the ROSLA students, often boys ... The theory of many of these courses, flawed from the beginning, was that such pupils were essentially of a different kind from their fellows. Accordingly they had to be catered for not only by a different time-table but by a quite separate syllabus from other students. On the face of things, it might seem very appropriate to provide a tailor-made curriculum for these reluctant students but in reality the need for such a radical step reflected just how inflexible main stream secondary education actually was ... Naturally, the kids saw through it from the start ...

Peter Armitstead 1971

In primary schools in the late Sixties there was considerable diversity ... Once the 11-plus examination had been abandoned, a set of targets had gone and individual schools and teachers had to exercise choice to an unfamiliar extent. An outcome was an immense amount of time and energy devoted to the creation of individualised workcards ... It called for skills of curriculum design and classroom management that few teachers possessed and was a mode of teaching which even uniquely talented teachers could scarcely manage with large classes ... This highly complex approach, was powerfully supported by influential educationists, including primary phase HMI and most obviously the Plowden Report as well as the overlong Bullock Report ...

Joe Trickey 1973

The work of the Modern Language Committee had a clear sense of direction, reflecting well-informed awareness of developments in the country. The range of courses we ran were themselves a reflection of this interest in practical developments in the subject. I directed ten national 16–19 courses, developing a mixture of lecture and discussion groups into a workshop course with the help of teacher trainers and teachers who were known to me as good practitioners. They were influential on practice in schools and led to changes in the form of the A level examinations, showing how a communicative approach to the teaching of modern languages could be rigorous even without the prose composition. The national courses inspired local ones run by universities and by LEA advisers. The changes were reflected in a publication on modern languages in the sixth form.

Alan Bassett 1976

The National Secondary Survey was, I thought, an impressive exercise. Certainly it exposed the vulnerability of some of our schools but it also showed the strengths. What emerged from a large team, well-focused, was that most schools contained elements of both. It became in effect part of that process driven politically to the league table approach ... *Ten Good Schools* was also a step in that direction. It was intended to offer models but inevitably led many to ask why only ten.

I think possibly the major effect of the Secondary Survey was to make HMI into a much more cohesive force. We benefited enormously from discussing as a large team the particular aspects of the work of a whole school. It enabled us to speak more authoritatively of a 'whole school approach', a mantra of the 80s. I do think it made HMI into a more professional body.

Tom Lilley 1977

Area Team Week plans were agreed at Divisional meetings. The exercises proved a useful means of extending HMI knowledge across the sectors of the education service. The weeks were particularly useful in tracking down the elusive 16 to 19 cohort, some in sixth form colleges and others in further education colleges. The weeks were also valuable in extending HMI knowledge of specialist areas and following up initiatives which extended across the schools and further education boundaries. Usually the schools and FE inspectors would make joint visits to schools and colleges. Typical topics which formed the basis of these visits might include: harmonisation of sixth form timetables; special needs provision; education within the prison service; TVEI; O level courses in schools and colleges; school links with industry and commerce; careers guidance in schools and FE.

David Soulsby 1975

Not long after I got to Newcastle (June 76) I was put on two First Call Centre teams. FCC was a response by the Inspectorate to dealing with issues-based inspection – something which reverberated throughout my career . . . My overall impressions of FCC were: it did enable us to do some policy-related inspection and this aspect developed very rapidly; it was poorly managed, since SIs at that time were not experienced in project management; the careers team spent much time on definitional questions, and on drafting and re-drafting; the work-loads for some of us were very unreasonable, although this was not the case for all teams; there was some difficulty over the coverage on the ground which was enfeebled in order to enable FCC HMI to get on with the centrally driven work. The main professional problem for me was that it disrupted my apprenticeship as HMI so that I had very little opportunity to develop the skills I had learnt in my first year (eg those of inspecting primary schools and of doing full inspections).

Jean Carswell 1981

In the early 1980s I was asked to take on a First Call Centre assignment, monitoring one of the Education Support Grants. Twelve LEAs were selected from 58 applications for grants to support projects designed to improve provision and standards in deprived urban areas . . . My brief was, initially, to offer advice on which projects to select, to visit the LEAs and to talk to their officers, then to meet and discuss the projects with the teams . . . Shortly after the projects were established I was asked to monitor the programme alone . . . The projects were dispersed throughout the country. Sunderland and Hartlepool were the furthest north, with Croydon and Swindon in the south. In between were Liverpool and Leeds . . . Unemployment, poverty, vandalism and petty crime created a setting in which the schools had had to become fortresses in which anything of value was locked in purpose-built strongrooms at night. Teachers were working with children whose families had little hope of moving out of this situation. The project teams were trying to introduce learning experiences which offered stimuli, colour and quality into the children's lives. They all brought enthusiasm, dedication and hard work to their task and I saw some very good practice. Unfortunately, not all were successful in providing long-term benefit, for when the support was withdrawn the momentum was lost. However, for me it was a period when I thought I was doing something very worthwhile.

Tom Marjoram 1966

APU – The intention was to engage research teams and to produce an overall picture of standards of achievement . . . and to identify weakness and strengths, areas in need of help and resources nationally . . . The problems were obvious. There were at least half a dozen ways of teaching reading, 57 varieties of maths ranging from the zaniest 'new' maths to the table-chanting 'trad maths', and a similar 'rich diversity' in other subjects . . . It gave Brian Kay a bad headache. In my view he took the only possible path which was not to check on subject knowledge but to devise ways of assessing 'ways of thinking' common to all curricula . . . which might occur in any subject or lesson: aesthetics in maths, language skills in history, maths in science and so on . . . I still regret that we were unable to get agreement to set up a serious monitoring project of national standards in the arts, music, social studies and physical development, or even to arrange experimental work on the testing of these admittedly sensitive, though also important, aspects of school work. This effectively narrowed the broad national monitoring focus envisaged by Reg Prentice, who set up the APU, to maths, language and science, though eventually limited surveys in technology and modern languages were performed.

Arthur Clegg 1967

By 1983 APU guidelines were laid down and the mathematics, English and science research teams were operating. My intention on reading the survey data was to attempt to digest it and to make the wisdom enshrined in it available to teachers. If teachers could be informed about common errors they could look out for them and focus attention on helping pupils over the hurdles. The APU produced many research monographs on what pupils could do, as well as many booklets for teachers . . . An assessment resource kit on practical mathematics, practical science, and listening and speaking, was sent to every teacher training institution and teachers' centre.

John Whinnerah 1966

In regard to most if not all the issues, it was not possible for HMI to sit on the fence. My colleagues and I had to form definite views supported by clear arguments. These views were the basis of my advice to the Department while at the same time I pointed out that some others might think differently . . .

In general my impression, gleaned from many FIs carried out by teams consisting of some local HMI together with others from various parts of the country, is that at the end of the inspections there was a clear consensus of views about the quality of the work seen, the organisation, the provision for pupils etc. That applied to the Science Committee in regard not only to inspections but also to our general views about the purpose of science teaching, aims and objectives, its content and process, and its quality – what constituted good teaching and learning and good provision. The ground had been well prepared by my predecessor, Norman Booth. He had established eight criteria for good quality science teaching and the Science Committee had readily adopted these, together with the premise that science in schools should include physics, chemistry and biology for all pupils up to 16 but at different depths of course, according to the ability of the pupils. These criteria had been published in Red Book One (together with a list of words – concepts – which should be understood by pupils as a result of a balanced school science course), and, again set out as a basis for the judgements reported in the National Secondary Survey.

Chapter 8   Special Education

Warnock and After

There was growing public concern at the end of the 1960s about special education and the arrangements made in schools and colleges – and in society at large – for the handicapped. The 1944 Act had extended the responsibilities of LEAs for special educational treatment for the 11 categories of disability itemised in the regulations: blind, partially sighted, deaf, partially deaf, delicate, diabetic, educationally subnormal, epileptic, maladjusted, physically handicapped and those with speech defects. For most of these conditions, separately or in combination, there were special schools; the post-war school building programmes had included many such specialised institutions and by the end of the 1960s there were many maintained and independent special schools. Most LEAs had an assistant education officer responsible for special education and there were about 20 HMIs with special education as their speciality.

The 1944 Act dealt with handicap in mainly medical terms – 'disabilities of body or mind' – and doctors were regarded as the main arbiters of need. Special education was never short of controversy. Experts argued fiercely about the teaching of the deaf – reflected inside the Ministry in the 1950s by the contending views of Dr Henderson, the chief medical officer, and James Lumsden HMI recruited as a young psychologist to strengthen the Inspectorate on special educational treatment.

By the end of the 1960s there were signs of a broadening of the approach to the subject. The concept of handicap was no longer exclusively medical; there was a greater awareness of the social and psychological factors. Parents increasingly wanted their children to be educated in ordinary schools rather than being segregated in special schools, if this could be made possible by giving them extra back-up. 'Integration' was the ideal to which everyone had to subscribe. All children ought to have the chance to enjoy the life of the regular school community rather than be labelled and shut off in special institutions. In the context of the time this was an extension of the idea of 'comprehensiveness' which dominated the debate on the organisation of secondary education. And indeed, this was a time when comprehensive schools were recognising the need to strengthen their remedial and special needs provision.

The emergence of a middle-class special needs lobby – a growing constituency led by articulate parents of handicapped children – was an

important development. For most of the time they made common cause
with the special schools professionals, but not always. The special schools
had their own vested interests in the provision of specialised institutions.
The campaigners wanted to avoid institutionalising special needs
wherever possible. They drew support from the irrational guilt felt by
members of the 'normal' public who sensed that some of the places to
which handicapped children were consigned might not bear close
examination.

The change in public attitudes was not confined to this country. Reform
was in train in Scandinavia and elsewhere in Europe, and in the United
States, where the treatment of handicapped people was treated as a
matter of constitutional rights and campaigners went to law to challenge
what was being provided. There were spectacular court cases where
American judges ordered the closure of institutions for mentally
handicapped adults on the grounds that such places did their inmates
more harm than good.

In 1970 Parliament transferred responsibility for children with severe
learning difficulties from the health authorities to the LEAs. The category
of 'ineducable' was abolished and a new set of institutions, many of them
independent, were brought into the educational net. Two new specialist
HMIs, Edith Cave and Winifred Curzon, had formerly been employed by
the Health Department. They now joined the Inspectorate and like anyone
else they had to go through the normal induction process under the
supervision of a DI and the guidance of a mentor, and learn to inspect all
types of primary and secondary schools as well as cover special
education.

There were practical difficulties in integrating Health Department's
Training Centre staff within the body of qualified school teachers. HMIs
played their part with a programme of inspections, visits, short courses
and advice. This became a major focus of HMI activity while the
education system adapted to the change. Not all HMIs greeted the
redesignation of the severely mentally handicapped with enthusiasm –
though it had long been awaited. As Winifred Curzon noted: 'When the
Council for the Training of Teachers of the Mentally Handicapped was
first investigated, several senior HMIs expressed astonishment at the
daring of such an organisation being set up under the jurisdiction of the
Ministry of Health, outside the DES. There was also disbelief that any
progress, especially educational progress, could be made with such
children. One HMI on a casual visit to a selected Training Centre had to

leave, saying it was difficult to stand the sight of the poor children, never mind think of schools for them. Happily this attitude became unacceptable and the Special Education Branch devised special teacher training courses and suitable learning programmes.'

Margaret Thatcher had been in no hurry to act on Conservative promises of a review of special education, but 12 months after the appearance of *Framework for Expansion*, she announced the setting up of a committee of inquiry to be chaired by Mary Warnock, a philosophy don at Oxford who had in her time also been head of a direct grant school, the Oxford High School for Girls. In September 1974 the committee held its first meeting. In May 1978 its report was published.

SI Cyril Cave wrote the brief for the Warnock Committee immediately before retiring and John Fish HMI, who succeeded him, became assessor to the inquiry, working closely with it throughout the four years of its deliberations. He had an office next door to the Assistant Secretary responsible for Special Education Branch in the DES and as he recalls, they were 'constantly exchanging views on problems and policies'. As SI, he planned the programme of inspections undertaken by his team to provide information and analysis for the Department and the Warnock Committee. The Warnock Committee's priority areas were pre-school, teacher training and post-16 provision (of which there was very little). These, along with Warnock's 'perceived stand on integration, dominated the work of the team in the 1980s'.

When it at last appeared, the report was a long and magisterial document with a lengthy set of recommendations for government, local authorities, schools and voluntary bodies. It was a unanimous report – no mean achievement on the part of the chair, seeing that this was a field in which strong personalities abounded. The Warnock Report was influential in the sense that it had mapped the territory in such detail that it became the starting point for all future policy discussion. It signed up to 'integration' within limits. The harder-headed members of the committee were all too aware how difficult it would always be to force the Government and the LEAs to meet the open-ended resouce implications of a commitment to supply the needs of handicapped pupils within the regular classrooms. Resources would hold the key to mainstreaming. (The story of 'care in the community' would show how much easier it is to close specialised institutions than to replace them effectively with alternative forms of support for the vulnerable.)

Much effort was directed towards avoiding stigmatising those in need of special help. The committee concluded that at any given time one pupil in six would be in need of special educational provision and that one in five – 20 per cent – would need such provision at some time in their school life. The intention was to avoid pejorative labelling and to play down the idea that special educational need was something shameful. But it is not clear that the adoption of such a wide definition did anything to alter basic perceptions – in the public mind, special educational need was equated with more or less severe learning difficulties, behavioural problems and physical handicaps. The committee was under no illusion that such perceptions could be changed quickly but insisted that all schools should play their part in meeting the varied learning difficulties of their pupils.

Related to questions of stigmatisation and designation were the procedures by which, under the 1944 Act, children and young people were 'ascertained' to be in need of special education. Warnock dealt at length with what the report called 'discovery, diagnosis and assessment', setting out the sequence of steps to be taken by the educational and medical professionals, together with the parents, in assessing the needs of a handicapped pupil.

Having been set up under a Conservative government, Warnock reported to a Labour minister, Shirley Williams, but before she was in a position to decide what to do, the Conservatives won the 1979 general election. It was Keith Joseph who took a bill to Parliament. According to Fish, the Conservative government was not keen on Warnock. 'Consultation was prolonged and the Report was only acted upon because legislation was seen as a low-cost activity to mark the 1981 International Year of the Disabled.'

The 1981 Act took up the Warnock recommendations for new multi-disciplinary procedures to determine the special needs of children who had formerly been dealt with under the ascertainment regulations. The new arrangements became known as 'statementing' after the statement which had to be issued to all interested parties setting out what the LEA would do to meet a pupil's assessed needs.

One of the members of the Warnock Committee was Dick Woodgate, an experienced head of a residential special school for maladjusted boys. As he put it – 'to work on such a committee was an honour and a privilege, even though one of the first things we were told (by a junior minister, I think) was that there would be no additional funding to implement our recommendations. That was my first introduction to that dreaded phrase "within existing resources" which was increasingly to be heard in school and local education authorities in the years that followed.' In the course of the four-year inquiry he and Fish got to know each other well and soon after the publication of the report, Woodgate joined the special education team of HMI.

Although the preamble to the 1981 bill asserted that it 'should not give rise to significant additional expenditure', it was obvious that the question of resources was at the centre of the development of special education. It was one thing to lay down a new procedure for 'statementing' but if there were insufficient resources to lay on the special educational treatment prescribed in the statement what was to happen? Inevitably local authorities dragged their feet in the statementing process and many children who had a legitimate expectation of being prescribed the treatment they needed, found they had to wait months or years before they could be fitted into the process. As with admission to hospitals, waiting lists were an effective way of rationing service.

There was no easy way out. The local authorities were strapped for funds and in some cases their budgets were capped by central government to stop them spending more. The chaos which was developing on statementing led parents to have recourse to the courts. Had an LEA acted reasonably if it failed to provide a service which a citizen had a right to expect because the Government refused to allow it to raise the money to pay for it? The courts were reluctant to force authorities to spend money they had not got or could not raise, and there was no definition of what an authority had to provide. There were examples of 'best practice' but how far did 'best practice' exceed the minimum an authority had to do to stay on the right side of the law?

Aggrieved parents complained to the Ombudsman who produced critical reports. In the end it took further legislation, the 1993 Act, to set up a new appeals process for dealing with disputes about the provision or witholding of help for SEN, new guidelines on statementing and an official code of practice. So long as the main cause of difficulty was limited resources, improved procedures offered a limited answer.

A joint study by the Audit Commission and HMI in 1992 had summed up the defects of the 1981 Act and its working in practice. LEAs had 'no guidelines as to the level of need with which the school should ordinarily be expected to cope, or the level of resource the school is expected to provide before referring the child to the LEA'. This made it very difficult for LEAs to budget 'because there is no firm basis on which to assess how many pupils will require extra help', or what the amount of the help would be.

The argument was as much about priorities as it was about money. It could be argued that, given the large resources which LEAs devoted to education as a whole, more could have been diverted to special education if this is what Parliament wanted, but this is not what Parliament had said and was not how most LEAs saw the underlying reality of the situation. What they saw was the Government passing legislation which increased demands for expensive services without any serious regard to the local consequences. Few would doubt that the potential demand for special educational treatment – in the wide terms which Warnock used to define it – was bound to be costly, nor yet that there were serious deficiencies within the existing services which needed to be remedied. Expectations had been raised which made it all the more difficult to accept that hope was yet again to be indefinitely deferred.

Woodgate observed what was happening to special education in Dorset and the south-west of England where many independent special schools – some of dubious quality – had sprung up presenting 'a plethora of problems and challenges'. There were many establishments which, for a variety of reasons, 'had been allowed to make a great deal of money and provide a service which was often sub-standard and occasionally abusive. Fortunately, as a result of undertakings given by Rhodes Boyson during the passage of the 1981 Act, there was initiated the system of approval of independent schools dealing wholly or mainly with children with special needs which enabled HMIs to require these schools to meet certain ... standards in order to stay in business. Although this involved many colleagues, including myself, in a period of frantic activity in every part of the country in order to get these schools looked at, it gave me intense satisfaction to know that we really made a difference ...'.

It is a strange episode. Of course the schools were subject to HMI inspection before Boyson gave his assurance and it is reasonable to ask how it was that the worst of these schools had been tolerated for so long? Why did it take a late night *contretemps* in the House of Commons to prod HMI into action? HMIs may not have seen themselves as watchdogs but Woodgate's story shows that when they got the chance to get their teeth into bad (private) schools they enjoyed the experience.

The proportion of young people who received 'statements' was 4 per cent
– twice what Warnock had foreseen. It was those with physical
disabilities, the visual- and hearing-impaired and those with moderate
learning difficulties which were most likely to be found in mainstream
schools including special units and specially reserved provision. Ironically
it was at this time that some large comprehensive schools were closing
down remedial units because of a misconceived reluctance to label those
sent to them. Had the same energy been devoted to summoning up extra
help for special needs as went into changes of nomenclature and political
correctness a great deal more might have been done.

Contrary to expectations, the numbers in the segregated special schools
remained high. Some who might have gone to such schools were indeed
retained within the mainstream, but their places were taken by others
with more complex and wide-ranging disabilities. As the Society of
Education Officers pointed out, this meant that LEAs were paying more
all round – SEN was becoming 'an increasingly expensive commodity'.

When HMI compared provision for disabilities in mainstream schools
with that provided by 'good' – and larger – special schools, they
concluded that segregated provision offered enhanced quality of
education and care. Eric Bolton, then SCI, told the House of Commons
Select Committee in 1987 of his concern for pupils previously in special
schools. There was a lack of overarching policy: a few individual LEAs
had articulated clear overall policies for all pupils with special needs;
many others had not. Special schools were uncertain about their future.
And where integration was being attempted there were often problems –
many secondary schools hived off their pupils into special units and there
was concern over assaults and bullying. Just being housed on the same
campus did not necessarily add up to meaningful integration.

What was clear was that any local authority which was minded to take
special needs seriously was facing what HMI called 'considerable
resource implications'. If it wished to do more than put paper plans in
place, there were costs to be met in providing ordinary schools with the
wherewithal to make integration a reality; there were costs for in-service
training, and for the training of non-teaching assistants and care staff.
There were also implications for initial teacher training.

The 1988 Education Act introduced another set of considerations, a
National Curriculum with regular assessment and league tables to
compare performance – these were going to do nothing to encourage

schools to keep, and provide for, children with special educational needs. The emphasis on assessment made SEN pupils a 'drain, not only on resources but also on the average scores'.[1] This was particularly true in the case of pupils with severe learning difficulties where the Act seemed directly in conflict with the inclusive Warnock approach. There were provisions in the National Curriculum for children with SEN to be allowed to pursue modified courses, but most special needs experts were not disposed to take advantage of these escape clauses and believed that the elements of the National Curriculum could form the basis of the work of children at many levels and under a variety of circumstances.

The side-effects which affected special needs were no part of Kenneth Baker's plan when he introduced the Education Reform Bill. The changes in the way education was financed – the steps taken to force local authorities to distribute most of the available money in the form of weighted per capita grants – gave another twist to the integration story. Not only were pupils with SEN likely to lower a school's score in the league tables, they were also going to pre-empt more of the budget. It was not that all schools were hostile to the idea of integration – many believed in inclusive communities, seeing integration as implicit in the idea of comprehensive education – but Baker's Act quite simply set up the wrong incentives. The economics of schools finance would make it logical for them to take as few SEN pupils as they could and spend as little as they could on them. Ministers hoped, of course, that they would continue to do their best for their SEN pupils – but if they did so it would only be because, perversely, they ignored the market signals. The same conflict of interest could be said to apply to grant-maintained schools – only more so.

Mary Warnock continued to take an interest in the special needs debate long after her report appeared. By 1992, her comments had taken on a decidedly revisionist tone:

> *The idea of a continuum of ability and disability, with only those at the very end identified by a 'statement' was too vague. It was all very well as an ideal; indeed it may have been beneficial in that it may have made children with disabilities seem less a race apart. But as a basis for legislation, especially at a time when LEAs were increasingly short of money, it was disastrous.[2]*

Notes

[1] Adams, F. J. (ed.) (1990) *Special Education in the 1990s: Written by Members of the Society of Education Officers*. London: Longman. Quote on page 61.
[2] Shaw, D. (1996) 'Special educational needs', in Docking, J. (ed.) *National School Policy: Major Issues in Education Policy for Schools in England and Wales, 1979*

Onwards. London: David Fulton Publishers in association with the Roehampton Institute London. Quote on page 77.

HMI Miscellany – 6
Extracts from HMI personal accounts

John Fish 1963

A unique feature of my period as SI was the work of the Warnock Committee, the production of its Report, and its development into the 1981 Education Act. As SI assessor to the Committee I worked very closely with the AS for SE Branch, constantly exchanging views about current problems and policies. Work on the Bill involved working with Parliamentary draftsmen, discussing provisions with Ministers and being present in the House for most stages. The Warnock Committee's priority areas, pre-school provision, teacher training and post-16 provision, together with its perceived stand on integration, dominated the work of the 18 or 19 colleagues in the special education team. Attention turned to more focussed inspections. These included groups of ESN(S) schools, schools for more than one disability and the inspection of whole LEAs' provision of special education. Although further education provision for young people with disabilities was neglected in the 1981 Act, Jean McGinty and Freddie Green made the running in supporting it by inspection and publication; special provision in FE colleges was recognised in the late 1980s.

Peter Wynn 1966

In the late 1960s the SEN field was strictly categorised and behaviourist philosophies had begun their long and (in my view) pernicious reign over the thinking of administrators and practitioners, and particularly medical people . . . It was an important part of HMI's work to caution against the ready acceptance of low standards. I recall the baffled and resentful anger of one Medical Officer when I pointed out that some partially-hearing pupils taught entirely in English were nevertheless bilingual, thanks largely to social and familial influences, and that other pupils categorised as ESN were able to act as interpreters when accompanying monoglot English HMI around special schools in Welsh-speaking areas. In the 1970s and 1980s an inordinate proportion of the time of specialist HMI was taken up with the registration and approval (or more often disapproval) of the independent special schools, and not always to good purpose . . . HMI had no illusions about the unreliability of some of the proprietors and did not mince words when reporting to them; but their visits were relatively brief, inevitably occasional – and nearly always announced in advance . . . Approval could be withheld, thus forbidding the admission of certain categories of pupil. But the demand for places was constant and insistent, as was the political pressure to allow the entrepreneur the fullest scope for business ventures. The result was the continuing existence of schools which HMI and the civil servants knew to be less than satisfactory in social and educational provision. These problems were only finally resolved with the implementation of the Children Act 1989 and the Education (Schools) Act of 1992.

The integration of pupils with SEN proceeded slowly in Wales. The work of inspecting SEN provision in ordinary schools was usually allocated to subject specialist members of inspection teams and SEN specialists became increasingly distanced from the inspection of initiatives and provision where their involvement would have been of benefit both to themselves and other HMI, and to the schools. There was inevitably some professional unhappiness with this state of affairs.

Dick Woodgate 1978

'Integration' was, I believe, regarded by many as a 'cheap option' both in national and local government, and special education, in either special or mainstream schools, as a last resort because it was expensive and because it was 'segregation'. The strongly expressed and positive views of parents in favour of special schools and the obvious advantages of concentrating scarce specialist expertise and resources in one place were often overwhelmed by what some of us saw as 'socio-babble' on the part of the media and others in influential positions. Those of us who were able to compare at first hand the greatly enhanced quality of education and care provided by good special schools with what hard-pressed mainstream schools were able to provide for pupils with identical special needs, deplored this exploitation of some children and parents.

Don Labon 1983

In the late 1980s, during my time as SI for special education, we continued our national surveys of particular aspects of this field, resulting in a number of publications (and follow-up) dealing with provision for the under-fives and over-16s, provision in ordinary schools, teacher training, assessment, support services, hospital education and IT . . . The ERA gave rise to a notable bone of contention over the education of children with severe learning disabilities. The Government's initial proposal had been to 'disapply' the National Curriculum with respect to these children, with the outcome that they would be expected to follow an alternative curriculum . . . This proposal met with much opposition in the field. In particular, it was seen to negate the principle, established as part of national policy and represented in the Warnock Report, of including children with disabilities as far as possible within the normal educational system. Eventually the issue was dealt with in part, but not resolved entirely, by adding downward extensions to the programmes of study and introducing the concept of 'working towards' the National Curriculum.

Chapter 9   James Callaghan and Ruskin

Alarms and Excursions. The Yellow Book. The Ruskin Speech.

In March 1976 Harold Wilson resigned, James Callaghan was elected leader of the Labour party in his place, and succeeded him as Prime Minister. The economic situation continued to deteriorate as the effects of the rocketing price of oil penetrated every corner of the economy. The pound was vulnerable to speculative pressure and unemployment was rising. The Government had a small majority in the House of Commons (which it was about to lose) and its attempts to control rampant inflation were dependent on the uncertain forbearance of the trade unions.

Callaghan was 64 – four years older than the man he replaced. The premiership came as a surprise – Wilson had given no public indication that he was going – the longer he stayed in office the less likely it had seemed that Callaghan would succeed. He had entered Parliament in 1945 from a white-collar union background, and made his way up the rungs of the Labour party ladder with solid right-wing, trade union support – support which he repaid when Barbara Castle tried to reform trade union law. He was the first Prime Minister born in the twentieth century who had not been to university, something he could never altogether forget. He was widely experienced, having been Chancellor, Home Secretary and Foreign Secretary, and his public persona was that of a capable and unflappable grandfather.

Bernard Donoughue who had worked for Wilson remained at Number 10 to serve as Callaghan's political adviser. He was clever and effective on a small scale – this was a time before political advisers had multiplied and the Policy Unit at Number 10 had assumed the importance it would acquire under Margaret Thatcher. Donoughue enjoyed the backstairs intrigue and gossip at the centre of government. In his autobiography he describes how he suggested that Callaghan should focus on education – a family-friendly theme which might capture the public imagination and illuminate his own political personality.

Callaghan wanted to take a wide interest in social policy – education was an issue on which he could mobilise non-political support at a time when public discussion was dominated by the economic crisis. Some were cynically tempted to assume that this is all it was – a piece of spin-doctoring. But Callaghan had been a junior minister in the Attlee government: he shared the commitment of the post-war reformers to educational opportunity; he wanted to give the next generation a better start in life than he had had himself; and as a former Chancellor he knew that education was a vital component in any long-term strategy to equip Britain to fight the economic battle as well as being something which was of value in its own right. He was above all else a shrewd politician. Opinion polling usually showed that education was a Labour issue: he wanted to keep it that way, not let the Conservatives pinch it.

There were other reinforcing reasons, public and private, why it seemed a good idea to focus on education. Callaghan had two grandchildren of primary school age – he was concerned about their future. More publicly, education continued to get a bad press and generate criticism of the Government. For the political opinion formers – especially in London, influenced by the London-based media – it had become the received opinion that the schools were in trouble. The educational professionals disputed this but with a growing sense of disillusion as the system lost the impetus of constantly increasing student numbers, and tried instead to adjust to falling rolls and budget cuts. Dr Rhodes Boyson, a former London comprehensive school head, now a Tory MP, had appropriated the Black Papers for the Conservatives and was pushing his party to sharpen their policy on education – in the 1975 Black Paper[1] he floated the idea of tests for all children at 7, 11 and 14.

Alarms and Excursions

In the early seventies education was never far from the headlines. Four news stories may be mentioned here. First, a Leicestershire high/upper school, Countesthorpe College, which opened in the late 1960s with the deliberate intention that it should be adventurous and try out new approaches, became a natural target for the local press and the local MP. The controversy came to a head in 1973 when the press discovered that one of the teachers had put pupils to work on a sociological survey of sexual mores in the locality. It made an excellent local newspaper story, offering the maximum of sensation with the minimum of solid facts, and it was enough to prompt Margaret Thatcher as Secretary of State to ask HMI to report.

There followed a full inspection which lasted 10 days involving 21 HMIs leading to a report, put out in the ordinary way (which then meant it was issued but not published) and discussed at length with the chief education officer. The report was severely critical. HMI commented on the wilful damage to the buildings and the lack of supervision and organisation which led to disruptive behaviour and a substantial minority missing classes. They also noted the good relationships between pupils and teachers, and praised the quality of some of the teaching. While the HMI report was carefully constructed to be fair to the good things as well as the bad, the impression the public at large gained was that the school had been hauled over the coals. It had an effect wider than the LEA itself not least in its implicit message that curricular experiments and classroom approaches had to be properly thought through, and pupil discipline maintained. It could also be said to have been an intensive learning experience for the senior HMIs involved – opening their eyes to the socio-political experiments which were taking place in schools.

Second, a book appeared in the autumn of 1975 by three lecturers at the North London Polytechnic[2] attacking the influence of left-wing teachers and students and alleging political bias in the teaching of such subjects as sociology and economics. The polytechnic had got into a bad way with dissension among the staff which was beyond the power of the Director to bring under control. The book – which an imaginative publisher had given the emotive title *Rape of Reason* – was written with more passion than objectivity but nevertheless made a big impression because it produced evidence to support the prevailing low opinion of students and teachers (there was a general assumption the 'polytechnocracy' was very left wing). It linked malpractice with left-wing politics and put Caroline Cox on the first step of the political ladder which would eventually take her to the House of Lords as a radical right-wing life peer. She and John Marks became zealous pamphleteers on educational topics for right-wing think tanks.

Third, Professor Neville Bennett of Lancaster University published a book on primary education in 1975 which sought to compare the effectiveness of different ways of teaching. *Teaching Styles and Pupil Progress* looked at classes and their teachers, grouping them with the most 'Plowden-type' progressive classes at one end of the scale and the most formal at the other. He then set the pupils' performance in achievement tests against the style of teaching, class by class. Pupils in more formal classes showed up favourably alongside those in the most progressive.[3]

The research was more sophisticated than a brief summary might suggest but, given the public mood, the conclusions which the media drew were simple – that progressive methods were short-changing children. The research was widely reported – in papers which would never ordinarily cover educational research, as well as in the educational press – because it appeared to give research support to the reaction against informal teaching methods. Like the book about the North London Polytechnic, it told people what they were hoping to hear. To the gut prejudice of the public bar, the saloon bar was now offered the luxury of research confirmation.

A few years later Bennett published a second report on his research, and having reworked his material concluded that his earlier findings were somewhat misleading. Not surprisingly, his second thoughts did not receive as much attention as his first.

The fourth episode was the most significant and influential: it showed that when progressive educational ideas are joined with left-wing politics, they could produce a peculiarly explosive mixture. In the summer of 1975, six months before Callaghan became Prime Minister, staff at a north London primary school, William Tyndale, were in conflict about teaching methods and organisation. The head effectively set aside his leadership responsibilities and turned the running of the school over to his colleagues acting as a self-governing collective. The regular curriculum was in abeyance and pupils were allowed to choose what and whether to learn.

William Tyndale was an inner city school serving a socially disadvantaged community and there were real difficulties to overcome which would, in any circumstances, have taxed the skills of a united and well-led staff. As it was in the summer of 1975, it became a *cause célèbre*, the consequences of which extended far beyond north London.[4] When eventually the Inner London Education Authority (ILEA) decided to become involved and send in their inspectors, the teachers refused to admit them, blaming all the school's troubles on the managers' failure to give the school the support it deserved. The key members of the staff were suspended and the inspection took place in their absence after which the school was reconstituted under a different head and new teachers and the ILEA asked a QC, Robin Auld, to conduct a public inquiry.

Concern about William Tyndale had been routinely reported by HMI to the ILEA but when the crisis occurred HMI were not directly involved. Arguably a full inspection by HMI at an earlier stage might have defused the situation and revealed to the managers and to the authority the need to take action to prevent the school from coming to grief. But this was not how it had seemed to Sheila Browne and her senior colleagues who argued, quite correctly, that the ILEA had their own highly professional inspectors (headed by a former senior HMI) and competent administrators. The root cause of the trouble at Tyndale, in her view, was political.

Auld's report appeared in July 1976.[5] It was extremely critical of the teachers, the managers and the ILEA – the teachers for the way they had mismanaged the school, excluded and alienated parents and obstructed the managers; the managers for leaking confidential matters to the press when unable to get satisfaction from the ILEA; the ILEA for ceding authority to the managers and through them to the teachers, without 'having set up a framework of school governance which could deal with extreme events such as those at Tyndale'.[6] His conclusion emphasised that an education authority's responsibility could be delegated but could not be abdicated – what children were taught or not taught remained the responsibility of the authority.

The fall-out from Tyndale was extensive. It contributed to the general sense that education was in trouble: if teachers and local politicians could behave as badly as this, there must be something rotten at the core. More specifically it pointed up the ambiguities at the heart of the system. If the ILEA could not evade its responsibility, what about that of the Secretary of State? Section 1 of the 1944 Act made him the person under whose 'control and direction' LEAs operated. Was it not up to him to make sure they executed 'the national policy for providing a varied and comprehensive educational service'?

The Yellow Book

Soon after taking over as Prime Minister, Callaghan set up a series of meetings with his departmental ministers as a way of getting into his stride. The first of these was with Fred Mulley, his Secretary of State for Education. At the meeting he broached the idea of a major education initiative and sent him away with a set of questions for the DES and a request for a memorandum spelling out the answers. Mulley returned to the Office with the Prime Minister's succinct message that he was to get a grip on education.

The Department's response took the form of a photocopied document running to 60-odd pages, with a yellow cover bearing the title *School Education in England: Problems and Initiatives*. It was dated July 1976. Two months earlier, William Pile had been moved to the Inland Revenue and succeeded as permanent secretary by James Hamilton from the Cabinet Office. Hamilton was an engineer, the civil servant most directly concerned with the building of the Anglo-French supersonic aircraft, Concorde. It was assumed that he was sent in to brace the DES for the demands which would be made on it by the Callaghan initiative and begin the task of reorientation.

He found the Department of Education a difficult place to come to terms with. He was a Scot and inclined (at first, at least) to suppose that what could be done in Scotland – where what the Scottish Education Department said, went – ought to be possible south of the border. This early misapprehension also coloured his view of the Inspectorate. The Scottish Inspectorate was a powerful body with its own authoritative tradition. It ran the secondary examination system. Its senior members slipped easily across into top jobs in the Scottish Education Department. Hamilton found it hard to understand when Sheila Browne insisted on distinguishing clearly between what the Inspectorate should and would do and what it should not and would not do. On one occasion, at a meeting attended by ministers, his irritation led to a famous clash between them.

The task of putting together a DES response fell to a group headed by John Hudson, the deputy secretary responsible for the Schools Branches inside the DES. Richard Bird, who had joined the Department from the Ministry of Transport a few years earlier, had become head of the new Schools Branch III in October 1975. The new branch had been formed to look after curriculum and examinations, a deliberate move to strengthen the department's capacity to take a more active role in the curriculum debate. The Prime Minister's request for a memorandum was an early vindication of the Department's forward planning.

The Yellow Book was a departmental document. There was a major contribution from the SCI and the CIs. If the document was going to say anything about what was happening on the ground, the main professional source of information had to be HMI. But the drafting was the Office's and, although outside it was widely regarded as an expression of the HMI view, it was more accurate to say it was a DES view which drew heavily on HMI.

The report was classified as 'For Official Use Only' – intended for the Prime Minister's Office and for internal use in the DES, but copies were later leaked to the *Guardian* and *The Times Educational Supplement* on the eve of the Ruskin College speech in October.[7]

The Prime Minister had asked to be told about: (a) the basic approach to teaching the three Rs (b) the curriculum for older children in comprehensive schools (c) the examination system and (d) the general problem of 16–19-year-olds who had no prospect of going on to higher education.

A brief historical introduction drew attention to past achievements such as the expansion of the education system, the raising of the school leaving age to 15 in 1947 and 16 in 1973–74, and the decade of reorganisation which the secondary schools had passed through. Turning to primary education, it noted that 'the press and the media, reflecting a measure of genuine public concern, as well as some misgivings within the teaching profession, are full of complaints about the performance of the schools.' The criticisms 'most commonly heard' concerned a lack of discipline and application, a failure to achieve satisfactory results in English and mathematics which the authors attributed to the changes in teaching methods recently endorsed by the Plowden Committee, and the 'child-centred approach' adopted to a varying extent by many teachers.

'In the right hands' this approach was capable of producing admirable results. 'Unfortunately these newer and freer methods could prove a trap for less able and experienced teachers.' The time had come, the Department believed, 'for a corrective shift of emphasis'. HM Inspectors had for some time stressed the need to make teachers conscious of 'the importance of a systematic approach'.

The criticisms of secondary schools were more diverse. These schools, too, were said to have become too easy-going, demanding too little work and inadequate standards in formal subjects. English and mathematical skills were most frequently criticised by employers and others. Some schools had allowed pupils to choose 'unbalanced and not particularly profitable' subject combinations and to 'opt in numbers insufficient for the country's needs for scientific and technological subjects'.

Observing that, in spite of these criticisms, 'examinations had held up very well', the Yellow Book listed other relevant factors – the demands of a plural society, the time taken to adjust to the raising of the leaving age to 16, the aftermath of comprehensive reorganisation. The last point drew a frank admission that there were 'currently weaknesses in secondary schools' some of which were 'by-products of the change to comprehensive education'. These made it necessary to work out new forms of internal organisation and curriculum and 'faced existing teachers, whose previous experience had been in teaching only part of the whole ability range, with difficult problems of professional adjustment. We are probably over the worst of the teething problems ...'.

There was a shortage of teachers in important specialisms like mathematics, physics and handicrafts. 'In the less definable qualities of skill and personality, while the best teachers are up to very high standards, the average is probably below what used to be expected in, for example, a good grammar school.' Some teachers, according to the memorandum, 'responding to the mood of the country', had over-emphasised social aims at the expense of economic. Here, as in the primary schools, the time might be ripe for a change.

There were concerns, too, about the mix of subjects pupils were choosing – for example the poor showing of modern languages and the physical sciences. 'The time has probably come to try to establish generally accepted principles for the composition of the secondary curriculum for all pupils, that is to say a "core curriculum".' This would also deal with problems arising from pupil mobility. 'Extensive consideration and consultation will be needed before a core curriculum could be introduced.'

More rigour without damaging 'the real benefits of the child-centred developments' was needed in the teaching of the three Rs. For older secondary pupils there needed to be more linked courses with further education and more opportunities for work experience. The Department and the Inspectorate had doubts about the Certificate of Extended Education which was being proposed by the Schools Council. As for the proposal to replace GCE and CSE with a new common examination, the aim was good but the Department had reservations shared by important sectors of the educational world.

It was clear that Callaghan's questions about 16–19 had landed in the heavily mined no-mans-land between the DES and the nascent MSC. All the DES could do was make a veiled plea for the power (already enjoyed by the MSC) to make specific grants to LEAs. (The DES was not merged with the Department of Employment till 1995.)

Two other sections of the report were particularly significant. The first concerned the Schools Council. By its terms of reference, the Council was to 'keep under review the curricula, teaching methods and examinations in schools, including the organisation of schools so far as it affects their curricula'. In the view of the Department it had performed indifferently.

Despite some good quality staff work, the overall performance of the Schools Council has, in fact, both on curriculum and examinations, been mediocre. Because of this, and because the influence of the teachers' unions had led to an increasingly political flavour – in the worst sense of the word – in its deliberations, the general reputation of the Schools Council has suffered a considerable decline over the last few years.

The second made it clear just how strongly the Department's hopes were pinned on HMI.

> *The Inspectorate is without doubt the most powerful single agency to influence what goes on in schools, both in kind and in standard.*

This was seen by Sheila Browne as pitching it a bit strong – a grandiose claim which could do HMI no favours. The memorandum then listed the Inspectorate's activities: inspection 'in its various forms', liaison with chief education officers and LEA administrators, publications, courses, assessorships and involvement in initial teacher training. Through these activities HMI were addressing the matters on the Prime Minister's list, as for instance in the Primary and Secondary Surveys which the Inspectorate had already put in hand.

The last paragraph was a plea for a more direct mandate to intervene.

> *It will also be good to get on record from Ministers and in particular from the Prime Minister an authoritative pronouncement on the division of responsibility for what goes on in school, suggesting that the Department should give a firmer lead ... Such a pronouncement would have to respect legitimate claims made by teachers as to the exercise of their professional judgement, but it should firmly refute any argument – and this is what they have sought to establish – that no one except teachers has any right to any say in what goes on in schools. The climate for a declaration on these lines may in fact now be relatively favourable. Nor need there be any inhibition for fear that the Department could not make use of enhanced opportunity to exercise influence over curriculum and teaching methods: the Inspectorate would have a leading role to play in bringing forward ideas in these areas and is ready to fulfil that responsibility.*

The memorandum was the Department's defence in the face of the implied criticism reflected in the Prime Minister's initiative. Donoughue's low opinion of the DES was shared elsewhere in Whitehall and in his capacity of backstairs intriguer and string-puller he had managed to hint to the SCI and at least one other key DES official that they had to come up with a satisfactory response or their jobs would be on the line. Neither was intimidated.

The Yellow Book was also the Department's bid for power: it was eager to seize the opportunities which might follow the Prime Minister's initiative. A new chapter was opening in which the old conventions were going to be replaced by new. Now was the DES's chance to emerge from the shadows and become a department which did things and made things happen, instead of leaving all the interesting work to the LEAs.

By putting HMI forward as the single most powerful agency to influence what went on in schools the Department was implicitly acknowledging its own limitations. As Sheila Browne told Anne Corbett (*Times Educational Supplement*, 29 November 1974) because the Department lacked legal powers it could only turn to the indirect influence of the Inspectorate and even this was qualified by an important and unequivocal statement from the Inspectorate rejecting any coercive intent on their part. There would be 'no exercise of power', the Yellow Book insisted, 'in this search for improvement; the Inspectorate, by tradition, exerts influence by the presentation of evidence and by advice'.

The Yellow Book concealed the extent to which the Inspectorate was under strength and overstretched to perform the duties already assigned to it, let alone the increased activities foreshadowed in the final paragraph. It made no attempt to pick up threads from the Select Committee Report by mooting the possibility of combining in some more formal and coordinated way with the local inspectors and advisers.

Why was the Yellow Book classified and not published? It is difficult to see what damage would have followed from putting it in the public domain. The main reason seems to have been the conventions of Civil Service secrecy which predisposed officials and their ministers to keep their hands close to their chest. It certainly would have caused a flutter in the dovecots – the LEAs and the teachers' unions would have been hostile – but this would only have caused Callaghan's speech to make more of a stir when he came to deliver it. If Donoughue and Callaghan had correctly interpreted public opinion, there would be wide support for a populist challenge to the professionals. But caution – and bureaucratic custom – prevailed and the Yellow Book (like the Board of Education's wartime Green Book) was quite unnecessarily withheld from public view.

Needless to say, the attack on the Schools Council produced a fierce come-back from Sir Alex Smith, chairman of the Schools Council, who dashed off an angry letter to Callaghan: if the DES had criticisms of the Council why had these not been raised with him and the rest of the Council – the Department was represented in its institutions and had every opportunity to speak up? As for HMI, what had 'this most powerful single agency, with a major commitment to improving the performance of the system' been up to while the weaknesses revealed in the memorandum had been developing? Both were good questions.

James Callaghan, Prime Minister, laying the foundation stone for a new
building at Ruskin College, October 18 1976.

The Ruskin Speech

The occasion for the speech was a visit by the Prime Minister on October 18
1976, to his friend, Billy Hughes, at Ruskin College, the trade union-
supported adult residential college at Oxford where many senior union
leaders had studied social sciences as mature students. The speech had been
much hyped in advance as an important, perhaps even a ground-breaking,
statement about government education policy. Things were never going to
be quite the same after Callaghan had spoken. Nor were they.

Callaghan struck a populist note at the outset as the plain man daring to
have views about education and sniping at teachers who thought it
wrong for anyone but professionals to lay profane hands on their
curriculum. 'There is nothing wrong with non-educationalists, even a
Prime Minister talking about ... [education] ... I take it that no one claims
exclusive rights in this field. Public interest is strong and will be satisfied.
It is legitimate. We spend £6 billion a year on education ...'.

In recent months he had visited a number of schools and 'first, let me say,
so there should be no misunderstanding,' he had been impressed by the
enthusiasm and dedication of the teachers and the variety of the courses
on offer in comprehensive schools. 'But I am concerned ... to find
complaints from industry that new recruits from schools sometimes do
not have the basic tools to do the job that is required'.

> *There is ... unease felt by parents and teachers about new informal methods of teaching*
> *which seem to produce excellent results when they are in well-qualified hands but are*
> *much more dubious in their effects when they are not. They seem to be best accepted, if*
> *I may judge from my own experience, where there are strong parent–teacher links.*

There is little wrong with the range and diversity of our courses. But is there sufficient
thoroughness and depth in those required in after life to make a living?
These are proper subjects for discussion and debate. And it should be a rational debate
based on facts. My remarks are not a clarion call to Black Paper prejudices. We all
know those who claim to defend standards but who in reality are simply seeking to
defend old privileges and inequalities.
It is not my intention to become enmeshed in such problems as whether there should be
a basic curriculum with universal standards – although I am inclined to think that
there should be – nor about other issues on which there is a divided professional
opinion such as the position and role of the Inspectorate ... To the critics I would say
that we must carry the teaching profession with us. They have the expertise and they
have the professional approach. To the teachers I would say that you must satisfy the
parents and industry ... For if the public is not convinced then the profession will be
laying up trouble for itself in the future.

He argued for a curriculum which did more to prepare young people for
future employment without becoming narrow and neglecting the wider
aims of education. It was no use looking for 'further increased resources'
– the challenge was to look at priorities and 'secure as high efficiency as
you can by the skilful use of the £6 billion of existing resources'.

He concluded by repeating his concern about improving relations
between education and industry and his concern about 'the methods and
aims of informal instruction'. He reckoned there was a strong case for 'the
so-called core curriculum of basic knowledge' and hinted at monitoring
the use of resources in order to maintain standards. He wondered what
might be 'the role of the Inspectorate in relation to national standards and
their maintenance'.

It was an interesting speech, some of it clearly based on the material
which the DES had supplied him, some of it equally clearly from sources
quarried independently by Donoughue, some of it echoing the Black
Paper critics he tried so hard to disown. There was certainly a feed into
the speech from the Board of Trade where Anne Mueller, a senior official,
chaired an inter-departmental committee[8] looking at the social and
cultural influences which were relevant to industrial and commercial
productivity – the kind of questions Martin Wiener and Correlli Barnett
had raised about the anti-industrial attitudes which caused university
students to prefer academic life or the Civil Service to jobs in industry and
commerce.

The speech put a number of balls in the air which ministers would juggle
with in the 11 years which divides the Ruskin speech from Kenneth

Baker's Education Reform Bill. There is nothing in Callaghan's speech which could be linked to the Conservatives' later attempt to unloose market forces in education, nor yet to their desire to give schools the chance to break away from LEA control. But he succeeded in putting down markers – his views about informal primary education became part of a new consensus like his wish to bring the content of education back into the public domain. His tentative thoughts about a national 'core curriculum' resonated politically and professionally. So too did his emphasis on preparation for employment.

The references to the Inspectorate are much more circumspect than the Yellow Book might have suggested. The future of the Inspectorate is included among the open questions at the end. Earlier there had been mention of 'other issues on which there is divided professional opinion such as the position and role of the Inspectorate' – an echo perhaps of the suggestions from the teachers' unions at the time of the Select Committee that the Inspectorate could be cut back because the teachers had 'come of age'. This somewhat less than enthusiastic endorsement of HMI suggests a canny political reluctance to lurch from one kind of professional control to another. Alex Smith was not the only one to spot the tinge of irony in the claims made by the Department on behalf of the Inspectorate. The educational world was well aware that HMIs had been at the forefront of the 'progressive' primary movement, and that the Inspectorate had supported the messages put out by the Plowden Report. Of this, the Yellow Book had wisely chosen to say nothing.

In reality, of course, to say 'the Inspectorate had supported the messages put out by Plowden' is an oversimplification – not all HMIs shared the same views – there were probably many who rejected the philosophical confusion which underlay the Plowden view of childhood attacked by Richard Peters and others in *Perspectives on Plowden.* Even so, they may, at the same time, have been favourably impressed by the many schools which made a success of informal methods – it was HMI who helped to choose the schools which Plowden visited, pointing them in the direction of what was then taken to be good practice. But this is not necessarily inconsistent with the subsequent doubts expressed in the Yellow Book with 10 more years of experience on which to base judgement. All such judgements, as Sheila Browne was wont to insist, were, to some extent, contingent and tentative professional assessments of a particular situation at a particular time.

Notes

1 Cox, C. B., Boyson, R. (eds) (1975) *Black Paper 1975: The Fight for Education*. London: Dent.
2 Jacka, K., Cox, C., Marks, J. (1975) *Rape of Reason: The Corruption of the Polytechnic of North London*. Enfield: Churchill Press Ltd.
3 Bennett, N. (1976) *Teaching Styles and Pupil Progress*. London: Open Books.
4 See also Gretton, J., Jackson, M. (1976) *William Tyndale: Collapse of a School – or a System?* London: George Allen & Unwin Ltd. Ellis, T., McWhirter, J., McColgan, D., Haddow, B. (1976) *William Tyndale: The Teachers' Story*. London: Writers and Readers Publishing Cooperative.
5 Auld, R., QC (1976) *The William Tyndale Junior and Infants Schools: Report of the Public Inquiry into the Teaching, Organisation and Management of the William Tyndale Junior and Infant Schools, Islington, London, N1*. London: ILEA.
6 Riley, K. A. (1998) *Whose School is it Anyway?* London: The Falmer Press. Quote on page 44.
7 A speech delivered by the Prime Minister, who laid a foundation stone for a new hall of residence, at Ruskin College, Oxford, on Monday, 18 October 1976. The Yellow Book appeared in *The Times Educational Supplement* on Friday, 15 October 1976, and a copy is held by the London University Institute of Education Library (o/s Ral GRE). The Ruskin speech is reproduced in Ahier, J., Cosin, B., Hales, M. (eds.) (1996) *Diversity and Change: Education, Policy and Selection*. London: Routledge.
8 Mueller, A. E. (1976) 'Industry, education and management', a Department of Industry discussion document dated 1976.

HMI Miscellany

Extracts from HMI personal accounts

Sheila Browne 1961

Yellow Book

There would never have been so much fuss about this, had it not been 'leaked' in near final form shortly before the Ruskin speech. It was a pity also that the Permanent Secretary chose to dress the thing up with a yellow cover, thus dignifying a pretty routine series of comments with a solemn identity that was all too easy to refer to.

We are talking about an essentially Office transaction. Number 10 asked the Minister for answers to a series of questions within a comparatively short time scale. Both questions and answers were classified Confidential. The Office composed the answers, at Dep Sec and Under Secretary level, drawing as they chose on sources of information, including probably HMI in the Office, without specifying the context. I was present at various discussions of the text round the Secretary's table and eventually with Ministers. The writing was not as some claim frantic or frenetic but very, very careful. The Office was visibly serving its Minister first and foremost. It was increasingly apparent that the document would have to have an appendix setting out what the Department thought could be done about those things which it was describing as not good enough. It was at that stage that Bernard Donoughue visited the Department and after a meeting at which I was present tried to put me on warning that the answers had better be right – or else.

My role in the meetings of the Yellow Book and its appendix was the classic HMI one. I was expected to speak up if HMI had evidence which would show that the facts or opinions in the draft could not be supported, and it was for me to say whether the Inspectorate was able properly to assume the role politicians – and some bits of the Office – would like to assign to it. The Secretary was, I think, disappointed to find that he could not direct the Inspectorate to turn itself into a sort of security police force or, still less, a political propaganda machine. He also had to come to terms with the fact that our numbers were not sufficiently great to give any sort of 'cover' in these sorts of role. Although he was irritated by my attitude, these early discussions about numbers of HMI were quite useful to us in the years that followed. On the whole the Office wanted the Inspectorate it had and most of the Ministers we had were inclined to trust us, the more so if they had any understanding of the complexities of the educational scene and the time necessary for successful change or development . . .

When the Yellow Book was followed in short order by the Ruskin Speech and the Great Debate, I took the brunt of the trekking around the country, involving small numbers of territorial HMI for each conference. Although the formula for the debate was pretty simplistic, it did preserve the notion of partnership and it probably did no harm – after the patronising effect of the leak of the Yellow Book – to bring together local authorities, teacher associations and local industrialists to try to get some forward movement on major matters of concern. Along with a whole series of informal conversations with teachers' associations, which I set up fast after the leak, the conferences made crystal clear that HMI were only party to the exercise, and not as so often asserted, the originators of it. Most of the time, HMI had easy relationships with the associations – even NATFE and HMC, though the latter thought it was definitely letting the side down to have a woman SCI – but recurrently one had to explain to them – as to Ministers and local politicians – where HMI was situated in the overall pattern. Both the NUT in my first year and Ken Livingstone at the time of the ILEA evidence report, cried 'political poodle' at me in public meetings but both learned otherwise. (I am not sure that most of the Ministers we had realised that HMI had to do their job, report accurately and remain on working terms with teachers, LEAs and all the innumerable associations that brought them together, including ESG(E).)

I know the above will appear simplistic. There were all sorts of political and Whitehall games and power struggles in the background but they were not HMI's business and my job was to do what I could to keep HMI decent and with some prospect of a future as well as able to make an appropriate contribution to education based on the facts as we experienced and knew them. I had the impression at the time – and remember that I was still learning how the DES worked – that it was a new sort of transaction for the Office to have to formulate such an overall assessment of one part of the field for which the Minister was responsible and then to speculate about how it could be improved free of any – visible? – policy proposal or even 'kite'.

[About the Green Paper the following year: *Education in Schools: A Consultative Document* . . .] . . . I was party to the drafting meetings on the usual basis of bringing HMI evidence to bear on the Office's drafts or explaining what the role of HMI could be but also had, with the help of a number of HMI, particularly Norman Thomas, actually to propose text for inclusion in those areas where the DES was not yet geared up to write for itself, e.g. Standards and Assessment, and Curriculum. Inevitably, since the Green Paper had to get past our own Ministers and Number 10, there were political meetings where it was quite a sensitive matter to preserve HMI's detachment.

Part 3:   Reform 1977–86

Chapter 10   Ruskin to Joseph (1) A Grip on the Curriculum

A New Consensus. The Great Debate. Strategy for Action. The Death of the Schools Council. A National Curriculum by Consent? Examinations.

A New Consensus

The decade which separates the Ruskin speech from Kenneth Baker's arrival at the department, is one of continuity of theme and direction, spanning party divisions. Labour's Shirley Williams replaced Fred Mulley as Secretary of State in September 1976 and served till 1979 when Margaret Thatcher formed her first administration and installed Mark Carlisle (1979–81). He was followed by Keith Joseph who stayed for five years – one of the longest stints by any education minister – from 1981 to 1986. They were three very different personalities.

Shirley Williams was a centre-right Labour politician who within a few years would throw in her lot with Roy Jenkins, David Owen and William Rodgers as one of the Gang of Four. Carlisle was a straightforward, steady and capable but unexceptional, Tory who, in the language of the eighties was branded as a 'wet' by the P.M.'s right-wing entourage. Joseph, a worried intellectual who cared deeply about education, was the man who had helped to found the Centre for Policy Studies to devise a strategy which would roll back the tide of socialism and state control. Different as they were, they worked on much the same DES agenda – looking for ways of getting a grip on the school curriculum. All three Secretaries of State were short of new money and resources. All were expected to make headway by maximising their influence rather than by taking new legal powers.

The Great Debate

Shirley Williams became Secretary of State six weeks before Ruskin, well aware that she had her work cut out. If the Government survived, she could look forward to at most, two and a half years before James Callaghan would have to call a general election. If Ruskin were to be taken seriously, the implications were huge: it was up to her to bring this home to the public in general and the educational world in particular. But as well as being Secretary of State for Education she held the office of Paymaster General, a sinecure which involved being chairman of

203

important Cabinet Committees. In this sense, the education portfolio had to take its place alongside her other Cabinet responsibilities in a Government living on a parliamentary knife-edge.

Moreover she had Margaret Jackson (better known later under her married name as Margaret Beckett) as one of her junior ministers, who was then an ardent left-winger. The two were at loggerheads. There was no hiding their political and personal differences from senior officials in the Department. Shirley Williams had had no part in the Prime Minister's speech. When she read it a few days before delivery, her main concern was that, in making his generalised criticisms of secondary education, Callaghan might unintentionally prompt attacks on the comprehensive school – one of the prime targets of the Black Papers. One reason why she welcomed the Great Debate was because she hoped that, on the contrary, it would generate a groundswell of support for comprehensive education from the silent majority of parents.

As a Secretary of State she had a great gift for listening to what people were saying and making those she talked with feel valued. The Great Debate ought to have been something which she could use to catch the public imagination, but in the event it was a bit of a damp squib. The Office and HMI prepared briefing papers on aspects of primary and secondary education and on the links between schools and work, and public meetings were held across the country chaired by ministers but most of the conversation ran on lines which could have been predicted in advance. All the usual suspects took a prominent part. The public impact was minimal.

Nor were the teachers much impressed. They had had a big 'catching up' pay increase brokered by a former Labour minister, Douglas Houghton MP, which briefly raised morale, but this was quickly eroded by high inflation and when the Great Debate was mooted it was received by most teachers with unrelieved cynicism. They interpreted Callaghan's speech as an attack on the teachers and their unions. However much he might deplore it, Callaghan's populism took on a distinctly anti-teacher tinge. The worse the economic news, the more attractive teachers became as scapegoats.

In noting a continuity of policy linking the Ruskin speech to the education reforms of the 1980s, it would be wrong to pretend that the politicians and their advisers had any clear idea what the path would be like. What they did have was an awareness that the politics of education had changed. For a quarter of a century in the post-war world, the focus had been on education and equality and the possible use of education as a liberating instrument to open up opportunity for the socially disadvantaged. This is what the comprehensive school had been about – was still about for Shirley Williams – combating poverty through access to education. Educational politics, like educational research, was dominated by sociology and the links between school performance and social class.

But now the mood had changed, focus had shifted to the nuts and bolts of schools and schooling. This was reflected in the renewed interest in basic primary education and the fundamentals of learning. Callaghan's Ruskin speech – though replete with references to the children of the ordinary men and women who, by definition, were the salt of the democratic politician's earth – did not resonate with grand statements about a brave new world of equality and justice. It projected a more immediate set of parental goals to do with getting a good job and keeping it.

The concentration on more limited aims echoed – at several removes no doubt – the influential studies in the United States by Christopher Jencks and John Coleman who demonstrated by large-scale survey research, the relatively small part education plays in the distribution of life chances compared with other social factors such as social class, wealth and family support. The short-hand interpretation of these elaborate studies had been: 'schools make no difference', a convenient argument in the North American context, to justify Richard Nixon's retreat from Lyndon Johnson's education policies.

On this side of the Atlantic, too, the devaluing of schools as instruments of macro-social change suited the more modest aspirations of the depressed 1970s. The response from those whose life and work was locked into the existing education system was simple: education reform might not, by itself, do away with the consequences of social inequality, but good schools were better than bad schools. It was time to move away from grand visions of social engineering and concentrate on the practical questions of how to make schools better.

Academics like Professor John Goodlad at UCLA began to talk about 'school effectiveness' and 'school improvement' and to work with schools on forms of self-examination aimed at raising standards of efficiency. By the mid-1970s Professor Michael Rutter was putting together a team to take a close look at how schools occupied the 15,000 hours pupils are compelled to spend in them. When it appeared *15,000 Hours* had a wide and immediate influence because, like HMI reports, it focused attention on what teachers could do to make a difference – including obvious things like starting lessons on time and marking homework – and the key role of heads in making these things happen. Here, too, was a theme which would persist; by the end of the century it would take institutional shape inside the Department of Education.

But the more attention came to be focused on ways of raising standards, the more it highlighted failure. Incremental improvement proved to be a step-by-step technique for articulating public anxiety. Both Williams and Joseph wanted to tackle the shortcomings of the service – not simply those pointed out by Callaghan, but in Williams' case, the long tail resulting from the way secondary education had been organised, and in Joseph's, the poor deal offered to the bottom 40 per cent. Both saw what needed to be done in terms of the modernisation of the education system. The outcome was 10 years of change and consensual reform which, by a paradox, paved the way for the sharp, unconsensual, changes initiated by Baker and his Education Reform Bill.

There were two sets of linked matters to be tackled. First, they had to bring the content of education back within the purview of ministers. And second, they had to confront the question of how to raise standards of achievement across the board. Ministers turned to HMI for help with both questions and the overlap between them.

Given the limited legal powers of the Secretary of State, there were no quick fixes. The agenda had to be worked through patiently. Little was wholly within the control of the Department: the teachers' unions and the LEAs had to be kept on board – any proposed initiative could be diverted or blocked by shifts in political or professional opinion. Too much clarity would frighten the horses and therefore be self-defeating. The public and private meetings set up by Shirley Williams gave many opportunities to air the concerns raised by the Prime Minister and to echo his criticisms of the schools.

The intention was that when the dust settled the Department would issue a discussion document, a Green Paper which would sum up the Great Debate and give the Government's response to it. The fact that nothing much had emerged from the travelling road-show did not matter greatly: what was important was to use the Great Debate as a peg on which to hang the outline of what the Government now intended to do.

The Green Paper appeared in 1977 under the banal title of *Education in Schools*. It echoed the Yellow Book with sections on curriculum, standards and assessment, teachers, and school and working life, rehearsing the by now familiar judgement on the primary schools: 'In some classes, or even some schools, the use of the child-centred approach has deteriorated into lack of order and application.' The answer was to 'restore the rigour without damaging the real benefits of child-centred developments'. The Green Paper saw a need to clarify teaching methods, establish target levels of achievement and teach the basics better.

As for secondary schools, the Green Paper restated the Government's commitment to comprehensive education, but noted that 'the pace of change has out-stripped the supply of appropriately trained and experienced teachers.' The 'balance and breadth' of each child's course was crucial – a phrase which would rise to a crescendo in Joseph's time. Options available to pupils in many schools did not ensure a broad and balanced course for every student – there was particular criticism of the options offered to girls – and the paper asked 'whether because there are aims which are common to all schools, and to all pupils at certain stages, there should be a "core" or "protected part"'. The hand of HMI is visible at various points in the document, since acknowledged by Sheila Browne. She put out a note to remind the Inspectorate that the independence of HMI 'is no more and no less than it has always been and is not changed by the Green Paper, even though I suspect it may put us on our toes'.

Strategy for Action

A clear strategy had emerged. Get the background facts about the curriculum debate out into the open, and confront LEAs with how they were (or rather, were not) carrying out their responsibilities; then further discussion of content and in particular, the common core. To force the pace, the Department would put forward some suggestions. And alongside these successive White and Green Papers, there would be a steady flow of reports from external bodies like the Bullock Committee on English and the Cockcroft Committee on mathematics. And from HMI there would be publications arising from the various surveys and inquiries already in hand. The outline is apparent in retrospect – how far ahead ministers and their officials could see at the time is not so clear.

First came Circular 14/77 to instruct LEAs to report to him on how they were attending to their own curricular backyard. As Shirley Williams wrote later in *Politics is for People*, this showed just 'how little LEAs knew about what was being taught in their schools, although they were legally responsible for the curriculum'. The intention was that the Secret Garden should be secret no more, so the information which the Department gathered was duly analysed and published in November 1979 as *Local Authority Arrangements for the School Curriculum*. By this time, Mark Carlisle had succeeded Shirley Williams but continuity was maintained.

Not surprisingly, local authorities were not enthusiastic: two out of three rejected the idea that they should exercise 'a formal system of detailed control over the curriculum of individual schools'. The picture which emerged was deeply disturbing: local authorities had abandoned their responsibilities; it was not that they had considered how best to proceed and then delegated control of the primary curriculum to head teachers and the secondary curriculum to the teachers and the examination boards. They had simply walked away, content to leave what happened to custom and practice. When challenged they rationalised their position with liberal sentiments.

The new Government was heavily preoccupied with economic matters and the main task of Carlisle, as Margaret Thatcher's Education Secretary, was to hold down expenditure. He pushed through cuts in spending on school meals, school transport and universities. Nevertheless, consideration of curricular matters continued at various levels. Notwithstanding the pressing financial concerns of the time, a series of documents from the DES were put out for consultation and the momentum was maintained. There was no attempt to close the discussion or to move towards radical action. It was still an exercise in trying to change the minds of the educators who remained deeply suspicious of political intervention in the curriculum.

In 1980, the Department issued *A Framework for the Curriculum*, as another discussion document. For the Office to issue papers on the curriculum was in itself a major break with the past. This was Schools Branch's attempt to move the discussion on, not in the tentative and discursive manner favoured by HMI but with proposals which might or might not lead to action. The *Framework* offered the Government's preliminary view of 'the form ... [it] ... should take and the ground it should cover', adding urgency by pointing out that falling rolls and financial cuts would also impinge on what the schools could and should teach. Every LEA should have a clear and known policy for the curriculum offered in its schools. The DES suggested *Framework* was built round a core of six subjects – English, maths, science, languages, physical education and religious education (RE) plus preparation for working life.

A few days after the *Framework* paper was published, HMI issued *A View of the Curriculum* in the 'Matters for Discussion' series, which was less prescriptive and drew carefully on the evidence of the Primary and Secondary Surveys. This was prepared in response to a Ministerial request for an overview of the curriculum and without knowledge of what the Office would put into the *Framework*. The difference in tone between the HMI paper and the Government's was inevitably remarked upon – the Government's prescriptive approach was not well received in educational circles whereas the document from HMI was less dogmatic and more clearly based on the situation on the ground. Nevertheless, the Inspectorate backed up the message that it was necessary to think again about 'a more explicit rationale for the curriculum as a whole'.

It saw a need for more work in the primary school to stretch the brighter children – there are references to French and experimental science – and, drawing on the Red Books, it argued for 'a broad curriculum for all pupils up to 16 ... [with] ... a substantially larger element than now in terms of the range of studies pupils carry forward to the end of the fifth year, but with suitable differentiation in detailed content and preparation, and still with some provision for choice, to match different abilities, aspirations and need'.

Already some LEAs were beginning to talk about 'curriculum-led staffing policies' – too often schools tailored the options they offered according to what they could staff – or could not staff – the teacher-controlled curriculum turned into a way of living with inadequate or inappropriate staffing.

A year later the DES back-pedalled. *The School Curriculum* was a better-considered paper which took account of the responses to the *Framework*. 'Neither the Government nor the local authorities should specify in detail what the schools should teach.' But on secondary education it advanced three propositions: the curriculum should be planned as a whole; all pupils should follow a broadly common curriculum from 11 to 16 to ensure a balanced education and prevent subsequent choices from being needlessly restricted; and schools should equip young people for life in a rapidly changing world.

Waiting in the wings – held back to give precedence to the DES document which overshadowed it – was *The Practical Curriculum* – the Schools Council's belated attempt to take a look at the curriculum as a whole. This offered schools a set of working papers, guidelines and principles intended to be useful in reviewing the curriculum as a whole and its design. Other influences were also at work, challenging the traditional outlines of the academic curriculum. A group based on the Royal Society of Arts produced a manifesto on *Education for Capability* which sought to bridge the gap between academic learning and the kind of skills which make for effective living.

Such ideas were also behind the Technical and Vocational Education Initiative (TVEI), lavishly funded by the MSC. David Young picked up ideas from the Jewish charity ORT which promoted work experience, technology and forms of active practical teaching. Joseph, a friend of Young, accepted the MSC initiative; many Labour-controlled local authorities were suspicious; others took the money and set about tailoring the scheme to their own needs. The MSC had no thought-through ideas on the content of secondary education, except to favour practical and technological developments, and were delighted when enterprising and opportunist teachers put their money to good creative use. Because of the generous financial arrangements, the scheme made a rapid and welcome impact, but the DES was always aware that it was 'not invented here' and when the time came to introduce the National Curriculum, less was heard of TVEI.

By halfway through Joseph's time at the DES, the cumulative pressure from ministers of both parties was beginning to tell (see box). Williams's Green Paper had highlighted the issues. Carlisle had kept them in play. Joseph had kept up the steady stream of documents – discussion documents, circulars, ministerial statements, HMI reports and surveys. At the end of 1983, he turned up the heat by sending out another circular (8/83) asking local authorities and school governors what steps they were taking to draw up curricular policies and to give them practical effect. The Circular made it clear that this was just another stage in what would be an ongoing process. ('The Secretary of State is regularly informed by HM Inspectors about developments in the curriculum nationally and locally: authorities are invited to keep district HMI in touch with the development of their policies for the curriculum.')

Not long before, Joseph had taken another milestone decision – to publish HMI reports on schools and colleges. Sheila Browne asked for the change, recognising that the time had come for more openness, and playing down the anxieties of some of her colleagues. The change caused much less stir than expected and came to be seen as an overdue move. There had long been a suspicion that reports, once filed in the recesses of the department,

Curriculum Strategy – Williams to Joseph: 1976–85

DES activity – Papers, Circulars etc

1977: Great Debate – eight regional public meetings on the issues raised in the Ruskin speech, with working papers from the Office and HMI. Attempt to mobilise public participation: use outcome of the discussions to inform –

1977: Green Paper – *Education in Schools* – setting out an agenda on curriculum, standards and assessment. After consultations, follow up with –

1977: Circular 14/77 – asking LEAs to report on how they managed the curriculum. The information collected is analysed and published in –

1979: DES Report – *Local Authority Arrangements for the School Curriculum* – an analysis of the LEAs' responses. To forward the discussion, the department offers its own first curriculum cockshy, the work of the Office, not HMI, published as –

1980: *A Framework for the Curriculum.* This too is discussed and consulted upon with the LEAs and the teachers who regard it as clumsy and over-prescriptive. A second attempt by the Office, more modest and better received, appears as –

1981: *The School Curriculum.* After more discussion DES issues –

1983: Circular 8/83 – asking what steps LEAs and governors are taking to follow up the *The School Curriculum.* Joseph keeps up the pressure with powerful speech at North of England Education Conference in January 1984 before setting out his stall in detail with –

1985: White Paper – *Better Schools* – the strategic White Paper which pulls together Joseph's plans for the curriculum, for examinations, for teacher training and for more parental participation in school government.

HMI papers, reports etc

1978: *Primary Education in England and Wales* (Primary Survey)

1979: *Aspects of Secondary Education* (Secondary Survey)

1980: HMI paper (Matters for Discussion) – *A View of the Curriculum*

1977, 1981 and 1983: 'Red Book' series

1984–8 'Curriculum Matters' series: 17 discussion papers: Number 2, entitled *The Curriculum 5 to 16*, offers an overarching rationale.

had no further use. Now they were to play a public role in school improvement – another move which raised the profile of HMI.

Death of the Schools Council

In 1982, Joseph announced that the Schools Council was to be wound up and replaced with two bodies of appointees, one for curriculum development, one for examinations. The last years of the Council had had a somewhat unreal quality – it was obviously out of favour with the Government, yet was allowed to go through a sequence of attempts to reinvent itself, during the last of which John Tomlinson, chief education officer for Cheshire, was chairman.[1] He worked hard to broaden its base to make it more sensitive to worlds beyond those of the teachers and local authorities.

In 1981, its future was reviewed by a committee chaired by Nancy Trenaman to which the DES gave evidence in private.[2] According to *The Times* (3 December 1981) it was 'particularly scathing about the Council's staff and Secretary. The Council required a competent, loyal and submissive staff . . . but now there seemed to be a serious danger of disorder through lack of control'. Ministers had decided to get rid of the Council: officials had to carry out the ministers' policy, even if this meant unjustly magnifying its faults.

HMI on the other hand, with first-hand knowledge of 29 Schools Council committees and 57 projects, gave public evidence in much more measured terms – praising much of the Council's work, noting that it had become more focused in line with general development on the curriculum, but complaining there were too many committees and too much politics. They would not have used the word 'mediocre' but were less than impressed.

Evidence collected by Peggy Marshall (CI secondary) listed among the projects which had been most successfully disseminated, Geography for the Young School Leaver, History 13 to 16, and the primary school project on Communication Skills. HMI cited the controversial Lawrence Stenhouse's Humanities project as an example of ventures which were not widely used in the classroom, but may have 'sharpened the view of teachers or have played a part in changing the climate of educational opinion'. The projects which had gained most acceptance by teachers were 'those which offered complete courses, including pupil materials; accompanied this with means of assessment or exam links; and have been aimed at easily identified "target" groups of teachers within a traditional age-range of schooling'. They also needed time – seven to ten years: 'the Council has yet to reap the full benefit of some of its large-scale projects funded before 1978.'[3]

In the event, Trenaman rejected the gravamen of the DES complaints, supporting the continuation of the Council with further proposals for reform. But Joseph's mind was already made up and he went ahead with his alternative arrangements. Tomlinson called it 'the saddest and most symbolic episode to occur on the education front during the Great War between central and local government (1976–?)'.[4] There is no doubt he personally had worked hard to save the Council and in other circumstances might have succeeded in prolonging its life. Its days were numbered because the climate had changed and the diffusion of power and responsibility which the Council embodied had ceased to be acceptable to a strong and opinionated Government.

A National Curriculum by Consent?

In his speech at the North of England Conference in January 1984, Joseph outlined his completed plan to an audience of local authorities, teachers and others. In spite of the bad-tempered atmosphere generated by the teachers' dispute (see box) he was well received as he expounded his case for ensuring breadth, balance, relevance and differentiation in the curriculum, with the Secretary of State in the lead but in partnership with the local authorities, school governors and head teachers. Another DES paper, *The Organisation and Content of the 5 to 16 Curriculum* (September 1984) now set out the Secretary of State's more considered views on what should go into the curriculum, outlining subject areas which should be covered including primary science and technology and a broad spread of subjects in secondary education including a modern language. After consultation, these were adopted as a basis for future planning, providing an outline which bears a close resemblance to the National Curriculum four years later.

Six months later Joseph brought his policies for the curriculum, teacher training and examinations together in what was intended to be a seminal White Paper entitled *Better Schools* (1985). After a critique of standards based on HMI school reports, it outlined the case for a publicly acknowledged, common curriculum arrived at by consent, based on the list of educational aims set out in *The School Curriculum* (see box). This was meant to state clearly what society expected of the schools.

By now LEAs had begun to draw up curriculum policies and consult on these with parents, governors and teachers. Even the ILEA, an authority uncompromisingly opposed to the Conservative government, responded with two excellent reports – one by David Hargreaves on London secondary schools, and another on primary education by Norman Thomas, a former CI. In *Better Schools* the Government expressly rejected the need for legislation to take more power over the curriculum.

Looking ahead, the White Paper envisaged a continuation of the process of discussion and reporting, led by Government policy statements and 'alongside these, but not normally coinciding in time, HMI publications

Teachers' Pay Dispute

A prolonged dispute with the teachers' unions over pay and conditions was a formidable distraction in the mid-1980s. It led to strikes and other forms of industrial action, with children sent home from school at short notice.

The teachers' contract had assumed that teaching was an open-ended professional occupation, the details of which did not need to be spelled out in a set of written contractual duties. Unfortunately it was easy for unions to exploit this for the purpose of industrial action without actually going on strike and losing pay. In the normal way, schools depended on teachers carrying out a variety of extra-curricular tasks – the most obvious of which was the supervision of children during the lunch break. By 'withdrawing cooperation' – ie refusing to supervise children outside their regular classroom duties – teachers were able to cause severe disruption without penalty to themselves. The local authorities and the Government were agreed that this obviously unsatisfactory contractual situation had to be ended – hence the extended negotiations and the failure to agree a pay settlement.

Members of the NUT did themselves enormous long-term harm with the public. Many of them, though supporting the union out of loyalty, were unhappy because of the manifestly unprofessional nature of the actions they were asked to take. The deadlock ended when Kenneth Baker stepped in with legislation to impose a settlement and deprive the teachers of collective bargaining rights.

designed both to inform and stimulate debate'. As a start, Government policy statements were issued for science (1985) and modern languages (1988), the year of the Education Reform Act.

The HMI publications came in a series popularly nicknamed the Raspberry Ripples (after the garish cover design), also known as the 'Curriculum Matters' series, two of which had already appeared before: *Better Schools*. These were *English from 5 to 16* and *The Curriculum from 5 to 16* which covered primary, secondary and special education, drawing on the Red Books for a rationale for the curriculum as a whole.

Six Aims of Education – from *Better Schools* (1985)

- to help pupils to develop lively, inquiring minds, the ability to question and argue rationally and to apply themselves to tasks, and physical skills;
- to help pupils to acquire understanding, knowledge and skills relevant to adult life and employment in a fast-changing world;
- to help pupils use language and number effectively;
- to develop respect for religious and moral values, and tolerance of other races, religions and ways of life;
- to help pupils to understand the world in which they live, and the interdependence of individuals, groups and nations;
- to help pupils appreciate human achievement and aspirations.

The *English* pamphlet caused a stir – as pamphlets on English always do – because it included age-related targets and because Joseph, who took a close personal interest, gave it his backing in a leaflet enclosed with the book – 'we endorse, subject to consultations, HMI's approach ... and commend the teaching styles, methods and approaches which they suggest'. Some HMIs felt compromised by the Ministerial *imprimatur*.

Between 1984 and 1988, 17 papers were published in the 'Curriculum Matters' series – edited by an SI and a small team in Elizabeth House. While most of the papers were subject-based, the subjects were broadly treated, within the general context of the knowledge, skills and understanding to be promoted; five were expressly cross-curricular: careers, health, environmental education, personal and social education and information technology. By the time the later ones appeared the

National Curriculum working parties were already getting under way, drawing on the work done by HMI.

One of the last drafts prepared came from the RE panel. It was never published, in spite of going through many drafts. By the time it was ready, RE and the daily act of worship had become matters of heated controversy in the House of Lords, where zealous peers were trying to strengthen the specifically Christian character of the legislation. The last thing Kenneth Baker who succeeded Joseph in 1986 wanted, when sensitive amendments were circulating in the House of Lords, was a 'stimulating' HMI paper on RE. Being in touch with what actually happened in schools, HMI knew only too well that the more tightly the religious clauses of the Act were drawn, the more likely it was that they would be honoured in the breach rather than the observance. But not unsurprisingly, ministers thought it impolitic to point this out at a delicate stage in the bill's journey. The 'Curriculum Matters' series was wound up without publishing the RE document. Its 'suppression' made brief headlines in the *Guardian* and caused dismay among the RE lobby.

Better Schools had left a lot still to be done. Joseph gambled on the ability of central and local government to cooperate – which, in effect, meant the willingness of local authorities to accept a lead from the centre even if this came from political opponents. It was no longer plausible to expect this. The old ideal of partnership was breaking up. Joseph was aware how much had been achieved in 10 years. The Department was much better equipped to influence what happened and his own aims had become more clear. Given time and a fair wind his strategy might just possibly have worked. Unfortunately there was no more time and the barometer reading was Stormy, not Set Fair.

The curriculum debate had already begun to excite interest in some left-wing local authorities: reminded of their legal powers over the curriculum, some felt an irresistible urge to impose their own priorities by, for example, deciding that the curriculum should be used to encourage a 'positive image' of homosexuals. It was clear that if LEAs became more active on the curriculum, some would use their powers to resist the Secretary of State.

Joseph, one of the most interesting and constructive politicians ever to head the Education Ministry, was genuinely opposed to taking legislative powers to give 'the holder of my Office' complete control of the content of education, because he shared the view which had predominated among his generation – that this would be a totalitarian move, inappropriate to a democratic Britain. Not all his senior officials understood this fully till they went back to the parliamentary debates on the 1944 Act and read speech after speech, equating central control of education with Nazism and fascism. Joseph saw it as raising a 'holocaust' issue: he continued to hold this view, opposing the National Curriculum from the back benches in the House of Lords.

Sir Keith Joseph, Secretary of State for Education and Science, 1981–86.

Ideally, he would have preferred to see the curriculum controlled by the market rather than by any executive action – it was not until he had been convinced that it was not possible to make rapid progress with a 'voucher scheme' that he was willing to pick up the threads of incremental administrative improvement. Walter Ulrich whom Baker called 'an intellectual bully' because he tied Joseph's political advisers up in knots on the practicalities of introducing vouchers, went on to be one of those on whom Joseph relied in his plans to achieve a common mind on the curriculum without legislation.

No minister had enjoyed a closer relationship with the Inspectorate; none had taken a closer interest in the curriculum or in pedagogy, none had read so voraciously in and around the subject of education – including HMI reports. He was genuinely concerned about the fate of the least successful pupils – the so-called bottom 40 per cent – but never fully recognised the extent to which their 'failure' was built into the examination system. The same certification process which celebrated those at the top of the heap, certified the failure of those at the bottom.

It has to be admitted that his strategy failed – overtaken by events and by the impatience of politics. It could not offer quick or decisive results. It aimed at an evolving curriculum rather than the sudden revelation of a new orthodoxy; it depended on a continuing process of development, reflection and in-service training. It assumed an intelligent teaching profession backed up by intelligent educational administrators. These were points in its favour for many traditional educationists. But there was no time to see if such an ideal could be realised. As the Conservative government entered the last 12 months before a general election was due, a disastrous by-election result at Brecon and Radnorshire stirred Margaret Thatcher into action. Joseph stepped down and reform gave way to more revolutionary change.

Examinations

Until the National Curriculum made it to the Statute Book in 1988, the external school examination system was the most powerful influence on the secondary school curriculum. It had become part of the liberal credo that the examinations ought to follow the curriculum not lead it, and bringing exams and curriculum together under a single roof (but on different floors) at the Schools Council reflected this ideal. It made it slightly easier to arrange for new syllabuses to have their own exams. But there was little doubt about the control exercised by the examinations, nor yet the fact that the Secretary of State could use them to promote curriculum change – a DES official's signature appeared on every GCE and though many of the responsibilities formerly belonging to the Secondary Schools Examination Council had been passed to the Schools Council, the last word still rested with the Secretary of State.

When Shirley Williams came to office in 1976, she found the Schools Council's proposals for merging GCE and CSE already on her desk. The

Council had been working for the best part of 10 years on plans to adapt the examination system to the logic of comprehensive schools, but there was still more work to do as the Yellow Book had noted. She conducted her own informal consultations and found opposition to the proposed changes from some who spoke for industry and commerce, and strong resistance from some of the more influential vice-chancellors – there was a memorable clash with the Cambridge Vice-Chancellor.

Given the precarious parliamentary situation in 1977, Shirley Williams could not risk anything which might arouse even minor opposition, so she resorted to the tried and trusted method for keeping the discussion going without precipitating a confrontation. She appointed Sir James Waddell, a retired civil servant, to head a small committee to look again at the proposals. An Educational Study Group (which included a team of HMIs) had been created to assist Waddell on the technical aspects. The group looked in detail at what was emerging from pilot studies set up by the Schools Council in cooperation with examining bodies to test the feasibility of merging the two systems. The conclusion was that a single system could work but that some subjects would need to offer differentiated papers to do justice to candidates at both ends of the ability range.

By the time Waddell reported in 1978 the Labour government was entering that period of half-life which precedes the calling of a general election and exam reform was put on hold. When the Conservatives took office they were inclined to see the proposals for a new exam as a sop to the comprehensive schools – a 'socialist' device to lower standards. But Mark Carlisle accepted the revised scheme, asking the examination boards to replace the separate GCE and CSE exams by a system incorporating a single scale of grades and national criteria for syllabuses and assessment procedures. HMI worked on these, building on a somewhat similar study already undertaken for the Red Book exercise. National criteria would yield greater consistency and clarity about what it was candidates would be expected to know, do and understand. Most important would be the subject or performance criteria, focusing on the qualities and competencies required of the candidates and recorded on a single scale.

Before the final decisions could be taken, however, a new Secretary of state, Joseph, appeared on the scene, and he and his political entourage had to be persuaded that a single system of examining was possible without lowering standards. After a series of lengthy discussions, Joseph accepted in principle in 1982, and work went forward on the national criteria and the administrative arrangements. Two years later, in 1984, Joseph told Parliament that the new exam would be introduced in 1988.

At his press conference following the announcement of his decision, Joseph was asked why he had decided to introduce the single system. He replied: 'the better to achieve my curricular objectives'. He had come to understand his new power over the secondary curriculum. He was not altogether sure it was safe in the hands of 'the holder of my Office' – 'What' he asked 'if he were mad?' Or as he might have said – a socialist instead of a scrupulous intellectual Thatcherite? Whatever his doubts, he had found one of the elusive levers of power and was not going to turn down the chance to pull it.

As time passed, it became clear that the old GCE yardstick would continue to be used as the yardstick of success – schools would continue to be judged only by the proportion of their pupils attaining five GCSEs at grades A–C. When the exam came into operation less than half the age group was staying on beyond the minimum leaving age and only about 20 per cent were getting GCE 'pass' grades and CSE grade 1. The introduction of the new system was followed by a rapid rise in the staying on rate which in turn was reflected in the numbers entering for the GCSE.

Reform of A levels was another matter. This too had been on the Schools Council's agenda since 1963. There was general agreement that the traditional sixth-form offering was too narrow – two or three, occasionally four A levels plus whatever was available as general studies. Numerous attempts to put something broader in its place had focused on a five-subject sixth form course and a revival of the idea of subsidiary papers like those once offered with the old Higher Certificate. The radical Conservatives invested heavily in A levels as symbols of their commitment to standards. A new 'half A level', the Advanced Supplementary (AS) level, was announced in Joseph's *Better Schools* but this only made limited progress in the schools. In 1987, HMI produced a report on *Experiencing A Levels* which found the sixth-form courses visited in schools and colleges, too narrow. Concentration on exams was crowding out potential contrasting and complementary courses. But by now A level had become the Gold Standard for Margaret Thatcher and when the Higginson Committee (1989) brought forward yet another variant on the five-subject sixth form it got short shrift. It was not till the turn of the century that there was another attempt, this time by Labour, to cut the knot.

Notes

1   John Tomlinson later became professor of education and director of the Institute of Education at the University of Warwick.
2   Department of Education and Science (1981) *Review of the Schools Council*. Report from Nancy Trenaman, principal of St Anne's College, Oxford, to the Secretary of State for Education and Science and for Wales and to the LEAs.
3   See note 2, Appendix III. Steadman, S. D., Parsons, C., Salter, B. G., 'The Schools Council, its take up in schools and general impact'.
4   Tomlinson, J. (1985) 'From projects to programmes: the view from the top', in Plaskow, M. (ed.) *Life and Death of the Schools Council*. Lewes: Falmer Press, 123–32, quote on page 123.

HMI Miscellany

Extracts from HMI personal accounts

Arnold Ashbrook 1968

The Cockcroft Report, *Mathematics Counts*, was published in January 1982 and it influenced the discussions, writings and activities of the Mathematics Committee for the next few years. Two particular paragraphs received a great deal of attention. The first (243) stated that mathematics teaching at all levels should include opportunities for exposition, discussion, practical work, practice of skills, problem solving, investigative work. The second (458) . . . gave a [Foundation] list of content which should form part of the mathematics syllabus for all pupils, and would constitute the greater part of the syllabus of pupils in the lowest 40 per cent of the attainment range. For other pupils the syllabus would be developed from the 'bottom upwards'. Para 243 was generally acceptable to mathematics teachers but many had reservations about recommending the content of the syllabus, as did HMI colleagues, particularly in view of the work of the APU and a recent study which had revealed a 'seven year difference' at age 11 . . . The Mathematics Committee saw the aims of teaching mathematics in terms of the development of concepts, skills and attitudes rather than the acquisition of a body of knowledge.

Fred Brook 1978

Much of the work consisted of survey inspections, centrally programmed in order to report on new Government initiatives . . . The inspection of TVEI, which ran for several years, was a good example. It brought a large team to Sandwell to look at schools and colleges. Business education was one curriculum area that most schools sought to enhance . . . Much of the work done in schools was worthy, using Business Education Council modules as vehicles for curriculum change. It enabled many of them to rediscover a lost School of Commerce tradition and to build up what is, today, a large and successful part of 16–19 provision by way of GNVQs.

Jack Dalglish 1963

In 1984 there was talk of 'benchmarks' and a tendency to believe precise standards could be laid down in all subjects . . . My response was later expressed in *English from 5 to 16* – number 1 in the 'Curriculum Matters' series: 'Assessment of work in English is not a matter of precise measurement, or usually simply a matter of marking right or wrong . . . It is subjective; but subjective judgements based on professional knowledge and experience and clearly stated criteria are far preferable to spurious objectivity . . .' On this basis I agreed to produce the pamphlet, with the help of the English Committee . . . It was 22 pages in length. It set out the aims of teaching English, the spoken word, reading, writing, and learning about language, 'some principles of English teaching'. There was a section on 'some principles of assessment' and a final section inviting comments and suggestions.

Most responses were to the section on learning about language and these were mostly hostile. The document suggested aims, objectives, principles and means of assessment of language study at all three stages – up to 7, up to 11 and up to 16 – asserting the importance of syntax, punctuation and spelling and the need to learn the names of some parts of speech in order to provide a nomenclature for discussing language. Far from suggesting any reversion to formal exercises, it suggested new ways of exploring the nature of language as, for various purposes, it is actually used, and drawing on insights derived from linguistics. The response exposed the fact that, having been told during their initial or post-graduate training that 'teaching grammar' was useless, many teachers were not open to new thinking. I was asked to discuss *English from 5 to 16* at a meeting of the National Association of Teachers of English, where the general opinion was that 'research had shown' that language study was useless. I asked for a show of hands of those who had read the research referred to (which, in fact had dealt only with formal exercises such as clause analysis and parsing). Only one hand was raised.

Pat Salisbury 1961

HM Inspectorate exerted an important influence upon the future content of the music curriculum in writings which were precursors of the 'Curriculum Matters' series that emerged from Elizabeth House under Eric Bolton's influence in the 80s . . . Curriculum Matters 4 placed considerable emphasis on the creative aspects of music-making in schools, and on learning to play a musical instrument an integral part of pupils' entitlement from the music curriculum. I am vain enough to have kept a letter from Sir Yehudi Menuhin and addressed to me as SI music, in which he states the *Music from 5 to 16* 'is one of the most comprehensive and civilised musical documents I have ever read'. [High praise also came from a different angle in the form of an article in the *Express* by Benny Green.]

Clive Goodhead 1981

The meetings to produce Drama from 5 to 16 in the 'Curriculum Matters' series are among the most stimulating educational meetings I have ever attended. They brought together colleagues from different backgrounds and different kinds of experience in drama. In a way they represented some of the widely various philosophies, techniques, practices and expectations that go to form the Protean content and background to the subject. Our common aim was to produce an agreed, nationally credible, framework for drama in schools ... The booklet successfuly attempted a difficult balancing act ... between theatre on the one hand and educational drama on the other ... It was the first attempt to codify drama in schools into separate but linked objectives for children at different ages, 7, 11 and 14.

Colin Richards 1983

My involvement in HMI's work on the curriculum began in 1984 or early 1985 ... with an invitation to an internal HMI conference at Buxton ... I realised that the leadership role in curriculum matters which HMI had been gradually assuming for some years was to be greatly enhanced by being linked to an initiative by the Secretary of State ... to achieve a national consensus about the aims and purposes of the school curriculum and to provide guidance to schools as to what might reasonably be expected of pupils at different ages ... The Buxton Conference debated drafts of some of the earliest papers – on the whole curriculum and on English. There was considerable heart-searching as to whether HMI should take such a public profile and in particular whether it was feasible (or educationally desirable) to attempt to provide age-related 'benchmarks' in terms of pupil's achievements. Sometime later I found myself on the FCC curriculum team ... [meeting] ... teachers concerned over possible infringement of their professional autonomy ... and HMI some of whom were equally distrustful of the exercise ... exemplified for me in the memorable words of a long-experienced home economics colleague who characterised a 'Raspberry Ripple' as a 'concoction of dubious nutritional value'.

Chapter 11   Ruskin to Joseph (2)

Teacher Education. FE – Preparation for Work: 16–19, Inspectorate
Changes. Other HMI Responses – Expenditure Surveys: Reports on LEAs.

Teacher Education

For 30 years after the end of the war, the dominant issue was how to train
enough teachers to staff the schools. During the 1970s this began to
change. Specific shortages remained but the general teacher shortage had
melted away. And as attention turned to the content of the curriculum
and standards of achievement, so too the quality of the teaching
profession and its ability to do what was required of it, came under
scrutiny.

Education has always been held in low esteem in the universities – the
(PGCE) never carried much academic or professional weight – but there
had been a professional assumption that teacher training needed to
strengthen links with the universities as the guardians of learning. This
was not an assumption which was peculiar to teacher training – other
occupational groups saw links with higher education as a way of raising
professional status.

The Robbins Committee had proposed a university takeover of teacher
education. This was resisted by the newly-formed Department of
Education because it was held that the Government had a direct interest in
what happened in the training of teachers and could not afford to put the
autonomous universities in charge. For one thing, the writ of HMI did not
run in the universities or in any of their activities, except those of the
extramural departments which were inspected as part of 'Other FE'. HMIs
did not report on PGCE courses – they might visit by invitation and
relations were generally good, but everyone was well aware where the line
was drawn. If universities took over the colleges they too might be out of
bounds for HMI. As it was, HMI continued to be regular visitors to the
colleges and closely involved in the traumatic events which overtook them.

In the colleges of education there was an obvious tension between
'discipline-based' courses and 'professional' courses – how much time
should be spent on the subject matter which students were being
prepared to teach, how much on equipping them with the skills to teach
it. By the end of the 1970s such matters were coming to the fore as the
evidence built up about the imbalance between teachers' specialist

qualifications and the subjects they were required to teach. Just as HMIs discussed the 'match' between children's abilities and the work they were given to do, so too, there was concern about the match between teachers' qualifications and the subjects they were engaged in teaching.

Such concerns reflected badly on the teacher educators, on the way in which they selected their students and constructed their courses and on the system as a whole. These were powerful technical criticisms to add to the widespread accusations that they had promoted the excesses of progressive education and the child-centred approach, filled students' minds with left-wing, anti-competitive ideas and used sociology to excuse failure. It would be a mistake to underestimate the strength of these sentiments in radical right-wing circles including many in the Number 10 Policy Unit in the Thatcher–Major years.

For Keith Joseph, the alarm bells rang with the appearance of an HMI publication *The New Teacher in School* soon after he became Secretary of State in 1981. This showed the limitations of the preparation of young teachers for their first appointments. It was always questionable whether someone coming out of college could reasonably be expected immediately to perform as a fully fledged professional teacher – other professionals were required to undergo formal periods of practical experience, like solicitors' articles or the internships of junior doctors, before being allowed to practise on their own. But in teaching there was the ridiculous assumption that the colleges and departments of education had to be able to serve up fully functioning professionals. (Some would say that most of what is wrong with teacher training – and with the measures introduced to improve it – stems from this absurdity.)

Joseph's reaction was to ask what was to be done about initial teacher training. The Office had been inclined to focus on in-service training as being a quicker way to get results. Pauline Perry became CI for teacher training shortly after the appearance of the *New Teacher* report. The focus of attention turned from in-service to initial teacher education and HMI launched a survey based on full inspections of a sample of colleges and visits to university departments. But long before this was completed Joseph had decided to act. (Philip Halsey, the deputy secretary under whose general responsibility came teacher training, was closely involved in the development of the policy and drafted the teacher training White Paper, *Teaching Quality,* which set it out. Halsey was not a typical official. He had been head of a London comprehensive school at Hampstead before joining the Civil Service.)

The strategy which Joseph adopted was to cut back the influence of the universities and CNAA and use his own powers to lay down what would-be teachers should learn and how they should be trained. He would thereby undercut the left-wing sociologists and diminish the extent to which the profession looked to the universities for leadership. And he would provide the central planning to match the supply of teachers to the work which had to be done. To put it in these terms, of course, exaggerates the coherence of the policy and implies an ability to look farther ahead than was possible in the hurly-burly of politics. To have spelled it out in such crude terms would, in any case, have been impolitic; by sugaring the pill in various ways, he softened the resistance which might otherwise have come from the universities and teachers' unions.

When he looked closely at the way power and influence were shared between the Government and the universities, Keith Joseph found that powers which the Secretary of State enjoyed under the Education (Teachers) Regulations had in effect, been delegated to the universities and CNAA. The academic authorities awarded PGCEs and validated the courses in the colleges. And ministers had been content to grant qualified teacher status (QTS) automatically to all who passed the exams and satisfied the probationary arrangements.

Joseph decided to take back the powers his predecessors had ceded. He would do this by laying down criteria which courses of teacher education would have to meet in order to receive his approval. In other words, he would tell the universities what they could and could not do in the preparation of teachers. No course which failed to satisfy his criteria would carry with it the award of QTS.

The *Teaching Quality* White Paper appeared in 1983 and was followed by the creation of a Council for the Accreditation of Teacher Education (CATE) whose job it would be to review what was provided, university by university, college by college and course by course in the light of the criteria laid down by the Secretary of State. As for the criteria themselves, Pauline Perry recalls the new experience of sitting down to write criteria in prescriptive terms. The criteria were securely based on the evidence gathered in the Primary and Secondary Surveys and other relevant HMI reports.

An HMI report on the content of teacher training reviewed what were seen to be the shortcomings of teacher preparation and suggested how training could be improved to meet the needs of the schools. This went to the Advisory Council on the Supply and Training of Teachers which accepted it. The criteria had to be formulated to serve as guidelines for CATE. They included the requirement that students should study a subject regularly taught in school for at least 'two full years', and receive adequate training in how to teach it to a particular age range. This had a direct implication for PGCE courses, limiting the range of students from whom they could recruit, and it was coupled with other conditions such as that requiring teacher educators to have 'recent and relevant' experience in the classroom. This last obviously sensible proposition caused consternation in the colleges of education and, particularly, in university departments of education: it was many years since some professors and lecturers had faced a class in anger.

The implications were far-reaching for all concerned. The detail was much less important than the fact that the Secretary of State (that is, the Department) was stepping in to take decisions which had hitherto been left to the universities and CNAA. As time passed the elaboration of the requirements increased. CATE, chaired by William Taylor, a former head of the London University Institute of Education who later become vice-chancellor of Hull University, included few members with direct experience of the teacher training system. It proved a willing instrument of the Secretary of State's policy – its terms of reference did not include considering whether the policy itself was wise or expedient.

The instinct of the university departments of education (UDEs) was to resist the direct intervention of the Secretary of State. They objected to him telling them what they must teach. The matter of compulsion was dealt with almost as a side issue: the Circular (3/84) simply made inspection by HMI a condition of approval – the official who drafted the paragraph had not realised it was a controversial matter. It suited Joseph, who was determined that if they wanted to have their course approved, universities must accept the criteria and inspection. No one was forcing them to give up their chartered rights – no one was forcing them to engage in teacher training – all that was being said was that if they wanted to do so, they would have to abide by the Secretary of State's rules, like everybody else.

In retrospect, Pauline Perry regretted that it had been thought necessary to force the issue – she would have preferred to rely on gracious invitations as in the past. But in any case, the pretence that HMIs only set foot in UDEs on sufferance had been wearing thin for many years. These events finished it off. If the UDEs had hoped that their universities would take up the cudgels on their behalf, they were quickly disabused of the idea. Some made representations, but behind the scenes there was some quiet encouragement for the new regime from the Committee of Vice-Chancellors and Principals.

There followed a period of intense activity for HMI inspecting every college and UDE and reviewing their courses – at first it was a matter of reviewing their plans – and sending reports to CATE. It remained a matter of resentment among some university teachers that HMI should pass judgement on their competence, but in practice, the teaching on most PGCE courses was found to be good; where there was criticism it was usually about the coherence of the course structure not the quality of the teaching.

FE – Preparation for Work

Employers continued to argue that young people were coming out of the secondary schools ill-prepared in basic literacy and numeracy. This was true. It was also true that they were probably better qualified than any previous generation but unfortunately this had no necessary connection with unemployment. Full employment had always depended on a large pool of unskilled jobs which was disappearing. The fact of the matter was that the rise in structural unemployment was causing employers to raise the educational threshold new entrants would have to cross. The schools were having to come to terms with the fact that young people would need a higher level of functional literacy and numeracy in future if they were to get, and hold on to, a regular job.

Meanwhile, the MSC and the Department of Employment set about improvising programmes for the young unemployed. Forms of job creation like the Youth Opportunity Programme offered short-term work and training of variable quality. There were no guarantees of future work. The schemes had an immediate effect on the unemployment figures and, within limits, were successful in keeping young people off the streets. But as could be expected, some employers were tempted to take on subsidised trainees to do jobs which might otherwise have been filled by unsubsidised young workers – the risk of 'substitution' was a feature of all the schemes.

The FE colleges, properly opportunist as ever, were eager for extra day-release students, but the outcome was predictably variable. The collapse of traditional apprenticeship and the failure of industry to replace it with more comprehensive forms of training for young workers, made it the more difficult to plug MSC Youth Training Schemes into the further education system. There were oft-expressed hopes that a properly organised youth training scheme might pave the way for a wider reform of industrial training and apprenticeship but progress was slow. The MSC was remarkably skilled in getting programmes up and running quickly but less successful in delivering a high-quality product, and there were damaging and continuing criticisms of the long-term results.

Throughout, the contrast between the go-getting MSC (with David Young, a brilliant political entrepreneur, as chairman) and the more deliberate and legally restricted Department of Education, was painfully apparent. The division of responsibility between the DES and the Department of Employment was more than one of interdepartmental demarcation – it was a difference of style, approach and priorities.

The clash of styles became most apparent when the MSC dealt with local authorities. The DES had no power to fund specific local projects but the MSC seemed to have unlimited funds and ample powers for making payments to LEAs and colleges. The MSC would launch a scheme first and work out the details afterwards – using the first year almost as an exercise in action research. The DES was more severely bound by the constraints of consultation and the need to dot every 'i' and cross every 't' before going ahead.

As the 1980s unfolded, the shortcomings of industrial training remained a matter of continuing concern, against the background of the realignment of British industry. Conservative Chancellors withdrew subsidies for failing industries, and there was a slow but steady increase in the numbers remaining in full-time education beyond 16. In 1989 a Task Force set up by the Confederation of British Industries published a clarion call to employers: 'The practice of employing 16–18-year olds without training leading to nationally recognised qualifications must stop'.[1] There was no instant response but as the century came to an end, continued economic recovery, and more 'schemes' took some of the sting out of the problem of youth employment.

16–19

What to provide for the students who stayed on in full-time education beyond the leaving age but were not suited to the traditional sixth-form A level course, remained a continuing topic of concern. It had been one of the subjects raised by James Callaghan when he asked Fred Mulley for a memorandum from the DES before the Ruskin speech, and was picked up in the Green Paper, *Education in Schools*.

It was not at all clear what curriculum should be offered to these students. In many comprehensive schools, various pre-vocational courses had come into being, leading to awards from such bodies as the Royal Society of Arts (RSA), City and Guilds of London Institute (CGLI) and the Business Education and Technician Education Councils (merged in 1983 to form BTEC). This confirmed the FE view that courses should be of a vocational nature, to be taken either by young workers, combining employment with part-time study, or by college-based students, working towards an occupational or professional qualification. The schools took a different view: they were keen to retain as many post-16 students as possible. There was a need, they argued, to consider what was best for 16-year-olds who had not formed any clear vocational ideas, and who might be thought to need another year at school in which to gain in confidence and maturity.

HMIs from both the schools and FHE branches of the Inspectorate were much involved in 16–19 issues. Students in this age range were to be found in the sixth forms of schools, in separate sixth-form colleges and in FE colleges, including tertiary colleges which offered a full range of sixth-form provision but operated under the FE regulations. The sixth form, the traditional jewel in the secondary crown, was for conservatives, a symbol of the excellence they wanted to defend. This went for many in the universities and in the Headmasters Conference; it translated easily into political support from the Conservatives. They placed great value on the maintenance of school sixth forms as talismans of value and quality.

An inquiry set up jointly by the DES and the Local Authority Associations with Neil Macfarlane, parliamentary under secretary at the Department in the chair, considered 16–19 provision at length.[2] (The joint sponsorship of the inquiry was in itself an interesting development.) The report (1980) was bland – avoided giving offence to the schools with their large vested interest in the sixth form, the sixth-form colleges or the nascent tertiary colleges. Those who hoped it would back the tertiary solution and propose a wholesale reconstruction of the system, were up against powerful political opposition. Any inclination to back tertiaries against all comers was countered by the facts of the situation on the ground. Too much was already set in concrete. Nor was it clear that tertiaries really did much to make cross-curricular choices easier. The Government's conclusion, set out in Circular 3/87 *Providing for Quality: The Pattern of Organisation to Age 19*, argued for sixth forms large enough to offer all 'commonly taken' A level options – a minimum of 150 students was proposed in a draft which went out to consultation – but the circular made it clear that on the main structural question, the Government had 'no preferred solution'.

In 1979 a new Certificate of Extended Education (CEE) was introduced. This was a school-oriented exam, based on school subjects augmented with content relevant to the world of work. Students were to be assessed in five subjects at the age of 17. Schools had financial incentives to hold on to students as long as possible. The CEE was intended to give them something to offer students as an alternative to repeats. By common consent it had to have a vocational flavour, within the limits of what the schools could offer or provide by joint schemes with a local FE college. The CEE was a compromise between the interests of the schools and the practicalities of staffing and resources.

Alongside this schools-oriented development, another initiative was being prepared by the Further Education Curriculum Review and Development Unit, usually known as the FEU. It was a DES offshoot which came into being in 1978 with Geoff Melling, an FE inspector, at its head, and began work on pilot schemes of unified vocational preparation. The FEU approach to 16–19 was markedly different from that adopted by the CEE. An FEU group led by Jack Mansell (who took over from Melling) produced *A Basis for Choice*, which outlined a modular framework of courses at various levels certified by City and Guilds and BTEC. This produced yet another set of initials – CPVE (Certificate of Pre-Vocational Education). The nature of the courses and the methods of assessment and evaluation linked in with other developments taking place in FE and vocational training and leading in time to the appointment of the review of vocational qualifications chaired by Oscar De Ville which reported in 1986. Offered a choice between the CEE and the CPVE, the Government came down firmly on the side of the latter. As its name suggested, this was to be more directly linked to preparation for employment. A common core of adult life skills was built into the package. It was more flexible than the CEE and more capable of being adapted and developed to meet rapidly changing needs.

During the 1980s, these relatively modest attempts to grapple with the needs of the 16–19-year-olds in schools and colleges, were overshadowed by the activities of the MSC and its successors within the Department of Employment. The De Ville review led to the creation of the National Council for Vocational Qualifications (1986) to coordinate and give shape to vocational qualifications in industry, but with the wider object also of constructing a framework into which all forms of vocational and professional certification could be fitted. From this emerged the concept of National Vocational Qualifications (NVQs) at five levels from level 1, certifying 'occupational competence in performing a range of tasks under supervision' up to level 5 for 'competence at a professional level'. The aim was to give employers 'ownership' of the vocational qualifications which were to be assessed, where possible, by tests of demonstrable competence in the workplace.

In the wake of the National Curriculum and the subsequent attempts to build more vocational options into the secondary school curriculum from 14 onwards, the search would go on for better ways of managing the deep divide between the academic and the vocational – between the realm of GCSE and A levels on the one hand and that of the Council for Vocational Qualifications on the other. NVQs were primarily vocational qualifications based on clearly defined jobs and job skills. As such they could not be used by schools. But there was a need to look at the years on both sides of the school leaving age and provide a framework of qualifications for those whose needs were not being met by GCSE and A Levels. A radical answer might have been to move to a baccalaureate system with several 'sides' or sections (which could include subjects drawn from both academic and vocational sides), but this would have meant challenging tradition and the primacy of A Levels. The alternative was to construct a parallel system of qualifications for vocational courses and to link these two separate systems at age 18.

General Vocational Qualifications (GVQs) were invented to provide such an alternative ladder. Initially, they came under the aegis of the Council for National Vocational Qualifications but they had to be tailored to the needs of the schools, sixth form and tertiary colleges. They could not be as dogmatically competency-based as NVQs and they had to contain enough general education ('knowledge and understanding') to make possible links with the academic mainstream and therefore offer a possible pathway to higher and continuing education. GVQs came into being at the three lower levels in the NCVQ table of equivalencies: level 3 – the advanced GVQ – would give recognition to vocationally oriented courses which also included sufficient academic content to equate with two A levels. After the merger of the DES and the Department of Employment responsibility for the supervision of examinations was brought under the reorganised Qualifications and Curriculum Authority.

Inspectorate Changes

In 1967 the two group designations – TCA (technical, commerce and art) and OFE (other further education) – were dropped, and all were joined together in the FE Inspectorate. (Later this became FHE in recognition of the higher education element.) TCA inspectors were heirs to the old 'technical education' tradition. They were an elite group, spearheaded, as Harry French insisted, by engineers of one kind or another, and their work ran from craft and technician courses to courses at degree and professional level.

Important developments were changing the face of FE. In many colleges there were empty places on engineering courses and more students in humanities and social sciences. There were changes, too, in the make-up of OFE. It remained a ragbag but priorities had changed. Adult education continued to be inspected, along with a wide range of middle-class recreational courses in FE colleges – including those lined up along the frontier between education and entertainment like bridge and ballroom dancing, not to mention Spanish for tourists. There were potentially huge inspectorial demands from the Youth Service – always in a state of major or minor crisis – and the other demands on the time of HMIs such as prisons and Borstals, Women's Institutes and Townswomen's Guilds.

As a result of a suggestion in the House of Commons Select Committee in 1968, a Departmental working party was set up to review the function, mode of working and recruitment policy of the FE Inspectorate, with Toby Weaver in the chair.[3] The draft proposals came from Harry French. He wanted an end to the traditional arrangements by which each FE inspector had general, district and specialist assignments. Instead there would be two groups: about a fifth would be district and general inspectors, with no specialist interests, who would liaise with LEAs and colleges. The remainder would be specialists, who would carry out specialist inspections and act as assessors and representatives of the Department.

The working party used the occasion of the annual FE Inspectors' Conference, held at Huddersfield in March 1970, to float these ideas and take soundings. Weaver's keynote address restated the Inspectorate's first responsibility to the Secretary of State which he insisted should take precedence over the service provided to LEAs and colleges. One of those present, Fred Parrott, recalls him painting 'a graphic mental picture of a central-heating system where a tangle of pipes painfully and noisily carries water from the boiler room in the basement up and round the lower floors until, by the time it reaches the upper floor radiators, no warmth is available'. The result was uproar in the hall and in the bar afterwards: 'to a man and woman, FE Inspectors are grotesquely overworked and if the Office isn't getting answers – that's because it's not asking the right questions.' In the folk memory Huddersfield became

'Shuddersfield'. The rank and file response may have been one reason why the working party never formally completed its work – it was, in Weaver's words, 'overtaken by events'.[4] This was the time when the Inspectorate as a whole was caught up in self-examination in the follow-up to the Fulton Report.

Weaver's answer to the question of how to free up some time was for HMI to give up their pastoral obligation to 'their' colleges. When the Working Party was over and done with, he circulated this suggestion as having a possible bearing on wider discussions of HMI's role. For much of the 1970s the FHE Inspectorate had kept out of the public eye. As FE expanded at all levels, the demands on the FHE Inspectorate changed. They gave up most of their executive functions which were taken over by the Regional Advisory Councils, though the course-approval system continued to be coordinated by a Regional SI in each division. This made possible a shift of emphasis and for HMI to spend more time inspecting and writing – an aspect of their work which had not been much in evidence hitherto.

Perhaps belatedly, a massive inspection programme was planned with a view to putting together a comprehensive picture of the work of FE in vocational training. Published in 1984, *Education for Employees* was intended to provide the evidence on which to base an intelligent discussion of industrial training and the work of FE colleges in building up the skill base in industry and commerce. The exercise had also served to bring to public notice the diversity of FE and the important contribution of the colleges.

At the other end of the spectrum the expansion of the polytechnics brought more work for HMIs in powerful institutions which did not necessarily relish being inspected by outsiders whose personal experience might not match the people and departments they were going to appraise. One of those who took part in this work was Clive Booth, formerly private secretary to Fred Mulley and Shirley Williams, who had left the Department in 1981 to become deputy director of the Plymouth Polytechnic. He returned to the DES and was made an 'HMI (Attached)' to work on the polytechnic programme. In the face of hostility from many poly directors, the Inspectorate made a breakthrough when Kenneth Green, the director of the largest poly – Manchester – agreed to cooperate and submit his college to the rigours of a full inspection, from which it emerged with a properly balanced but in the main favourable report.

Terry Melia became CI for further education in 1985 and pressed ahead with the inspection programme and the publication of reports on part-time advanced FE, and in 1986, the biggest programme of inspection ever mounted in FE, gave rise to *Non-Advanced Further Education in Practice*. This showed the astonishing variety to be found within the FE colleges and their entrepreneurial character. Some would say the appraisal was less than rigorous, though it was, of course, a judicious report, drawing attention to some inefficient practice along the way and the unacceptably small size of some teaching groups. This was followed up a year later with a survey of *Tertiary Colleges* – seen, inevitably, by the media as another round in the tussle between the tertiaries and the sixth-form colleges – especially when it was found to be possible to make favourable comparisons between some tertiary colleges and some top public schools.

Other HMI Responses: Expenditure Surveys

Along with getting a departmental grip on the curriculum, the secondary school examinations and the training of teachers, the Government was also tightening its hold on education spending by local authorities – and therefore, curbing their ability to push off-message independent policies of their own. The main cause of this was economic: Chancellors of the Exchequer of both parties insisted that the Treasury must have total control of public spending of all kinds – that restraint in times of economic stringency must extend beyond central government departments to all other major public spenders, including local authorities – and that the Public Borrowing Requirement as a measure of the Government's requirement for credit must also include local authoritiy loans. Hence the squeeze on local spending and borrowing which followed the financial crises of the 1970s.

Denis Healey's economy campaign under the Callaghan government included harsh measures for education, signalled by tough negotiations each year with the local authorities on the Rate Support Grant, the government grant-in-aid which supplemented the income authorities raised from the property tax known as the rates. The negotiations were complicated because the formula on which the grant was calculated was complicated and controversial, weighted for a variety of social and economic factors and revised from time to time to reflect the central Government's political as well as economic priorities.

The 15 years which separated the crisis of 1976 and Margaret Thatcher's poll tax debacle saw a steady deterioration in local–central government relations on finance. Confrontation became more fierce after she had become Prime Minister and Michael Heseltine, the secretary of state for the environment, took powers to impose penalties on recalcitrant authorities by 'capping' their budgets.

The Inspectorate became involved early on. It was agreed that the SCI should produce a report on the impact of cuts on local provision, for the Rate Support Grant negotiations. Thus in 1977 began the series of reports for the Expenditure Steering Group (Education) – known by its initials as ESG(E). These were based on inspection visits carried out the previous autumn and on the annual reports from district inspectors, aimed at assessing the resourcing of the schools and colleges and the impact of cuts on quality.

To report on these matters was squarely within the remit of the Inspectorate. From the beginnings of the Inspectorate it had been HMI's job to report on how public money was spent and what value was being achieved as a result. But it was inherently dangerous for the SCI, all the same. Sheila Browne was being invited to take up a position between the Government and the authorities – both would use her report polemically if they had half a chance. The exercise would call on all the resources and experience of the Inspectorate; it would demand courage as well as drafting skill, to do this in such a way as to retain the confidence of all concerned without sacrificing integrity. It is a measure of their skill that this was done without any breakdown of relationships. And it may well be that the very existence of these reports affected the level of the financial settlements during these critical years.

The early reports were confidential to ESG(E) – authorities were not identified by name and the information was collected on this assumption – but the inevitable occurred in 1981 when Sheila Browne was quizzed on her report by the House of Commons Select Committee chaired by Christopher Price MP, former parliamentary private secretary to Anthony Crosland when he was Secretary of State. Price thought the reports should be public not private documents and pressed the SCI vigorously to disclose the names of LEAs where it was found that expenditure had been cut below the level needed to maintain a satisfactory level of service.

After a lengthy exchange in which the SCI maintained her refusal to divulge the names, the matter ended. But by then, Price had primed the education correspondent of *The Times*, Lucy Hodges, who rang round all the authorities and winkled out the names – Gateshead, Somerset,

Norfolk and Wiltshire. (According to Price, Charles Morrison, one of Wiltshire's Conservative MPs, came up later to congratulate him (Price) on doing more for Wiltshire education in 48 hours than he had been able to do in 30 years.)

Thereafter the reports were published – the question of publication was already under discussion and plans were being made to go public before the incident with the Select Committee. The reports became a major annual commitment for the Inspectorate, with a team led initially by an SI, Geoffrey Elsmore, engaged in collating the material at Elizabeth House, followed by a delicate drafting task in which the SCI took a particularly close interest. The first published report (1980–81) put LEAs into three bands reflecting effectiveness of education and availability of resources: for schools, 20 per cent fell in the upper band; 65 per cent in the middle band and 15 per cent in the 'cause for concern' lower band.

After Sheila Browne retired a year early to become principal of Newnham and Eric Bolton had succeeded her as SCI, the ESG(E) report was superseded by an annual report from the SCI on the work of the Inspectorate as a whole. The first such report appeared in February 1989 by which time the Education Reform Act had been passed and the powers of local authorities had been curtailed.

The whole episode illustrated both the strength and the vulnerability of the Inspectorate – its strength, because it was trusted to carry out a difficult and demanding task with professional impartiality, its weakness in that it could not expect to act as arbiter between the Government and the local authorities and emerge unscathed. No one believed that Government – any government – would find it tolerable, indefinitely, to employ candid critics, experts licensed to provide ammunition for their political opponents.

And there were even then, some complaints from Conservative backwoodsmen who objected to HMI telling them they were not spending enough, when what they were doing was holding down expenditure on the Government's instructions. The protest seems to have been a damp squib though Bob Dunn, a junior minister, and Stuart Sexton, a political adviser, had helped to stir up Tory education committee chairmen in a few LEAs.[5] It was an incident which had no immediate consequences but in the light of later events it showed there were elements in the Conservative Party which had it in for HMI.

Reports on LEAs

Another development connected with the centralist tendencies at work in the education system at this time involved HMI in inspections of local authorities. The Rayner Report had recommended a planned rolling programme of LEA inspections spreading over some years. It was obvious that the politics of such a programme would not be easy. People were bound to question why a particular authority had been chosen – hence the desire for a regular programme which would not be restricted to what might be called 'authorities at risk'. On the other hand, there was no escaping the fact that it would be politically tempting for ministers to 'send in the Inspectors' to an authority which hit the headlines.

Such inspections had begun before Rayner. There was an inspection of the ILEA in 1980 which Peter Newsam insisted on publishing in full because he trusted the Inspectorate a great deal more than he did his own education committee or the education ministers in the Thatcher government. Others followed for the Toxteth district of Liverpool in 1982 (following urban riots), Dudley (1982) and Norfolk soon after. Both the last two had appeared in the SCI's annual ESG(E) reports as low spenders.

Carrying out such inspections was a considerable test for HMI. Those who took part in the early ones complained that they received little guidance on how to proceed; all they could do was feel their way, using normal HMI methods to arrive at judgements on the institutions in question. Guidelines were issued later but not till a major part of the programme had been completed. For these single authority exercises, it became the practice to mount a series of full inspections concentrated within a limited period, and to augment these with information gathered from earlier inspection visits. It meant assembling teams from far and wide in order to bring together the specialist expertise required. This did not happen without some ill feeling. DIs and district inspectors in whose areas the relevant authorities were located, resented having so much of the planning, and eventually the final writing, taken out of their hands. Practice improved with experience but the exercise was not good for morale.

The inspections included sections on local administration and finance but HMI were anxious not to stray outside the area of their own expertise, and the main focus was squarely on educational effectiveness. As with reports on schools, the practice was to make sure critical points were discussed in advance with those directly involved – chief education officers and local inspectors or advisers – who were invited to Elizabeth House to read the draft reports before publication. HMI were also prepared to meet the education committees in the inspected authorities and discuss the report with them after publication.

Brent was one of the authorities inspected on the peremptory instruction of Kenneth Baker. As Brian Arthur, the CI in charge of the programme, recalls: 'we were particularly proud of the Brent report, a contentious exercise completed in six months during which all the reports on individual institutions had been published ahead of the overall report.' In Brent, meetings with parents as well as with the authority and its officers, were included in the exercise.

Altogether, 13 LEAs were inspected in this programme before ministers lost interest and an aside from David Hancock, the permanent secretary, at a conference of senior HMI broke the news that it was at an end. Ministers liked the idea of HMI reports which heaped criticism on 'loony-left' authorities. They were less keen when it was their own kith and kin who found their way into the pillory.

How successful was the venture – was it worth the effort which it entailed? The political delicacy of the exercise from the point of view of the Inspectorate cannot have made for plain speaking. And as for their primary client, the Secretary of State, HMI failed to deliver thunderbolts when they might have been politically convenient; in preserving their own reputation for fairness they did him credit as well as themselves. Joseph, in particular, though sometimes disappointed by what HMI served up, valued their integrity and refusal to bow to political pressure. Kenneth Clarke, when his time came, had no taste for the hair shirt and was less impressed.

Notes

1. *Towards a Skills Revolution*, report of a Task Force set up by the Confederation of British Industry, London, 1989, para 21.
2. DES/Local Authority Associations (1980) *Education for 16 to 19 year-olds: A Review Undertaken for the Government and the Local Authority Associations*. London: DES/Local Authority Associations. Chairman, Neil Macfarlane.
3. DES Working Party on FE Inspection, first draft report considered by 15th meeting, 1 January 1971. Chairman, Toby Weaver, PRO ED 213/5.
4. Letter to Secretary, 25 July 1972, 'Review of the Inspectorate'.
5. See interviews with some chairmen of Conservative LEAs concerning the value of HMI expenditure reports, *The Times Educational Supplement*, 15 June 1984.

HMI Miscellany
Extracts from HMI personal accounts

Roy Prideaux 1967

The DES has spent 50 years in largely inconclusive debate about the line of demarcation between training and education, with the result that very important aspects of child and adolescent development have been widely neglected, with widespread economic and social consequences . . . As a secretary to the 16–19 Committee in the lead-up to the DES's joint study with the Ministry of Labour of this issue in 1975 (which became a detailed report with costed options for a Cabinet committee by 1976), I know how much effort HMI put into the presentation of policy issues which might easily have led (but for political and financial considerations) to a combined Department of Education and Training by 1978 . . . Various HMI surveys and studies, of FE or sixth form provision singly, or of overall provision involving both sectors, led to critical views of provision and the waste of resources. Conferences, courses and seminars seemed to me to be highly productive in the encouragement of change, with the exception of structural change . . . We worked strenuously to persuade heads that small sixth forms were uneconomic, lessened choice for their pupils, and were often staffed at the expense of large junior forms. FE and schools HMI worked together to expose the waste of resources within single or adjoining LEAs. Conferences that presented the facts on the economic size for sixth form (A level) work were slow in producing collaboration between schools and colleges or in discouraging the initiation of small sixth forms for status reasons.

Ken Hastings 1970

Problems and unrest seemed to be springing from an ever-growing variety of sources. One of the most traumatic innovations was the onset of training courses promoted by the Manpower Services Commission, to which the colleges began to respond in line with Government policy. I can still remember the concern felt by my own colleagues, who feared that their own work was to be undermined by the arrival of a new army of bureaucrats who knew little about education, even if they knew slightly more about training. I was frequently surprised, sometimes appalled, to discover what inadequate accommodation had been put into use for certain youth opportunity or vocational preparation courses in colleges that were already overcrowded but under pressure to respond to government training initiatives. Often, too, such training courses were being staffed by the least experienced college lecturers, though many of them at least believed in the validity of helping the young unemployed. I sometimes found it difficult to report objectively on such courses when I felt they were mainly a means of reducing the

240

unemployment statistics for the age groups between 16 and 18. (From *In a Right State* by Ken Hastings, The Book Guild Ltd, 1998*)*

Peter Brown 1973

From the mid-80s the old, self-managed, idiosyncratic lifestyle of HMI gave way to new, centrally driven, systematic, efficiency-conscious methods of working. The general changes in HMI organisation (particularly the merging of specialist teams) and inspection policy that occurred from the mid-80s onwards reduced significantly the opportunities for the intensive team working of earlier years. Many centrally-driven exercises required specialists to work singly or in pairs . . . forcing the focus of specialist HMI away from subject practice towards educational principle. At the same time the number of HMI days allocated to each inspection was reduced significantly. HMI's touch during inspections thus became lighter quantitatively as well as qualitatively. Critical comments offered to colleges were now more generalised and less discerning of specialist strengths and weaknesses than formerly. This trend was reflected in inspection reports which, though more numerous and now published, became more repetitive in the broad messages they conveyed. These changes represented a major improvement in HMI's productivity. HMI was now focusing much more on assessing and reporting overall educational standards. But their teeth had been drawn. No longer could they be expected to 'mix it' with teachers on the more specialised aspects of courses (for example, advanced practical teaching); no longer did they provide short courses for teachers; nor, from the mid-80s, did they have any say in the approval of courses, buildings or equipment; above all they no longer offered possible solutions to problems identified through 'eye through a microscope' specialist inspection and 'ear to the ground' pastoral visiting to anything like the extent that they had done in the past.

Tom Wylie 1979

Policy command for the Youth Service, of course, remained with the Department. Here it was anchored in the shifting sands of Ministerial and official interest. Youth and Community HMI, although relatively few in number, were often at the sharp end of intelligence gathering for the Inspectorate and the Department about street-level community-based activity designed to ameliorate youth issues. This activity went well beyond the responsive capacity of most formal educational institutions, whether schools or FE. It was, in part, a major task for the country's Youth Service with its diverse and unbiddable organisations. HMI's specialist knowledge, advice and professional judgement were welcomed on specific matters such as the Department's grants to over 70 national voluntary youth organisations or on the development of specific initiatives, such as youth work apprenticeships in the inner cities. It was less welcome when HMI raised questions about the Department's overall stewardship of the Youth Service, in particular its unwillingness to give unequivocal statutory underpinning and decisive policy leadership to a diversifying sector ... The much enhanced inspection activity both across the country and across the range of needs which the Youth Service was endeavouring to meet had exposed the feebleness of Government policy. This was not a comfortable message for the Inspectorate to convey. Its heightened profile in the field, its involvement as assessors on a range of national youth-related bodies, its short course programme and willingness to speak, however judiciously, on public platforms, all risked illuminating tensions between the Department and the professional advice its Inspectorate offered on policy development (or its lack). But, by 1992, disputes between youth specialist HMI and the Policy Branch were swamped by the waves which overwhelmed the Inspectorate as a whole.

Mark Todd 1979

The 16–19 work was of great interest though there were minor but persistent frustrations stemming from the position of 16–19 inspection in the HMI structure, which never seemed to be able to come to a fixed conclusion of how to organise inspection of the work: the question of who had responsibility for mounting inspections of, say, humanities A levels was never definitively answered. Was it the schools' subject committees in English, French, history etc? the FE general studies group? the 16–19 Divisional groups with a joint commissioning structure at EH? or the FHE humanities committee which later came into existence? I would not want to make too much of the frustrations nor certainly to criticise HMI for its failure to come up with a definitive way of handling them. The HMI situation (and its reported tensions) exactly mirrored the one on the ground within LEAs and within FE colleges and between sixth forms, sixth form colleges and FE colleges. The 16–19 Divisional Committees with support from the centre mounted many interesting exercises. Nationally, I especially remember the inspection of tertiary colleges which led to a publication during the late 80s. The evaluations we received from those who attended our courses were nearly always extremely positive.

Prys Owen 1963

How many colleges of education were we going to close in Wales? Hugh Harding was the 'hatchet man' in the DES and in my meetings with him I really came to think he enjoyed the role and the media publicity that went with it. He took the line that it was better to cut hard and leave colleges of a good size – if possible amalgamated with polytechnics and universities. We had real problems in Wales with this policy. We had to have a Welsh language teacher training base and we could not eliminate the Church role ... Meeting Lord Crowther Hunt and Hugh Harding to discuss the detail of numbers, the Minister was anxious to avoid too much political tension and the Principal of one of the colleges had cleverly invited him to do openings and give speeches. Hugh Harding did not want small numbers. At one point when we seemed stuck I said, 'We could keep another college alive by only cutting entry by . . . ' The Minister grabbed the chance. 'Yes, what do you think of that, Harding?' 'Not much', replied Hugh in a lordly tone and accent which I can still imitate but not describe.

Gilda Everson 1980

The work in teacher training brought HMI into close dealings with the Office. None of the civil servants had experience of teacher training. They were clear analytical thinkers, able to interpret Ministers' thinking but shrewd enough to seek professional advice to support the policies they were implementing. The advice given rested upon the findings of the inspection of all teacher training courses, set up by CI Mrs Pauline Perry and completed after four years by CI Mr Alan Marshall under whose guidance all primary professional courses were reinspected. He was quick to detect an interest in on-the-job training which came partly out of the definition of the basic content of an ITT course in the CATE criteria and partly from the dissatisfaction being voiced by non-teacher trainers on the CATE Committee. He followed the time-honoured practice of taking a critical look at the practice of other countries to help inform our own, and set up a visit to the New Jersey Articled Teacher Scheme. We were aware that this was an important issue and not blind to the implications of such a change.

Roger Hennessey 1973

In spite of the considerable progress made in establishing a team (for local authority inspections) to cover primary, secondary, FHE and LEA experience and in establishing 'custom and practice', a hard core of problems remained. First, HMI in the field persisted in perceiving LEA inspections as 'whole LEA inspections', almost PhD theses, and hankered after huge evidence bases, numerous inspections and lavish manpower which could not be afforded. The centre, on the other hand, wanted economical exercises and brief, punchy reports. Eric Bolton had produced such a report on the Toxteth area of Liverpool and it remained his model. Meanwhile, one HMI calculated that a report on Leeds (never attempted, in fact) would require 'five million HMI days'. The second problem was that to produce the more austere version still required an irreducible minimum of evidence drawn from inspections, but such were the pressures on HMI, the vagaries of the 'matrix system of management' and the CI heptarchy heading it, that even to obtain a barely respectable minimum of coverage caused massive horse trading. Although it seemed sensible to divert inspection towards the LEAs being reported on, in practice this was never easy. The CIs and their teams had their own priorities . . . In the course of running the LEA inspections we learned a great deal in a short time – and just in time – about such matters as performance indicators, CIPFA criteria, systems analysis etc. This was at a time when HMI, as well as drawing on LEA expertise in the inspections, were being increasingly seconded to management consultants who in turn found that HMI had useful insights to offer.

Alan Bassett 1976

In 1981 inner city riots in Brixton and Southall jolted us all. Eric Bolton and I discussed briefly the events of the week-end and he suggested drawing up a list of the LEAs where the problems were roughly of the same order. I was asked to contact the district inspectors in each to ask them whether they could suggest why their area had not rioted (contra-history in action and, as far as I know, entirely Eric Bolton's idea). The returns were highly significant in their unanimity. Each felt that he/she was waiting for an explosion to happen. The next week-end it did and, as I remember, HMI predicted all of them. What was of considerable satisfaction to us was that the Home Office asked immediately to be informed of our evidence. The enquiry brought a range of responses but there was clearly an identifiable thread through each: relationships between young teenagers in particular and the police were at their nadir. I believe it was salutary for the Home Office and the DHSS to realise that HMI had a network of intelligence which, because it was close to schools and was not associated with authority, gave insights they had failed to perceive. In the follow-up it became even more clear that the schools were perceived by the youngsters as refuges. Only one school had been the victim of the rioting. Many young people had been disturbed by the violence they had witnessed and needed to talk about it with their teachers: the schools could perform a true counselling job. I had been constantly surprised at the hard attitude of some of the Home Office and DHSS civil servants towards schools which they saw as exacerbating the problem of delinquency through a failure to deal with truancy. The sad part was that there was political mileage to be made from this attitude. I also believe that HMI thinking butted up against the mind-set of some of the mandarins in the DES, reflected in (later) pressures to get a more amenable SCI. The 'independence' of the Inspectorate was severely under threat when I came to leave HMI in 1985.

John Brierley 1959

An odd job (health education); but one that loomed politically, largely because of drugs and sex education. I did not like it, not because of HMI colleagues, but because of large numbers of people who appeared to me to be trendy. I thought my role was to find out what was happening in schools and to avoid some of the hot air at meetings and lectures. So the Panel (Committee) set about, following HMI Mrs Holmes' lead, inspecting and producing reports – reality as opposed to ideas. We based many of our courses on what we had seen and what we thought.

Ministers (Dr Boyson) were then much concerned with sex education and what should and shouldn't be taught in schools. There was much tension between the Health Department's views and those of the DES. At the Health Education Council meetings (which I attended often on behalf of the DES officials) I wore two hats: speaking to a DES brief and giving an HMI view. Eventually a Curriculum Matters paper (6) was produced on health education – with much on abortion, homosexuality and contraception. The drugs scene became increasingly difficult for HMI to monitor. The Home Office ran the meetings and turned to HMI for a 'field view'. In those days (1981–85) alcohol was more of a problem than drugs.

Part 4: Revolution 1986–92

Chapter 12   The World Turned Upside Down[1]

Education Reform Act 1988. National Curriculum. Markets and Management. ILEA Inspection Criteria.

Education Reform Act 1988

Reform gave way to revolution in 1986, when Keith Joseph was replaced as Secretary of State by Kenneth Baker. It was a bloodless affair. Ten years of incremental reform had prepared the ground. Without tackling the teachers and the local authorities head-on, the Department of Education (with the active participation of HMI) had successfully taken back the initiative and engaged their grudging acquiescence. This had exposed the poverty of leadership and imagination among the teachers' unions and the local authority associations and when the Thatcher government decided to apply to education the kind of radical treatment which had been dealt out to the trade unions and nationalised industries – and would in due course be applied to the health service – there was remarkably little fuss.

Does this mean that it was not really a revolution   simply a further step along a road which had already become familiar? The answer must be that it seemed like a revolution at the time. It was tied up with a general attack on the values of the welfare state, the values which underpinned the post-war education system. It was a comprehensive break with the past and a conscious rejection of the regime which had been in place since 1944.

The Baker revolution was dominated by a few powerful ideas:

● distrust of local democracy and the institutions of local government
● distrust of professional autonomy
● belief in market mechanisms as applied to the public service sector – eg education and health.

Hostility to local government was an essential ingredient – the Government refused to accept the democratic credentials of locally elected representatives. Ministers concluded that the tension between the local and the national franchise had ceased to serve a useful purpose; elected or not, local councillors were impediments to national policy.

Had the Government continued to pursue incremental reform it would have been necessary to frame a consensus by argument and persuasion and only as a last resort, by legislation. The essential element in revolutionary change was the rejection of consensus – the creation of sharply defined issues on which a general election might turn – and then the imposition of a new orthodoxy by means of a parliamentary majority.

Local government reached a low ebb in the 1980s. The electoral mechanism had left many authorities with no effective opposition. Welfare benefits had removed the link between voting and taxation – in many authorities large numbers of voters paid no local taxation. As the American colonists had attacked taxation without representation, so now ministers resented representation without the obligations of taxation. The antics of extreme left-wing local authorities – in education as in other matters – brought local democracy into disrepute.

The anti-professional animus was not confined to education – there was a generalised, populist, antagonism to the professions on Shavian lines: the belief that professions were organised conspiracies against the public. There was an assumption that they must be regulated because if left to themselves they would short-change their clients. In education this was extended to a blanket attack on the 'educational establishment' – teachers, educational administrators, university professors and principals of colleges of education – as self-regarding participants in policy-making who arranged things with their own convenience in mind. Officials in the Department of Education – and HMIs who were teachers turned civil servants – came under the same anathema. They too were infected with dangerous egalitarian ideals. There was also a discernible hostility to public service as an ideal left over from an imperial past, an idealistic refuge from the rigours of wealth-creation and competitive endeavour. The mood had changed since Martin Wiener wrote his *English Culture and the Decline of the Industrial Spirit*. The new Right was aggressively commercial and believed the public good was best served by the pursuit of private wealth.

As for the market, the new Right, led by the Institute for Economic Affairs, the oldest of the right-wing think tanks, had for more than a quarter of a century been promoting the idea that the public services should be subjected to the disciplines of competition and the market place. Joseph had reluctantly been persuaded that a voucher scheme to hand schools over to the free market raised too many practical problems in the short term, but he remained intellectually convinced that

consumers in the market place would make better decisions than
functionaries of the managed system.

This was one of the basic tenets of the Thatcher government. To increase
competition and choice was an aim which applied to all policy areas. It
was inevitable that when education came to the top of the agenda,
ministers would try to make schools compete in an educational market
place, giving consumers as much choice as possible. Needless to say, it
was impossible to create a real market and ministers, whatever their
ideological position, betrayed an old-fashioned desire to remain in charge.
Alongside the desire to use the market – albeit rigged to achieve the
results they wanted – ministers also relied on authoritarian, top-down,
policies which embodied what they thought would be best for the
education system.

The Education Reform Bill included measures which were clearly market-
inspired such as open enrolment, financial delegation (which became
known as local management of schools), grant-maintained schools and
city technology colleges, while the National Curriculum is the most
obvious example of the attempt to use top-down enforced procedures.
Other provisions spring from a variety of sources – the abolition of the
ILEA was a paying off of old scores, a direct reflection of the
Government's dislike of local government, focused on the largest and
most troublesome authority. The removal of the polytechnics from local
government provenance was both a put-down for the local authorities
and a move to make the colleges more independent and therefore
competitive. The replacement of the University Grants Committee with a
Funding Council was part of a plan to make the universities more
accountable, more commercial in their outlook, and generally more
sensitive to external influences and financial pressures.

The 1988 Act left loose ends which were quickly followed up. Having
taken the polytechnics away from the local authorities, the next stage was
to merge the Polytechnics and Colleges Funding Council and the Higher
Education Funding Council and create a single funding council for higher
education, thereby abolishing what was known as 'the binary line'. The
reorganisation of FE was completed with the removal of post-16 colleges
from local authority control, to become charitable corporations funded by
a new FE Funding Council.

Baker was one of the successes of Margaret Thatcher's governments. He
had earlier been a supporter of Edward Heath and backed his policies for

The Revolution – 1986 and After

Education Reform Act 1988

National Curriculum, Open Enrolment, Financial Delegation (Local Management of Schools), Grant-Maintained Schools, City Technology Colleges, HEFC, PCFC, Polytechnics removed from local authority control, Abolition of the ILEA.

(The sections on higher and further education were quickly reviewed and in due course the binary divide was ended, all polytechnics and some other colleges becoming universities or parts of universities, funded by the HEFC with other post-16 further education and sixth-form colleges taken out of local authority control and funded by an FE Funding Council.)

Related legislation

Education Act 1992 – Creation of OFSTED, Education Act 1993 – Schools Funding Agency, Education Act 1994 – Teacher Training Agency.

Kenneth Baker, Secretary of State for Education and Science, 1986–89.

Britain in Europe as well as his commitment to modernising Britain. He was a competent and entertaining speaker, sociable, friendly and ambitious. A 'coming man' soon gets fingered as a possible future prime minister. In Margaret Thatcher's last years, he was on the shortlist of those who might succeed her if she decided to retire of her own volition – quoted at 2:1 by Ladbrokes. The suggestion was fanciful but it dogged him as he moved into the upper reaches of government and to some extent diverted attention from his undoubted achievements at Environment, Education, the Home Office, and eventually as Chair of the Conservative Party.

His first post in the Thatcher government was as a junior minister in the Department of Trade with a special interest in information technology where he made a name for himself as an energetic and ebullient minister. He launched a successful 'Micros in School' programme of cheap computers in schools, but felt he was only getting lukewarm support from the DES which glumly drew attention to the lack of teachers trained in IT and the limited range of software available for schools. This sounds very much like someone passing on the cautious comments of HMI and the Council for Educational Technology – sage enough as far as they went but missing the point: Baker's scheme was an important *political* statement which demanded a *political* response from Elizabeth House, meaning support at Ministerial level. The response was typical of the feeble attitude which the Department took, over many years, to the challenge of educational technology. No doubt the events of 1981 lingered in Baker's memory when he took over the DES in 1986.

Not only did he grasp the economic importance of computers, but his political sense also convinced him of their social importance. He was personally excited by the new technology; he understood its appeal to the younger generation and therefore its political significance. He was sure that computers would fascinate the young and help them learn. A visit to a prototype ITeC in Hammersmith brought him hurrying back to the Department of Trade (and off to Number 10) to mobilise support for a nationwide chain of such post-school centres where young people, including many with no appetite for conventional study, could get their foot on the employment ladder by becoming computer literate.

Baker was a man who wore his ideology lightly – he was neither a wet nor yet ideologically 'one of us' – but became without any difficulty a loyal Thatcherite when the political winds changed. He could best be described as having liberal views about social policy while giving full support to the economic policies pursued by Geoffery Howe and Nigel Lawson. He was a good deal tougher than his bland exterior might suggest. At critical points in his career he knew when to fight and when to back down. He could make up his mind and impose his will on officials in a large department. If he had an obvious weakness, it was that his flair for publicity and populist appeal could undermine his judgement and lead him into folly and ridicule. When home secretary he did himself no favours by responding to a fit of tabloid panic with instant and unthought-out legislation on dangerous dogs. He was thought of as a politician who was not averse to gimmicks and stunts.

When Margaret Thatcher said farewell to Joseph, Baker was 52. He had masterminded the privatisation of British Telecom and the abolition of the Greater London Council and had faced down the militants in Liverpool. He had also prepared the plan for the introduction of the poll tax: had he had his way, he says it would have been introduced by stages and at a much lower level. He was chosen to take on education because he had the kind of political and communication skills which Joseph lacked and which were needed if education was to be placed at the top of the next election manifesto.

The Prime Minister gave him no blueprint or steer. He was told to get a grip on education – instructions not unlike those Fred Mulley took back to the DES from James Callaghan a decade earlier. He understood the political timetable: there would have to be a general election not later than 1988 – sometime in 1987 was more likely – and it was clear that he was not appointed simply to go on doing what Joseph had done. He had no close understanding of just what Joseph had achieved – on the curriculum, for instance.

Joseph had an undeserved reputation for refusing to take decisions: his agonised expression and his painstaking concern for evidence were continually misunderstood. His honesty and loyalty were at times disabling – as when he would pull his punches in negotiations with the Treasury because he sympathised with the Chancellor's aim of curbing expenditure. Margaret Thatcher, in spite of her high regard and affection for him, saw the political need for a change of direction without having a clear-cut alternative agenda. The change came as a relief to Joseph himself who was ready, after five years, to step aside. He knew his days in office were numbered and was tired of speculation about when and where the axe would fall.

Baker described the move from Environment to Education as 'like moving from the manager's job at Arsenal to Charlton' – a step down in the world. Margaret Thatcher had warned him about what to expect and passed on something of her own unhappy experiences at the DES. As he put it: she seemed to have had a 'searing time' with senior officials and she believed they had thwarted Joseph too. For his part, Joseph had left him with one last piece of advice: 'Don't make the same mistake I did of attacking the teachers.'

Baker knew that his first task was to settle the teachers' dispute and used his appointment and the new political importance of education to secure the Prime Minister's backing for a financial package for teachers. He pushed through a short bill to abolish the Burnham Committee, the body in which teachers' pay and conditions were negotiated, and then imposed a new teachers' contract. The dispute had soured the atmosphere for so long that there was an almost audible sigh of relief when the bill became an Act. The new contract spelled out the teachers' duties in greater detail – 195 days (1,265 hours) a year. As an unintended consequence, its immediate effect was to bring to an end many of the out-of-school activities teachers once ran in their own time.

Joseph had allowed the dispute to blight his relations with teachers – and not just union leaders – by constantly carping at them and their unprofessional behaviour. He believed that teachers and local administrators (and DES officials) had covered up the shortcomings of the system and felt he could not say nice things about them without perjuring himself. It went against the grain for him to engage in the innocent flattery of teachers which oils the wheels of politics for education ministers. When he tried to do so in carefully crafted phrases, slipped into major speeches, the media did not listen or did not want to know. (Having become a hate figure for militant teachers through his own misguided honesty, there was not much he could do about it: after the HMI report on the Wigan LEA in 1985, Joseph was so impressed he wanted to go to Wigan to congratulate the teachers on their good work. But the local chief education officer would not hear of it – if Joseph came, he said, there would be noisy demonstrations and ugly scenes of confrontation.)

Baker on the other hand could make mildly soothing noises to the teachers while consigning them firmly to the sidelines. Baker wrote later: 'As Environment Minister during the rate-capping disputes I had marginalised the local government unions and their leadership by reducing the frequency of meetings ... It had been a successful strategy ... I decided to adopt it at Education. While I would of course meet with the unions, these meetings would not be as frequent as in the past and none of the unions should feel they could just drop in to the Department and see me at any time.' *(The Turbulent Years*, page 172). There was a similar distancing between Baker and the authorities.

Baker's verdict on the Department in his memoirs conveys the Thatcherite message:

> *It soon became clear that not only was Departmental morale poor – teachers' walk-outs, Keith's unhappiness, and shortfalls in funding had all contributed to that – but ministerial morale was also low, due in no small part to an inability to push distinctively Conservative policies past powerful civil servants' opposition. Of all Whitehall Departments, the DES was among those with the strongest in-house ideology. There was a clear 1960s ethos and a very clear agenda which permeated virtually all the civil servants. It was rooted in 'progressive' orthodoxies, in egalitarianism and in the comprehensive school system. It was devoutly anti-excellence, anti-selection, and anti-market. The DES represented perfectly the theory of 'producer capture', whereby the interests of the producer prevail over the interests of the consumer. Not only was the Department in league with the teacher unions, University Departments of Education, teacher training theories and local authorities, it also acted as their protector against any threats which Ministers might pose. If the civil servants were the guardians of this culture, then Her Majesty's Inspectors of Education [sic] were its priesthood. Reports on schools were written with an opaque quality which defied any reader to judge whether the school being inspected was any good or not. (page 168)*

Baker was quick to size up the situation. At the Environment Department he had been a member of Committee H, the Cabinet Committee in which educational developments were discussed. There were also sweeping plans for the nationalisation of education germinating in the Treasury where Lawson, the Chancellor, flirted with taking education off the rates as a way of making local taxation manageable.[2] The news that Thatcher intended to make education the centrepiece of the 1987 general election had already reached the DES before Joseph's departure; work had already begun on plans for a national curriculum and local financial management. Ideas mooted by Joseph and his colleagues (and worked on intensively within the Department) resurfaced in different form under Baker. One was for creating new forms of direct grant school – there was speculation about a string of direct grant primary schools – and a search for other ways of diminishing local authority control. This was the germ of grant-maintained schools. Margaret Thatcher welcomed any proposal which reduced the role of the local authorities. Baker developed close relations with Brian Griffiths, the head of the Number 10 Policy Unit, who helped him keep the ear of the Prime Minister. Baker led a ministerial steering group which included Angela Rumbold, Nicholas Ridley (and Ferdinand Mount from the Policy Unit).

The scene was set for a fundamental reappraisal. There was to be a paradigm shift: a radical and revolutionary redesign. For some years there had been desultory discussion of the need for a new Education Act. The pros and cons were canvassed but without much urgency or enthusiasm. The 1944 Act had proved flexible enough for most purposes: like an old jacket, it had been let out and patched at the elbows, adapted to changed conditions without challenging its essential outline. Now the old garment was to be thrown out. Education was to get a new basic law, different principles and a new distribution of power.

A condition precedent for such a revolutionary measure was a continuing belief that the schools were failing their pupils. There was, in fact, a lot of evidence to suggest that more pupils were attaining higher standards – measured by exam results – than ever before but this evidence was cheerfully swept aside. In the years since 1970 in Britain, as in the United States, the failure of the education system had become one of the convenient clichés of received opinion – an unexamined assumption lodged in the back of the collective mind – propagated by the media and the opinion formers and strongly held by employers and employer bodies. Baker was sensitive to these unexamined assumptions and took their political potency for granted.

Not only was there an unshakeable conviction that the education system was failing, there was an explanation for this supplied by the new Right in politics. Thatcher and Baker spelled it out in their comments on the DES – the blame was to be laid on socialism and soft-centred liberalism. Schools were failing because teachers were tarred with a socialist brush. Worse than this the whole educational establishment was implicated in a *trahison des clercs* led by the professors and teacher trainers.

This analysis had the great virtue of fitting into the frame of policies which had come to be recognised as Thatcherism. The assault on union power and the privatisation of public sector industries were ways of attacking collectivism and socialistic expectations; so too was the attack on professional autonomy in the name of consumers and their rights. Baker's reforms would be rooted in this ideology: he would claim to be the parents' representative, the consumers' friend, taking their part against the self-interested professionals and local politicians.

National Curriculum

Baker had a year in which to prepare his package before the election in May 1987. He was quick off the mark, going over his plans with the Prime Minister a month after taking office, when he discussed the possibility of a national curriculum and received warm encouragement. Three months later he secured her support for delegated school budgets. He floated out titbits as he went along: at the Conservative Conference in September 1986 he announced his scheme for city technology colleges; when he made it clear these were to be independent and have no links with the LEA the cheering rose to a crescendo. He broke the news that there would be a national curriculum on a TV programme, 'Weekend World' – this before he had cleared it formally with his colleagues. Baker reckoned (rightly) that the much abused Department 'was glad to be given the green light to develop proposals for a National Curriculum' referring directly to Eric Bolton, the SCI, who gave 'much help'.

There was little consultation on the main outline of the bill. A series of discussion documents was issued in July 1987 inviting replies by the end of September, the most substantial being *The National Curriculum 5 to 16*, which produced about 10,000 comments in spite of the timing. The bill itself was published in November so there was little enough time to read and consider the tens of millions of words which flowed into the Department. But in reality the time for consultation had passed. The election mandate was clear. When Baker announced that he was going to introduce a national curriculum the news caused little stir. Only two years previously (in *Better Schools*) the Government had expressly rejected the idea. Baker had correctly judged the public mood; the National Curriculum was accepted as a *fait accompli*. Most of the debate thereafter was about the content and the arrangements for testing and publishing the results.

The bill provided for two bodies to be set up – the National Curriculum Council (NCC) and the School Examinations and Assessment Council (SEAC) – composed of individuals nominated by the Secretary of State to advise him on the preparation of the necessary Parliamentary Orders. The National Curriculum drew heavily on the work which had been undertaken by the Inspectorate and by Schools Branch III in the years leading up to 1986. During that time a clear difference had arisen between the approach favoured by the Inspectorate and that adopted by the Department. HMI had sought a rationale for choosing the content of study. They did this by considering the areas of learning and experience which would need to be covered to provide the mix of cognitive and affective learning for a broad and balanced education, and going beyond traditional subjects to 'cross-curricular themes'. The Office was more direct, dealing in traditional subjects and what and how much should be included. The differences could be seen in the succession of publications – those of the Department and of HMI – discussed in Chapter 10.

Academic study of the curriculum had led to the proliferation of theories which added to the background noise. The quest for a rationale was important, but HMI had always acknowledged that, in practical terms, subjects were the main ingredients of the curriculum because they were there in the schools, in the teachers' expertise and in the parents' expectations. By the time Baker appeared on the scene, the Inspectorate had already published *The Curriculum from 5 to 16* and the 'Curriculum Matters' series was well under way. All this was available to the subject working parties which the Secretary of State would set up.

It was always intended that testing and assessment at the end of each key stage would be an integral part of the National Curriculum and in five months in the autumn of 1987, while the bill was on its way through the House of Commons, a Task Group on Assessment and Testing (TGAT), worked out a common format for setting out the content of curriculum subjects and testing pupil progress. The bill required the curriculum to be expressed in terms of pre-stated attainment targets. TGAT, chaired by Professor Paul Black, had to accept this but wanted to ensure as far as possible that these targets and profile components arose out of the curriculum content rather than *vice versa*. Norman Thomas, the former CI for primary, was a member of the group.

The report was an extraordinary piece of work, given the time available. It provided for pupils' progression through 10 levels. It assumed that there would be some external assessment, using 'standard assessment tasks' (SATs) augmented by teachers' own assessments based on classwork. It assumed extensive in-service training of teachers for the new responsibilities they would have to undertake and called for a realistic timetable for the introduction of the new regime. It concentrated heavily on making the assessment procedure 'education friendly' – for instance it envisaged SATs which primary school children might take in the course of their ordinary work rather than under exam conditions. In fact, it tried to do the near impossible – square the circle by combining formative and summative assessment in a single, complex, system.

The proposals were quickly accepted by Baker who secured the acquiescence of Number 10 in spite of instant doubts in Margaret Thatcher's private office about the over-elaboration of the scheme. The report had been well received in the educational press and by teachers' leaders – this was enough to set alarm bells ringing in Downing Street. But the bill was coming under pressure in the House of Lords and Baker needed to divert criticism by accepting the TGAT report. Moreover, Black was very persuasive. Baker was beguiled by his advocacy and impressed with the rationale he presented.[3]

Baker was determined to press ahead as fast as he could and to trim the TGAT model of its frills and furbelows as he went along. The case for simplification was made stronger when some of the subject working groups proposed over-elaborate combinations of attainment targets and profile components. In effect, therefore, Black's TGAT report was accepted but not carried through – or, rather, only enough was carried through to assure immediate progress at breakneck speed. Bolton was one of those who, from the first, had been sceptical about the chances of the TGAT Report being implemented in its original form. It gave too many hostages to fortune. Black was left an angry and disillusioned man by the time the School Examinations and Assessment Council had done with it.

Baker had accepted the DES view that if you were going to lay down a national curriculum, it would not be enough simply to make a few core subjects compulsory and leave the rest to the discretion of the schools. If you did that, he believed, many schools would neglect the non-compulsory part. This was a view shared by HMI and by most of the subject associations. Baker wanted to make sure that technology, foreign languages, history and geography were protected and felt he could not leave out art, music and physical education.

Margaret Thatcher, on the other hand, wanted a more limited operation – a defined core of, say, English, mathematics and science. She had warned Baker against over-elaboration in March 1987, but Baker persisted. His July Consultative Paper, produced in haste but agreed in detail with Griffiths and Number 10, included a cockshy at a time allocation for the 10-subject curriculum which, omitting religious education and making no provision for extra science, maths or a second language, claimed 75–85 per cent of the time. It was prepared by Jenny Bacon, an under secretary drafted in from the Civil Service Department to work on the bill, with no previous contact with the curriculum debate. Baker did his best to evade questions about the amount of time the National Curriculum would absorb. He gave the House of Commons the meaningless, but incontrovertible, reassurance that it was unlikely to take up less than 70 per cent of the time available.

Talking about it 10 years later, Baker thought one of his mistakes had been not to increase the number of hours pupils spent in school to accommodate the enlarged curriculum. An HMI study had revealed that, though the average length of the school day in England and Wales was broadly comparable with that in other advanced countries, there were wide discrepancies from school to school. Whatever Baker thought in retrospect, however, the fact of the matter was that he had only just introduced the new teachers' contract amid much indignation and grumbling. It was far too soon to think of extending the number of contract hours.

Baker had many torrid times in the Cabinet Committee where the details of his plans were settled. His technique with the Prime Minister was to maintain his fixed smile when she hectored him. If he could not get his way first time, he would take his proposal away and re-present it at a later meeting, with an excess of supporting paper. On one famous occasion on October 28 1987, he clashed with the Prime Minister in Cabinet Committee E(EP). Again the argument was about how detailed and extensive the National Curriculum should be. She was pressing for it to be limited to 70 per cent of the time available and for art and music to be left out of the compulsory part (though not cut out altogether – 'I so enjoyed them myself at school'). When the 70 per cent figure appeared as a decision in the minutes of the meeting, Baker challenged them, and says he told the Prime Minister that if she wanted him to continue as Education Secretary she would have to stand by the plans he had announced. The Prime Minister backed down. Her instincts may have been right – the first version of the curriculum enshrined in Parliamentary Orders was hopelessly overloaded and a few years later, the ineffable Ron Dearing had to be called on twice as a one-man trouble-shooter to prune it. Baker's defence was that it was important to press ahead with a complete curriculum, knowing that it would be easier to loosen the reins later than to tighten them.

Duncan Graham became the first chairman and chief executive of the NCC. According to Graham, when Baker offered him the job, 'he (Baker) stressed the importance of the independence of the Council.' This may have given Graham a misleading impression – the NCC was to be independent but its job was circumscribed. The setting up of the NCC and SEAC was without prejudice to the Secretary of State's powers and the part he expected the Department to play in shaping the curriculum. It was the Secretary of State who chose and appointed the members of the subject working groups. With a large input from HMI, the working groups prepared their reports which they submitted to him. Their suggestions were then worked on by the Department – with HMI – and when the Secretary of State was satisfied, the proposals were sent to the NCC which would organise the consultation process and advise on the eventual Order.

The NCC did not, therefore, come into the action till subject proposals had been knocked into shape by the Office: it was a matter of grievance for the NCC that they only came into the picture at this late stage. A prime object of the Education Reform Act was to give the Secretary of State a controlling voice in the curriculum – it would be he who presented the Orders to Parliament and, therefore, it was to be expected that he would want them to incorporate his policy. Baker did not emphasise this in his conversation with Graham but he left his top officials in no doubt about what he wanted and it was not to be thwarted or delayed by the NCC or SEAC.

In his account of these events Graham asserts that senior officials wanted to run the curriculum themselves with some help from a subordinate HMI.

> *I became acutely aware that in its implementation and substance this was a Civil Service driven curriculum and not the property of HMI. This was the first evidence of a huge de facto power shift in the way education was controlled in England and Wales. The HMI were adjuncts and the inspectors on the working group were extremely helpful, but they were not the driving force: that was the civil servants. The national curriculum was their baby, the first major educational reform in Britain that had not been created by the educational professionals.* (A Lesson for us All, *page 30*)

This is an exaggerated way of restating the underlying fact about the new Act – that it gave the Secretary of State a position of authority in curricular matters and that he exercised this authority through the Department as an extension of himself. HMI played a major part in the work of the working groups but it is true, the power of decision did not lie with them – nor had they ever taken decisions about the curriculum. Graham's quarrel was with the Act and the spirit behind it. His attack on the civil servants was misdirected.

The arrangements could only work if the NCC and SEAC were made aware of what the Secretary of State wanted and were willing to go along with it. The political importance of the Chairs became obvious when, at a critical point, both the technocrats who had been installed at the beginning were sacked to make way for people who were closer to the ideology of the Secretary of State.

The Inspectorate could be described as being collectively in favour of the National Curriculum while having reservations about the methods by which it was being introduced, notably the speed with which decisions were being taken and implemented. Among the rank and file there were more doubts. HMI had been called upon in the early days to help the NCC get off the ground, but its relationship with Graham and the NCC was ambiguous. Graham did not want to be dependent on HMI, some of whom he thought were hostile to what was going on, and too anxious to stress their independence. There were clashes between his staff and members of the Inspectorate: 'We were told early on that HMI considered they had a right to inspect the National Curriculum Council.' Someone clearly got hold of the wrong end of a fairly large stick – there was never any question of HMI 'inspecting' the NCC; perhaps someone misunderstood the function of the NCC's HMI assessor.

HMIs disliked the method of working backwards from attainment targets and they counselled against laying out the National Curriculum in too much detail. But they were also made aware that they had lost those battles. Brian Arthur, who was the CI in whose lap curricular matters had come to rest, recalled discussions with Griffiths, the head of the Number 10 Policy Unit, followed by a meeting at Downing Street where he (and a colleague from Schools Branch III) were told, in terms, that 'our rationale and framework would not do.' The Office whose priority, according to Arthur, was to defend Baker's concept of a 10-subject curriculum against the minimalists, 'was not going to trammel itself with any HMI rationale'.

Few HMIs had a clear idea of what was happening. The senior members of the Inspectorate were unable to keep the rank and file informed of what was going on because they were deeply involved in confidential discussions with ministers and senior DES officials. As Arthur recalled:

Perhaps because we were unable to take them into our confidence sufficiently, many HMI in the field were unaware of the pressure of policy machination and thought we were sacrificing 'independence', failing to see that, within the welter of advice coming from all directions, the Government was not duty bound to heed HMI. The Act went through very speedily, given its far-reaching and controversial nature (not only in respect of the National Curriculum); it was a remarkable political achievement. The dissension was apparent in all quarters. The work of elaboration went on. Initially the brunt was borne by the working groups (including SIs and other HMIs drafted in to help the groups and SEAC). Their job was to recommend attainment targets, levels of performance and programmes of study. There were heated arguments within the working groups, with the NCC, and with successive Secretaries of State who came to deal with them (and the NCC) more and more peremptorily.

Some subjects ran into more difficulty than others. The maths working party was a near disaster, whose membership had not been selected as carefully as some. Sig Prais from the National Institute for Economic and Social Research (who cheerfully told his fellow group members that he was Margaret Thatcher's appointee), wanted long division and plenty of it. It was he who a few years earlier had set alarm bells ringing with articles comparing maths standards in English and West German schools. Others such as Hugh Berkhart and Hilary Shuard (who had been a member of the Cockcroft Committee) were determined to resist what they saw as a reactionary prescription.

All subject groups had difficulty – notably English, history and technology. A year earlier, Baker had set up a committee on English chaired by a scientist, Sir John Kingman, vice-chancellor of Bristol University. Its report had not been to the liking of the Conservative hard Right. It had refused to bring back formal grammar and, though it insisted that every child should be taught to speak and write Standard English, it was seen by the coterie of right wingers who made themselves the self-appointed guardians of the traditional curriculum as 'the work of educational professionals'. In the minds of the ideologues, therefore, it was the job of the working party to ditch Kingman and vindicate the old-fashioned values of formal English teaching.

Chairman of the English working party was Brian Cox, professor of English at Manchester University. He seemed to have impeccable credentials, having been one of the original Black Paper editors. Unfortunately he turned out to have rather liberal views on how English should be taught in schools and to be anxious to distance himself from the back to basics right wing. The Conservative camp thought he was insufficiently wedded to formal grammar teaching and dangerously inclined to believe children should enjoy learning. The English proposals were only sent on to the NCC after the Department had worked hard to make them acceptable to Baker (and Number 10).

It had been clear all along that the questions raised by subjects like English and history were political dynamite – selecting what to teach would depend in part at least on political and sociological judgements.

Such questions could provide relatively harmless diversions for teachers and academics, but put to an official working party for national answers they could quickly lead to confrontation. Cox's English curriculum was referred back to the NCC for review almost as soon as it had been introduced: there had been a change of Secretary of State and it was not to his taste nor that of his unofficial advisers.

History was a particular concern of Baker, who was aware that his right-wing colleagues had strong views about the function of history teaching in creating a sense of national identity. School history had come a long way since *1066 and All That* – so too had the national identity in the post-imperial age and an increasingly multicultural society. Given the universal tendency for lay people, including politicians, to hark back to their own school days, there was no shortage of experts on the school history curriculum, one of whom was lodged at Number 10.

The main technical issue was the relative weight to give to 'understanding and skills' as against 'knowledge'. The working group elected not to have 'knowledge' as an attainment target. The programmes of study would make clear the ground which courses would have to cover, but the attainment targets would be framed in terms of understanding and skills. Right-wing critics were quick to interpret 'understanding' as a code word for woolly-minded cop-outs such as 'empathy' – which involved asking children to use their historical imagination to see things through the eyes of others. Michael Saunders Watson, the Tory landowner Baker had chosen to chair the history group (home address, Rockingham Castle, Northants) was an Englishman whose castle was his home. He was Tory enough to recognise the objections to history as a government-selected list of events – objections which became clearer than ever when the Prime Minister waded in with a demand for more emphasis on the learning and testing of historical facts. The working group refused to be coerced and came up with a terse and telling response: 'Names, dates and places provide only the starting points for understanding. Without understanding, history is reduced to parrot learning and assessment to a parlour memory game.'

After a cooling-off period the DES drafted proposals which the next Secretary of State, John MacGregor, could send to the NCC and the history order was completed. Another damaging hitch which showed how undesirable it was to put critical curricular decisions in the hands of ministers, occurred after MacGregor was replaced by Kenneth Clarke. The new Secretary of State suddenly came out with an arbitrary ruling that history, as such, should end for any generation of students, 20 years before their school days began.

Graham's blow-by-blow account of the making of the National Curriculum gives a bitter account of his experience. His narrative has therefore to be read with caution. What to him was unwarranted interference by the Department with the working of the NCC was, to the Department, the proper pursuit of the Secretary of State's interests. When appointed, he had misunderstood what the Minister wanted and misconstrued what was meant by the independent advice of a respected council.

When Graham decided to complain, his only way to see Baker quickly was to track him down to Betws-y-Coed in North Wales where on 16 June 1989, he confronted a Secretary of State, clad in running gear, a helicopter waiting to whisk him off to run a half marathon. It was a hilarious scene. Baker turned away his wrath with a soft answer, repudiated the Department's intrusive ways and promised Graham his firm support like the chairman of a football club assuring his manager of his total confidence shortly before sacking him. Things continued without much change.

All this time Nick Stuart and his staff in the Department were being pressed hard by ministers to deliver the National Curriculum in short order. Whatever Baker might say to Graham, he wanted the curriculum on time and in a form he could approve. The timetable was ridiculously tight. Baker certainly would not have got his finished article if members of the NCC had been allowed to drag things out.

The NCC had realised that it would become more difficult as they worked their way up the age range – Key Stage 4 problems had been put on the back-burner. The NCC's attempts to look at cross-curricular themes and whole curriculum problems had been choked off by the Office to stop effort from being diverted from the immediate work in hand. When John Patten took over from Clarke as the fourth Secretary of State in six years, the chickens were on their way back to the roost – the curriculum was overloaded, the assessment procedures were too onerous and Key Stage 4 was unmanageable. Patten's health suffered, as did his finesse – he managed to defame a national parents' organisation and was at the receiving end of an action for slander brought by Tim Brighouse, the last surviving educational administrator with flair.[4] As already mentioned, a troubleshooter had to be imported to slim down the National Curriculum and provide some breathing space. As the century wound to its close, the

10-subject National Curriculum set out in the first 25 sections of the Education Reform Act was effectively curtailed at the end of Key Stage 3 and the search was on for a more flexible, differentiated and inclusive 14–19 curriculum which would still provide breadth and balance.

HMI had not been cast in the leading role in the drawing up of the National Curriculum but they had put in a lot of work on the foundations. Their publications provided a starting point for the working groups. If the Office continued to rely heavily on HMI during this period, it remains true that a sea-change had taken place: there was undoubtedly a greater confidence among ministers and senior officials in their own judgements. There was a sense in which the Education Reform Act was a liberating experience for the Department, a rite of passage which brought with it a new, enlarged role in the post-revolutionary world. The fact that this revolution bore a particular political stamp was not important – the main revolutionary changes would outlast the politics of Thatcherism.

Markets and Management

The attempt to create a market in education was a relatively half-hearted affair. There was no real confidence that standards could be raised and maintained by the market alone. Schools would be assessed, results would be published and parents would have the freedom to vote with their children's feet, if they believed that the school their children attended was failing on the job. This was all right in theory but lacked conviction in practice.

Of course, there were bound to be shortcomings in the market. Parents could only know so much about the schools from which they had to make a choice. Markets depend on transparency. The Reform Act followed up what had already been done to make the publication of information a statutory duty laid on governors.[5] Had ministers really trusted the market all this might have been enough – political advisers like Stuart Sexton thought it should be: he would have liked the National Curriculum to be less detailed and for schools to be left enough market-constrained freedom to interpret it in their own way. That way a more lively market would have developed and parents would have been given more real choice.

The Conservative government, however, wanted belt and braces. They wanted to impose market disciplines but they also wanted the kind of administrative accountability appropriate for publicly funded institutions.

They knew that whatever they might say, the man in the street – and in the voting booth – would expect them to retain responsibility. New Labour, when their turn came, dropped the market rhetoric and concentrated on the central controls.

Questions of accountability came up in a different form in connection with the local management of schools (LMS) – one of the most successful and popular innovations in the 1988 Act. The idea was not original – several counties, among them Cambridgeshire and Cheshire – had been bringing in phased schemes of financial delegation, but the requirements of the Act went farther and faster than anything tried out at local level, and systematised it. Local authorities were required to hand over most of the 'general schools budget' to the schools themselves. The proportion which LEAs were allowed to retain for central services was progressively reduced, and increasingly, such central services as remained had to be charged out to schools, as and when the schools chose to use them. Much responsibility was being transferred to the schools but there remained open questions of accountability. What public authority was to hold them accountable? And who was to support, or ultimately bail out, failing schools?

The Government's attitude towards the LEAs was fundamentally hostile but it needed the authorities to play an essential part in the transition period when the Act was being brought into operation and when governors, heads and local administrators were learning what was expected of them. It remained uncertain for a long time what would be the long-term responsibilities of the LEAs for monitoring the progress of their schools and providing them with the support they needed. Baker was pragmatic about short-term matters: he required the LEAs to provide the back-up for in-service training in the new assessment procedures and in the early implementation of the National Curriculum. His response was to make four-year grants for 400 supplementary local authority advisers and to make speeches stressing the importance of local authority support staff (see Chapter 13).

All this raised looming questions for HMI and for their future. Baker liked to use the metaphor of the Department as the hub of the education system and the schools (not the local authorities) as the rim. He devised his model without spending too much time working out what form the spokes would take. One reason for this was the developmental nature of the system he was putting in place. Important matters were left in the melting pot – as for instance, with regard to grant-maintained schools. He created the means for schools to opt out of local authority control. He then had to sit back and see how many schools decided to apply. The Education Reform Act was based on the assumption that the LEAs were holding the schools back with red tape and political interference. This being so, it was logical to expect the schools to welcome the grant-maintained escape route. But this expectation had to be put to the test. The proposals sprang from a coterie of political advisers. Only a narrow circle of like-minded people with knowledge of the system were consulted – how much wishful thinking lay behind the grant-maintained initiative?

It was in the nature of things that grant-maintained schools would be unpopular with supporters of the old order – which meant most teachers, chief education officers and local authority members. There was strong opposition, not only from most local authorities and teachers' organisations, but also from the Churches – particularly the Roman Catholics – who were major stakeholders in the system. Applications were slow in coming forward. After the general election of 1992 the pace was expected to pick up but this did not happen, and as the fortunes of the Conservatives declined, fewer governing bodies were prepared to chance their arms in the face of unremitting hostility from the government-in-waiting. All in all, in the seven years which followed the passing of the Act, some 1,100 schools opted out – less than 5 per cent of all maintained schools.

Both Margaret Thatcher and John Major would have liked to see grant-maintained status become the norm. Some saw the arrangements for grant maintained status as a stepping stone to a voucher scheme. There was talk of forcing every school to ballot its parents at regular intervals till they voted the way the Government wanted. But other ministerial statements insisted on the right of parents to make up their own minds. There were many reasons why a school and its parent body might decide to opt out. Ministers imagined that schools in 'loony-left' urban areas would do so to avoid political interference. Few did. Some of the schools which applied had ambitious heads who wanted the increased freedom which grant-maintained status might bring – and the financial benefits built into the scheme as incentives. When such heads could call on powerful business people as chairs of governors, their chances of going grant-maintained were likely to be strong. But grant-maintained status was also seen as a last resort for schools threatened with closure or merger because of a surplus of places. How ministers dealt with these schools would be a test of their integrity and the principles of opting out.

Proposals for closures and mergers and for grant-maintained status brought requests from the Office to District HMIs for on-the-spot advice. There were established arrangements between HMI and the officials who dealt with reorganisation schemes and HMIs were accustomed to working with territorial principals, visiting schools involved and giving professional advice on the merits of whatever was proposed. Often closures were part of larger schemes involving several schools and, as with comprehensive plans, requiring judgements about the direct and indirect impact on the schools of a neighbourhood. But applications for grant-maintained status were handled by a different group of officials, whose success was measured in the number of schools which they could bring into the grant-maintained corral. As Richard Brake, the SI who was closest to this episode put it:

> There were difficulties. The whole principle of GM schools aroused passions among individual HMI who were reluctant to make recommendations in a development of which they disapproved. Pointing out that what they wrote would actually be seen by Ministers and acknowledged often eased their anxieties. More disagreeably HMI were often caught in the crossfire between two Schools Branches. Schools 1 was charged with taking out surplus places and closing schools ... Schools 3 had the responsibility to get as many GM schools as possible to meet the Government's targets. As many of the schools applying for GM status were doing so to avoid closure or amalgamation there was considerable room for conflict ... I recall a most uncomfortable morning about a school with the two heads of Branch, one of whom wanted to close it, the other to give it GM status, arguing over examination results and how they should be interpreted, and each, by putting his own 'spin' on the factual data, trying to enlist HMI support on his side.

The Treasury's desire to see surplus places taken out was frequently at odds with the policies for competition and market choice. The competition policy depended on there being spare places. It was a not unfamiliar situation – unresolved tension between two ministerial objectives, neither of which the Secretary of State wished to give up. The two policies went forward side by side, each case being taken on its merits in a pragmatic manner. From the outside it looked like a muddle.

It was never easy to get local authorities to tackle redundant schools. The legal procedures were cumbersome, and involved the publication of notices and the consideration of objections by the Secretary of State before he could give approval. One reason why local authorities held back was because, too often in the past, it had been the ministers who had backed down in the face of political pressure from their own back benchers. Teachers and their unions did all they could to resist closures having no taste for, or experience of, redundancy. Some authorities like the ILEA unwisely signed no redundancy agreements with their teachers.

Of the first 350 applications for grant-maintained status, more than one in six were from schools threatened with closure. There were no clear pre-stated criteria. All there was to go on were a few ministerial statements from which aspects of policy might be inferred. HMIs would give their advice on the local impact of any proposal on the quality of education and quality was initially regarded as a prime criterion. But the pressures built up and increasingly the Office recommendations had to reflect the Government's political imperative that opting out should go forward. When primary schools were invited to apply, size and viability came to be seen as more important than standards and quality of work and 'in the end, only very small schools or those with rapidly falling rolls were refused.'

The grant-maintained school was the single most vulnerable innovation in the Reform Bill package, the one which would not survive a change of government. Many opting-out campaigns were bitterly fought, but once a change of status had gone through, grant-maintained school parents knew that so long as the Conservatives remained in power grant-maintained schools would face life on favourable terms: in most cases they were well placed for recruitment, and not only was going grant-maintained thought to give them an elite status they enjoyed financial benefits as well. At first they were funded directly by the DES and later by the Funding Agency for Schools. When grant-maintained schools moved out from under the LEA umbrella, their progress was monitored by HMI under a programme set up for the purpose. Support groups were created for the handful of schools – Stratford School in east London, being the best known – which ran into serious trouble. HMIs also took an interest in the city technology colleges. The department's architects got a new lease of life working on designs for city technology colleges with, as ever, participation from HMI.

ILEA

The decision to abolish the ILEA came at the end of a long campaign Baker had made his own. In 1980, before becoming a member of the Thatcher government he had, as a London MP, headed a group which produced a report for Mark Carlisle, which recommended getting rid of the ILEA and the transfer of education to the inner London boroughs. Secretary to Baker's group was Stuart Sexton, who later was a political adviser at the DES in Joseph's time. The report was not well argued and

Peter Newsam, the ILEA education officer 'sandbagged it' (Baker's phrase) without much difficulty. This rankled with Baker. He clearly recognised that Sexton's report to which he (Baker) had put his name, was a poor thing, and smarted under Newsam's barbs. After the Greater London Council was abolished in 1986 – the legislation was taken through by Baker as Secretary for the Environment – the ILEA became an *ad hoc* authority for education with a directly elected membership. It was the first such *ad hoc* education authority in England since 1903 when the last one – the London School Board – was abolished.

Baker hesitated before making a frontal attack on London in his bill – he knew there would be strong establishment support for the ILEA but believed that the left wingers who provided its political leadership would, if given enough rope, volunteer for the hangman's noose. Following a manifesto promise, the bill originally allowed boroughs to opt out of the ILEA if they wished to do so. He was delighted when a back-bench amendment promoted by Michael Heseletine and Norman Tebbit settled for immediate abolition rather than death by a thousand cuts.

The ILEA was subject to two HMI inspections, one in 1980 which Peter Newsam decided to publish – this was before the routine publication of HMI reports on schools – and one for Baker. Both reports were a disappointment to ministers because of the balancing act which was second nature to the Inspectorate. London had always had some of the best and some of the worst schools in the country. Looking at a sample of schools across inner London, Inspectors were bound to find good, bad and indifferent, and while they were quite prepared to draw attention to weaknesses where they found them they felt equally obliged to record the good things as well.

Baker's attitude was less stoical than Joseph's. HMI's second report on London touched on the implications of the abolition of the ILEA, and concluded that to do away with the London authority would have serious adverse consequences. In a separate paper, Bolton set out the strengths and weaknesses of the ILEA as HMI knew them, emphasising what might be lost with the abolition of the authority – eg the ILEA's music provision, its excellent youth service, and provision for adult education which was second to none. This Paper was leaked to the press, presumably by one of those mysterious 'sources close to' ministers who know how to do these things discreetly. It had become a common phenomenon for ministers to leak documents to the press through their political advisers for their own purposes. In this instance, HMI was wrongly suspected. The leak may have been intended to pre-empt some of the professional opposition to what was happening in London, while casting the Inspectorate in a bad light in Conservative circles. In a matter of months, the climate inside and outside the Department had changed out of recognition and being the bearer of uncongenial news was becoming a more and more dangerous task.

After the Act had gone through, HMI were alerted to difficulties in one of the newly formed inner London boroughs, Hackney. In the term before the borough took over, two HMIs had paid a routine visit to a Hackney voluntary aided secondary school and, as a result, a full inspection was carried out. This produced a devastating critique which was picked up by the press and persuaded the SCI to send HMIs in to every school in the borough of Hackney.

In inspecting the schools, HMI were also inspecting the area. Hackney was an inner city area, where living costs were high, and it was hard to recruit and harder to retain sufficient experienced teachers to work with a school population affected by severe social and economic problems. Those who opposed putting education back to the boroughs had conditions like these in mind. Hackney had also for many years been a hotbed of Trotskyites and members of the Socialist Workers Party – many of them radical teachers and members of Rank and File. The report which followed was very critical. The episode was seen by some of those involved as a vindication of a new, tougher, inspection style which, having found a bad situation, was prepared to do something about it.

By the time the report was published, however, its authors were disappointed to find it had been toned down. It was a delicate situation with strong political overtones where it was appropriate to tread with great care. Hackney was a brand-new LEA with more than its share of social problems. Perhaps it deserved a little time to shake down before being put through the wringer. Perhaps also there was an awareness that the new Education Secretary, Kenneth Clarke, did not start with any great respect for the independent traditions of the Inspectorate.

After the break-up of the ILEA, the metropolitan HMIs continued to work as a team and to monitor the situation. They made sure the Office knew about the central activities of the London authority – like the ILEA Teachers' Resource Centre and the Research and Statistics unit which were at risk when the ILEA was removed from the scene. Their efforts did nothing to stop the break-up from going ahead; nor did they endear themselves to the Secretary of State.

Inspection Criteria

Other important developments in the way HMI went about their work were coming to a head in the middle and later 1980s. HMI were affected by the managerialism which swept through the Government machine. Working patterns were reviewed and formalised with emphasis on targets and individual annual assessments. This was part of a larger concern with evaluation – evaluation of individual institutions (schools and colleges); evaluation of the impact of government policies on the education service; and the evaluation of all aspects of Inspectorate activity.

Translated into questions for HMI this meant asking how to define and identify 'educational quality', 'levels of attainment', 'quality of teaching and learning' and all the other elusive concepts which HMIs spent their lives pursuing. Historically, HMI had managed to develop an inspection process which relied on accumulated experience and trained observation to form the basis of judgements. It was only at the end of the 1970s that some of the criteria used in different aspects of the inspection process began to come out. An HMI was more like a music critic than an analytical chemist. Judgements were formed from all the inspector saw and sensed as well as from the evidence presenting itself in objective form.

This said, the art of inspection had not stood still over the years. For a combination of reasons it had been refined and extended with a view to increasing consistency and regularity of practice. When the number of full inspections declined in the 1960s and early 1970s it was said that there was 'a significant loss of experience'; as older HMIs retired they were followed by new entrants who did not have the same grounding. As we have seen, when the policy changed again in the mid-1970s, it was necessary to provide more detailed guidance on basic principles, on how to write up and conduct an inspection. Inspection techniques had to develop as HMI were confronted by a wider range of tasks demanding different kinds of inspection – for example, the short ('dipstick') inspection which was brought in for the follow-up Secondary Survey in the 1980s. In the 1970s, more formality had been introduced into the Note of Visit, the HMI's bread-and-butter record, to make it easier to retrieve information. This was the beginning of a process: Notes of Visit became even more highly structured using numerical gradings, as the use of computers spread.

The ever wider use of surveys (particularly in divisional area teamwork in the 1970s) focused attention on what information HMIs should collect

and the way it should be reported. There was also concern that the
process of collecting the information should not itself affect what
happened in school. In the Primary Survey, for instance, HMIs were
asked to note whether dictation was being used in the teaching of literacy.
In the Secondary Survey information was required in comparative form
on the amount of oral work (and listening) which was going on in each
class. A check-list was needed to build up a consistent picture of practice
across a range of schools. But there was no intention of publishing this in
advance because that would have changed the nature of the exercise.

There was much talk of setting down the criteria to be used in inspection.
But 'criteria' was not used in the true sense of the word. As Norman
Thomas, who had used scales and grades in the Primary Survey, put it,
'what most people call criteria are in fact elements of behaviour/action
that the observer makes a judgement about in terms of effectiveness. They
are no more objective; ie observer-free, than more general judgements.
They are simply a more specific list of matters on which subjective
judgement is to be made.' Nor, he might have added, does putting
numbers to them make them more precise than the judgements on which
they are based; making them spuriously quantifiable may facilitate
specious comparisons.

Giving advance notice of 'criteria' might have led teachers to draw the
wrong conclusions – conclusions which could distort their behaviour as
teachers. In fact, none of these refinements in inspection procedures led to
the *publication* of the criteria HMI would use in judging quality. But as the
use of criteria became widespread in work on secondary school exams, in
the late 1970s the science HMIs agreed eight criteria they would use for
inspection purposes. They were happy to discuss these openly with the
staff of science departments when they came to carry out formal
inspections.

Writing about the accountability of HMI in 1979,[6] Sheila Browne had
defended the lack of any rigid definition of inspection. HMI, she said,
were concerned with what an institution was doing, not with what it was
not doing. They were not imposing set standards but engaged in open-
minded inspection and reporting.

> *HMI's accountability is a somewhat delicate plant; the service is always fully extended;*
> *it is highly selective; it samples continually but does not provide cyclical cover; it*
> *depends for results on complex communications and the decisions and actions of others,*
> *which may well not be taken on educational grounds. To protect and foster its*

accountability HMI must therefore keep under constant review the detail of its programme, the conclusions it derives from inspection and its means of communication. It must be sure that it is in a position to see clearly what is there to be seen and to report accurately and compellingly. That is what is expected of it.

This, of course was written before the publication of HMI school reports. David Soulsby was one of those who argued that: 'to make criteria explicit, however difficult, is arguably essential among professionals; and the more HMI reports are published the more untenable the position of operating without explicit criteria.' But he added an important, if implausible, rider: 'To make criteria explicit does not entail their publication outside HMI.' If they were important, they were bound to come out.

If the criteria used by HMI were not to be published in advance, was it possible to deduce them retrospectively? Michael Salter HMI was asked to answer just that question. (He was one of the HMIs who had the unenviable job of reading and summarising all the published reports of school inspections – not even Joseph had been able to maintain his resolution to read them all as they came in.) In an internal HMI paper, *Judging Quality and Effectiveness* (1986) Salter sought to identify the criteria used by HMI in their assessments.

In fact, the real criteria proved elusive. It was possible to list the objective elements – to make a checklist of factors making for good (or poor) schools, teaching, teachers. It was possible – though difficult – to go some way towards adducing performance indicators, which could be used (with reservations) for making comparisons between schools. But these did not constitute criteria in the sense of revealing the basis of an HMI's judgement of what is 'good' or 'bad'. If HMI could not define their criteria, they could exemplify their judgements after they had been made – in publications such as *Ten Good Schools* and the 'Education Observed' series. This was not the same as going into an inspection with a list of possible statements against which to measure what was good or bad, true or false. As one of the published HMI papers on inspection practice put it (in 1990), 'Inspectors' observations and judgements of what is going on [are not] decided by pre-determined criteria. When Inspectors have decided what they think of what they have seen, they work out criteria, and where appropriate, apply them.'

Perhaps such a formulation attempts to make up in inspectorial self-confidence what it lacks in objectivity. But the value of not being tied down to pre-stated (and probably relatively banal) quality criteria was very real. It was summed up in an aphorism which Murray White distilled from long experience. HMI, he said, must never ignore 'the irritating success of the wrong methods'. If there were to be criteria they would have to be drawn sufficiently widely to recognise merit in a wide variety of circumstances, and identify the second-best as second-best even when it conformed to the criteria.

One of the SIs involved, Roger Hennessey, felt that the attempt to make more transparent the inspection process was 'a vital task, albeit fifty years late'. Nothing could hide, however, the dangers attached to tampering with the mystique of inspection. HMIs had a particular kind of unauthoritarian authority, a particular kind of wisdom; they went out of their way to claim nothing but a conscientious willingness to report, fairly, what they saw when they visited schools and colleges. They were not part of the line management or command structure. Essentially, HMI's stock-in-trade was judgement. Its reputation was built on a perception of fairness and integrity. These were qualities ascribed to the Inspectorate collectively even when human frailty marred the performance of individual HMIs.

To put such perceptions of authority and wisdom under the microscope was dangerous indeed. The fact that this seemed to be necessary was a sign of the changing times, the revolution which was taking place. A case could be made out for saying that this was the writing on the wall which spelled out the passing of the old Inspectorate. In a real sense the authority of HMI had existed in the eye of the beholder. In the 1960s, cynical old-lag HMIs would pass on to new recruits the maxim – 'its good, because I say its good,' knowing this to be a travesty which contained a grain of truth. By the mid-seventies, in an age of evaluation and accountability, HMIs were going to be asked to show the colour of their money. Why is it good? What would it have to satisfy to be counted as good? Is that the view of the Inspectorate or just your subjective opinion? If you know what is good, why not tell us in advance so that we can learn what to do to satisfy the most fastidious inspector? And the conscientious HMI knows that to reduce teaching and learning to a set of measurable performance indicators is reductionist and ends up with a sheet of boxes to tick. Bolton was well aware of the dangers. But the exercise had to go forward and not only were general criteria advanced, but SIs did the same for their subjects.

HMI were also implicated in the Department's response to a Treasury-led evaluation initiative. This concerned moves to make civil servants evaluate the policies and programmes for which they were responsible.

David Hancock, the DES permanent secretary, circulated a paper on evaluation which referred explicitly to the part HMI would play in evaluating education policies:

> *For many of the Department's policies the most important instrument of evaluation is HMI. Evaluation is their business ... Relevant HMI should be involved in planning policy evaluation ... What is required should ... be ... built into HMI's programme of work.*

Performance indicators were also a matter of widespread interest – the subject of an OECD project, as well as of concern in the United States and at the DES. They seemed to offer a painless way to provide statistical measures which could be used for audit purposes. Other fields of activity such as the health service were engaged in a similar search for simple measures of performance. In education there were attempts to build up a package of indicators, some academic, some financial, some community-based, some relating to conduct such as truancy and delinquency, which could be used to assess school performance. The social context continued to present stubborn difficulties and the attempt to describe the playing field more fully did nothing to make it more even. The quest for simple ways of measuring 'value-added' ran into the same social problems.

Anthea Millett was the CI responsible for management and Richard Brake, the SI whose brief included work on evaluation. By 1988 the HMIs' bible – an orange-coloured ring-binder containing *Inspection and Reporting: Working Notes for HMI* – was a bulky assembly of A4 pages. Two kinds of reporting inspections were described: those of individual institutions (all or partial) and surveys (phase, aspect, subject or area , or a combination of any of these). Particular forms were provided for particular types of reporting inspection.

For full inspections schools could be asked for an *aide memoire* of factual material about the school in question – there was no set form in which this should be set out – and this was not intended to be a big production. If possible one lesson taught by each member of staff was to be observed – 'observation and description are the necessary foundation on which evaluative judgements are based ... they are not in themselves the purpose of the exercise'. In a large school or an FE college it would not always be possible to observe all the teachers. The traditional disclaimers are included: HMIs do not report on individual teachers and if there are any implied criticisms they are to be discussed with the individual concerned first; HMI are not involved in the appointment, promotion or dismissal of teachers.

There is a lot about the writing of reports – the need to avoid dogmatic prescription, to relate any recommendations to evaluation, to make sure assessments do not appear to come from the 'rigid application of a ready-made blue-print or template,' but from an impartial consideration of what is happening in the institution. 'There is no role for an "HMI pontifex" making sententious pronouncements about the purposes of education.' HMIs are enjoined to stick to Plain English and their own house style.

As well as the instructive text on what to do and what not to do, the Working Notes provided a set of headings for school reports – one for primary, one for secondary – augmented by illustrative lists of the topics which might be treated under these headings. Other sections dealt at length with higher and further education reporting. With the lists of 'possible topics for inclusion' under each heading, the 1988 instructions provided a long and detailed specification for the visiting inspector. An important caveat was attached: 'all of these papers are to be regarded as evolutionary, and circumstances may well lead to further revisions.'

The formalisation of the inspection process had gone a long way, in the sense that a step-by-step procedure had been laid down and the headings for a full inspection report had been exhaustively listed. By so doing, the senior managers had removed much of the scope for inconsistency. If HMIs obeyed the guidelines they were given, all reports would follow the same pattern and judgements would be made about the same matters, even if there were no definitions of quality or 'criteria' as such. As the next chapter will show, the groundwork was in place for what would become the first OFSTED Handbook.

Notes

[1] See *Oxford Review of Education*, Vol. 24, No. 1 dated March 1998 – *Through the Revolution and Out the Other Side* – edited by Stuart Maclure.

[2] Lawson, Nigel (1992) *The View from No.11: Memoirs of a Tory Radical*. London: Bantam Press, 608–9.

[3] By an unhappy coincidence, the TGAT Report and the Higginson Report on *Advancing A Levels* arrived on Kenneth Baker's desk about the same time. Baker, knowing Margaret Thatcher would dislike both, decided to shelve Higginson and focus his persuasive powers on TGAT.

[4] Tim Brighouse was chief education officer for Birmingham, before that chief education officer for Oxfordshire and professor of education at Keele University.

[5] The Education Reform Act built on important legislation in 1980 and 1986. In addition to strong parental representation on governing bodies, provision had been made for more members from the local community, and for LEA representation to be curtailed.

[6] Browne, S (1979) 'The accountability of HM Inspectorate (England)', in Lello, J. (ed.) *Accountability in Education*. London: Ward Lock, 35–44.

HMI Miscellany
Extracts from HMI personal accounts

Colin Richards 1983

When preparations for the National Curriculum got under way, we worked extensively on co-ordinating HMI responses to the multitude of requests for advice from civil servants unversed in these matters and faced for the first time with the complexities of curriculum design and implementation. I remember countless discussions with extremely able civil servants whose logic was impeccable but whose grasp of the only partly rational world of schools was almost non-existent. HMI's task was as much to educate the DES in curricular issues as to provide detailed inspection-based professional advice in the intricacies of curriculum implementation . . .

I think the subject SIs had a major influence on most of the working groups . . . SIs were regarded as authoritative sources of advice on good practice, on what was feasible in schools and on contemporary standards and quality. The 'Curriculum Matters' documents were widely 'mined' in pursuit of the working groups' tasks. When, later, revisions became necessary the SIs were again consulted. I suspect that on most working groups the subject SI was the most influential single individual, with the possible exception of the Chair.

In the early years of the implementation of the National Curriculum HMI were carrying out their classic function – evaluating the impact of government policies on policy and practice in schools. I don't believe HMI saw themselves as 'key stage cops' enforcing compliance! They endeavoured to see which things were going well and which were going less satisfactorily, so as to feed back to the Department and the National Curriculum Council what further needed to be done to ease implementation problems, and which aspects of the National Curriculum needed revising. HMI evidence was a major factor in bringing about the Dearing review of 1993.

George Hicks 1976

By the time the Technology Working Group was appointed, pressure from the profession caused the title 'Technology' to be changed to that of 'Design and Technology' for work which involved the use of materials – listed in the Group's terms of reference as wood, metal and plastics. This was something they thought they understood. Confusion returned, however, when the term 'Technology' was later re-introduced to describe the combination of D & T and Information Technology. The Working Group by this time was responsible for both. But its original terms of reference, which clearly described CDT, were never strictly referred to or ever completely met and D & T was said to mean something quite different from that which had been going on so successfully in schools for almost 20 years. The majority of the Group had no experience of teaching or studying D & T and the voice of the minority, including HMI, was quickly discouraged. Challenging and constructive criticism was ignored. Warnings from the HMI observer to the Group, to the DES and to CIs . . . of the unworkable nature of the emerging proposals and the assessment model went unheeded . . . After just one term of the implementation of D & T in the National Curriculum, the failure of the Statutory Orders was acknowledged and a revision called for. Now, ten years and three revisions later D & T is still struggling to regain the ground lost at that time.

Joan McLean 1978

After returning to HMI from secondment to Schools 3 I was asked to collate colleagues' notes of visit on the introduction of National Curriculum science. I tried to explain the science and the picture on teaching, training, materials and accommodation was weak. I was asked to justify the skewed picture . . . I focussed on the evidence, quoting 30 examples of really bad provision in named primary schools – mainly in the London area. The distortions in the national picture were due to lack of science training, absent staff, sick senior management, thin evidence and weak judgements. It was agreed that the problems were real and had to be addressed . . . Some weeks later I was asked how much money was needed to put things right . . . The figures I gave were based on my knowledge of TVEI programmes which I had monitored previously.

Terry Dillon 1984

HMI had close and important links with the ILEA, which was by far the biggest LEA in the country. A district inspector led the HMI team and an HMI was responsible for each of the ILEA Divisions, liaising with the ILEA Divisional Inspector. Meetings were held regularly and were extremely useful. For example, the participants drew up lists of schools in difficulty or performing well, and discussed the implications of ILEA policy. Relationships between HMI and ILEA were not always easy, however. For example, the famous Hackney 'sweep' of the late 1980s was not well received by the ILEA. Most one-day visits to schools by HMI had revealed serious weaknesses. Consequently, SCI ordered the inspection of every school in the Borough. The resulting reports listed a catalogue of failure in most of the schools. A number of interesting points emerged from this exercise. First, it demonstrated HMI's ability to bring a national perspective to a local situation; many Inspectors used in the 'sweep' were from outside the Metropolitan Division. Secondly, it highlighted HMI's naivety in its relationships with the press: Hackney managed to convince part of the national press that HMI was victimising the Borough, a view supported by at least one national newspaper. Thirdly, it showed how little HMI could influence practice: the ILEA and the Borough largely ignored the major issues identified in the final report. OFSTED's adverse report on Hackney in 1999 demonstrated their limited response. The ILEA's headteachers often saw HMI as a critical friend with whom they could share their problems and from whom they could seek advice. I remember instances of overstaffing and staff discipline which caused headteachers great difficulties with the powerful teachers' unions and over political pressures from the Authority, which could negate heads' decisions.

Peter Brown 1973

If FE HMI needed a new source of leverage, it was to come from the publishing of quality grades based on inspection. This action offered a more effective lever for quality improvement than anything that had gone before, influencing, as the grades do, the colleges' levels of funding and their competitiveness in the market for students. The financial welfare of the colleges had now become a direct outcome of inspection. It was therefore no longer acceptable for HMI judgements to be based on undefined criteria and standards. Too much was now at stake: the criteria and standards used by HMI had now to be systematically defined and disseminated. The process of achieving this definition took a lot of time; indeed some of the transformation remained to be done when the work of the FHE Inspectorate was transferred to the Funding Councils in 1993. Nonetheless, the newly emerging parameters for HMI assessment of quality had a marked impact on the process and style of inspection itself. Some saw a danger that inspection would become driven by a checklist of items to be ticked off mechanistically and that HMI's ability to judge the complex interactions of all the factors that combine to influence 'quality' would be attenuated. Their concern was exacerbated by the pressures of a sharp increase in the number of inspections each HMI was required to make, coupled with a reduction in the time allotted for the completion of each inspection and report.

David Grant 1980

During my time in Derbyshire I aimed to see that all the secondary schools (80 before re-organisation) had at least one visit a year, while about 25% of the 400 primary schools were visited. Being the kind of unambitious HMI rarely asked to do work of 'national importance' I was usually able to do this. Increasingly, however, this kind of visiting was questioned by the centre: it tended to be insufficiently 'focussed', a term becoming increasingly fashionable. I estimate that I must have been RI about 15 times, mostly in the County, and been a team member about 35 times, all around the country. Occasionally one made a difference. Towards the end of this period I was RI of one of the last of the 'blockbusters' – a full inspection of more than 20 colleagues ... When we reported back to the head with, on the whole, largely favourable messages, he challenged virtually every judgement made. But, as later transpired, as soon as the inspection was over he set to and implemented every recommendation. One of the first secondary schools for which I had to run an inspection – a 'dipstick' in those days – locked all but one boys' toilet except at break, sat boys and girls separately for assembly and offered prayers that HMI would give the school a good report. There was plenty of caning also. At a country primary school a few years later an elderly primary teacher was quite outraged when I had to point out to her that under the new National Curriculum legislation then being introduced she would be breaking the law if she continued to forbid all oral work by pupils in her classroom.

Jean Carswell 1981

In 1985 I was asked to take on the responsibility for monitoring the DES's commitment to the European Schools' nursery and primary sections. Although I had a colleague responsible similarly for the secondary sections, and 11 colleagues from the other member states of the European Community (as it was then known), much of my work was carried out alone . . . Most of the schools were very big with one of the two in Brussels having over 3000 pupils aged from four to 18 years. The teachers in the English speaking sections welcomed and looked forward to a visit from HMI. We were expected to provide many of the features of an LEA advisory service and also professional and pastoral care when problems arose: grievance and disciplinary procedures, transfers for career and personal reasons and support on the break-up of marriages.

As a new member of the Primary Board of Inspectors I had to learn quickly to hold my own in what was a long-established male 'club'. No quarter was given in debate and discussion of issues which touched on territorial imperatives or national traditions . . . I learned never to disclose my hand too early in a debate. During my time the Board of Governors, who were high-ranking civil servants from each of the member states, decided that some form of group inspection of the schools should take place. Knowing that HMI was involved in formal team inspections, they asked me to outline our procedures and to lead the first group inspection of the European School at Culham . . .

It was a demanding but exciting exercise . . . It provided a basis for discussion amongst the inspectors on what constituted good practice. It was reassuring to find that, in spite of different approaches to some aspects of organisation and teaching, there was considerable agreement on what constituted weaknesses and strengths in the work we had seen. The Board of Governors decided the exercise was a success as it gave them some useful evaluations of the work of the School. I also regarded it as a success, for my colleagues had generously accepted my leadership and genuinely welcomed the introduction of HMI's British style of inspection. The exercise, in different forms with differently composed teams, became a regular feature and was later adopted by the Secondary Board.

Michael Webb 1981

Inspections of degree courses in polytechnics around the country took place rapidly over about a three year period. As with teacher-training institutions, HMI's verdict could, and often did, have funding implications, a feature that sometimes made willing co-operation and open debate with directors, principals and lecturing staff more problematic . . . It was a sector of education particularly fraught with the demands made on it and its eagerness to establish reputation, credibility and respectability. Degree courses had been expanded but polys smarted under their perceived inferior, second-class, non-professorial status, while at the same time taking pride in the 'inclusiveness' and the range of their courses for adult students, part-timers, foreign nationals and special-entry students – or those without conventional A levels . . .

In extreme form, the less adequate provision presented serious weaknesses of assessment and quality assurance. At more than one polytechnic department of English and media and communications (it could rarely be English alone), the piles of student essays we scrutinised were depressingly similar in tone, style and sometimes content. A few brave students confessed, in talking to us, that they felt it necessary to write in the nearly-incomprehensible jargon they had been taught, or had absorbed, in order to be sure of decent grades, or even of retaining their place on the course. There was frequent frustration and dissatisfaction. Yet there was also pressure on the institutions to return good degree results, even where standards of writing, speaking and general literacy were disgracefully low. A few colleges and polytechnics ran remedial courses in writing and critical reading; many did not, but needed them. The external examiner sytem was subject to concomitant pressures: some externals colluded, some protested and were ignored, a few resigned. Most had been selected, after all, by the department or institution itself; therefore they were likely to be favourably disposed. Some students, in some cases even a majority, got a raw deal and an inferior higher education; some managed to show talent despite the limitations of their courses – but perhaps it is ever thus. HMI produced reports and digests, perhaps pulling punches but usually endeavouring not to. It was often a considerable and testing expectation, on the basis of a brief visit, some observations and interviews and a scrutiny of many papers and documents.

Anthea Millett 1978

Before an inspection was programmed by the Work Programme Team, the Divisional Committees put forward names of institutions to be inspected to the National Primary, Secondary, FE, HE and ITT Committees. These proposed the actual content of the central programme in part on the basis of the Divisional submissions and in part on the basis of national priorities. There was always a battle royal between the CIs about which exercises should be programmed and which should not. Manpower was not always rationally distributed and the lion's share of HMI on the schools side were either secondary or primary. The two schools phase CIs saw that work-force as theirs but three other CIs – for ITT; SEN, ethnic minorities and educational disadvantage; and curriculum and assessment also needed schools HMI to cover their exercises. The two CIs for FE and HE managed things better but then they had fewer calls on 'their' HMI. The tradition which allowed HMI to hold a multiplicity of roles exacerbated the problem and it wasn't until the imminent arrival of OFSTED that HMI began to work in dedicated project teams. In my view the change to dedicated project team working was the most significant management break-through. It allowed the Inspectorate to cover a great deal more ground but it was not popular with an HMI field force used to playing demands off against each other.

Martin Foster 1980

My recollection is that at the beginning of the 1980s HMI saw their task as being to judge the quality of work. Examination results were peripheral to HMI's business, partly because they reflected pupils' ability at least as much as teaching, still more because they told nothing of the educational experience leading to the examination. It was quite a shock when in the later 1980s word came down that what concerned Ministers was 'standards', 'performance', or even 'output', not quality ... In 1990–91 all HMI subject committees were required to draft criteria for judging the quality of work seen, as part of the general drive to achieve greater precision and objectivity in reporting. In apparent conflict with this, I believe we remained faithful to the principle that what matters is whether a lesson observed works in practice. The Modern Language Committee spent one year on a noble experiment: grading each lesson for learning opportunities in four or five key aspects; for standards achieved in four or five key activities, and for overall quality – all of which was retrieved and analysed at national level, a mammoth task. There remained a strong consensus view that the essence of HMI's role lay neither in assessing teachers nor in examining the students but in judging the quality of the learning. I argued that what HMI, sitting at the back of a classroom, is principally equipped to judge is: how well are the students learning that which they should be learning.

The years 1980 to 1992 were characterised by a continual sharpening of the focus of inspection and systematising of procedures, in parallel no doubt with other areas of British society during these 'Thatcher' years. I see the changes as mainly constructive, a transition from gifted amateurism to professionalism. In 1980 there were still some HMI who saw their role as dispensing wisdom in the course of random visiting on their 'patch', who rarely wrote notes of visit, and who resented central programming as an unjustifiable constraint. The establishment of a standard note of visit format in the early 1980s was thought by many to be a mental straight-jacket, and RIs felt free to invent their own grading systems for whatever survey or inspection they were currently organising. The Inspectorate's national view was formed (as far as I could see) through the coalescence of subjective impressions: discussions in local committees were summarised in local reports, and these were summarised in Divisional reports, which again were summarised in SCI's report. The first attempts to systematise and objectify reporting were the Secondary Survey in the late 1970s and the Expenditure Reports in the early 1980s, which required the grading of individual lessons seen. It was not until 1987 that a five-point scale with grade descriptors was finally made standard. The OFSTED framework was closely modelled on these developments, though whether OFSTED has at the same time been able to maintain the same expertise in judging quality, which HMI nurtured through the 'common pursuit of true judgement', is another question.

Bob Young 1976

When I joined the Inspectorate and began what was to be, over the next eight years, a vast number of relatively informal one-day visits to schools (about 100 a year) in my various 'patches', the gist of my DI's and others' advice was that I should encapsulate on one sheet of A4 (I was allowed, I believe, to use both sides if necessary) the essential and distinctive features of the particular school, concluding always with my own assessment, however tentative it might need to be, of its most significant strengths and weaknesses and the overall quality of its performance . . . I enjoyed for some years an enviable freedom to plan my own work; in return, both I and the Inspectorate gained a very broad (and, if I was any good, an accurate) overview of the quality of education in my area.

Ten years later, the situation had drastically changed. In the misguided belief that, if sufficient detail were committed to print on every aspect of every visit, then someone, some day, would have the means, time and inclination to 'retrieve' it, we were gradually driven to spend more and more time writing longer and longer notes on even fewer visits . . . All that happened was that, as the 'trees' proliferated, the 'wood' became more opaque.

The requirement, over the years, for more and more detail to be included in inspection reports was accompanied (and to some extent prompted) by two other, and even more pernicious, developments: the demand for published 'inspection criteria' and the heavy reliance on 'performance indicators'. HMI, when I joined, had a common understanding of the sort of things their inspecting should properly take into account; but, having done this, they knew they must ultimately use their own judgement to decide whether what they were seeing was praiseworthy or poor ... Yet time and again the view was being expressed during my time as HMI that inspection could only be carried out fairly and consistently if all parties, inspectors and inspected, were equipped in advance with a list of 'criteria' – ie a collection of possible statements about the school that could be identified as true or false – as if value statements can be derived from factual statements without going through the process of actually making a value judgement ... The ready availability and apparent objectivity of 'performance indicators' ensured that, quite regardless of their validity, they would erode and finally eliminate, the scope for professional judgement.

Geoff Robson 1980

One of the ironies of Keith Joseph's decision to publish HMI reports was that they increasingly became a commentary on previous government policy and therefore gave unwelcome evidence of its shortcomings ... An attempt was made to limit the damage by insisting that the Secretary of State's Office should scrutinise all HMI reports before publication. I heard that the occasion for this was a report ... on the education of children from travelling circus families. The question asked was why are HMI 'wasting their time' on such concerns which were not part of the political agenda. The answer, of course, was that these children had just as much right to education as any others in British society and a great deal more difficulty than most in getting it. Alarm bells, however, had been rung and the next published report would have to be 'non-controversial'. Unfortunately for me this was the survey of schools serving predominantly ethnic minority pupils, which had been printed and was awaiting distribution. There was nothing new in it, as each individual school had already received a published report, but it attempted to draw together the lessons we had learned for a wider public. As a sop to Ministerial susceptibilities this report was simply withdrawn.

Chapter 13   The End of One Road and the Start of Another

Inspection. HMI and Local Advisers. The Road to the Citizen's Charter. Setting up OFSTED. Handbook.

Inspection

The Education Reform Act, for all its 220-odd clauses, left many loose ends. A series of lesser bills followed, completing the changes initiated by the abolition of the University Grants Committee. Second thoughts on the funding and management of FE and the decision to make the polytechnics into universities – all required legislation and the early amendment of the 1988 Act. (The expansion of higher education – admissions doubling in a decade – must rank among the greatest achievements of educational policy in the Thatcher–Major years.)

The last instalment came in 1994 with the Act which completed the task of bringing teacher training under central control begun by Keith Joseph. This set up the Teacher Training Agency, responsible to the Secretary of State for all aspects of the recruitment and training of teachers, and the allocation of funding for that purpose. An HMI who had transferred to OFSTED, Anthea Millett, became the first chief executive.

Another loose end concerned inspection. Kenneth Baker's priority was the bill and its implementation, particularly the National Curriculum which absorbed his total energies and those of the Office. HMI was involved at every stage. Except for a late amendment (after intensive lobbying led by Lady Young, a former DES Minister of State) which obliged the Secretary of State to provide assistance, including inspection, for British schools abroad, the Act did not refer to inspection or the Inspectorate. The Secretary of State's duty to cause inspections to be carried out remained in the unrepealed sections of the 1944 Act. Baker certainly assumed that there would have to be far-reaching changes for the Inspectorate – he was not one of those who thought the National Curriculum would be self-policing. There would have to be some method of reporting on schools' progress: he would want this as Secretary of State and he thought parents would want it too. In his autobiography, he reproduced the 'Blueprint for Education Reform' dated December 1986 which summarised his plans for the Reform Act as they had then taken shape up to that date. Paragraph 3 (page 480) reads:

> *Once established the curriculum will have to be inspected on a more regular basis than*
> *now. We will need a much enlarged national inspectorate. This will mean taking into*
> *central government employment the local inspectors and advisers.*

At Eric Bolton's suggestion, Baker decided to meet the senior members of
the Inspectorate to get to know them and tell them about his plans. He
gave a dinner at the Carlton Club in the late autumn of 1986 attended by
the SCI and the CIs. Somewhere in a wide-ranging discussion he
mentioned the fact that they would need a new system of inspection – one
capable of inspecting every school every few years – a cyclical system of
reporting inspections the like of which had long since been far beyond the
resources of HMI.

Eric Bolton, Senior Chief Inspector, 1983–91.

This was not the main topic of discussion and there are varying accounts
of what happened from those present. Terry Melia, who was then CI for
FHE and who would eventually serve as the last SCI after Bolton's
retirement, recalls the Carlton Club dinner as a lost opportunity. When
Baker raised the possibility of an extended role for HMI, Bolton had
opposed the idea if it meant simply expanding the present Inspectorate –
expansion on the scale required would change the whole character of
HMI by making it less coherent and more diffuse. Melia took this
negative response to be a strategic error. Instead of picking up the bone
and running with it, exploring all available ways of providing what the
Minister wanted without sacrificing the quality of the elite group of HMI,

Terry Melia, Senior Chief Inspector, 1991–92.

Bolton and his schools' colleagues, Melia thought, had preferred to restate the traditional case against dilution.

This was Melia's interpretation. Bolton and some of the others who were present have different recollections. Bolton had already discussed inspection with Baker. They were agreed that a big expansion of HMI was 'just not on'. Bolton understood quite well that parents would need up-to-date information about schools. It was the need to keep succeeding generations of parents informed which dictated a four- or five-year cycle. But how this was to be organised – and what relationship HMI should have with local authority inspectors and advisers in managing an enlarged system – all this was wide open. Nothing specific was proposed by Baker and nothing specific rejected by Bolton.

What was said at the Carlton Club dinner lies in the grey area of unspoken communications and depends on reading between the lines – not of written text, but of after-dinner conversation. Many of the discussions which Bolton was engaged in at this time were confidential at the highest level in the Department and could not be divulged even to the CIs. It is a matter of fact that Bolton's actions following the Carlton Club dinner showed he was fully aware of the need for HMI to adapt to the new situation and that he had a good idea what should happen. What he did was fully consistent with this. What he failed to do – and could not have done – was to inject sufficient urgency and radicalism into the discussion of alternatives, to bring things to a head quickly, when Ministers and the Department had their hands full with the National Curriculum and were content to mark time.

If the implication of Baker's comments was that HMI would have to expand to take on the whole job, the negative reaction of the HMI hierarchy was predictable and generally shared. Both Bolton and his predecessor had difficulty in filling posts with the quality of HMI they required and the idea of a mass recruitment campaign was far from attractive. But that was not necessarily what Baker had in mind, nor yet was it the only option.

Bolton continued to reflect on how the Minister's requirement could best be met. Early in 1987, Bolton put up a paper to the permanent secretary, considering the merits and demerits of three possible lines of development:

- The first was to enlarge HMI to the size required to undertake the whole job – which would mean expanding the Inspectorate to 2,000 or more. He thought such a proposal would be thrown out by the Prime Minister who wanted fewer civil servants, not more. It was very expensive and would destroy the collective judgement of HMI which was based on the cohesion possible in a relatively small collegial body.

- The second might be to adopt the French model with regional inspectorates organised and supervised by an elite national inspectorate. Among the objections to this was the fact that it conflicted with the Government's Conservative instincts and seemed too much like an expression of Gallic centralism.

- The third was to let HMI oversee LEA inspectors and manage a combined HMI–LEA inspection system, while continuing to act as professional advisers to the Secretary of State and his department.

In Bolton's view only the last of the three was a realistic runner.

Bolton's analysis was fed into an exercise initiated by a request from Baker to the permanent secretary for a paper describing a new model inspectorate capable of inspecting all schools and colleges regularly. David Hancock put forward what became known as the 'managerial' model. This proposed the creation of a grant-aided, non-departmental commission, reporting to the Secretary of State, which would oversee inspection. The commission would be composed of appointed worthies – a few employers, a chief education officer, an FE principal and other members of the somewhat Great and fairly Good. The Inspectorate would be organised in two tiers – with 500 HMIs to oversee the process and carry out some of the inspecting, and seven regional inspectorates of 300, to do the bulk of the work under the guidance and supervision of HMI. The annual cost was estimated at £100 million.

This was what Baker had asked for and it went to him with a mandarin note from the permanent secretary to the effect that, though it was a workable model, it was opposed by all his senior colleagues, and that they had convinced him, also, that it was not a good idea.

Margaret Thatcher records in *The Downing Street Years* that in September 1988, Baker put up a proposal for

> *comprehensive monitoring of the National Curriculum by the recruitment of 800 extra LEA inspectors, who themselves would be monitored and controlled by the HMI who would doubtless have to be expanded as well. I noted: it is utterly ridiculous. The results will come through in the tests and scores.*

This was another example of the divergence of view between Margaret Thatcher and Baker: she wanted simplicity and economy of effort – with a national curriculum limited to the core subjects which relied on the publication of results to enforce compliance. Baker (and the Office) wanted a broad and balanced curriculum of 10 subjects, prescribed and tested, with regular inspection to make it stick. Faced with her rebuff, Baker adopted a familiar strategy – he smiled and took his proposals away. The future of the Inspectorate went into the pending tray while he got on with more pressing matters.

Baker never returned to the topic, and neither did his successor, John MacGregor. Nor did the Office press ministers to take any action. There was plenty to get on with and no need at that juncture to confront the difficult institutional vested interests which would have to be appeased, accommodated or defeated. The following year, 1989, two other developments showed the inspection issue was not going to go away. The Labour Party briefly floated the idea of an Education Standards Commission which would incorporate HMI in a larger organisation concerned with raising school performance. And Bob Dunn, a former junior minister at the DES, put down an early-day motion on the House of Commons Order Paper, calling for the Audit Commission to take over school inspection.

HMI and Local Advisers

As we have seen both Baker in his December 1986 'Blueprint' and Bolton in the model which formed his preferred option, had envisaged a combined HMI–LEA Inspectorate overseen at the national level by HMI. The need for closer working relationships between HMI and the local authority inspectors and advisers – known in the Department as the 'LEAI' – had been around since before the House of Commons Select Committee inquiry in 1968. It will be recalled that the Select Committee had thought that much of what HMIs did could be done as well or better by local authority inspectors and advisers.

But in 1968, the Inspectorate had had no desire to become a small elite force working alongside a more numerous local authority inspectorate. HMI valued their relationship with schools and the quality of intelligence which their day-by-day contact with schools gave them. Traditionally this had been the basis of their expert knowledge and advice. The Office took the same view.

If, following the Select Committee Report the Government had forced the LEAs to reorganise their local inspectorates and bring them up to a first-class standard; if they had devised a system which articulated the work of HMI with that of LEAI; if they had thereby created a powerful, efficiently organised, national inspection service, the situation two decades later would have borne little relation to what Baker found in 1986. But none of this happened. Instead, the aim of cooperation with local inspectors received regular commendation from SCIs and senior HMIs, but little was seriously done about it till the mid-1980s.

There were many other things to think about and in practical terms, genuine cooperation was not easy – the local authority inspectorates were a mixed bunch, some first class, others less satisfactory. A few local authorities such as the ILEA, West Riding, Oxfordshire, Manchester and Lancashire, had well-developed advisory teams but there were many authorities which still had few advisers. There were also significant difficulties where local inspectors had direct influence on the advancement of teachers. There were obvious limits to what HMI could do unless and until it became ministerial policy to confront the practicalities head on. The matter never received that degree of priority in the thinking of the department.

Quality (and costs) rose with improved salary scales but the picture remained extremely uneven. At the time of the Select Committee it is estimated that there were about 1,260 local inspectors and organisers.[1] Sir William Alexander, who was eminently numerate, produced a back-of-an-envelope figure for the Select Committee of 2000, a wild exaggeration. The number was growing but even eight years later a working party set up by the DES and the LEAs only found 1,819 local inspectors and advisers. There was also a growing number of 'advisory teachers'. Only 50 out of 97 LEAs thought LEAI should carry out inspections. Unlike HMI, local advisers and inspectors had no statutory right of access – though it would have been a strangely feeble LEA which tolerated heads and assistant teachers refusing to admit members of the authority's support staff. (At the William Tyndale Primary School it had been the teachers' refusal to cooperate with ILEA inspectors which finally led to the suspension of staff members.)

In many areas, secondary heads succeeded in preventing local inspections, and promoting a culture in which local advisers saw their role as being confined to advice and in-service training. Many of them believed that if they were seen as inspectors it would damage their work as advisers. On the other hand, heads who resisted inspection by local inspectors, generally valued inspection by HMI: what made the difference was HMIs' independence of the LEA management structure and the authority attributed to them by the breadth of their experience.

At a personal level relations were often good and there was ready cooperation in teachers' courses and conferences. There was a small but steady inflow of former local authority advisory staff into the Inspectorate. In some specialisms such as Craft, Design and Technology cooperation was particularly good. But the Rayner Report in 1982 could still refer to a 'lingering condescension' on the part of HMI in their dealings with local authority counterparts. This may well have been a considerable understatement. The attitude of some local advisers was coloured by their resentment of the fact that their work could be evaluated by HMI. And though it was freely conceded that the quality of local advisory staff was improving, HMI remained an elite body whose *esprit de corps* was based on the unassailable conviction that they were the best in the business. It was not surprising if HMI were a bit condescending if they were convinced that relatively few of their LEA opposite numbers could meet the kind of standards demanded of the Inspectorate.

The policy statement issued by the Department and the Welsh Office on *The Work of HM Inspectorate in England and Wales* underlined the importance of local advisory services, complementing and enhancing the work of HMI. It responded to the Rayner Report which had pointed out the need for HMI and LEAI to work together to 'translate HMI's national findings into local action and development' (page 32). The Department's efforts to persuade LEAs to turn their attention to the curriculum put the spotlight on the work of local advisers. Just as HMI had gained in influence inside the DES when ministers became interested in the curriculum, so too local advisers would have a bigger part to play if LEAs did the same. In the Primary and Secondary Surveys there was a wealth of information on which local in-service trainers could draw: one thing HMI and the Office could agree on was that local advisers could helpfully do more to disseminate HMI material.

HMI continued patiently to explore how best cooperation could be organised – an inquiry launched in 1985 asked district HMI and subject and phase SIs to update the material on file, augmenting their answers with information from other sources such as the SCI's annual expenditure surveys and assessments of the effectiveness of what was available at the local level. Following the Rayner Report arrangements had been made to bring in a number of LEA advisers to work with the Inspectorate to mutual advantage – some went on to become HMIs; among LEA officers who were seconded was Jennifer Wisker, an up-and-coming deputy chief education officer in Leicestershire, who was enlisted to add to the Inspectorate's expertise in matters of management, local administration and finance. She was particularly influential in developing policy about local management of schools.

Working together more closely undoubtedly threw up real difficulties – the most obvious of which was the fact that they were reporting to different masters. Suggestions for joint inspections ran head on into problems arising from different lines of accountability and reporting, and in any case, could only be considered where local inspection was accepted. It is hardly surprising that there were practical problems – they were two quite different bodies of men and women. They had quite different responsibilities, were subject to quite different systems of management, had been trained in quite different traditions and started from quite different professional experience. They were never going to get anywhere without much more radical consideration being given to structural questions – unless, that is, ministers and their senior advisers were prepared to consider from scratch what kind of unified inspection and advisory service was needed, and how such an organisation could be created by combining the resources of HMI and the LEA inspectorates.

Negotiations between the Department, HMI, the LEA associations and the National Association of Inspectors and Educational Advisers (NAIEA), produced the first draft of a joint statement which was intended to establish the basis on which HMI and LEAI could work together. This statement was widely discussed and frequently amended. It set out the different areas of responsibility of the Department, HMI and the LEAs; described the tasks now performed by the LEA advisory services; identified future demands; and called on LEAs to review the role of their advisory services in the light of present and future needs. It was intended to provide a way through the maze of conflicting lines of accountability and reporting, and lead to a concordat which could regulate the complementary functions of HMI and LEAI. But progress was painfully slow and it was overtaken by events before it was ready for publication.

The arrival of Kenneth Baker, the promise of a major bill, the general election of 1987 – all combined to cause a hiatus during which the impetus was lost. New factors entered the equation. The announcement that there was going to be a national curriculum and that the LEAs' managerial control of schools was to be sloughed off left many questions unanswered about monitoring and support. The LEAs had every reason to be apprehensive because of the uncompromising hostility towards them which ran through the Education Reform Act, and the rhetoric used to promote it. But as more details of the National Curriculum emerged, any doubt about the central importance of local inspectors and advisers disappeared. In the short term, at least, the Government's plans for the implementation of the National Curriculum – and the system of assessment and testing which was integral to it – would depend on the active participation of local authority educational support services.

Baker's instinct was to leave till later consideration of the long-term part LEAs should play in monitoring and supporting the schools. He had a better chance of enlisting their help with his immediate concerns if he concentrated on the here and now – giving the LEAs enough encouragement to keep them hopeful, without making any lasting commitments.

This became the policy which the Department pursued. The first indication came in September 1987. Nick Stuart, the deputy secretary in charge of the bill, wrote to the General Secretary of NAIEA explaining that, although inspection had been left out of the bill, LEAs were going to be required to put the National Curriculum into operation, and that the expectation was that inspectors/advisers would play an important part in this. Baker took this further in January 1988, addressing the Society of Education Officers, stressing the need for local advisory staff to monitor and evaluate schools' performance as the National Curriculum was being introduced and provide back-up. It was here that he announced the funding of 300 additional advisory posts to meet the extra demands which would arise from the changes.

Two more speeches the following summer – by David Hancock to the NAIEA executive and by Angela Rumbold, the minister of state, to the Council of Local Education Authorities – followed the same line and were calculated to give medium-term encouragement to the authorities. Even so, ministers spoke with forked tongue – out of the other side of their mouths they were castigating authorities which sought to hold back money for support services instead of distributing it to schools under LMS.

It was no secret that there were differences of view in the Department and in the Government about the part LEAs should play when the initial phase was over. Bolton continued to favour a combined HMI–LEAI inspectorate supervised by HMI. There were many open questions about support for schools, and in particular for failing schools, which went beyond the matter of inspection. And LEAs remained problematic institutions: if grant-maintained status really took off (or was thrust on schools whether they wanted it or not) who would need LEAs? There were many in the Conservative Party (including Nigel Lawson and Margaret Thatcher) who would be happy enough to see the local authorities bow out of education altogether.

An Audit Commission report – *Assuring Quality in Education* (1989) reviewed the mixture of advisory services and inspection provided by the LEAs, which now had some 2,500 staff in these categories. It acknowledged the usefulness of performance indicators and evidence from examinations and other forms of assessment, but still saw the need for inspection – that is, classroom observation – by suitably qualified and trained inspectors. The report recommended that local authorities should provide more systematic monitoring, and that they should actively manage their advisory services to ensure that advice was soundly based and to the point. An HMI, Gordon Barratt, was seconded to the Audit Commission, along with a deputy chief education officer, Clayton Heycock, and the DES and HMI were among those consulted. The report confirmed the view that the LEAs had a long way to go before they could be relied upon to monitor the National Curriculum.

This was probably an opinion shared by both major parties – the gulf between the Conservative and Labour Parties on the role of the local authorities was never as wide as the parliamentary exchanges suggested. A later Act (1993) contained opaque provisions for 'educational associations' to take over and run schools which were judged to have failed. Time would show these clauses could be expanded to provide support from sources independent of the LEA. Other devices would be developed to send in outside consultants to take over the responsibilities of failing LEAs. All that can be said with certainty is that at the end of the 1980s, there were endless possibilities for consideration and ministers saw no reason why decisions should be hurried.

Attempts by HMI and local inspectors to get closer continued. HMI used the joint draft statement as the basis of more developments at divisional level: in an attempt to get more coherence there were further discussions with LEAI of how chief education officers and authorities were responding to the changes brought in with the National Curriculum and other provisions of the Act. But the caveats remained: there could be no discussions of existing practice without the prior agreement of the chief education officer; HMIs were not to get involved in training schemes for LEAI without reference back; and there could be joint informal visiting for specific in-service training purposes, but no joint reporting inspections because of the recurring objections arising from different lines of reporting and accountability.

The next – and as it transpired last – development in this particular saga came in 1989 when a joint pilot scheme was set up with seven LEAs (one in each HMI division) to explore whether HMI and LEA teams could cooperate in the inspection of individual schools. The HMIs involved were given fairly free hands to cut red tape and explore how far cooperation could usefully go. The aim was to report in 1991. Eric Bolton asked Bob Young, the SI in charge of the project, 'to produce a confidential blueprint for how a national system of inspection could be organised and how its reliability could be guaranteed'.

In Young's words:

> Quite suddenly [in the middle of 1990] and without explanation, the mood changed. At a meeting of SCI and CIs (I was temporarily acting as CI at the time), the possibility of a cooperative system on which so many of us had been working for so long and with such strong encouragement, was brusquely dismissed as unrealistic. My impression, confirmed by subsequent events, was that Ministers had ruled out anything which appeared to acknowledge the competence of LEAs by offering them a continuing stake in the inspection process and that SCI felt unable resist the pressure.

Bolton had evidently concluded by this time that the Government was so adamantly opposed to any LEA participation in a national inspection system, that nothing was to be gained from the pilot projects. This was six months and more before Kenneth Clarke and the Number 10 Policy Unit pushed the inspection issue to the top of the agenda. It is not clear what prompted Bolton's decision at this particular time. It was still assumed the best solution would be one built on the resources of HMI and the local inspectorates, but this did not necessarily imply a continued role for LEAs.

The Road to the Citizens' Charter

Time had run out. Baker had come and gone, handed the poisoned chalice as Thatcher's party chairman. In had come the thoughtful and moderate John MacGregor who wanted to consolidate progress and gather professional support rather than kick on with radical ideas. This made him an immediate target for the radical Right, who like Baker, thought it was essential to maintain the momentum of reform. Thatcher was deposed in November 1990 and John Major became Prime Minister.

Kenneth Clarke, Secretary of State for Education and Science, 1990–92.

MacGregor became Leader of the House where his courtesy and emollient manner were useful to the in-coming Prime Minister.

Clarke, who had already shown his versatility and competence at

Employment and Health, continued to hold the fort at Education. He was one of those who had told Margaret Thatcher she should go while others prevaricated. He was blessed with a formidable lack of self-doubt, bearing the burdens of office lightly. He shared the belief that the new Government should press ahead with its education reforms and keep up the pressure for radical change.

It was said of Major that his first and greatest asset when he became Prime Minister was the fact that he was not Thatcher. He spoke of the need for moderation and tolerance – he wanted 'a country that is at ease with itself' – and tried to live up to this in his early dealings with the House of Commons: at Question Time he began by deliberately lowering the temperature and discarding, if only for a while, the confrontational techniques of his predecessor.

Like James Callaghan before him, he found himself looking for a theme for his premiership and Sarah Hogg, whom he made head of the Policy Unit at Number 10, and Jonathan Hill, who became his political secretary,[2] came up with several. One of these was the ill-fated 'Back to Basics' call – part of the attempt to present Major as an exponent of simple, decent, values – which foundered when the tabloids pretended it was a campaign for moral purity and were then hypocritically delighted to discredit it by finding moral laxity in Conservative high places.

Educational reform was still in the forefront of politics. Education was not a subject Major had ever had occasion to give much practical consideration – either in local or national government – but he saw it was central to his Government's programme. As Prime Minister he bought into the radical thinking which had put the Education Reform Act on the Statute Book and adopted without much questioning the right-wing ideology of the Centre for Policy Studies – using their platform for an important early speech. In many aspects of social policy he belonged to the liberal tendency within the Conservative Party. Perhaps that was why he was so anxious to demonstrate his Thatcherite credentials on education.

When, just two months into the new administration, he met his newly formed Policy Unit for a working supper on January 29, John Mills, a career civil servant on secondment who looked after education in the Policy Unit, had spoken with 'fire and force' on the need to tackle 16-plus education and training. This was taken up in the first of a series of policy reviews held at Chequers with Clarke and the Employment Secretary, Michael Howard, who agreed to prepare a joint White Paper – *Education and Training for the 21st Century.* This backed the development of General National Vocational Qualifications and introduced proposals for training credits to create a market in industrial training by holding out a financial incentive for employers to take on young trainees. Launched during a recession, the response was disappointing.

Hill and Clarke were on the same wavelength – Hill had been Clarke's political adviser at Employment, Trade and Industry, and health. Clarke was thought to have an uphill struggle at the DES with the education reforms at a 'crucial stage', opposed by the teachers, and made more difficult by the excessive bureaucracy which the Department was said to have built into the National Curriculum. (Here was another echo of Margaret Thatcher's running battles with Baker whose determination to prescribe and test the full 10-subject curriculum, was now blamed on the Department.) Also on the Policy Unit's agenda for Clarke's meeting with Major were how to get more schools to go grant-maintained, and how to make the Inspectorate a real 'quality control' organisation – one which stopped identifying with the teaching profession. It was already clear that the Department of Education was being lined up to be the first Department to face the challenge on inspection. According to Hogg and Hill – Clarke was an 'open door' and would find the pressure from Number 10 helpful in dealing with opponents of the policy in the Department of Education.

The Policy Unit had already – in February 1991 – begun to work on what eventually became the Citizens' Charter. The quest for a unifying idea led them on from Thatcherite achievements such as privatisation to quality-of-life issues – 'choice, opportunity, responsibility'. The germ of the policy was to be found in a speech by Major two years earlier to the Audit Commission when he was Chief Secretary at the Treasury. In commending the commission's quest for value for money, he said flatly that 'shoddy public services should not be an option, nor should they be tolerated.' Hogg and Hill saw this as a way of turning the spotlight away from resources and onto efficiency and the human factors which make the difference between good and bad public services.

The idea appealed to the Prime Minister for two reasons. It was down-to-earth – it suited his self-image as the kind of man who might actually travel on the underground, have breakfast at a Little Chef, or attend an NHS surgery. And it was also attractive because it could be applied across Whitehall, local government, public transport and the public utilities – in fact, wherever members of the public came into contact with the providers of public service.

Education, Health and Transport were seen as the departments which would be in the front line, but Major was determined to demand a response from every department – a letter to that effect was duly sent out by his private secretary to the private secretaries of all other ministers and they were then bullied till they did something about it. Francis Maude, a Treasury minister, was put in charge of the Charter programme, and everything was set in train for a launch in July. This Citizen's Charter would be the foundation stone of a structure of consumer protection, the building blocks of which would be many subsidiary Charters, setting out the rights of, for example, people who used the health service (the 'Patient's Charter') or the schools (the 'Parent's Charter').

As a means of levering up standards in the public service, the Charter movement had a lot to commend it. It focused the attention of managers on the quality of service and provided a stimulus for self-review and internal audit. There was also a lot of publicity and media interest – it presented the new Prime Minister in a consumer-friendly light – but at the expense of exposing him to a certain amount of ridicule when things went manifestly wrong: it was never possible to take it entirely seriously – it always seemed a public relations substitute for the real thing.

Clarke was close to Major from the beginning of his premiership. According to Bolton, Clarke's attention shifted almost wholly to establishing a domestic policy for Major that would be sufficiently different from that of his predecessor, and coherent enough to attract the electorate at the election due in 1992. Concern about quality and standards in education justified education's prominence in that policy, and choice, diversity, accountability and inspection were seen as the means by which it would be addressed.

'Independent inspection' gathered importance as the Charter idea took off. The consumer needed a friend at court, a guarantor of standards and quality. Often the market, underpinned by legislation on monopolies and unfair trading, could provide the safeguards needed. Privatisation had produced the useful concept of the 'regulator' – an independent referee who holds the ring on behalf of the consumer. Public services like education, the police, prisons and social services had inspectorates of one kind or another. The question for education was what, in the context of the

Citizen's Charter, would happen to HMI if they were to become part of a
national inspection service acting as a real 'regulator' for education. To do
this HMI would have to accept new responsibilities towards parents as well
as towards the Secretary of State and rethink relationships with schools.

Of critical importance was what was meant by 'independent' inspection.
HM Inspectorate was proud of its own particular kind of independence:
nobody could tamper with HMI reports. But the Inspectorate was located
inside the DES, its reports went to the Secretary of State who decided
whether or not to publish them. The Royal Warrant was of symbolic
rather than practical value. There was an honourable tradition of
independent thought which for the most part the Office and ministers had
respected. Clarke was not like Joseph who defended HMI even when
their judgements rebounded on him. As Bolton noted, Clarke 'found it
hugely irritating to determine policies for education and then "have HMI
running around the country critically commenting on them" '.[3]

Between the end of March and the beginning of July 1991, the decisions of
principle about the future of the Inspectorate were taken in Downing
Street – that is to say, the essentials of the Citizen's Charter were settled –
and Clarke accepted the implications of the charter for HMI. This was only
known at the highest level – the CIs, who with the SCI, formed the senior
management team for the Inspectorate, were unaware of what was going
on and still had hopes for a two-tier system run by HMI from the DES.
Inside the Department there were continuing attempts to make sure the
Inspectorate would still report to the Secretary of State even if its
independence were increased. There were suggestions that the
Inspectorate should become a 'Next Steps' agency – a public sector agency,
with its own named head, operating within the framework of government
but set up to deliver particular services. This change of managerial
structure would still be consistent with HMI working in close association
with the Office as professional advisers and intelligence gatherers.

Those at the top of the DES who were aware of which way the wind was
blowing had no doubt of the importance of the questions at issue. John
Caines had succeeded Hancock as permanent secretary in 1989. In a letter
left for his successor, Hancock had written: 'HMI is absolutely the heart
of the Department; without it the Department will have very little
solidity. It is the way we know what is happening in education.'[4] Caines
received the same advice from his top officials. Caines was an incomer to
the Department, chosen (like Hancock before him) as someone who
would make up his own mind. He was unlikely to expend too much

energy resisting what was clearly the policy his minister wished to implement.

Simmering on the back-burner were the three models outlined in Bolton's 1987 paper. The preferred solution continued to be one which combined the resources of HMI and the LEA support services with or without the participation of the LEAs. Aware that things were beginning to hot up, in the early spring of 1991, at Eric Bolton's request, four of his CIs, Terry Melia, Anthea Millett, Mike Tomlinson and Jim Rose, put together a paper entitled 'Quality Assurance in Education'.

To achieve quality assurance, they reckoned the inspection process would have to examine all the available objective evidence – examination and test results and other measures of performance – and for a proper evaluation, there would have to be 'observation and inspection of pupils' and students' work in classrooms and lecture theatres, laboratories and workshops, as displayed in written and practical work, tests and exams. Evaluation and thorough inspection which is conducted in this way across the nation as a whole, and which seeks to identify those factors which contribute to the standards achieved, is the unique contribution of HMI.'

The paper assumed that most primary schools would remain under the LEAs which would therefore be responsible for 'quality audits' of primary schools. HMI would oversee the process and report on it. Secondary schools, on the other hand, would require other arrangements because the assumption was that opting out and local management would decrease the role of the LEAs. A central core team of HMI would be responsible for 'planning, organising and managing' inspection on a regular basis. The inspection work would be carried out by a field force of non-HMI inspectors whose work would be directed from the centre. HMIs would lead the individual inspection teams which might include former HMIs, LEA advisers, people from industry and commerce, and some former and some practising heads.

Sensing the political need for radical measures, they argued that this would make it possible to cut the Inspectorate to 110 HMI – 40 secondary, 40 primary, 10 SEN and 8 FHE, and 12 for teacher training. HM Inspectorate would thus become an elite, highly professional nucleus within a nationwide quality assurance system. They made four 'key assumptions' about the role of HMI within such a system:

- the constitutional links with the Secretary of State would be retained;
- HMI should get more independence as an agency linked to the Department;
- that HMI's powers in relation to non-HMI inspectors should be clearly articulated;
- that HMI would retain their statutory right of access to educational institutions.

In Bolton's account of these events,[5] he says he continued to believe that 'the logical route was to make use of a re-jigged LEA inspectorate overseen by HMI', recalling the 'seven pilot projects ... in which HMI worked with LEAs to explore ways and means to bring about workable and rigorous arrangements'. But, as he also noted, neither the Thatcher nor Major government was in the business of giving more power to LEAs. Moreover it became clear that Clarke was willing to go along with the Prime Minister's wish for a new system conspicuously independent of the Department and of the local authorities. Every twist and turn of the education news machine brought more pressure – when an HMI report described a primary school[6] as typical of the 20 per cent of primaries where reading standards were unsatisfactory, it was another stick with which to beat HMI – their lack of sanctions was shown to be a crucial weakness which called for a revamped Inspectorate and more protection for parents.

Bolton's position was getting more difficult by the day. Events were moving fast – only those at the top of the Department knew how fast – and he was unable to keep his colleagues fully informed because of the confidential nature of the discussions which were taking place. It was at this point – the beginning of May – that he decided to retire four years early, leaving at the end of the summer to take up a chair at the University of London Institute of Education in September. (He had always envisaged going early to do other things rather than staying on to 60.) As far as he was concerned things had gone badly wrong and he had no wish to preside over what would now take place. It was inevitable that Bolton's action should be misinterpreted by some of his colleagues. There were romantic suggestions that he should have stayed and gone down with the ship. But plainly his position was becoming untenable. Political decisions were being taken over his head. There is no suggestion that had he stayed he could have altered them: it was not a case of being able to do more to oppose by remaining on the inside than by getting out. So long as he remained SCI he was obliged to support government policy.

His resignation raised the question of what sort of a job should be offered to his successor. Two Civil Service competitions were held but no appointment was made. Shortly before his departure was announced, an internal review was set up in the DES to be conducted by Mark Neale, a Grade 5 civil servant, and an HMI, Judith Phillips, to consider what should be the outline of the future inspectorate and the job description of Bolton's successor. On May 5 1991, Clarke used a debate on the Teachers' Pay and Conditions Bill (which introduced teacher appraisal) to break the news that he intended to reduce the number of HMI from 480 to 175. Melia, CI for further and higher education, became acting SCI, and later was confirmed as SCI.

Presumably the paper which Bolton had asked the four CIs to prepare was fed into the Neale–Phillips review. This had a deadline of July but was still in the pipeline when decisions were brought forward to fit in to the timetable for the Citizen's Charter launch planned for July 10. The launch was preceded by a Chequers meeting. One session was devoted to inspection, introduced by Judge Stephen Tumin, then HM Inspector of Prisons, who argued strongly for a completely independent inspectorate, capable of standing up to the entrenched power and prejudice of the Home Office and the people who ran the prisons. Pauline Perry (by now Vice Chancellor of the South bank University and soon to be made a Conservative Life Peer by John Major) also spoke about an independent schools inspectorate – independent of ministers, LEAs and independent of professional cosiness. (*The Times Educational Supplement* carried a piece by her along the same lines, a couple of weeks later.[7]) It had been her experience towards the end of her time in the Inspectorate that pressure on HMI brought by ministers and, particularly, senior officials, had increased.

A constant Charter theme was the need to include lay men and women in the inspection process in the belief that their common sense would help to prevent inspectors becoming part of the professional conspiracy. With this went the emphasis on inspection as consumer protection – the inspector acting as the eyes and ears of the parents as well as of the Secretary of State. 'I want,' said Major, addressing the Centre for Policy Studies, a week before the Charter was published, 'to turn the school inspectorate into the parent's friend.'[8]

When the Charter appeared it promised parents 'regular and independent inspection', school reports and league tables of results – see box.

Citizen's Charter – Inspection

Regular and independent inspection of all schools with the results reported to parents ... Rigorous and independent inspectors and auditors can perform a vital role in checking how performance compares with both local and national standards ...

The inspectorate's ... central responsibility is to check that the professional services that the public receives are delivered in the most effective way possible and genuinely meet the needs of those whom they serve. In the past, inspectorates have often been staffed exclusively by members of the profession they oversee. Under the Citizen's Charter programme the Government will change this balance ...

If an inspectorate is too close to the profession it is supervising there is a risk that it will lose touch with the interests of the people who use the service. It may be captured by fashionable theories and lose the independence and objectivity that the public needs. Professional inspectorates can easily become part of a closed professional world ...

Decisions following the review of Her Majesty's Inspectorate of Schools will be announced shortly. However, in line with the Citizen's Charter, the changes which result from this review will reflect these principles:

- the need for independent judgment about schools, teaching and learning based on objective inspection and analysis of performance measures;
- the need for the inspection process to involve lay members with a range of expertise and experience other than teaching or educational administration;
- the need to ensure that inspection is carried out independently of the producer interest.

The deal had been clinched between Clarke and Nicholas True of the Policy Unit on July 1, and this changed the context of the Neale–Phillips review. But it seems that having rehearsed the other options, the review came down in favour of a model which bears a close resemblance to what appeared in the bill which Clarke later brought forward, with the important difference that it would have kept HMI within the Department of Education. Under such a scheme, the Secretary of State would, in Bolton's words:

establish national criteria for school inspection, give a much smaller HMI the job of controlling the quality of school inspection; give schools the money for inspection and let the governors choose their inspection teams from a register of independent inspection agencies.[9]

It was significant that Scotland decided to wait and see what happened in England before deciding whether to follow suit. In spite of regular prodding, the Scottish Education Department was determined not to give up control of the Inspectorate, on which it relied heavily, to an independent body. Ian Lang, the Secretary of State for Scotland, stonewalled successfully and OFSTED's writ did not run north of the border or in Northern Ireland. Wales has its own HM chief inspector (HMCI).

While the DES began preparations for a short bill, the finishing touches were put to the Parent's Charter which spelled out the service guarantees which were now to be given to parents. The results of the Neale–Philips review of HMI were included with the publication of the Parent's Charter, and used to underpin the approach pushed by Number 10 and endorsed by Clarke. The report itself was suppressed though a partial account was leaked to the *Independent* later in the year.

Also in the autumn, John Burchill, the LEA chief inspector for the London Borough of Wandsworth, wrote a pamphlet for the Centre for Policy Studies in which he sketched the outline of an inspection set-up much like that created by the bill. To what extent, if any, Burchill influenced events is not clear. Wandsworth was a new Right Conservative LEA flagship and Donald Naismith, the Wandsworth chief education officer was one of the few local authority administrators with access to Number 10 and the Policy Unit. Through him, Burchill may well have been among those who were aware of what was being discussed and eager to air his view in a Centre for Policy Studies publication. But by the time his pamphlet appeared in print the key decisions had been taken and it was these key decisions which shaped the bill.

In the event the final outcome was influenced by the need to get the bill through both Houses of Parliament before the 1992 general election. Clarke believed strongly that governors should be allowed to pick their own registered inspectors from an approved list so that there should be little bureaucratic intervention by the office of HMCI. The proposal had merit on strict market grounds but Major's advisers were prepared to forego market principles to head off the common-sense criticism of those who thought schools would find a way of choosing 'soft-touch' inspectors. The provision was ridiculed and defeated in the House of

Lords: Clarke had eventually to give way and give the HMCI the bureaucratic apparatus for scheduling inspections and inspectors for schools – putting each inspection out to tender and making a choice among the available registered inspectors.

In reflecting on these events it can be seen that the reconstruction of the Inspectorate was inevitable, given the general agreement that the schools needed a system of quality control which would maintain a regular cycle of external inspection; inevitable, too, that it would require some sort of two-tier system with HMI supervising the people who actually carried out the inspections. Nobody thought the whole job could be done by the Inspectorate as constituted in the mid-1980s. The Education Reform Act simply brought the issue forward: the introduction of the National Curriculum raised questions about enforcement and the policing of performance in individual schools and this, too, would alter the character of the inspection process. But even without a National Curriculum there was a case for more inspection and better monitoring on behalf of the consumer – it was no longer thought to be a serious option to trust the professionals without better audit and more inspection.

We have seen that Baker broached the subject at the outset but set it on one side because he needed the undivided attention of the LEAs and their advisers to usher in the National Curriculum. We have also seen how the inspection issue returned with the election of Major and his espousal of a Citizen's Charter for consumer protection as a major theme of his administration. Had the Policy Unit come up with a different bright idea, the context for the eventual review of inspection might have been very different, but as it was, when Clarke sent for the file marked 'Inspection' and the DES dusted off the choice of models, inspection had become ideologically loaded and politically significant. Clarke, urged on by Number 10, favoured a market model, with a small, elite, HMI supervising teams of self-employed inspectors.

The key question concerned the relationship of HMI to the Secretary of State. The Department continued to believe that HMI should report to the Minister, and act as advisers to the Office. The aficionados of the Charter made 'independence' into an overriding principle, a matter of dogma. They wanted the Inspectorate taken, physically, out of the DES and given a new identity as regulator and parents' watchdog. This would press home the ideology of independence. And to make the new status plain for all to see, they wanted the new HMCI to report directly to the Prime

Minister, and not to the Secretary of State for Education. The future of HMI became a test case for the Charter. The important thing was to give public vindication to a general principle – to provide a way of spinning the message of the Charter to the wider public – this consideration took precedence over the future consequences for education.

It was this definition of independence which brought about the divorce of the Inspectorate from the Department and ended HMI's historic role as professional advisers to the Secretary of State. It was this which marked the great gulf fixed between the pre-1992 HMI and the post-1992 HMI. Bolton clashed with Clarke in the columns of *The Times Educational Supplement*. 'I fear,' wrote Bolton,[10] 'that HMI is being shunted into a siding ... its work will in future be directed away from the Government and the DES and towards the schools ... The threat to HMI ... does not arise from attempting to enhance the quality and up the strike rate of institutional inspection, but from downgrading, almost to vanishing point, inspection intended to inform policy-making.' Clarke[11] defended the change as an enhancement of the role of HMI 'yielding far more inspection evidence' than before and dismissed out of hand the suggestion that the creation of a separate organisation would reduce the day-to-day contact between HMI and the Office. Reports from the new HMCI 'will be as critical to the work of the legislators and policy-makers as was the advice tendered during Eric Bolton's tenure as Senior Chief Inspector'.

Events quickly proved both men right. OFSTED proved to be a powerful body with a strong impact on schools and the new HMCI's voice resonated in high places. But the day-to-day contact of HMI and the Office came to an end. And, as if to underline the significance of the change, one of the first actions of the New Labour Secretary of State who took office in 1997, was to install his own professional advisers – academics with a taste for politics and such other advisers as he chose to call upon – to supply the expert advice which would otherwise have been available from HMI. Such an arrangement was likely to be to the taste of an incoming minister, who could dismiss one set of academic and professional advisers and install his own without any fuss. The price to pay was the loss to the Department of its own national intelligence-gathering organisation, a tradition of impartial, evidence-based counsel and the presence of senior professional advisers working cheek by jowl with senior officials. Number 10 was also urging that the HMCI should have a strong independent voice and use it to speak out publicly on issues thrown up by the practice of inspection. The first HMCI was recruited through a headhunter. Professor Stuart Sutherland who was appointed to do the job on a part-time basis, was principal of the University of London and had been involved in the attempts to introduce quality assurance schemes in higher education. It was he who coined the acronym OFSTED for the Office of Standards in Education, to join the other, similarly named regulatory bodies spawned by privatisation. OFSTED which began as a noun, soon became a transitive verb. Sutherland oversaw the setting up of the organisation, keeping a relatively low profile while doing so. In 1994 he left to become principal of the University of Edinburgh.

Great weight was attached to the inclusion of lay people in inspection teams – a Charter principle. There was a naive optimism that lay common sense would prevail over professional prejudice – that lay people would somehow be able to take the definition of good practice out of the hands of the professionals and that this would be beneficial. It was duly included in the Act that every team of inspectors should include one with no professional experience of schools as a teacher or administrator.

Enough of the market philosophy survived for no one to be able to say for certain where the inspectors would eventually come from. There were hopes that a new breed of inspector would come to market – ideally ministers would have liked to see the big management consultancies bidding for contracts – but firms like Coopers and Lybrand, Touche Ross, and Deloittes saw no profit in it at the rates countenanced by the Treasury. It was unlikely that many working business people would be tempted either. (The Treasury figures envisaged fees of £300 a day; the consultants were looking for £600.) The irony was lost on no one that in the end the new arrangements would depend on local authority staff bidding for the work – the self-same professionals that the market model was intended to bypass.

Setting Up OFSTED

Setting up the new system of inspection required work on two fronts. The new HMCI's office would have to be set up within the conventions of the public service and the necessary administrative arrangements made. And preliminary work would have to be done on the technical side to prepare for an inspection process approved by HMCI and carried out by registered inspectors, working to instructions. This would be work for HMI before and after the transition.

On the administrative side, a DES official, Petra Laidlaw, headed a Planning Unit charged with the task of creating the OFSTED organisation structure. There were staffing levels and grades to settle. There was the transfer of funds within the public expenditure to negotiate, accounting and information technology systems to set up and premises to find and equip. At the same time there were staffing questions for HMI – the allocation of the mass redundancies among existing inspectors and decisions about the 175 HMI posts which would be created at OFSTED.

For HMI it was a bitter time, with recrimination on the part of some who felt that, somehow, the worst could have been averted if the Inspectorate had been more astutely led, and uncertainty about who would transfer to the new organisation and who would not. It was a shattering experience, made worse because few HMI had ever supposed they were in a job where their security was at risk. Many were within the age bracket in which early retirement was a possibility. Others could consider applying to stay on at OFSTED. HFE inspectors were not quite so immediately affected – some of them might be able to continue when responsibility for FE inspection passed to the Funding Council. (OFSTED did not take over FE till 1999.)

In the words of one official, 'it was a rough job – especially cutting back the Inspectorate's top-heavy senior management structure in the teeth of covert – and often overt – opposition.' HMI had their own stories to tell of the speed and ruthlessness with which the task was accomplished – there was no way of undertaking surgery on this scale without blood being spilt.

The First Division Association had written to Clarke making representations on behalf of members of the Inspectorate who would be made redundant by the changes. Clarke wrote back with fulsome praise for HMI for whom 'I have the highest regard'. He went on: 'I have gone out of my way to emphasise the key role of HMI in extending their professional standards to all school inspections. It is simply perverse to infer that I have doubts about the credibility of HMI while proposing an enhanced role for the new office of Her Majesty's Chief Inspector of Schools.' Less gracefully, he linked his praise for HMI with a sideswipe at local authority inspectors – most of the criticism of inspectors which he had heard at the mouths of teachers, he said, was aimed at them not HMI.

There were queries from HMI about references and about procedures for applying for other jobs – normally civil servants were subject to certain rules when leaving to take other jobs, to ensure that there were no conflicts of interest. In the case of HMI, the conditions were waived for those applying for academic posts and jobs with the Funding Councils, and for those proposing to set up as self-employed consultants.

The bill became an Act in March 1992, to come into force after the April general election. Victory for the Conservatives was by no means certain: had Labour won, would they have scrapped the Act, having attacked it on its way through Parliament? In the event the Conservatives got back against the odds and no one can say what Labour might have done. Letters went out at the end of April to all HMIs about the transfer of employment of HMIs from September to the Office of the HMCI. Some would be taken on by the HMCI, others would become redundant. Volunteers for early retirement were invited and arrangements made with an employment consultancy for the counselling of HMIs seeking other jobs or planning to set up as independent consultants. A group of HMIs including CIs John Everson and Sally Twite, set about forming a network of retiring HMIs with a view to possible mutual support – a form of 'outplacement self-help'.

About 150 HMI who did not move over to OFSTED were made redundant when the legislation came into force. About 100 FHE inspectors remained till April 1993 when the HEFC took over responsibility for quality control and created 25 jobs for which the FHE inspectors were invited to apply. A further 25 transferred to the FE Funding Council. The remainder were made redundant.

Handbook

It was agreed that a system like that envisaged for OFSTED would require an operating handbook setting out everything a member of an inspection team would need to know. Some 200 HMI in OFSTED would be working through subordinate teams of inspectors, led by registered inspectors who would probably have professional qualifications but little or no experience of inspecting. (And as it turned out, they would have a very brief training period.) The handbook would have to set out step by step what the inspector had to do, what he/she was to look for and how he/she was to evaluate what was seen.

In a paper prepared for an international conference in 1987, with the National Curriculum already on the horizon, Bolton and his senior colleagues reflected on the consequences for inspection if ensuring compliance became a prime function of an Inspectorate. The paper touched on the question of criteria for HMI judgements:

> *In the final analysis the countless judgements made by individual inspectors are inherently subjective ... Talking to teachers is always an important feature of our work and is intended to ensure that those whose work is being reported on have confidence*

311

that the inspectors' judgements are reasonable and fair and relate to a situation they recognise.

That confidence is also helped by the use of criteria which relate to HMI's observations of good practice in a range of circumstances. The criteria are not externally imposed and HMI have in recent years endeavoured to make them known through explicit use of them in their reports and in their publications.

A lot had been done to improve the consistency and comparability of reporting, not only of full inspections, but also of Notes of Visits and the reporting of surveys. HMIs had a clear set of headings under which to organise their reports. These were filled out with questions to prompt observation and assessment, and amounted to a check-list of things to consider and factors to take into account. (The official line, however, was to deprecate terms like 'check-list' which seemed overly mechanical, preferring instead to think of these headings and questions as aids to 'sustain, temper and refine judgements made on the basis of observation of work ...'.)

The work of the HMI Management Unit under Anthea Millett and later, Sally Twite, served to focus these efforts, exploring the possibility of restructuring to create a single-line management and a further reduction in the number of divisions. In parallel with these developments, HMIs working in further and higher education who had been engaged in a similar process of self-examination, organised an invitation conference at Heythrop College in June 1989 on *Quality in Higher Education* attended by polytechnic directors, vice-chancellors, college principals, members of validating bodies and representatives of the Funding Councils, to share ideas and experience. As Melia put it, it was the first time HMI had revealed the criteria they used in inspection.

The paper from HMI, which forms the first section of the report of the conference, made the main concern the quality of learning – premises and equipment and management and all the other aspects of colleges as educational institutions, were only of interest insofar as they impinged on the students' quality of learning. The underlying concept was 'fitness for purpose'. Different courses and methods might be fitted to different purposes – HMI would make their assessments in the light of these differences, using five gradings ranging from 'generally good' to 'many shortcomings, generally poor'.

It is important to stress that there was nothing particularly surprising in what was made known – it would have been very odd indeed if HMI had not used some such categorisation, as Melia said, for 'internal purposes'.

The idea of gradings was not new – numerical grades had already been introduced into the format of Notes of Visits some years before. What broke new ground was the decision to go public – it was this which marked a break with tradition and signalled changes ahead. The FHE inspectors were striking a blow for openness and transparency in response to the spirit of the times. HMI were now called upon to be accountable like everyone else – how could HMI be accountable if they refused to explain the values behind their judgements?

There was, however, more to it than this. It was becoming part of the consumerist political culture to demand league tables and all manner of numerically expressed measures of success or failure – hence the intensifying pressure to use 'objective' school performance indicators (expressed in tabular form), in order to facilitate comparisons between schools. HMI was under the same political imperative to increase the appearance of objectivity of reporting by translating subjective assessments into grades and numbers. (There had also been murmuring of a different kind from academic educational researchers like Desmond Nuttall and Neville Bennett, for HMI to be more open about the evidence on which they formed their judgements. Educational research had embraced the apparatus of social science and was disposed to use the same apparatus to appraise the work of HMI.)

By 1992, grade descriptions similar to those revealed by Melia for FHE, were appearing in the material used by HMI for the school inspection programme. A reporter from *The Times Educational Supplement* was invited to sit in on an inspection of a secondary school in the Midlands. Each member of the team had a ring-binder with pages outlining the matters to be reviewed. The right-hand pages set out the topics and provided spaces for the inspector's notes with a small box where a grade was to be inserted. The left-hand pages had the questions which indicated what was to be covered. It was a highly structured document covering every aspect of the inspection and pre-inspection procedures.

A draft *Framework for the Inspection of Schools* was prepared by HMI for the Secretary of State (at his request) in December 1991 – while the bill was going through Parliament. It was put together in three months following Clarke's statement in September. It was incomplete and amendments to the bill as it went through altered the content of the final version which appeared in August 1992, a month before HMCI took over. It was aimed at registered inspectors and devotes 22 pages to the statutory conditions they must sign up to.

Also issued in 1992 was the *Handbook* in the same format, largely concerned with organisation, but also containing detailed sections exemplifying the criteria for judgement. It detailed the record of evidence the inspectors were to compile and return with their report to support their judgements. Further guidance on inspection stressed the need to arrive at collective judgements, and amplified descriptions of 'good' and 'poor' to pinpoint grade differences.

It had, of course, been an axiom for HMI that what was being inspected was the pupils' learning not individual teachers. The new regime would assess both the quality of learning and the quality of teaching. The *Handbook* placed the quality of learning under 'main findings' and teaching quality under 'factors contributing'.

This was the pre-1992 HMI's last bequest to OFSTED, a gift carried over by those HMI who went on to set up the new organisation. The style was more direct and assertive than that hitherto. It was aimed at people who were coming to the task without lengthy training and was meant to provide them with an all-purpose *vade mecum* to be followed in detail. Things which HMI took as implicit as part of a tradition going back generations, had to be made explicit in these pages with the comfortable ambiguities removed, but much of the content was a direct reflection of traditional HMI thinking. It did not pretend to be the last word; revision began almost immediately and revised editions appeared in 1994 and 1995.

Notes

[1] Pearce, J (1986) *Standards and the LEA: The Accountability of Schools*. Windsor: NFER-Nelson, 19.

[2] Hogg, S., Hill, J. (1995). *Too Close to Call*. London: Little Brown and Co.

[3] Bolton, E. (1998) 'HMI – the Thatcher years', *Oxford Review of Education* **24**(1): 45–55. Quote on page 52.

[4] Seldon, A. (1997) *Major: A Political Life*. London: Weidenfeld and Nicholson. Quote on page 186.

[5] See Bolton, note 3, 53.

[6] Culloden Primary School, Tower Hamlets, which had been the subject of six 30-minute programmes by the BBC, 'A year in the life of a city primary school', was broadcast in spring 1991. It was also inspected by HMI in March 1991 (No. xx/91).

[7] Perry, P. (1991) 'Inspection: quality assurance or quality control', *The Times Educational Supplement*, 12 July 1991, 16.

[8] Speech by the prime minister, the Rt Hon John Major, 3 July 1991, to the Centre for Policy Studies, Cafe Royal, London, on 'Education: all our futures'.

[9] See Bolton, note 3, 52.

[10] Bolton, E. (1991) 'Charter bears a closer inspection', *The Times Educational Supplement*, 18 October 1991, 10.

[11] Clarke, K. (1991) 'Power to the people's HMI', *The Times Educational Supplement*, 1 November 1991, 6.

HMI Miscellany

Extracts from HMI personal accounts

John Everson 1968

Throughout this period increasing demands were made upon the manpower of the Inspectorate as well as sharp time-scales for responses. For example, a very great deal of inspection power was taken up by the introduction of the inspection of all ITT institutions . . . Later, HMI time was needed to support the work of all the subject committees set up to take forward the introduction of the National Curriculum and associated assessment. In fact the initiatives that Ministers wanted us to take and the range and depth of the advice they needed on, for example, less able pupils, inner city problems, the polytechnics, 16–19 education, overseas educational developments, independent schools and INSET, forced the Inspectorate to inspect and visit more widely and to ask more and more from individual Inspectors . . .

Time, too, was taken up in pushing forward without disaster Ministers' favoured plans: a considerable amount of the time of senior secondary HMI was taken up in helping to set up the CTCs. HMI were good at guessing Ministers' likely requirements for advice, helped by well-placed officials, although attempts to get the Office to state its needs for a coming year or so collapsed after a few long and inconclusive meetings. Towards the end of the period the pressure on HMI was very great and tested to the full the experience and expertise of some Inspectors who were not entirely suited to the new, more frenetic, ways of working.

When Sir Keith Joseph decided that all HMI inspection reports on schools should be published I was strongly opposed to it, thinking that it would be impossible to obtain all the information needed from the school and to write a proper report. I was quite wrong. The development undoubtedly improved our writing of reports and speed of production. It also meant that considerable benefit was gained by schools and LEAs.

When the National Curriculum had to be introduced to a fierce timetable, corners had to be cut and the Office began to make educational decisions about the shape and nature of the curriculum that it did not have the expertise or experience to take. Some Ministers, too, became more reluctant to accept honest comment about their schemes.

Things began to get really difficult when officials were placed under severe pressure to introduce a Ministerial scheme notwithstanding the effects on the

315

whole educational system and other parts of the Government's policy and whether or not the particular aspect of the initiative harmed other desirable goals. When this pressure also became associated with the targets set by senior officials as part of the DES appraisal scheme, problems began to arise.

Bob Young 1976

During the late 80s the future role of LEA advisers came to the fore. Given, on the one hand, increasing pressure from the Government for each individual school to be inspected regularly, reported on and 'held to account' and, on the other, the incapacity of HMI, with its existing work-force, to fulfil this task unaided, the obvious question was whether the vast force of LEA advisers could somehow supply the deficiency. Some LEAs were already well down this road and were using their advisers, often retitled 'inspectors', to conduct formal inspections. Other LEAs, and a great number of individual advisers, were totally opposed to any such move, being convinced that their advisory role, as friend and supporter of the school, would be contaminated if they were also involved in inspecting and reporting on the school's performance. I was convinced that this was to under-value their own professionalism and that the two roles both could be, and should be, combined ... If LEA teams were to have a place in a reliable and nationally acceptable system of inspection, then two things at least were essential. They would need to be trained, and subsequently monitored and assisted, to undertake the role; and their relationship with HMI would need to be much closer than (officially at least) it had traditionally been. A valuable, though small-scale, precedent had already been set in the secondment of senior LEA officers to work alongside HMI in Elizabeth House. They brought a detailed and up-to-date knowledge of LEAs and their problems and procedures and gained in return a potentially fruitful insight into HMI methods and values.

Sally Twite 1980

From 1985 until 1992 all the procedural areas underwent considerable change, with the overall aims of increasing efficiency and thus tightening up systems, streamlining them and making criteria more transparent. Work programming conventions and travel and subsistence regulations were difficult to administer within the matrix structure; changes towards greater centralisation took place and were often resisted. A bone of contention at the time was the introduction – Civil Service-wide – of performance-related pay. Even the earliest version – performance bonuses – was much disliked (except by some of those who received them). The later versions, imposed centrally in the Civil Service, were also unpopular in many ways, even though the recipients gained permanent and pensionable increases thereby. Among the most telling arguments against the introduction of PRP were its perceived divisiveness and unfairness of rewarding individuals for what was often achieved through team effort. Needless to say, HMI's attitudes to annual reporting changed greatly over the period: though some appreciated the greater rigour and consistency of the procedures and the attempts to link it with in-service provision, there remained uneasiness about the link with pay.

The Framework in effect drew on HMI expertise developed and refined over ten to fifteen years. Until the early 80s much HMI work had been implicit, an effect of osmosis, and development consisted largely of making explicit HMI principles and practice, basically the criteria for inspection and its practice. The thinking underlying the practice started to emerge in guidelines, in the booklets explaining HMI practice, in the development of a standard format for notes of visit, and in new forms of inspection, notably the short ('dipstick') inspection. These matters received much attention in the 80s so that when HMI were set the task of elaborating an inspection 'model' the work was quickly resolved and is basically still in place. What was a good 'management' format allowing both an individual school focus and a wide overlapping coverage of subjects and aspects was ruined by the piling on of current issues ('piggy-backing') . . . Irrespective of the debate about the future of HMI, the depressing work of management went on in its own right. It stopped in 1992 when the world fell round our ears . . . Curiously, at a time when the Inspectorate was under fire at home, abroad, other countries were continuing to appreciate our ways. *(In interview with Brian Arthur)*

Jim Rose 1978

The publication of reports had given HMI 'teeth'. *Better Schools* relied heavily on them, particularly for judgements about uneven provision, identifying a continuum of practice varying from excellent to poor, the latter shown up in sharp relief, making all the more urgent the need to close the gap. Some reports, notably three on reading, were seminal contributions to the debate on standards. Following the last of Eric Bolton's Annual Reports (1990–91) an MP had asked 'Are we likely to lose reports of this quality?'

HMI were inevitably involved in policy evaluation; Eric Bolton had no choice. This meant criticising policy, albeit 'in camera', on the basis of what HMI were finding in schools, and giving Ministers considerable discomfort. Hence the new direction taken by OFSTED: from survey-type work to a role of regulating a contracted-out system of inspections of individual schools. This was a sea-change. It fulfilled the policy interest of focusing on relevant information and getting it where it needed to be: to parents and to the schools. This could not have been done before: how else could 20000 primary schools have been inspected on a once-in-a-child's-lifetime cycle, identifying quickly those schools below the line and applying 'special' or 'serious weakness' measures to them. These requirements represented a very marked shift from what went before; and it constituted policy change, requiring a political decision. A multiplicity of functions was replaced by a much more focused one. And an expert system was translated into a wider world. With that came the danger of losing the quality of judgement since there were doubts about the calibre of others to do the job. Hence the need for a framework, which ran the risk of being prescriptive. *(In interview with Brian Arthur)*

David Taylor 1978

In the end the change happened very rapidly. Not many HMI were prepared for their new role although consultants and advisers were available for career counselling for those who were considering early retirement. Probably too little was done to ensure the notion of continuity and stability. On the contrary, the insistence on a structural break, abolishing the Divisions and the old committee structure headed by phase, subject and aspect SIs, gave a deliberate impression of discontinuity, designed to make HMI sharply aware of the new order. Too much was perhaps left to the Framework: HMI's experience in quality evaluation (criteria and standards) was neglected. The dismantling of the field force meant the loss of regional intelligence, which had been one of HMI's strengths in building up a body of evidence of performance. This evidence was also seriously affected by HMI's withdrawal from INSET and notably from the teachers' short course programme, a prime source of evidence, a means of carrying out 'improvement through inspection' and a very enjoyable aspect of HMI work. *(In interview with Brian Arthur)*

David Soulsby 1975

There was no doubt that the management unit was an important innovation and that some central co-ordination of the increasingly complex management issues was becoming essential. However, such was the nature of the Inspectorate, even after a good deal of more centralised work, that this was very difficult to achieve; many HMI felt that a management unit was simply another obstacle to the proper conduct of their professional business. If it had happened some five or ten years before, it might have succeeded in grappling with the issues sufficiently swiftly to enable a more streamlined Inspectorate to do a better job and respond more swiftly to the increasing pace of change. As it was, it was overtaken by political events and by the new Secretary of State, Kenneth Clarke.

Fred Brook 1978

Eventually, the intentions of the Education Bill were made known to us. The FHE Inspectorate was to be cast adrift and the Schools side severely reduced. There would be more inspection of schools than ever before but it would be done by contractors. The shock to the FHE Inspectorate was enormous. Many people felt that what was being proposed could not be done, since we were Crown Officers. For many colleagues who had recently joined it was Hobson's Choice: stay on as HMI until such a time as the FHE Inspectorate was abolished and future arrangements were clearer, and then become redundant. We awaited the outcome of the 1992 General Election with acute concern. If the Conservatives lost the Bill would fall; if they won the Bill would go through. I had to chair the meeting of Northern Division FHE HMI the day after the election . . . The meeting was short and grim . . . What a way to go! But there was much to be proud of. The HE sector had prospered and the polytechnics became universities in the summer of 1992. I was proud to attend Sunderland University's vesting day ceremony, my last 'official duty' as HMI . . . My last week in the Inspectorate was spent at a conference in Llandudno to give those of us retiring the opportunity to qualify as registered inspectors or team inspectors under the new arrangements – to make us qualify for work which many had been doing for over 20 years. And this was being done to us by our own people! Not surprisingly, reality was suspended during much of that week as we went through the motions.

David Grant 1980

For me it was a disappointment when the local focus of HMI was cut off at the end of the Inspectorate's life. There was a particularly chilling moment when District Inspectors were, in effect, told to throw away all their school and district files. Perhaps OFSTED would not want this material, but the idea of disposing of such crucial local history in this way seemed appalling. The Derbyshire County Records Office at Matlock were keen to take possession of them. We agreed to a 50-year embargo, to cover the files which might mention teachers by name, and I drove them up to Matlock. For me that was the moment when Her Majesty's Inspectorate ended.

Tom Wylie 1979

I eagerly seized the invitation in 1990 to become SI for Educational Disadvantage – taking on responsibility for two teams and a whole raft of issues concerned with the local management of schools, urban schooling, school attendance, behaviour, and, before long, the education of ethnic minorities. All this work lay in the Inspectorate's schools command; indeed, predominantly in the secondary schools command but there was just enough cross-phase involvement to make it intellectually coherent. Notwithstanding the setting, the policy tasks were similar – the provision of the best possible advice to Ministers and SCI and CIs, and the shaping of inspection activity – individual and collective – to these ends. Some of these inspections were very specific exercises, looking, for example, at behaviour or provision for pupils excluded from school, or at the education for travellers' children or young people held in secure accommodation for other reasons, or at travellers' children. Many of the messages were bleak but Ministers were rarely concerned to hear how their policies were working in practice.

Before the waves from the Schools Act 1992 swamped the Inspectorate, one major, unique inspection task was undertaken under the Educational Disadvantage aegis. It was to inspect and report on the educational experiences – from cradle to grave – of people growing up in disadvantaged areas. Seven urban areas – predominantly peripheral housing estates – were identified, one in each Division, and by dint of persuasion of HMI Divisional and other planning systems, inspections undertaken of all or most of the education provision for their residents. It embraced nursery, primary and secondary schools; FE; youth and adult provision from Manchester to Hull, Bristol to Derby. The overall RI, Frances White, straddled the schools/FE divide. Unusually, it made use of socio-economic data skilfully marshalled by George Smith, the Inspectorate's attached research consultant . . . Published as 'Access and Achievement in Urban Education', 1993, the outcome was a penetrating snapshot of the quality of the educational experience offered to some of the most disadvantaged communities and their people . . . Such a holistic inspection could never be repeated. Published by OFSTED, it was, nevertheless the last hurrah for HMI's unique approach and educational reach.

Afterword

A Janus Look

This narrative has followed the scenario sketched at the front of the book; plotted the transformation of the education system in England and Wales from the post-war period to the 1988 Education Reform Act and its consequences; recorded the changes which replaced a highly decentralised system, run by powerful local authorities and a weak Ministry of Education, with a centrally controlled national education machine with local authorities on the sidelines; and observed the part played by HMIs in the shaping of education policy from the end of the Second World War to the setting up of OFSTED.

The role of the Inspectorate has always been determined by what is happening in education generally. In the century and a half which preceded the passing of the 1992 Act, HMI went through various metamorphoses and fulfilled the various functions given them by the governments of the day in accordance with their policy requirements. By the middle of the nineteenth century the Inspectorate had established that its reports could not be rewritten by the Minister or his/her minions. This was the pre-OFSTED Inspectorate's one unchallengeable mark of independence. Otherwise, HMI was at the disposal of the Minister and over the years, this has meant that HMIs have had to tailor their working lives and their professional expectations to meet ministers' policy needs – whether these were 'payment by results' or keeping the elementary schools in order, or progress-chasing for the Ministry or helping to get a grip on the curriculum. It was always to the Minister that HMI reported.

There were two sections to Martin Roseveare's post-war Inspectorate: an FE Inspectorate looked after FE in all its forms providing regular inspection of technical colleges. In the fifties there were major developments in technological education in which the Inspectorate played an important part.

About three-quarters of the Inspectorate focused on the inspection of schools. The immediate priority was to set up reporting inspections for all the schools to provide a post-war baseline. This provided the post-war affirmation of the district HMI and his team of colleagues, out in the field in a given area, devoting themselves to the visitation and oversight of the schools and teachers on their 'patch', and to liaison with the chief education officer and local authority. Under Roseveare's successors, the focus of school visiting had begun to shift, with fewer full inspections and more surveys directed at specific questions or different aspects of the system. It had ceased to be practical to think of inspecting all institutions on a regular, cyclical, basis – the Inspectorate did not have the manpower.

The essence of the work of HMI was visiting and reporting on schools and passing on advice and encouragement. Many HMIs continued to think that was what it should always be about, long after priorities changed. Every HMI was also a specialist with an academic subject to keep up or a phase to focus on. Regular inspection visits formed the basis of their professional expertise, their knowledge of the schools, their understanding of the tasks the teachers were confronting, their experience and knowledge of good practice in different circumstances, their ability to report what they saw, without imposing their own or someone else's orthodoxy. This was the classic ideal to which HMI as a whole subscribed. This is what HMI stood for in the schools. Like many classic ideals its appeal may have grown as time passed. If it ever existed in reality, it was never static and soon began to change and develop.

One feature of the Roseveare Inspectorate was the relatively weak central management which reflected the strength of the periphery in the education system. HMI were organised in regional divisions. DIs were respected figures, but individual HMIs had a large measure of freedom to plan their own work. They acted like independent professionals for much of their time, though they would expect also to take part in programmes of inspection organised both at divisional and national level.

There were guidelines laid down for inspection procedures. These became more detailed as time went on but an HMI was expected to exercise his/her own subjective judgement in assessing school performance. There were no pre-stated measures which HMIs were to use, no set of tests which schools could know in advance that HMI were going to apply. They knew all schools were different and faced different challenges as a result of factors beyond their control. They were connoisseurs of schools, using judgement educated by experience and collective wisdom, to look at schools in the round and make their assessments of good and not so good practice. Any authority they wielded was attributed to them by those with whom they had dealings: they were not part of any schools management structure and had no executive authority.

They backed up their programmes of school visiting and their pursuit of specialist interests in two ways. First, the specialists met regularly in panels and committees to share knowledge and experience gathered in the course of their work as inspectors, and to review developments, publications, innovations. This was a time-consuming and, judging from the minutes of the meetings, unexciting, activity but it to kept people in touch and created a sense of belonging. SIs could use it to build up a team. It was a necessary activity but only went some way towards sharing a common base of knowledge and experience.

The second way in which HMI fire-power was brought to bear was through the in-service training programme, the courses which were organised by the subject and phase specialists each year. Many HMI regarded these as among the most important (as well as the most enjoyable) activities in which they engaged. Though the programme grew and occupied a significant fraction of HMI time, it could never have touched more than a fairly small proportion of the teaching force, but it had a disproportionate influence among those in the schools who had responsibility for the curriculum.

What was important was the orientation of the Roseveare Inspectorate. The theory was quite clear. Inspectors were the Minister's eyes and ears. They reported to him/her. But this is not how it seemed to be in practice. HMI looked outward to the schools and the teachers. To all intents and purposes, it was as if the schools and the teachers were their principal clients. In the course of their duties, in and out of schools, they spread good practice, offering (but not imposing) advice and encouragement. This was their pastoral role and explained their gentle approach and cautious manner. They seldom threw their weight about or in Roseveare's terms, raised their voice. Maintaining good relations with teachers was a priority. When they left a school, they were meant to leave the teachers feeling the better for HMI's visit.

There was, somewhere in their brief, the watchdog role but it was rarely emphasised and when they encountered what would later be called a 'failing' school, the typical follow-up was a quiet word in the chief education officer's ear, a discreet chat with the local adviser and, probably, a return visit in six months or so. In many cases – most cases? – this was an effective if muted way of working. Often in the case of schools which were not making the grade, it was the chief education officers who took the initiative and asked for a full inspection to back up action which was already planned.

So here were the main elements of the classic Inspectorate – elements which, as we have suggested, began to change almost as soon as they were established, but which continued to be present in the make-up and personality of the Inspectorate. They included its orientation towards the schools exemplified by pastoral visiting and in-service training, and by the degree of professional autonomy enjoyed by rank-and-file HMI. To this might be added its devotion to the writing of reports on schools which, for the most part, were read and then filed. (The use made of them by schools and LEAs was not monitored.)

This is, of course, only part of the story because there were also senior HMI working alongside the senior officials in the Department who were much more concerned with policy issues and who, with the SCI, were drawn into consultation at many points when, for example, a White Paper was being prepared. The duty to advise the Minister remained but for much of the time the Minister felt relatively little need for such advice and successive SCIs complained about being kept out of the top management net till eventually, in 1969, Bill Elliott was elevated to the rank of deputy secretary.

Out of these components came the style – the set of characteristics which defined the Inspectorate in its relations with the schools and with the Office. It was cautious and understated in its public pronouncements. Its reports on schools were issued but not published. There was an emphasis on etiquette and courtesy in relations with teachers and local educational administrators, and collegiality in relations within the Inspectorate. It was more inclined to encouragement than blame. It operated from within the system – HMI were (with rare exceptions) teachers turned inspectors and remained members of the profession operating within the Civil Service. In due course this would be one of the charges brought against them – that they were part of the 'producer culture' not guardians of the consumer interest.

When, therefore, the background to educational policy-making changed in the mid-1970s, there were corresponding changes in the role of HMI. It was a process which took place over time. An important landmark was the reorganisation of the Departmental Planning Organisation at the DES which included HMI. After 1969, the SCI had direct access to the Secretary of State. After seven years of review upon review, a new and determined SCI in the person of Sheila Browne, tackled the need to reorientate the Inspectorate, to make clear its prime obligation was to meet the needs of the Minister and the Office.

The key to this was to turn HMI into a managed group of professionals whose work could be centrally coordinated and directed towards supplying answers to the questions thrown at them by ministers and officials. It meant challenging the notion of the laid-back, self-directed inspectors who spent their time visiting 'their' schools – and curbing the freedom of the DIs, in their quasi-independent fiefdoms. As for many HMI the pastoral role was one of the attractions of the job; this redirection of effort was not generally welcomed by the old guard, but newer members of the Inspectorate had less difficulty in recognising that it was necessary. The Inspectorate was vulnerable if it failed to respond.

The adaptation equipped the Inspectorate for the period described in this narrative as 'Reform' – the years between James Callaghan's Ruskin speech and the end of Keith Joseph's time as Secretary of State – and on into Kenneth Baker's 'Revolution'. It involved the centralisation of authority summed up in the First Call Centre arrangements which put a third of HMI manpower at any time at the disposal of the SCI and through her the CIs and SIs. And the centrally driven programmes were governed by central considerations – the priorities, determined by the Office through the Planning Organisation, and by the leaders of HMI in their anticipation of future demands.

Well before the Ruskin speech there was an awareness at the top of the DES that the context for educational policy-making was changing. The time was coming when ministers would wish to take a more proactive role. To do so they would be dependent on HMI for knowledge of what happened at school level. It would be up to the Inspectorate to supply the intelligence service and professional advice which the Department would need if it were decided to move into policy areas hitherto regarded as outside the purview of ministers or civil servants – areas like the school curriculum, of which George Tomlinson had memorably – and proudly – claimed ministers knew 'nowt'.

This was made clear – overstated, in fact – in the famous Yellow Book prepared at Callaghan's request, which embodied the Department's bid for a major role in the new dispensation. The Department, aided by the Inspectorate, began the process by which the curriculum was brought back into the public domain – a lengthy exercise in changing the mind-set of the education community. Over the decade which followed the Callaghan speech, three Secretaries of State took steps to seize the initiative on the school curriculum, examinations and teacher training, drawing heavily on the work of HMI in the process. Joseph, the last of the three who had the longest sojourn at the Department, used political stick and carrot to bring the local authorities into line with what was essentially a centralising programme.

The narrative has shown something of what HMI contributed to the execution of these policy manoeuvres by the material they prepared for publication – from the Primary and Secondary Surveys and the Red Books exercise, through the various curriculum discussion documents of the late seventies and early eighties which progressed and sharpened the debate, to the important 'Curriculum Matters' series of pamphlets from 1985 onwards which focused attention, subject by subject, on the content of study and what pupils might be expected to have learnt at specific points in their schooling. With this had also gone the work on the subject criteria for the General Certificate of Secondary Education, which was complementary to the curriculum debate.

The essential characteristics of the Inspectorate in this period – 1976–86 – included some which were different, some which were carried over from the earlier period.

- The Inspectorate was still firmly located within the Department of Education and continued to report to the Secretary of State.

- The majority of HMIs continued to be part of a field force, organised on a territorial basis and spending most of their time visiting schools. There would be less routine visiting, less 'dropping in', more visits with a specific objective to answer questions put by others. HMI would be spending enough time in schools (it was hoped) to keep in touch, and a programme of full inspections continued which provided some necessary experience of in-depth, whole-school reporting.

- HMI was now positioned to look to the Minister and his needs for priorities and programmes and organise their work accordingly. The emphasis had moved away from what HMIs could do in their schools to spread sweetness and light, to what they could glean from their schools to support the work of the Department. They retained the obligation to do good as they went, but the change of emphasis was plainly important.

- The management of the Inspectorate had become more centralised, FCC being one of a number of ways in which the hand of the SCI and CIs was strengthened and the myth of the 'self-employed' HMI was buried.

- One significant change concerned publications. The post-Ruskin Inspectorate was even more committed to writing and publishing papers, pamphlets, reports, emerging from its collective endeavours. It also continued to support an extensive programme of in-service training for teachers; often the priorities for in-service courses would be related to the publishing programme and the dissemination of ideas developed, or reported on, in the publications.

- As for inspection, work went forward on the criteria to be applied in the inspection of schools and colleges. The confidence in HMI's tutored, but subjective, judgements remained, but the pressure was building up for more objective performance indicators and for HMI to organise their conclusions in ways which minimised inconsistency and maximised quantifiable judgements.

This was the Inspectorate which entered the fourth, 'Revolution', period of this scenario. For five years, the Inspectorate was fully employed supporting ministers' revolutionary plans, most notably in the making of the National Curriculum. But because the Baker Act transformed the powers and functions of the Secretary of State, it was also bound to entail major changes for the Inspectorate. The arrangements initiated by Sheila Browne had been geared to the needs of ministers and officials operating under a system of distributed power and the consultative conventions of the 1944 Act. What sort of Inspectorate would a minister need, who sallied forth armed with the powers and responsibilities of the 1988 Act?

If formal inspection was to be put on a four-yearly basis, it would be necessary to simplify the process, and speed up attempts to translate the subjective judgements of HMI into marks out of five and boxes to tick. A simplified written inspection procedure, working to published 'criteria', would be a necessary step towards a system of quality control which could be run by an elite Inspectorate and a supporting cast of what, for want of a better term might be called, registered inspectors. In fact the old HMI's last bequest to OFSTED was the first edition of a Handbook and Framework for just such an inspection regime.

What is clear is that writing it all down and systematising each step in the inspection process was incompatible with the philosophy and the style of the old Inspectorate. It meant giving too many hostages to fortune. The mystique of HMI was wrapped up in the idea of professional judgement, refined by experience and deepened by the shared wisdom of colleagues, applied without prejudice or dogma. One of the things which made HMI acceptable was their claim to approach schools with something like an open mind and their willingness to accept that good education came in many different shapes and sizes. By not stating the criteria of their judgements in advance, they were able to report what they saw and value quality even when it came in controversial or politically incorrect forms.

It is worth noting that an HMI inspection of Summerhill – the one-off, progressive school founded by A. S. Neill – under the old regime, was capable of understanding and appreciating what was being done in a school which was like no other. All the post-1992 inspectors could do when they went to Summerhill was apply their rigid template to prove what was plain in the first place – namely that this was a school which did not obey the ordinary rules. They had no alternative but to recommend the closure of Summerhill. In the event, the school was rescued by the Secretary of State who allowed common sense to prevail at the last moment. It was no fault of the inspection methodology that the Minister and the Department escaped without international egg on their faces.

When the time came in 1991 to choose a new model for the national school inspection regime, the search was on for a suitable two-tier system. Eric Bolton had looked for ways of combining the resources of HMI and the local authority inspectorates, with HMI in charge. Other schemes were floated to take account of uncertainty about the future of local authorities in the aftermath of the new Act. All the DES/HMI-originated schemes envisaged HMI continuing to report to the Secretary of State and acting as his/her professional advisers.

This remained the Office view to the end. But by the spring of 1991 a different approach had been formulated in the Number 10 Policy Unit which derived from preliminary thinking about a Citizen's Charter. Independent inspection was elevated to an essential element in John Major's campaign for consumer protection. It so happened that consideration of what should be done about the Schools Inspectorate happened to come to the top of the in-tray at the same time as the Charter. It was from this that the physical and administrative separation of HMI from the Department for Education and Employment became a matter of principle, accepted by Kenneth Clarke against the advice of the department.

There was in this a large element of bad luck and bad timing. It helped Number 10 spin the Citizen's Charter, and there was an obvious tabloid appeal about presenting the old HMI as a toothless lapdog grown fat and indolent sitting on the Secretary of State's knee and contrasting this with the head of the new inspectorate, HMCI, like a rottweiler straining at the leash, as the single-minded champion of parents' rights. Scotland wisely held back and did nothing, and as it happened other Government inspectorates like that for social services continued to report to the relevant Minister. Only education got the full treatment.

It was part of the rhetoric from early on to insist that HMCI should speak out and use the independence which was so conspicuously attributed to the holder of that office, fearlessly and publicly, to expose the shortcomings of the system. Outspoken critical comment by HMCI has been one of the hallmarks of the new regime. This was seen as an indication – and a vindication – of new-found independence.

There must, however, be more than a suspicion that this owes less to the Inspectorate becoming independent of the DfEE than to the fact that it has become wholly dependent on the Prime Minister. The independence of the HMCI will be of little value if he/she is wholly dependent on pleasing the Prime Minister.

The Inspectorate is now in a much more exposed position. Its raised profile has made it stand out as a political target. Its prestige and that of the Prime Minister are now interlinked. What HMCI does is now a matter of direct interest to the political advisers and media manipulators of Number 10. It is difficult to resist the conclusion that the real independence of HMI was much more likely to be safeguarded when the Inspectorate was an integral part of a great Department of State than out on a limb with the Prime Minister as patron.

The new arrangements have involved a deliberate change of style. Style is important, as both the Roseveare and the Browne Inspectorates showed. Just how important became evident after the old Inspectorate was replaced and the former civilities were set aside. It is plainly necessary to find ways of restoring the civilities and reshaping the pattern of the inspection of schools on a more education-friendly basis.

Personalities apart, there is no reason why an effective system of inspection need be abrasive or hostile. At issue are questions of professional performance and how to operate an inspection system which protects the public, but does so in such a way as to build up the professionalism of teachers not undermine it. No one who has read this far will need persuading that the watchdog role of HMI was underplayed for far too long. There is no doubt that ministers (and the public) would expect the inspection process to be sharp and for there to be coherent and systematic follow-up procedures. But the fundamental truth remains that the teachers in the schools are the only teachers there are to do the job, and their competence and confidence cannot be enhanced – nor can parents be protected as consumers – by subjecting them to inspection procedures which undermine them.

Such matters will doubtless be attended to over time, as the education system as a whole domesticates OFSTED and its ways are tempered by day-to-day realities. New organisations and new chief executives start with energy and enthusiasm to cut a swathe through the system, but in the course of time the realities win and this will be true of the inspection arrangements. The new arrangements are orientated towards the schools and the parents not the Secretary of State. This is what will determine how they develop and the style which comes to epitomise the inspection regime.

The point on which to end must be the fundamental mistake which Major and Clarke made in taking the Inspectorate away from the DES – the sheer irresponsibility of making a fundamental change in a trusted organisation with 150 years of history behind it, for no better reason than to give an extra spin to an ephemeral political gimmick.

The pretence was that HMI would continue to advise ministers even though the new inspection organisation was separate. This was never likely and, of course, it never happened. Instead an incoming Secretary of State hastened to import his own professional advisers, unhindered by the HMI tradition of impartiality which might on occasion confront him/her with unwelcome advice. No doubt the academics ministers bring in will be honest men and women who do their excellent best, but none of them will have served the apprenticeship which HMIs served. They will be supplemented by others whom the Minister decides to invite. They too will serve at the minister's pleasure. Politicians, of course, will appreciate having their own picked advisers to help them: whether it is something the rather larger group of citizens who are not ministers will have cause to appreciate is another matter.

This has all the appearance of an irreversible change – one which ministers will not regret and one to which the educational system has quickly adapted. But if there is no going back to the Inspectorate which served ministers well between 1976 and 1992, there is no reason to believe that the arrangements set up under the 1992 Act are the last word.

There will be many who regret the passing of the old HMI. They will include some of those who have thrown in their lot with OFSTED and loyally taken part in the transition from the old to the new. They will include all who remained unconvinced that public education needs to be under the thumb of national politicians as a closely controlled system; who do not want a compulsory curriculum to be laid down by

Parliament; who distrust the desire to centralise decision-making; who believe that only indifferent teachers will put up with excessive central direction and oppressive inspection; who believe that ministers need sound evidence-based advice, and advisers who have learned their trade in day-to-day contact with schools *and* in using their judgement in observing and reporting on schools.

The time will come when the received wisdom of the National Curriculum will be challenged and people will look for a less authoritarian model – one which can accommodate the broad public interest and yet leave room for more originality and imagination at school and classroom level. One of the lessons to be drawn from the shaping of educational policy in the second half of the twentieth century is that all policies are interim and incomplete. This will be true of the next 50 years too, but there is just a chance – who knows? – things might be better done.

A Note on the HMI Personal Accounts

Following a general invitation from the original steering group to retired and serving HMI to contribute written and spoken accounts of their experience, well over 200 personal accounts were received, from English and Welsh HMI appointed between the years 1937 and 1988. As is described in 'About this Book', these individual contributions and the papers accompanying them have been drawn on to build up a picture of the Inspectorate's work.

A full list of the contributors, including those interviewed, is given below, linked chronologically to the decade of their appointment and showing the time-span of the individual and collective experience which the book has quarried.

With the agreement of the contributors, the personal accounts and accompanying papers are to be lodged in the AHMI (Jack Kitching) Archive at the University of London Institute of Education and made available for future research.

1930s

Direct contributions: GC Allen, CBE; Lady Helen Asquith, OBE.

Other papers: JEH Blackie, CB; L Clark, OBE; WR Elliott, CB; Sir Martin Roseveare, OBE; P Wilson, CB.

1940s

Direct contributions: RH Adams, TD; FA Arrowsmith, OBE; AB Baddeley; JW Banes; LJ Burrows, CBE; R D'Aeth; Miss EM Davies, OBE (Wales); HJ Edwards; RW Evans (Wales); WJ Evans; HL (Tim) Fenn; HW French, CBE; AH Howlett, OBE; TR Jenkyn; Miss G Jones (England & Wales); LS Laid; Miss M Lockyer; RW Morris; DIR Porter; Miss EM Sharman; EJ Sidebottom.

Other papers: EI Baker, CBE (contributed by Mrs R Baker); CH Barry, CBE; P M Burns (contributed by Mrs J Burns); Sir Cyril English; Miss MML Lewis (Wales) (contributed by Miss BJ Lewis); JCG Mellars; JW Morris contributed by Mrs N Morris; GSV Petter; R Tanner; GE Trodd (contributed by Mrs C Trodd).

1950s

Direct contributions: KL Ashurst, OBE; JK Brierley; Miss BS Briggs; Mrs BM Brook; WJH Earl; DW Emery; Lewis Evans, OBE; DRT Goodwin; EA

Greatwood; Miss WM Hopkins-Jones (Wales); DM Hopkinson; PH Hoy; WJF Jeff; Miss ME Johnston; Miss MD Lewis; Miss MT McBride; HES Marks; Miss MJ Marshall, CBE; Mrs B Parr, OBE; Miss M Rayment; JV Shelby, MBE, TD; H Taylor; WW Taylor; Miss KM Tobin; A Wigglesworth; CL Williams.

1960s

Direct contributions: TWF Allan; JP Allen, OBE; Mrs MI Ambrose; TI Ambrose; A Ashbrook; A Bell; JM Birchenough; DMW Boulton; G Bowen (Wales); Miss MI Brogden; Miss SJ Browne, CB; DG Buckland; AG Clegg; J Dalglish; M Edmundson; KT Elsdon; JA Everson; J Featherstone; JR Fish; TJ Fletcher, CBE; WH Francis; WG Hamflett; BWV Hawes; GM Hearnshaw, OBE; JA Hill; D Hollingsworth; EH Hutton (Wales); RA Jeffery; HR Jones; LJ Kay; FR Kitchen; IR Lloyd (Wales); DTE Marjoram; PE Owen (Wales); F Parrott; Mrs DM Penn; P Phillips; Miss EG Pollard; DR Prestwich; RM Prideaux; JCD Rainbow, CBE; D Ll Rees; CD Roberts; IA Robertson, DFC; IP Salisbury; KJ Sargent; CH Selby; JG Slater; JL Swain; N Thomas, CBE; AF Turberfield, CBE; RA Wake, KSG; Miss R Wallis Myers; Miss P Walters; ER Wastnedge; PC Webb (Wales); JB Whinnerah; CG White, MBE; AJ Wiles; M Wylie; MJF (Peter) Wynn (Wales).

Other papers: TA Burdett (contributed by Mrs P Burdett); KT Elsdon; GW Elsmore (contributed by Mrs D Elsmore); E Sims.

1970s

Direct contributions: SJ Adams (Wales); Mrs GMV Alexander, PT Armitstead; BC Arthur, CBE; D Baillie; AM Barnes; EA Bassett; Rev G Benfield, OBE; EJ Bolton, CB; RG Booth; RJ Brake; EH Brittain; F Brook; P Brown; Mrs E Cave; EC Cordell; Miss M Corlett; AT Cox, CBE; LS Crickmore; Miss S Crisp; Mrs WF Curzon; JD Dale; B Denton; T Dickinson, OBE; JM Evans; Mrs B R-D Fisher, OBE; B Gay; M Hart, CBE; KN Hastings; GJ Haworth; RAS Hennessey; PM Hesketh; GA Hicks; MW Himsworth; JB Hurn; AR Ivatts; DA Jones; GNE Lageard; EH Leaton; Miss BJ Lewis; TL Lilley; AG Loosemore; Mrs J McLean; PF Marlow; CP Marshall; TP Melia, CBE; Ms AC Millett; Ms H Moffatt; RW Mycock; H Myers; J Ounsted; Mrs RW Peacocke; Lady Pauline Perry; TG Prosser (Wales); AJ Rose, CBE; E Scott; BD Short, CBE; PJ Silvester; P (John) Singh; Mrs MM Smart, OBE; DE Soulsby; JW Steel, OBE; DW Sylvester; DW Taylor; M Todd; JE Trickey; DH Watts; DL West, CBE; Miss S Whitworth; JB Willcock; DP Woodgate; T Wylie; RE Young.

1980s

Direct contributions: Mrs J Carswell; PR Clarke; T Dillon; Mrs G Everson; DHM Foster; C Goodhead; DI Grant; DP King; D Knighton; D Labon; Ms SM Nicholls; C Potts; Mrs BF Pratley; CM Richards; G Robson; BJ Smith; Mrs E Soulsby; J. Stanyer; R. Storrs; Mrs JW Turner; Mrs SP Twite; Mrs AP Warren; MR Webb; R Whitburn; C Wightwick.

The following organisations and individuals also deserve particular mention for their professional and administrative support for the project:

The Association of Her Majesty's Inspectors of Schools; Colin White; Mrs Barbara Fisher; and the donation inspired by the late Tim Fenn.

The HMI History Advisory Group: Brian Arthur; Miss Sheila Browne; the late Tim Fenn; John Hedger; Terry Melia; Don Porter; John Slater; Nick Stuart; Norman Thomas; Roy Wake; Tom Wylie.

DfEE Library: Ms Arabella Wood.

Institute of Education Library (AHMI Jack Kitching Archive): Ms Jenny Haynes;

The Derbyshire Record Office, Matlock: Dr M O'Sullivan.

Select Bibliography

1. Public Documents

Royal Commission (1868) *Report of the Schools Inquiry Commission.* Lord Taunton, Chairman. See Maclure, *Educational Documents*, 92–5.

Royal Commission (1969) *Report of the Royal Commission on Local Government in England.* Cmnd 4039. Lord Redcliffe-Maud, Chairman.

House of Commons Select Committees

Select Committee on Education and Science (1968) *Her Majesty's Inspectorate (England and Wales)*, 2 vols.

Select Committee on Education and Science (1969) *Teacher Training*, 5 vols.

Expenditure Committee, Education, Arts and Home Office sub-committee (1976) *Policy Making in the Department of Education and Science.* HoC 621.

Education, Science and Arts Committee (1981) *The Secondary School Curriculum and Examinations with Special Reference to the 14 to 16 year old Age Group.* HoC 116, 3 vols.

Education, Science and Arts Committee (1986) *Achievement in Primary Schools.* HoC 40, 2 vols.

Education, Science and Arts Committee (1987) *Special Education Needs, Implementation of the Education Act 1981.* HoC 201, 2 vols.

2. Board of Education, Ministry of Education, Department of Education and Science, Department for Education

Circulars

1652, Emergency recruitment and training of teachers, 15 May 1944.

73, The organisation of secondary education, December 1945.

144, The organisation of secondary education, June 1947.

323, Liberal education in technical colleges, 1 March 1957.

10/65, The organisation of secondary education, 12 July 1965.

10/70, The organisation of secondary education, 30 June 1970.

15/70, The Education (Handicapped Children) Act 1970, 22 September 1970.

14/77, Local authority arrangements for the school curriculum, 29 November 1977.

15/77, Information for parents, 25 November 1977.

6/81, The school curriculum, 1 October 1981.

1/83, Assessments and statements of special educational need, 31 January 1983.

8/83, The school curriculum, 8 December 1983.

3/84, Initial teacher training: approval of courses, 13 April 1984.

6/86, Local Education Authority training grants scheme: financial year 1987 88, 29 August 1986.

1/87, Follow up to HMI Reports, 18 February 1987.

3/87, Providing for quality: the pattern of organisation to age 19, 6 May 1987.

Green Papers, White Papers

(1943) Educational reconstruction (White Paper), Cmnd 6458.

(1956) Technical education (White Paper), Cmnd 9703, February 1956.

(1972) Education: a framework for expansion (White Paper), Cmnd 5174.

(1974) Educational Disadvantage and the educational needs of immigrants

(White Paper), Cmnd 5720, August 1974.

(1983) Teaching quality (White Paper), Cmnd 8836.

(1985) Better schools (White Paper), Cmnd 9469.

(1977) Education in schools: a consultative document (Green Paper), Cmnd 6869.

(1981) A new training initiative: a programme for action (White Paper), Cmnd 8455, December 1981.

(1984) Training for jobs (White Paper), Cmnd 9135, jointly with Department of Employment.

(1984) Parental influence at school: a new framework for school governance in England and Wales (Green Paper), May 1984.

(1986) Working together: education and training (White Paper), Cmnd 9823, July 1986.

(1991) Education and training for the 21st century (White Paper), 1536.

(1992) Choice and diversity: a new framework for schools (White Paper), Cmnd 2021, July 1992.

Reports

Lewis (1917) *Juvenile Employment in Relation to Employment after the War*. J Herbert Lewis, MP, Chairman. See Maclure, *Educational Documents*, 168.

Hadow (1926) *The Education of the Adolescent*. Report of the Consultative Committee on Education. Sir W H Hadow, Chairman.

Hadow (1931) *The Primary School*. Report of the Central Consultative Committee on Education. Sir W H Hadow, Chairman.

Norwood (1943) *Curriculum and Examinations in Secondary Schools*. Report of the Committee of the

Secondary School Examinations Council appointed by the President of the Board of Education in 1941. Sir Cyril Norwood, Chairman.

McNair (1944) Report of a Committee appointed by the President of the Board of Education to consider the *Supply, Recruitment and Training of Teachers and Youth Leaders*. Sir Arnold McNair, Chairman.

Percy (1945) Report of a Special Committee appointed in April 1944 on *Higher Technological Education*. Lord Eustace Percy, Chairman.

National Advisory Council on Education for Industry and Commerce (1950) *The Future of Higher Technological Education*.

(1951) *Training and Supply of Teachers*. First report of the National Advisory Council covering the period July 1949 to February 1951. London: HMSO.

Gurney-Dixon (1954) *Early Leaving*. Report by the Central Advisory Council (England). Sir Samuel Gurney-Dixon, Chairman.

(1956) *Three Year Training for Teachers*. Fifth report of the National Advisory Council on the Training and Supply of Teachers.

(1957) *Scope and Content of the Three Year Course of Teacher Training*. Sixth report of the National Advisory Council on the Training and Supply of Teachers.

Crowther (1959) *15 to 18*. A report of the Central Advisory Council for Education (England). 2 vols. Sir Geoffrey Crowther, Chairman.

(1962) *The Demand and Supply of Teachers 1960–80*. Seventh report of the National Advisory Council on the Training and Supply of Teachers. J S Fulton, Chairman.

(1962) *The Future Pattern of Education and Training of Teachers*. Eighth report of the National Advisory Council on the Training and Supply of Teachers. J S Fulton, Chairman.

Newsom (1963) *Half our Future*. Report of the Central Advisory Council for Education (England). John Newsom, Chairman.

Robbins (1963) Report of the Committee on *Higher Education* appointed by the Prime Minister under the Chairmanship of Lord Robbins 1961–63.

(1965) *The Demand for and Supply of Teachers 1963–1986*. Ninth report of the National Advisory Council on the Training and Supply of Teachers. A L C Bullock, Chairman. Minority report by Sir William Alexander and a note of dissent by Eric Robinson, supported by John Vaizey and Charles Carter.

Plowden (1967) *Children and their Primary Schools*. Report of the Central Advisory Council for Education (England). 2 vols. Lady Plowden, Chairman.

Fulton (1968) *The Civil Service*. Report of the Committee on the Civil Service, 6 vols, Cmnd 3638. Lord Fulton, Chairman.

Gittins (1968) *Primary Education in Wales*. Report of the Central Advisory Council for Education (Wales). Professor Charles Gittins, Chairman.

James (1972) Report of a Committee of Enquiry into *Teacher Education and Training*. Lord James of Rusholme, Chairman.

Houghton (1974) Report of a Committee of Inquiry into the *Pay of Non-University Teachers*. Lord Houghton of Sowenby, Chairman.

Bullock (1975) *A Language for Life*. A report of the Committee of Inquiry appointed by the Secretary of State

for Education and Science under the chairmanship of Sir Alan Bullock FBA.

Auld (1976) *The William Tyndale Junior and Infants Schools*. Report of the public inquiry [by Robin Auld, QC] into the teaching, organisation and management of the William Tyndale Junior and Infant Schools, Islington, London, N1.

Taylor (1977) *A New Partnership for Our Schools*. Report of the Committee of Enquiry appointed jointly by the Secretary of State for Education and Science and the Secretary of State for Wales. Tom Taylor, Chairman.

Warnock (1978) *Special Educational Needs*. Report of a Committee of Enquiry into the Education of Handicapped Children and Young People. Cmnd 7212. Mrs H M Warnock, Chairman.

Waddell (1978) *School Examinations*. Report of a Steering Committee. Cmnd 7281. Sir James Waddell, Chairman.

Keohane (1979) *Proposals for a Certificate of Extended Education*. Cmnd 7755. Professor Kevin Keohane, Chairman.

Macfarlane (1980) *Education for 16 to 19 year-olds*. A review undertaken for the Government and the Local Authority Associations. Neil Macfarlane, Chairman.

Trenaman (1981) *Review of the Schools Council*. Report from Mrs Nancy Trenaman, principal of St Anne's College, Oxford, to the Secretaries of State for Education and Science and for Wales and to the Local Authority Associations.

Cockcroft (1982) *Mathematics Counts*. Committee of Inquiry chaired by Dr W H Cockcroft.

Rayner (1982) *Study of HM Inspectorate in England and Wales*. London: Sir Derek Rayner, Chairman.

Hargreaves (1983) *Improving Secondary Schools*. Report of the Committee on the Curriculum and Organisation of Secondary Schools. London: David H Hargreaves, Chairman.

Fish (1985) *Educational Opportunities For All?* Report of the Committee reviewing provision to meet special educational needs, chaired by John Fish.

Thomas (1985) *Improving Primary Schools*. Report of the Committee on Primary Education chaired by Norman Thomas. London.

TGAT (1988) *Assessment and Testing*. Report of the National Curriculum Task Group. 13 January 1988. Professor Paul Black, Chairman. Appointed 30 July 1987.

Higginson (1988) *Advancing A Levels*. Report of a Committee appointed by the Secretary of State for Education and Science and the Secretary of State for Wales. Gordon Higginson, Chairman.

Departmental and Other Official Publications

(1949) *Story of a School. A Headmaster's Experiences with Children aged Seven to Eleven*. Pamphlet 14. [A L Stone, Headmaster of Steward Street Primary School, Birmingham]

(1950) *The Future of Higher Technological Education: Report by the National Advisory Council on Education for Industry and Commerce*.

(1950) *Challenge and Response: An Account of the Emergency Scheme for the Training of Teachers*. Pamphlet 17.

(1950) *Reading Ability: Some Suggestions for Helping the Backward*. Pamphlet 18.

(1950) Chapter 8, 'HM Inspectorate', *Report of the Ministry of Education for the Year 1949*, 87–96.

(1951) *Cost Study*. Building Bulletin 4.

(1959) *Primary Education: Suggestions for the Consideration of Teachers and Others Concerned with the Work of Primary Schools*.

(1965) Biggs E *Mathematics in Primary Schools*. Schools Council Curriculum Bulletin 1.

(1967) Porter D I R *A School Approach to Technology*. Schools Council Curriculum Bulletin 2.

(1967) HM Inspectorate. *Reports on Education* 37: 1–4.

(1970) *Output Budgeting for the Department of Education and Science*. Education Planning Paper No. 1.

(1976) *The Government's Reply to the Tenth Report from the Expenditure Committee, Session 1975–76 (HC621), 'Policy Making in the Department of Education and Science'*. Cmnd 6678.

(1976) *School Education in England: Problems and Initiatives*. Yellow Book. Confidential and unpublished, photocopy.

(1978) *Management Review: Report of the Steering Committee*. London: [One of a cycle of reviews of major government departments begun in 1972 to assist departments improve effectiveness and efficiency.]

(1979) *A Basis for Choice (ABC): Report of a Study Group on Post-16 Pre-employment Courses*. FEU.

(1980) *A Framework for the School Curriculum*, departmental consultative paper.

(1981) *The Practical Curriculum: Schools Council Working Paper 70*. London: Methuen.

(1983) *The Work of HM Inspectorate in England and Wales: A Policy Statement by the Secretary of State for Education and Science and the Secretary of State for Wales*.

(1983) *HM Inspectors Today: Standards in Education.*

(1984) *The Organisation and Content of the 5 to 16 Curriculum: A Note by the Department of Education and Science and the Welsh Office.*

(1986) *Reporting Inspections: HMI Methods and Procedures.* [3 versions for maintained schools, independent schools and further & higher education institutions.]

(1988) *Her Majesty's Inspectors of Schools: Their Purpose and Role.*

HMI Publications

(1970) *HMI Today and Tomorrow.*

(1970) *Launching Middle Schools: An Account of Preparations and Early Experiences in Division No. 15 of the West Riding of Yorkshire.*

(1970) *Towards the Middle School.* Education Pamphlet 157.

(1972) *Open Plan Primary Schools.* Education Survey 16

(1973) *Careers Education in Secondary Schools.* Education Survey 18.

(1977) *Ten Good Schools.* Matters for Discussion 1.

(1977) [Red Books] *Curriculum 11–16* and subjects: *Geography* (1976); *Home Economics* (1978); *Modern Languages* (1978); *Supplementary Papers* (1979).

(1978) *Mixed Ability Work in Comprehensive Schools.* Matters for Discussion 6.

(1978) *Primary Education in England: A Survey by HMI.* [The Primary Survey.]

(1979) *Aspects of Secondary Education in England: A Survey by HMI.* [The Secondary Survey.]

(1980) *Educational Provision by the Inner London Education Authority: Report by HM Inspectors.* Confidential [HMI Report published by the Education Officer of ILEA.]

(1980) *A View of the Curriculum.* Matters for Discussion 11.

(1981) *Report by HMI on the Effects on the Education in England of LEA Policies, Financial Year 1980–81.* [4th annual HMI Report for ESG(E), first three unpublished.]

(1981) *The School Curriculum: A Statement.* [results of consultations on 1980 Framework] March 1981.

(1982) *The New Teacher in School.* Matters for Discussion 15.

(1984) *English from 5 to 16: Curriculum Matters 1*; and *The Responses* (1984).

(1984) *Education for Employees: An HMI Survey of Part-time Release for 16–19 year olds.*

(1985) *The Curriculum from 5 to 16: Curriculum Matters 2*; and (1988) *The Curriculum from 5 to 16: Responses to Curriculum Matters 2. An HMI report.*

(1986) *Educational Provision in the Metropolitan Borough of Wigan,* an HMI report, carried out 1983/84. Report 84/86.

(1987) *Non-Advanced Further Education in Practice: NAFE Practice (General)*; 1 Science; 2 Hotel & Catering; 3 Business Studies; 4 Agriculture; 5 Child Care Course; 6 Computing and Maths; 7 Art and Design; (1988) 8 Engineering; 9 Hairdressing; 10 Construction.

(1987) *Educational Provision in the Inner London Borough of Brent, Autumn 1986–Spring 1987,* an HMI report, 168/87.

(1987) *The New Teacher in School: A Survey by HM Inspectors in England and Wales 1987.*

(1988) *Report by HMI on Crookham Court Independent School, Newbury, Berkshire,*

Inspected 23–27 November 1987. IND 3/87.

(1989) *Report by HM Inspectors on Holte School, Birmingham LEA, inspected 7–11 November 1988*, 135/89.

(1989) *FE in Practice: Tertiary Colleges*, an HMI survey.

(1989) *Post-16 Education and Training: Core Skills*, an HMI paper.

(1989) *Standards in Education 1987–88: A Report by Her Majesty's Senior Chief Inspector of Schools Based on the Work of HMI in England*, a report by HMI. London: DES. September 1987–August 1988, following the 10 ESG(E) reports.

(1989) *Implementation of the National Curriculum in Primary Schools*, an HMI Report. 332/89.

(1990) *Hackney Free and Parochial Church of England Secondary School, 13–15 December 1989*. 46/90.

(1990) *Quality in Higher Education: A Report on an HMI Invitation Conference held at Heythrop Park, Oxfordshire*.

(1990) *The Implementation of the National Curriculum in Primary Schools: A Survey of 100 schools*, autumn term 1989, a report by HMI.

(1990) *Schools in Hackney, Some issues, Hackney LEA, A report by HMI*. 200/90. Visits between 1988–90.

(1990*) HMI in the 1990s: The Work of HMI*.

(1990) *Assessment Recording: Reporting the National Curriculum*, a Report by HMI.

(1990) *National Curriculum and Special Needs*.

(1991) *Education Observed: The Implementation of the Curricular Requirements of ERA, An Overview of HM Inspectorate on the First Year, 1989–90*.

(1991) *Performance Indicators in Higher Education, January – April 1990*, a report by HMI.

(1992) *Framework for the Inspection of Schools: Paper for Consultation*. August 1992.

3. Other Government Departments

Carr. Ministry of Labour, Joint Consultative Committee (1958) *Training for Skill*.

Bains. Department of the Environment (1972) *The New Local Authorities: Management and Structure*. M A Bains, Chairman.

Manpower Services Commission (1981) *A New Training Initiative: An Agenda*.

De Ville MSC/DES (1986) *Review of Vocational Qualifications in England and Wales*. A report by the working group, April 1986. Oscar De Ville, Chairman.

Department of Employment (1988) *Employment for the 1990s* (White Paper).

Audit Commission (1989) *Assuring Quality in Education: A Report on LEA Inspectors and Advisers*.

Audit Commission, HMI (1992) *Getting in on the Act: Provision for Pupils with Special Educational Needs, the National Picture*.

4. Other Sources

Adams F J (ed.) (1990) *Special Education in the 1990s: Written by Members of the Society of Education Officers*. Harlow: Longman.

Ayerst D (1971) *'Guardian': Biography of a Newspaper*. London: Collins.

Baker K (1996) *Turbulent Years: My Life in Politics*. London: Faber. Appendix 2, 'The Blue Print for Education Reform, December 1986', 479–82.

Barnett C (1986) *The Audit of War: The Illusion and Reality of Britain as a Great Nation*. London: Macmillan.

Bennett N (1976) *Teaching Styles and Pupil Progress*. London: Open Books.

Blackie J (1970) *Inspecting and the Inspectorate*. London: Routledge and Kegan Paul.

Bolton E (1991) 'Charter bears a closer inspection', *The Times Educational Supplement*, 18 October 1991, 10.

Bolton E (1998) 'HMI – the Thatcher years', *Oxford Review of Education* 24(1): 45–55.

Brierley J (1999) *Her Majesty's Inspector of Schools: Some Personal Memoirs of a Diverse Life*. Salisbury: Swift Press.

Browne J D (1969) 'The balance of studies in colleges of education', in Taylor W. (ed.) *Towards a Policy for the Education of Teachers*. London: Butterworths for the Colston Research Society, 99–109. Proceedings of the twentieth symposium of the Colston Research Society.

Browne S (1979) 'The accountability of HM Inspectorate (England)', in Lello J (ed.) *Accountability in Education*. London: Ward Lock, 35–44.

Bruce M G (1985) 'Teacher education since 1944: providing the teachers and controlling the providers'. *British Journal of Educational Studies* 33: 164–72.

Burchill J (1991) *Inspecting Schools: Breaking the Monopoly*. London: Centre for Policy Studies.

Butler R A (1971) *The Art of the Possible: The Memoirs of Lord Butler CG CH*. London: Hamish Hamilton.

Carr R (1958) 'The Changing Pattern of Apprentice Training': Seventh Annual Conference Report. East Midlands group, British Association for Commercial and Industrial Education.

Chasty H, Friel J (1991) *Children with Special Needs: Assessment, Law and Practice Caught in the Act*. London: Jessica Kingsley.

Clark L (1976) *The Inspector Remembers: Diary of One of Her Majesty's Inspectors of Schools 1936–1970*. London: Dennis Dobson.

Clarke K (1991) 'Power to the people's HMI', *The Times Educational Supplement*, 1 November 1991, 6.

Cockerill G (1985) 'The Middle Years', in Plaskow M (ed.) *Life and Death of the Schools Council*. London: Falmer Press.

Coleman J S, Campbell E Q, Hobson C J, McPartland J, Mood A M, Weinfeld F D, York R L (1996) *Equality of Educational Opportunity*. Washington, DC: US Department of Health, Education and Welfare and the Office of Education.

Confederation of British Industries, Task Force (1989) *Towards a Skills Revolution*. London: CBI.

Corbett A (1974) 'Tentative about means, firm about ends'. *The Times Educational Supplement*, 29 November 1974. [Interview with Sheila Browne.]

Cox C B, Boyson R (eds) (1975) *Black Paper 1975: The Fight for Education*. London: Dent.

Cox C B, Dyson A E (eds) (1977) *Black Papers 1969–77*. London: Maurice Temple.

Crosland S (1982) *Tony Crosland*. London: Jonathan Cape Ltd.

Dent H C (1944) *The Education Act 1944: Provisions, Regulations, Circulars, Later Acts*. Fourth edn. London: University of London Press Ltd.

Dent H C (1977) *The Training of Teachers in England and Wales 1800–1975*. London: Hodder & Stoughton.

Docking J (ed.) (1996) *National School Policy: Major Issues in Education Policy for Schools in England and Wales, 1979 Onwards*. London: David Fulton Publishers in association with Roehampton Institute London.

Donoughue B (1987) *Prime Minister. The Conduct of Policy Under Harold Wilson and James Callaghan*. London: Jonathan Cape.

Dunford J E (1998) *Her Majesty's Inspectorate of Schools since 1944: Standard Bearers or Turbulent Priests?* London: Woburn Press.

Ellis T, McWhirter J, McColgan D, Haddow B (1976) *William Tyndale: The Teachers' Story*. London: Writers and Readers Publishing Cooperative.

Elsdon K T et al (2001) *An Education for the People? A History of HMI and Lifelong Education 1944–1992*. Leicester: National Institute of Adult Continuing Education.

Floud J E (ed.) with Halsey A H, Martin F M (1956) *Social Class and Educational Opportunity*. London: William Heinemann Ltd.

Fowler G (1974*) Decision Making in British Education System*. Unit 3, policy finance and managment, E221, Educational Studies, a second level course. Milton Keynes: Open University Press.

Green A, Stedman H (1993) *Educational Provision, Educational Attainment and the Needs of Industry*. London: National Institute for Economic Research.

Griffin-Beale C (ed.) (1979) *Christian Schiller in his own words*. London: Private subscription by A and C Black.

Gosden P H J H (1972) *The Evolution of a Profession: A Study of the Contribution of Teachers' Associations to the Development of School Teaching as a Professional Occupation*. Oxford: Basil Blackwell.

Gosden P H J H (1976) *Education in the Second World War: A Study in Policy and Administration*. London: Methuen & Co. Ltd.

Graham D with David Tytler (1993) *A Lesson for Us All: The Making of the National Curriculum*. London: Routledge.

Gray J (1997) 'A Bit of a Curate's Egg? Three decades of official thinking about the quality of schools'. *British Journal of Educational Studies* 45(1): 4–21.

Gretton J, Jackson M (1976) *William Tyndale: Collapse of a School – or a System?* London: George Allen and Unwin Ltd.

Hall V (1990) *Maintained Further Education in the UK*. Bristol: FE Staff College.

Harris J (1990) 'Enterprise and welfare states: a comparative perspective'. *Transactions of the Royal Historial Society* 40: 175–95.

Hastings K (1998) *In a Right State: The Reflections of an Education Inspector*. Lewes: The Book Guild Ltd.

Healey D (1989) *The Time of My Life*. London: Michael Joseph.

Hegarty S, Pocklington K with D Lucas (1981) *Educating Pupils with Special Needs in the Ordinary School*. Windsor: NFER-Nelson.

Hencke D (1978) *Colleges in Crisis: The Reorganization of Teacher Training 1971–1977*. Harmondsworth: Penguin.

Hennessy P (1992) *Never Again: Britain 1945–1951*. London: Jonathan Cape Ltd.

Hogg S, Hill J (1995) *Too Close to Call*. London: Warner.

Hoggart R (1957) *The Uses of Literacy: Aspects of Working-class Life with Special Reference to Publications and Entertainment*. London: Chatto & Windus.

Hudson J (1986) 'Whatever happened to technical schools?' *The Times Educational Supplement*, 3 October 1986.

Jacka K, Cox C, Marks J (1975) *Rape of Reason: The Corruption of the Polytechnic of North London*. Enfield: Churchill Press Ltd.

James R R (1993) *Chips: The Diaries of Sir Henry Channon*. London: Weidenfeld & Nicholson.

Jencks C, Smith M, Acland H, Bane M J, Cohen D, Gintis H, Heyns B, Michaelson S (1972) *Inequality: A Reassessment of the Effect of Family and Schooling in America*. New York: Basic Books.

Judd J (1991) 'Major settles old score', *Independent on Sunday*, 20 October 1991.

Judge H (1984) *A Generation of Schooling: English Secondary Schools since 1944*. Oxford: Oxford University Press.

Kogan M (1971) *The Politics of Education: Edward Boyle and Anthony Crosland in Conversation with Maurice Kogan*. London: Penguin.

Kogan M, with Katherine Bowden (1975) *Educational Policy-Making: A Study of Interest Groups and Parliament*. London: George Allen & Unwin.

Kogan M (1978) *The Politics of Educational Change*. Manchester: Manchester University Press.

Kogan M (1979) *Education Policies in Perspective: An Appraisal of OECD Country Educational Policy Reviews*. Paris: OECD.

Lawlor, S (1993) *Inspecting the School Inspectors: New Plans, Old Ills*. London: Centre for Policy Studies.

Lawson, N (1992) *The View from No.11: Memoirs of a Tory Radical*. London: Bantam Press.

Lawton D, Gordon P (1987) *HMI*. London: Routledge & Kegan Paul.

Maclure S (1984) *Educational Development and School Building: Aspects of Public Policy 1945–73*. London: Longman.

Maclure S (1986) *Educational Documents: England and Wales 1816 to the Present Day*. 5th edn. London: Methuen.

Maclure S (1998) 'Through the revolution and out the other side'. *Oxford Review of Education* 24(1): 5–24. Volume edited by Stuart Maclure.

Major J (1999) *John Major: The Autobiography*. London: HarperCollins.

Marwick A (1982) *British Society since 1945*. London: Allen Lane.

Medd D (1976) 'Designing buildings as a resource', paper given at a summer school for teachers, Eaton Hall College of Education, Retford, Notts., mimeo.

Middleton N, Weitzman S (1976) *A Place for Everyone: A History of State Education from the End of the Eighteenth Century to the 1970s*. London: Victor Gollancz Ltd.

Monks T G (1968) *Comprehensive Education in England and Wales: A Survey of Schools and their Organization*. Slough, Bucks: NFER.

Mueller A E (1976) 'Industry, Education and Management', Department of Industry discussion document.

Neave G (1977) *Equality, Ideology and Educational Policy: An Essay in the History of Ideas*. Occasional Paper 4, Institut d'Education, Fondation Européenne de la Culture.

Organisation for Economic Cooperation and Development (1975) Review of National Policies for Education:

Educational Development Strategy in England and Wales. Paris: OECD.

Pearce J (1986) *Standards and the LEA: The Accountability of Schools*. Windsor: NFER-Nelson.

Pearson E (1972) 'Trends in school design'. *British Primary Schools Today*. Vol. 2, Anglo-American Primary Education Project/Ford Foundation. New York: Macmillan, 270–337.

Perry P (1991) 'Inspection: quality assurance or quality control', *The Times Educational Supplement*, 12 July 1991, 16.

Perry P J C (1976) *The Evolution of British Manpower Policy 1563–1964*. London: British Association for Commercial and Industrial Education.

Peters R S (ed.) (1969) *Perspectives on Plowden*. London: Routledge and Kegan Paul.

Pimlott B (1986) *The Political Diary of Hugh Dalton, 1918–40, 1945–60*. London: Jonathan Cape in association with the LSE.

Plaskow M (ed.) (1985) *Life and Death of the Schools Council*. London: Falmer Press.

Prais S J, Wagner K (1983) *Schooling Standards in Britain and Germany: Some Summary Comparisons Bearing on Economic Efficiency*. Discussion Paper 60, Industry Series 14. London: NIESR.

Ranson S, Tomlinson J (eds) (1986) *The Changing Government of Education*. London: George Allen & Unwin.

Redcliffe-Maud J (1981) *Experiences of an Optimist: The Memoirs of John Redcliffe-Maud*. London: Hamish Hamilton.

Richards P G (1975) *The Reformed Local Government System*. London: George Allen and Unwin, 2nd edn.

Riley K A (1998) *Whose School is it Anyway?* London: The Falmer Press.

Rogers R (1980) *Crowther to Warnock: How Fourteen Reports Tried to Change Children's Lives*. London: Heinemann Educational Books in association with the International Year of the Child.

Roseveare M P (1984) *Joys, Jobs and Jaunts*. Blantyre Print.

Rowan P (1983) 'No going back to a quiet little world'. *The Times Educational Supplement*, 29 July 1983, 9. [Interview with Eric Bolton.]

Royal Society of Arts, Tyrrell Burgess (ed.) (1986) *Education for Capability*. Windsor: NFER-Nelson.

Rutter M, Mangham B, Mortimore P, Ouston J with Alan Smith (1979) *Fifteen Thousand Hours: Secondary Schools and their Effect on Children*. London: Open Books.

Sanderson M (1994) *The Missing Stratum: Technical School Education in England 1900–1990s*. London: The Athlone Press.

Seldon A (1997) *John Major: A Political Life*. London: Weidenfeld & Nicholson.

Shaw K E (1966) 'Why no sociology of schools'? *Education for Teaching* 69: 61–7.

Silberman C E (1970) *Crisis in the Classroom: The REMAKING of American Education*. New York: Random House.

Silver H (1990) *A Higher Education: The Council for National Academic Awards and British Higher Education, 1964–1989*. Basingstoke: Falmer Press.

Simon B (1965) *Education and the Labour Movement 1870–1920*. London: Lawrence and Wishart.

Simon B (1991) *Education and the Social Order: 1940–1990*. London: Lawrence & Wishart.

Steadman S D, Parsons C, Salter B G (1978) *Impact and Take-up Project: An*

Inquiry into the Impact and Take-up of Schools Council-funded Activities. First interim report to the Programme Committee of the Schools Council, May 1978.

Stevens A (1976) 'HMI: secretive, futile or prophets in the gloom?' *Times Educational Supplement*, 17 September 1976, 2.

Tanner, R (1987) *Double Harness*. London: Impact Books.

Thatcher M (1993) *The Downing Street Years*. London: HarperCollins.

Thatcher M (1995) *The Paths to Power*. London: HarperCollins.

Timmins N (1995) *The Five Giants: A Biography of the Welfare State*. London: HarperCollins.

Tomlinson J (1985) 'From projects to programmes: the view from the top', in Plaskow M (ed.) *Life and Death of the Schools Council*. Lewes: Falmer Press.

Tomlinson J (1993) *The Control of Education*. London: Cassell.

Tomlinson J (1997) 'Her Majesty's Inspectorate in the 1980s and 1990s: An exemplary tale' in Watson K, Modgil C, Modgil S (eds) *Educational Dilemmas. Debate and Diversity*. Vol. 3. *Power and Responsibility in Education*. London: Cassell.

Vernon B D (1982) *Ellen Wilkinson, 1891–1947*. London: Croom Helm.

Vernon P E (1952) 'Intelligence Testing', *The Times Educational Supplement*, 2 January, 1 February 1952.

Vernon P E (ed) (1958) *Secondary School Selection: A British Psychological Society Inquiry*. London: Methuen & Co. Ltd.

Walden G (1999) *Lucky George: Memoirs of an Anti-Politician*. London: Allen Lane.

Weaver T (1979) *Central Control of Education?* Educational Studies, a second level course E222, Unit 2. Milton Keynes: Open University Press.

Weiner M J (1985) *English Culture and the Decline of the Industrial Spirit, 1850–1980*. Harmondsworth: Penguin.

Wilcox B (1990) 'Is there a role for site visits in monitoring systems? A UK perspective'. *Evaluation and Research in Education* 4(2): 81–91.

Williams S (1981) *Politics is for People*. London: Allen Lane.

Wilson P (1961) 'Snakes and ladders in English higher education', in *Views and Prospects from Curzon Street: Seven Essays on the Future of Education*. Oxford: Blackwell, 79–87.

Wrigley J (1985) 'Confessions of a curriculum man', in Plaskow M (ed.) *Life and Death of the Schools Council*. London: Falmer Press, 41–53.

Yates A, Pidgeon D A (1957) *Admission to Grammar Schools: Third Interim Report on the Allocation of Primary School Leavers to Courses of Secondary Education*. London: Newnes Educational Publishing Co Ltd. for the NFER.

Index